JIM RUSTON

A COCKNEY KID
IN GREEN WELLIES

J.R.M.

First Published in Great Britain by
J.R.Marketing
41 High St. Chipping Sodbury
Bristol BS 37 6BA

The Author asserts the moral right to be
identified as the author of this work

A CIP catalogue record for this book
is available from the British Library

ISBN 0-9540430-0-6

Printed in Great Britain by South Western Printers
Trecenydd Business Park Caerphilly CF83 2RZ

The publisher would like to thank Popperfoto and Joke Quarles Van Ufford
for giving permission to publish photographs to which they hold copyright

To Joyce
A country girl with such a gentle way.

Also
for our daughters
Jane Karen and Rachel.

Anchor and Treble Clef
From a painting by Jack Russell based on an idea of mine.
Signifying the influence shipbuilding and music had on my family.

CONTENTS

ACKNOWLEDGEMENTS

They say everyone has a book in them. This is mine. It has taken me five years to research and write it. During my research I discovered things about my ancestors that humble me somewhat. I have had a wonderful life and regret very little. I owe a great deal to my family for their unfailing support; I have led them a merry dance at times. My wife, children and grandchildren, brother and sisters, more worthy than I deserve.

My new found cousins and kinfolk, Alan Ruston, who led me to Janet Austin, Walter Ruston, Adrian Puller and Jean Barron. They each gave access, without hesitation, to documentation they had collected over many years of research. Without them, I would still be buried in the Family Records Centre in Islington! I thank the archivists at Bancroft Library, The London Metropolitan Archive, The Family Records Centre Islington, National Newspaper Archive Collingwood, and the Somerset Records Office and Archive, Taunton. I spent a great deal of time in all of them. I want to thank the East of London Family History Society; it was through them that I met Alan; and Prebendary Arthur Royall who gave me a newspaper article on Father Raven. My thanks to Claire Struthers, for wading through my manuscript and offering constructive advice. Thanks also to Steve Noble, computer wizard, for tuition and for rescuing chapter 11 from the bowels of my PC. I thank my business associate and close friend Jack Russell, for the challenge of the past nine years, and for his seemingly endless faith in me. Finally, Mum and Dad – a promise kept.

THANKS ADOLPH

Thanks Adolf. We 'ad buggerall an' you bombed it! The siren sounded 'All clear'. The wail of a siren, for those of us who heard it in wartime, never to be forgotten. We had come up from the underground shelter. Mum, Maisie, Stella, Evelyn, Betty and me. We stood there a little dazed but thankful the bombing had ceased, at least for now. It had been a routine we had followed many times already. First the siren warning of an impending attack, then hurrying to the nearest shelter. As the time wore on trips to the shelter were more orderly with less rush and tear. We simply had gotten more used to it, finding also, that there was generally more time between the air raid warning and bombs falling. Indeed sometimes there were no bombs and the 'all clear' sounded almost as soon as you were underground. Other times we would stay in the shelter for hours. There was never much room so people were encouraged to keep their belongings to a minimum.

It was incredible what some folk would try to take down the shelter with them. The ever, vigilant Air Raid Prevention, wardens would be heard 'you can't take that now, can you luv' as some poor old dear tried to take a cage down with her budgie in it. The shelters were damp and dingy. Cold at first, they would become hot and clammy with the amount of bodies in them. The aroma far from exotic would defy separation by ones senses, a melting pot of every odour the body can emit, and sprinkled with Evening in Paris (my dad called it Midnight in Wapping) lashings of slap and peroxide as some of the ladies were wont to use. 'Well I wouldn't go down the shelter without me face on, now would I!' Us kids took little notice of the all too familiar routine. The adults did the worrying, some more than others. Our mum Elizabeth, Liz to everyone, was an exceedingly tough lady. Although under 5feet she could square up to most with a look followed by a flying shopping bag if need be. She would make sure that we were as comfortable as possible, but she wouldn't put up with any moaning either. She was an advocate of instant retribution; a swift smack around the ear was her preferred deterrent. If by chance she had meted out the discipline to the wrong child she justified her actions by saying: 'Well, you must have done something wrong that I don't know of, so it will serve for that.' Arguing with mum was futile.

We stood in a group on a small patch of green opposite the entrance to the shelter, the five of us, and mum. The sky was black with smoke and there were fires everywhere. This time we had not been so lucky. Our street had copped it; so had Elsa Street where we were all born, it was in ruins. For the first time in her 37 years of life, our lovely mum didn't know what to do. Like the amazing woman she was, after a few minutes, composed, she turned to Stella and Maisie, the two eldest, and told them to look after Eve and me. She scooped Betty up in her arms saying to us, 'Wait there I will find out what's happening.' Each direction she tried to take ended with her return after a few minutes. She would say 'Don't worry kids I won't be long' and off she would go again. The whole area had been flattened. Fire hoses wriggled along the ground like snakes, as they were pulled from building to building. Fractured water mains spurted fountains of water high in the air. Emergency supplies had to be pumped from the Regent's canal. Firemen, ambulance crews, civil defence members, and the heavy rescue teams were going about their work. The smoke stung your eyes, the dust got in your mouth and the acrid smell of gas lingered in your nostrils. Civilians, those uninjured and able to help others did so.

As if a vision, dad appeared. He seemed to come from nowhere out of the smoke and dust. With a look of panic on his face he asked 'Where is your mother?' 'Its all right' said Stella. 'She has gone to find somewhere for us to go and taken Betty with her.' His relief was instant. He asked if we were all right, then touched each one of us on the head just to make sure. His face was black, his blue overalls covered in grime, under his arm he held a helmet with the letter R for rescue painted on the front. For that is what he did throughout the Blitz. Defiant, he would never go down a shelter. Mum came back with Betty in her arms. 'Liz I thought something had happened to you.' With tears in his eyes he continued 'My London's on fire. I never thought I would see this day.' Like most East-Enders, dad thought London exclusively his. He would have died for her.

We gathered up the few things we had. Little did we know at that moment, it was all we had left in the world. Then we found our way to a reception centre. This one was a church hall, which was utilised as a shelter for those families who had been bombed out and now homeless, as indeed were many such places of worship. And very glad of them we were. The largest congregation most of them had seen in a long while! Dad remonstrated with mum, 'Liz I told you not to come back from King's Lynn, didn't I.' 'You did Jim, but my sister Vi said nothing was happening here.' Mum responded.

We had been evacuated early in September 1939 soon after Britain had declared war on Germany. We stayed on a small farm in King's Lynn in Norfolk. The setting was idyllic. It was harvest time and the weather was warm and sunny. London seemed a long way off. It was a whole new experience for us. We were excited, but mum was bored. Dad had joined the war effort and insisted we evacuate. Reluctantly mum agreed. When war broke out everyone thought we would be either bombed or invaded almost immediately. All the emergency services were put on standby, a Home Guard was formed and conscription was implemented. The men in the countryside also were doing their bit. Those who were in reserved occupations such as farm workers joined the Home Guard (formed in May 1940). Blackouts went up; and regulations about lighting were issued and enforced by the ARP wardens. Some were far more officious than policemen. Some girls joined the Women's Land Army, others volunteered for the ATS, WRENS or WAAF – Army, Navy and Air Force respectively – in a wonderful show of patriotism. Later the 'joining up' became compulsory. The Women's Voluntary Service (WVS) held meetings to recruit more members and plan their strategy. Wherever there was want, these wonderful ladies in green would appear. We as a family were grateful beyond words to this organisation.

The nation, alert, stood by. Apart from the to-be-expected false alarms, the siren would sound, people would rush to the shelters, and almost as they took cover, the 'all-clear' would be heard. As they came out of the shelters some would be angry at the seemingly unnecessary disruption, others would feel silly thinking they had over-reacted. And then there were those who would boast they would never go in a shelter. This cavalier attitude, whilst admirable, got many of them killed. It was a period of 'waiting for something to happen' and became known as the phoney war. Mum received a letter from her sister Violet with whom she had been corresponding and airing her feelings of boredom and loneliness. In her latest letter Vi wrote, 'All's quiet here; come home Liz.' Its all mum needed. 'Right kids pack your things, we're going home'. 'But mum we only just got here!' We responded. And so back to London we went, amid the cries and protestations of the authorities warning us we would be doomed. Too late. Mum had made up her mind.

Back in Elsa Street Maisie and Stella returned to school. Eve and I played in the street with Betty and Bob, dad's collie, sitting on the step of the front door. Mum could visit the neighbours, and Eve and I could wander off with our friends, Betty was safe and happy with Bob; he wouldn't let anyone near her. Dad had had him some years and Bob had looked after each of us in turn sitting by our pram when we were babies. Although there was always food for him at home he rarely ate there, preferring to go off and find his own. He would get into the odd fight and was often chased, never caught, by butchers and bakers for obvious reasons. On hot summer days he would go for a swim in the Regent's canal which ran nearby. Bob was never gone for long, and would never desert if on duty!

A COCKNEY KID IN GREEN WELLIES

Tales of Bob the collie are family legend. But there is one that will always stand out in my mind. A Billie-goat had arrived in the neighbourhood (it's amazing what East-Enders' kept in their back yards) and he took an instant dislike to our dog. Every time Bob passed near him, the billie threatened to butt. Bob was never shy of a fight, and had had enough of this scraggy smelly chap. The next time the goat ran at Bob he stood his ground, but brave though he was, Bob was no match for the horns of the billie, and got bowled over. This happened several times before Bob worked out a strategy. The next time the goat charged, Bob waited until the very last moment before the contact, then, as nimble as you will ever see, leapt over the head of the charging billie and landed on his back, biting him on the bum for good measure. They say Bob was laughing as he trotted off, triumphant!

With summer approaching London seemed so peaceful, at least it did to us kids. The adults viewed things differently, listening to the wireless, reading the newspapers and speculating as to when the bombing, or indeed invasion, would start. Rumour was rife. Few families had a wireless set. Those who did passed on the latest bulletins. By the time these had been relayed and re-told they didn't bear much resemblance to the original broadcast. There is the story of an old lady running in to her local pub and announcing, 'The Russians are in Trafalgar Square.' When asked why she thought they were Russian she exclaimed, ' 'cause they still had snow on their boots!'

Dad had a small garage close to where we lived, well more of a shed really. He kept his car there, an Armstrong Siddley. I loved to sit in the car pretending to drive it. With petrol on ration, it was laid up on blocks. Dad was a motor mechanic who had recently found popularity as an entertainer. After the First World War, he played the piano in a local pub, to amuse himself. He struck up a friendship with another cockney, Alex Steel. Just for fun they sang the odd song together. Before long they had the resemblance of an 'act.' They performed in local pubs and in a matter of weeks they had a small following. Alex Steel loved all of us. He would call at the house in the morning and say; 'Got any breakfast Liz.' Mum's reply was usually, 'What do you think.' Alex would disappear then return in a few minutes with bread, eggs, bacon, and milk. 'Alex where did you get all this?' Mum would ask. His reply, always the same 'Don't ask'. Sometimes he would bring Biegles.(Cockney pronunciation) When as an adult, I heard people talking of Bagles, I had no idea what they were and it was a long time before it dawned on me that they were one and the same! I will talk more about dad and his partnership with Alex Steel in the next chapter.

THANKS ADOLPH

About the middle of July 1940 the German *Luftwaffe* started attacking our airfields in an attempt to gain air supremacy, or at least to diminish our ability to attack their invasion force poised across the Channel waiting for the order to sail. So what did the cockneys do? They went hop picking of course. They were not going to let Hitler ruin the only holiday most of them ever had each year. 'Goin' down 'oppin was a ritual. Late August the exodus to Kent would begin. People packed all they needed, and travelled by rail or road, to the Kent hop fields, or to use their correct name, Hop Gardens.

The kids would get an extra couple of weeks off school, and have a lovely time. Dad had a lorry and would make several trips with different families and their chattels on board. Dad often recalled the occasion when, on his way back to London at the end of the hop season, laden with pickers and their luggage, his presence of mind and coolness averted an almost certain disaster. Having left Sevenoaks behind he was negotiating the notoriously steep River Hill, when the brakes failed. He used his considerable experience and strength to keep the vehicle straight. With skilful use of engine speed and double-de-clutch, he managed to drop down through the gearbox, eventually bringing the lorry to a halt. None of his passengers realised the danger they were in, their only comment being, 'Just what was the bloody hurry Jim? The pubs ain't open yet!'

We mostly went to Paddock Wood. Whitbread and Guinness had big farms there. Each family would be allocated a hut. These were made of corrugated iron, but could, with a little flair, be made quite attractive. In the hut there would be bundles of brushwood which, when laid on the floor, formed the base of your bed, on top of which a mattress would be placed. Then with sheets and blankets it would become quite inviting. After long days in the fields we would sleep like logs. There was a block of toilets and a communal cookhouse. After cooking our meal we would return to our hut and eat. Sometimes in, more often than not, outside, weather permitting.

When it rained conditions became challenging to say the least. There is a fair amount of clay in the sub-soil of Kent, a yellowy, slimy, sticky substance. When wet, it sticks to everything and builds up on the heels of your boots so that everyone is walking around on high heels. I hated this and was continually teased 'Look Jimmy's wearing high heels', girls doing most of the teasing. Mum, Maisie and Stella spent long hours picking at the bin. This was a large sack-like affair supported on a trestle. The hop plants were grown in rows and the bines trained up 10-foot poles, four to a pole. It was a wonderful sight looking down the avenues of hop bines ready to harvest. Bins were placed between the rows, and the adjacent bines pulled down and across the bin. Having stripped the hops from bines pulled, the bin was lifted and moved forward to the next pole. And so you worked your way down the row. Once you had filled your bin the recorder would be summoned, hops weighed, and the resulting amount marked in a book and tallied up at the end of each day.

Some pickers would wait until the end of their stay before collecting what was due. This could be quite a lot of money depending of course on how many bins you could fill. Others took subs on their dues and were left with little at the end of the season. Some of the big families with a number of teenagers would clear an enormous amount of hops. We mostly had just three picking. Dad would come at weekends and help. With hindsight, whilst it was heaven for the small children, playing all day in fields instead of the East-End streets, it couldn't have been so much fun for Stella and Maisie. Mum did the bulk of the picking, as she did the bulk of just about everything else. We took a picnic into the hop garden and like everyone else sat by our bin to eat lunch. Mum would make tea; she couldn't function without her cuppa. The kids would drink water, sometimes lemonade if we were lucky. Rationing was in force so there really wasn't much of anything to eat. Our diet had become quite plain, but we had got used to it by now. If it's not there you don't ask, soon you don't expect, eventually you stop thinking about it.

When mum thought she had had enough, she would tell us to collect our things together, load up the pram and make ready to move. But not before tidying up around our bin would she allow us to set off. With tired legs we made the long trek back to our little hut. Mum cooked a hot meal, helped by Stella and Maisie. After eating we washed in a bowl of hot water and went to bed, exhausted but happy. In the evenings mum sat outside of the hut talking with her friends. The men went to the local. It was a holiday atmosphere, waited for all year, yet still having to be earned daily. There were records to be broken, how many bins filled, by how few pickers, in such and such a time. I really don't know where my mother found the strength for all this. She never ceased to amaze us with both her fortitude and resourcefulness.   In the coming years she would surpass even this.

None of us missed out spiritually during our time in the hop fields, Father Raven saw to that.   An East End priest, he spent more than 40 years in the service of his parishioners, even travelling with them to Kent each year where he had his own hut, and picked from the bine; side by side with his flock. He held services of worship in the fields on Sunday mornings. And he could often be seen walking through the streets of Five Oak Green with 20-30 kids all linking arms. Together with father Richard Wilson, affectionately known as the 'hopper's parson', they ran the hopping mission. When children were sick they were looked after there. We East-Enders called it 'The Little Hopper's Hospital'. Dad was involved in raising funds for this facility.

Dad, and the cleric, who had been ordained by the Bishop of London in St Paul's Cathedral, were firm friends. Father Raven officiated on the occasion when dad married his first wife at St Saviours in Poplar, even though it wasn't his parish. His was St Augustine in Stepney. Dad had helped the Father raise money for a hospice. They both cared passionately about the people in the East End, and loved children. Now with war imminent, they feared for the future of them all.

There had been enemy aircraft in the vicinity already and bombs had fallen in the neighbouring countryside. The coastal towns had already suffered damage and Maidstone had been bombed. It was the middle of September, the weather perfect; blue sky with the occasional puffy white cloud. Dad had come down the night before. We had risen early, had breakfast and made our way across the fields to our bin. Some mornings a mist would rise from the ground. Running eagerly forward we called to mum 'Can you still see us?' She would answer 'No'' even if she could. The countryside with all its mysteries was an adventure for us kids. Our love for it all would grow from here, and eventually change our lives forever. Dad, mum, Stella, and Maisie were picking. Evelyn and I were playing nearby. Betty was in her pram close to mum, where else. She was a marvellous baby, so content. On the way to and from our bin, mum would sit me on the side of Bet's pram, and push us across the heavy ground. The pram was used to transport just about everything. We each had taken our turn in it; now it was Betty's, and she would be the last. We would tie our gas masks to the handles to save carrying them on our shoulders. Tiresome but essential, it was an offence in wartime to be without a gas mask. Ours were of the Mickey Mouse variety, with a tongue and ears, so designed to make us kids eager to wear them when told. Nothing would induce me to wear mine. I felt as though I was choking in it.

It must have been mid morning. We could hear a drone from overhead getting steadily louder. Then, there they were hundreds and hundreds of black shapes, like the migration of a million blackbirds. They covered the sky, blotting out the blue. The blood drained from my dad's face. Mum said quietly, 'My god Jim, is this it?' Apart from the pulsating drone of aircraft, not a sound came from any of the hundreds of pickers in the fields. We stood, numb, looking skywards. It was Stella's distinctive voice, 'Look, look everyone, silver dots, what are they?'

She had been looking into the sun, something mum forbade us to do for fear of damaging our eyes. 'Spitfires, that's what they are, Spitfires!' shouted dad. They came out of nowhere and pounced on the enemy bombers. All hell was let loose. People scattered in every direction, bins went over and hops were trampled in the earth. Dad grabbed Betty in one arm and me in the other, 'Run kids' he shouted, and off we went to one of the many trenches that had been dug in the event of an air raid. We reached the trench in no time; Dad hurled us into it. We fell on top of each other. For good measure dad grabbed hold of an old iron bedspring that happened to be close by, and threw it over us. An enemy bomb never hit us, but the bloody bedspring nearly brained the lot of us!

From the cover of huts and trenches, people looked skywards and witnessed what was to become known as The Battle of Britain - now commemorated each year on 15 September as being considered the decisive day of the battle. It was the most amazing sight. Planes were shot down, pilots bailed out. Enemy planes that had been hit turned for home and dropped their bomb load at random. There was devastation in the hop gardens, bomb craters appeared everywhere; amazingly very few people were badly injured. We were on the way back to see what had happened to our hut when a bomb fell nearby, and the blast threw Evelyn up against the corrugated iron cookhouse. Unconscious, she had lost one shoe and all the buttons off her dress. Dad picked her up, and much to the great relief of everyone she eventually re-gained consciousness. Apart from some bruising, she was all right. However, we were all badly shaken. Dad and mum held council with a few close friends and made the decision to return to London.

Dad packed our belongings and loaded the lorry. With mum Betty and me in the cab, and Stella and Maisie in the back, dad started the motor. The lorry was a Ford with a canvas covering the back. It was a pretty bumpy ride, but I loved it. Motors of any kind fascinated me; I think most small boys were – still are no doubt. I would grab any chance of going for a ride with Dad. He never said much to me. He doted on the girls, but hardly seemed to notice me. We headed back to London, to the cries of 'Don't forget to come for back for us, will you Jim?' Many of our neighbours would only 'go 'oppin' if dad drove them in his lorry. He spent the next week bringing families back to London. It still eludes me why they thought they would be safer in London, which was being bombed daily. There was little rationalisation in wartime; people followed their hearts. You could get killed anywhere, so perhaps it might as well be in your own home.

THANKS ADOLPH

The bombing of London had begun on 7 September. One of the first buildings to be hit was the Coliseum Picture Theatre, in the Mile End Road, where dad and his partner Alex had performed so many times. Being in close proximity to the docks the East End was having more than its fair share. There was bomb damage all over. We took up residence and joined those making the nightly trek to the shelters. There was a permanent pall of smoke over the city, and a red glow, so that it never looked completely dark. Whilst spirited, ever-resilient and resourceful, the Cockneys were taking a pounding; and it was showing on the faces of many. Especially the mothers of children still in London. Evacuation was not compulsory once the intensified bombing had abated, the evacuees gradually drifted back.

At the reception centre, mum was having one of her migraines. When they fell upon her they were savage. She was lying down with brown paper soaked in vinegar wrapped around her forehead. It was the only way she found to ease the pain. We had seen her like this many times before and instinctively remained quiet. Stella sat close to mum comforting her and offering to get her whatever she asked for. Commotion and confusion ruled. The comings and goings of people looking for lost loved ones, the crying, and arguments, too many demands being made on the too few voluntary helpers. After a couple of days we were told we could be evacuated once more. We didn't know where, and we didn't much care.

The few things we had in the bags we carried were the only possessions we had in the world. Dad's 'garage', and the Armstrong Siddley? Flattened by a bomb! Mum dressed us in the warmest clothes we had. She was a bit stuck when it came to me. Being the only boy, my 'wardrobe' was limited. She put me in a jumper, coat and a pair of my sister's navy blue knickers! (I have had a penchant for them ever since. The frilly kind that is; preferably with a female still inside!) I was teased about this for years. With others, we were marshalled together by the well-meaning ladies in green, the WVS. 'Where are we going?' mum inquired. 'Paddington Station' was the reply.

From the time we had returned from Kent, I don't think there was one night without a raid of some kind. Our church, St John, Halley Street (named after Edmund Halley, the famous comet is also named after him), where we had all been baptised, was badly damaged. Bombing was indiscriminate. Whole streets were disappearing day by day. Houses with the front facade blown out, yet the interior seemingly intact. A wardrobe with its door open and dresses hanging inside gently swinging in the breeze. A gas cooker suspended in mid air, supported only by the pipe connecting it to the gas main. Unreal, and highly dangerous. Cherished possessions, scattered like so much jumble across the bombed-out ruins of what had been home. There was Mrs Dove, affectionately called 'Mother Dove' standing in her backyard waving her fist at enemy bombers and shouting; 'come down 'ere you bleeders, I'll 'ave 'yer.' She had just hung her washing out, and the dust from the bombing was making it dirty! Dad said if Hitler could have seen her, he would have packed it in right then!

Men, women and children were searching through piles of rubble looking for the things that meant most. Family records, photographs, a doll with a china face, some lead soldiers. The East End would never be the same again. Centuries of tradition would gradually disappear. Could England take it? She had to. She just bloody well had to. These were our darkest days. Everyone who lived through them would take the experience to their graves. Fifty years on I visited a museum in Cornwall called Flambards, where they have re-created a scene from the Blitz. It is incredibly authentic. As I walked with others through the reconstructed street scene, the sights and sounds, and that ever-pervading smell of gas hit me, sending shivers down my spine. The guide, a lovely lady about my age, walked over to me and said. 'You were there, weren't you.' 'Yes', I said. She continued 'I can always tell. Hundreds of people come here and I can always pick out the ones who were in it; it's the look on their faces, unmistakable. You see, I too was there.' Filled with emotion, I walked out into the sunshine of a beautiful day, and thanked God to be alive. It is a privilege and not a right to live in this wonderful country. Others died for it.

My mother was one of 11 children. Her mother, Alice Hare, was known throughout the East End as a nurse and midwife. People said that she delivered half the kids in Stepney. When she died in 1962, mum and I attended her funeral. The streets were lined with people, you would have thought she was royalty, she was held in such high regard. My grandfather, William Charles Hare, I hardly knew. I do, however, remember that he wore a three-piece suit with a gold watch and chain, which had been presented to him for loyalty and long service by the firm where he worked as an oil refiner. Mum always said he was a wonderful father to her, and she loved him dearly. When he died mum went alone to his funeral to be with the rest of her family. When she returned she brought with her my granddad's pipe with the remains of his last smoke still in its bowl, and his tobacco pouch. It's all she wanted. My sister Betty still has it intact.

FROM WHOM I AM DESCENDED

In the Ruston family there is a long tradition of shipbuilding and the sea. As the records show, a number of early Rustons were from Devon. Over a dozen between 1569 – 1624. Interestingly they all came from the Bideford area, an important seaport at the time.

Among the first London entries is the marriage of Christian Ruston, a minor, who married Gabriell Trayman a mariner of Poplar, at St Dunstan's Church, Stepney, in 1626. At that time Christian was not a common name. Bartholomew Ruston is the first shipwright to be mentioned (but shipwrights ship's carpenters and mariners were, of a class.) Bartholomew was a 40-year-old bachelor of Wapping when he married in 1707 at St Dunstan Stepney. In 1737 Robert Ruston left a will. He was late of the Parish of Wapping, and a mariner. He left his money to his loving friends, the Walker family, victuallers of Wapping! Another sailor was Caleb Ruston. He came from Worcester and died a bachelor in 1748. He belonged to the private ship of war the *Winchelsea*.

Our branch of the family is descended from Joseph (a shipwright) and Martha. They married in October 1749. Joseph was a bachelor from the parish of St Nicholas Deptford, and he married Martha Beveridge at St Paul's Deptford. They had two children – Martha (b. 1751) and Samuel (b. 1758.) At that time they were living in Grove Street.

In the year 1750 a frantic re-armament plan was in progress. Britain had just finished the war with France in 1748, but it was not a proper conclusion. The seven years war began in 1755. Every yard along the front at Woolwich had a new battleship on the stocks. Deptford was also full of partly built ships. History tells us that navy recruitment was mostly by impressment. There is also the fact that ship's carpenters often sailed with the ships, if the work had not been fully completed. This could be the reason why there were only two Ruston children, baptised seven years apart.

In August 1777, Samuel Ruston married Martha Rawlinson in Shoreditch, St Leonards. Their children were Margaret (b. 1784) Joseph (b. 1786) and in July 1789 Samuel. They were all baptised at St Dunstan's, Stepney. Samuel the father was still described as 'a shipwright' of Poplar.
Between the years 1811 and 1823 John Charles Alfred and Samuel were born. They all became shipwrights. Their father was Samuel (b. 1789).

In 1807 Joseph Ruston, brother of Samuel, married Ann Smith at St George in the East. (Much later, in 1842, Joseph appears as licensee of the Anchor & Hope public house at 198 High Street Wapping.) In January 1807, Joseph and Ann had their daughter Ann baptised at St

11

Dunstan's, Stepney. A year later in Poplar a son, Joseph John Ruston was born. He was to have a distinguished career.

Like his forebears, Joseph John became a shipwright and also trained as an engine builder at the engineering works of Boulton & Watt. He was invited by John Andrews, himself a Londoner, who had recently co-founded the Danube Steamship Co., to go to Austria and help in his new enterprise. The following agreement was drafted and signed on 22 November 1832.

* Memorandum of agreement made this 22nd November 1832 between; JOSEPH RUSTON of Boulton & Watt Co on the part of Mr. J. ANDREWS of Vienna, the former agreeing to undertake the building of one or more steam vessels at Vienna or elsewhere and to act in the capacity of shipwright and do every duty relating thereto for and during such time as the vessels shall be completed or as long as Mr Andrews may require his services he agreeing to pay to the said Joseph Ruston a salary of Three Pounds per week also his reasonable travelling expenses out of home, his said salary to commence from leaving England and to conclude when Mr Andrews shall have no further occasion for his services.
Witnessed and signed by John Andrews and James Brown and for Boulton & Watt A.F. Stonebridge and Joseph Ruston.

Joseph's passport was issued on the same day, and a few days later he started out on his trip, which led to a fabulous career. (The original of the above agreement is kept in the archive of the Technical Museum in Vienna.)
This is a translation made by my relation Walter Ruston, who lives in Brussels, of a biographical entry in Sonderdruck Osterrreichisches Biographisces Lexikon.

RUSTON JOSEPH JOHN boat and engine builder, and manufacturer, born in Poplar London on March 3 1809, and died in Vienna March 2 1895. He was the eldest son of Joseph John Ruston owner of a shipyard in Poplar and was apprenticed as a ship's carpenter and also trained as an engine builder.

In 1832 he became a master boat builder in the shipyard of Andrews, a fellow founder of the first Danube Steamship Company in Wein-neu-Leopoldau. From 1833--6 three steamships were built, the *Pannonia, Zrinyi* and *Nador*, which was designed by Ruston. In 1839, he completed the steamship *Sophie* for Andrews from his own plans, destined for the Traunsee. In 1840 Ruston designed for Andrews, who had been granted a licence for transport on the Moldau and the Elbe. The *Bohemia* was built between 1840 and 1841 in Karolinenthal (Karlin) near Prague. It was the first steamship in Bohemia. Joseph later went on to build the paddle steamer *Gisela*. Which to this day sails on the Traunsee, still powered by its original engine

After the death of Andrews in (1847), Ruston married his widow, and after her death in 1848 he came into possession of all ships' transport of the Elbe, which he gave up in 1851 after the building of the Dresden to Prague railway.

In 1854 Ruston took part in schemes to acquire transport on the Inn and until 1859 he built ships on the Danube near Klosterberg. From 1857 to 1873 he also controlled the shipyard taken over from Breitfeld and Evans in Schwarzlackenau. From 1862 he owned all transport on the Traunsee (his brother John R Ruston, 1820 – 1873, was a sleeping partner) which his nephew Joseph J Ruston, (1857 – 1934) continued. In 1850 the Ruston Brothers acquired an engine-building concern near Prague (Ruston & Evans -- from 1854 Ruston & Co), which produced excellent results, in particular building of steam power plant, machinery for sugar factories, mills, maize spirit distilleries, mines, iron industry, china factories and saw mills. And from 1863 bridge building. Numerous new machines were constructed for sugar factories, using their own inventions.

In 1858 the first steam traction engine was produced, and in 1863 the first water turbine. Apart from all that, from 1852 the business was engaged in building ships' and their engines, and from 1863 also steam dredgers. However, it was impossible to maintain the building of ships continuously because of lack of demand. In 1869 the Prague Engine Co., formerly Ruston & Co., took over the concern. Ruston was a technical and commercial pioneer of the development of industrial transport in Austria. In Vienna Joseph Ruston is commemorated with the naming of a thoroughfare, Joseph Rustonstrasse, with a further street bearing the name Rustonstrasse in Gmuden upper Austria.

Joseph John Ruston played an important role in the mechanisation of both shipping and industry in Austria. He lived for 45 years in a house he purchased named 'Grunberg', next to the Imperial Palace Schonbrunn in Vienna. He was befriended by Emperor Franz Joseph, and named three paddle steamers, *Sophie*, *Elizabeth*, and *Gisela*, after members of the royal family. (I have sailed on the steamer *Gisela,* and have also met Marcus Habsburg, a direct descendant of Franz Joseph, who owns and still lives in the Kaiservilla in Bad Ischl, Austria.)

Joseph John's first wife Isabella (formerly Andrews) had been born a Hepburn; she claimed descent from John Hepburn, Earl of Bothwell. She died in 1847 without having given birth. Joseph married Barbara Victoria Belha with whom he had four children: Joseph John Victor, Isabella, Victor John George and Henrietta. However he divorced his wife after the birth of their fourth child. The children grew up hardly having known their mother. They were rich kids with quite a high opinion of themselves, and seemed to prefer to infer that Barbara Isabella Hepburn had been their mother and not Barbara Belha – thereby laying claim to a 'royal connection'.

Joseph John Victor Ruston (the grandfather of Walter Ruston) had a brother Victor John George, and he in turn had one son Joseph Victor Anthony Ruston born on 21 November 1889, who married the Dutch Baroness Ella van Heemstra. They had one child, Audrey Kathleen Ruston born in Brussels on 4 May 1929. She latter became a world-famous film star, under her stage name Audrey Hepburn. Without any legitimate reason, her father called himself Hepburn-Ruston. It is of course possible that both he and Audrey believed that Isabella Hepburn had been both their grand- and great-grandmother respectively.

Much has been written about Audrey's father, and how he simply walked out on her and her mother in 1935.
My kinsman, Walter Ruston, a distinguished engineer now living in retirement in Brussels writes:

It is totally untrue that Joseph simply walked out on his family, never to be heard from again. They lived together in Brussels until 1939. Audrey attended an English boarding school. Only at the outbreak of war did they part. The Baroness van Heemstra took Audrey back to Holland where she thought they would be safer. As it turned out of course Holland was invaded and they endured a particularly hard war. Joseph was interned with many others for the duration of the war because of his association with Oswald Mosley and his hard line Fascist beliefs. After his release from internment, Joseph settled in Dublin. (It had been written that he had Irish or even Scottish forebears, they can't seem to make up their mind which! All nonsense, he could be described as Anglo Austrian perhaps.) He began to use the name Anthony Hepburn.

Joseph Victor Anthony's old mother who still lived in Vienna had his address all the time. However, Audrey's mother systematically intercepted all the letters, which Joseph wrote to his daughter. He was very well aware of his daughter's fame and I am in possession of his last letters to his mother in which he bitterly complained about the fact that his ex-wife made all contact between him and his daughter impossible.

FROM WHOM I AM DESCENDED

I am not certain that Audrey was aware of that. In the mid 1950s, whilst her grandmother still lived in Vienna, Audrey came to visit, and on that occasion my father showed her the portrait of Joseph Ruston's first wife which he called 'old Hepburn' but did not have the heart to tell her she was not her great-grandmother. The old lady was not even born a Hepburn.

Ella van Heemstra was a peculiar woman. Her animosity toward the Austrian Rustons dated from the time of a visit she had made with her husband to Austria and Bohemia when the newly weds presented themselves to the family. Unpleasant events poisoned the atmosphere during their visit and all later attempts at reconciliation failed.

If Ella had not returned to Holland in 1939 she would probably have been interned with Joseph Victor. Diana Mosley (one of the Mitford sisters) the wife of Oswald, was interned for three years in appalling conditions in Holloway Prison, and she was a cousin of Winston Churchill! Ella was actively involved in the British Union of Fascists and wrote articles for 'Blackshirt' (the official news journal of the BUF) yet it is difficult to find any written reference whatsoever to Joseph in BUF literature. Surprisingly he is not mentioned even once in the autobiography of Oswald Mosley (1968) or Diana Mosley (1977), or even in Robert Skidelsky's book on Mosley (1975). It seems that Ella loved the thrill of it all, but deserted the sinking ship when things got warm. Certainly Audrey would have been better off in England during the war. She nearly died in Holland.

Audrey's father Joseph has been portrayed as the villain of the peace by most biographers, who have further sought to exonerate her mother Ella, suggesting that she was led into it all by Joe. I maintain that had Joe had any deep hidden resentment of Britain, which would have been understandable given he spent five years in prison without charge or trial, he would have had ample opportunity to vent his anger whilst living in Northern Ireland for the remainder of his days. I am sure he could have found plenty of sympathisers there. The internment of political prisoners was a disgrace, many of whom played incredibly minor roles in the BUF. One of the most ironic reports to be heard at the time was of a lady member of the BUF. Whilst in Holloway Prison she was sent a telegram by the War Office telling her that her son had been killed in action whilst serving in the British Army. Was she then released on compassionate grounds? No, she was not.

In 1918 the First World War had come to an end. The weary servicemen returned to what they thought had been promised: 'A land fit for heroes.' It fell far short of their expectations. They were disillusioned. By the early 1930s instead of improvement the economic situation had worsened.

Oswald Mosley stated his policy at the inception of the BUF, of a 'Greater Britain'. 'Our main policy, quite frankly is a policy of "Britain first" but our very preoccupation with internal reconstruction is of some guarantee that at least we shall never pursue the folly of an aggressive Imperialism. It will never be necessary to stimulate the steady temper of Britain in the task of rebuilding our own country, by appeals to flamboyant national sentiment in foreign affairs. We shall mind our own business, but we will help in the organisation of world peace as part of that business'. Mosley wrote these words in 1932. That same year, fired with hope and imagination, my father, James Alfred, joined the BUF.

Dad was born in Cayley St Limehouse in 1900. As a child he preferred the company of his grandfather Charles, a shipwright, to that of his father Alfred James. He loved going to Victoria Park. Vicky Park as it is affectionately known, is a haven of green in the heart of London's East End. Our family have fond memories of summer days, spent feeding the ducks, sometimes lying on the grass listening to a band playing or more energetically, dancing to it. Swimming, boating, cricket, fetes, exhibitions and, oh yes, political rallies, they all happened in Victoria Park.

Back in 1880, grandfather Charles had built a model boat. With his father Charles, also a shipwright, they experimented with various models of steam engine by which to power it. They then hit on the idea of fixing a plumber's blowlamp in the stern. After priming and pumping, the lamp was ignited. Once a good flame was under control, and with the rudder fixed, they let go of the boat. Much to their delight it shot across the lake at considerable speed. Father and son together had discovered the principle of jet propulsion, but sadly did not see the significance of what they had achieved.

The boat was still around when dad was a boy. Grandfather Charles was an elegant man who wore a cape, top hat and carried a cane with a silver top. In 1861 he had married Margaret Elizabeth Shirt, whose father John was a violinist, and a professor of music. Her mother was Elizabeth Margaret Addis, related to the famous Addis brand name; they had four children, one of who was Alfred James, my grandfather. Taught in the classical style, he became a fine pianist. He used his talent on the music halls and it was there that he met my grandmother Hannah Rust. She was also an 'act' and played the accordion. In 1866 a financial crisis shut most of the shipyards and caused widespread unemployment. Grandfather Charles was forced to seek new employment. So he learned the bakery business and worked for Meredith & Drew as a journeyman biscuit baker. Later, when becoming foreman, he was in a position to offer jobs to many of the family, and so a long line of biscuit bakers followed. The decline in the shipbuilding industry, together with the influence the Shirt family musicians had on us, brought to an end the 200-year family tradition of shipwrights. As far as I am aware, no member of our family entered the shipbuilding industry again.

My dad was nine years old when his grandfather, Charles, died. Uncle Arthur, a soldier, came home for the funeral. He was stationed at Victoria Barracks Portsmouth serving in the Devonshire Regiment. The trips to Vicky Park with the boat came to an end. Under the guidance of his father Alfred James, Dad started to play the piano. It was to be a major influence in his life.

Another influence was his Aunt Minnie Rose Shirt. She brightened his life with her whistle-stop visits from America. She had married a David Wood and emigrated to the States early in the century, but never lost contact with her family in London. Arriving in England via a Cunard Liner, Aunt Minnie installed herself at the Dorchester hotel, and would visit in a chauffeur- driven car. This impressed Dad greatly, and his aunt further encouraged him saying, 'Young man, you should be in America'. Aunt Minnie and her husband had started a business, which had become very successful. Her son, Leonard, had an engineering works in Beaumont Street London W1. She wrote to her younger brother Claude, now in Australia:

England certainly has something on her plate. It makes my heart ache, with practically the whole of Europe against her. Whilst the States are drafting men, I don't think there is any danger of them going to war, although they are keeping England with material – perhaps the draft is only to keep the men at home. This is only my idea of course but is a good way to find employment for them. Don't take me too seriously on the subject, but they are just showing any country that they are ready for them. I cannot help it, but England is on my mind, night and day. I sometimes wonder if any of our family has been bombed. (We had!)

Leonard sent a cable this spring asking if Ethel could take 15 children of his employees. The fathers were willing, but when they asked their wives they didn't want to part with their children, so there was cabling to and fro, then more waiting, through red tape. At last a cable arrived saying there were seven children coming for Ethel to sponsor. So she found a home among her friends for them. She took two, a girl aged 12 and a boy ages 13, brother and sister. The other five went to three homes. Leonard paid the children's fares £25 each – bought them clothes for the trip and gave each £10 for landing expenses.

As I have never been naturalised and am not a US citizen, I could not take any. Perhaps you heard about the boat being torpedoed with children leaving England. There were three boats that left at the same time, the boat that these children came over on was one of them, and arrived in Quebec safe.

I felt rather touched, when I heard of the *Empress of Britain* being bombed and sunk. It was a beautiful ship and the last one I crossed to Canada in. Lillian Ethel and myself are doing knitting and giving our time for war work for the British war relief. Lillian and Ethel are making bandages and sewing two days a week. It is awful to think such things have to be made for the imminent destruction of the living. Tonight it is snowing fast, and it makes me shudder to think of England and what might be taking place in that chilly, damp climate, with helpless sick, sleeping underground while their homes are going up in flames and destruction. But material things don't matter if lives can be saved. Leonard is in England and that means a great deal for me to worry about. Of course his business is at a standstill, as naturally it would be. Although they are making some kind of gadgets for planes which does a little to help the cause.

Perhaps I might mention that every country is looking out for itself, and as the States is not a British colony, there are a great many people who think the British children should not be sent here as they have enough poor of their own to look after. I am sending you a British Christmas card this year. Its sale is for the British war relief. They cost 15 cents apiece and the proceeds go to the relief fund.

When I was in Germany it was plain to see the Germans were up to something, because most of the ones who wore pants were in uniform, while other countries were asleep. After the last war they silently went ahead to prepare for the brutal one, now sweeping everything before them.

This country [America] has every race of people, and there is a surface and an undercurrent of hate of anything that is British. They will never forget the revolution, and the Irish will see to it that they never will. While Roosevelt has been with the British-- that white-livered Lindbergh is another one who went round the world to spy for Hitler, at least that is the way I see through him. His father was a German American and naturally the Germans back him. As soon as the Irish put their foot on this soil they become politicians and support anyone the priest tell them to, or as they say, when an Irishman arrives, he is met at the boat with a policeman's uniform, and he intends to run the country.

FROM WHOM I AM DESCENDED

We lost all contact with Aunt Minnie. When she visited England in 1948, there was not one Ruston abode left standing in the East End. From her letters we know that she came looking, but couldn't find any of us. My regret is that I never met this remarkable woman. Had I done so, I think I just might have followed her. Dad spoke of her until the day he died. Our family had lived in the East End for more than 250 years. Hitler moved us out in two!

There has been much written about the East End of London, much of which bears little resemblance to the people and place I knew. Anita Dobson, the star of the original East-Enders TV soap, wrote her account of the East End she remembered as a child. The book is called *My East End*. It rekindled many memories for me. As well as Anita's memoirs, the book contains a potted history of London's East End, its people and the Cockney language. You have to be born there to understand it. However, she does give an insight into the dialogue. Coincidentally, Anita's grandmother was a close friend of my mother's.

Dad left school at the age of 14 with a basic education. Undaunted by this he set out to teach himself. He read every book he could get his hands on, but much preferred those written by people of imagination and achievement. For a short time he worked as a porter in Billingsgate market. Motorised transport was in its infancy; there were still more horse and carts around then. His father, Alfred, bought him a racing bike. Extremely light, it had cane wheels. Dad didn't drink or smoke and was very fit. He often rode around Vicky Park and was challenged to race. This he always refused to do – that is, until one day someone suggested that he was frightened of being beaten. That did it. His father laid down a challenge to all comers; bets were taken. Dad wasn't a bit worried he was a distance rider, and cleverly suggested a race of 20 laps. The local lads were mostly used to sprint racing, and had no idea how to pace themselves. They hadn't calculated exactly how far it was going to be. Some had very good machines with gears, whereas dad's bike was fixed- wheel. The race started. Dad let the others tear away. One by one he caught and passed them until he had eventually lapped them all, much to the delight of his father, who had won a few bob on the race.

Dad had an aunt in a sanatorium near Southend-on-Sea. She had tuberculosis, which was quite common then. His mother Hannah made a few custard pies, wrapped them in a muslin cloth and gave them to him to take to his aunt. It was Sunday, there had been a hard frost during the night, and the road was still icy when dad set off. He got to the sanatorium, where his Aunt was so pleased to see him, but he could only stay a short time, before starting back. On his way home, hungry and tired, he saw a cyclist in the distance. Standing up in his pedals, he made an attempt to catch the bike in front. This took longer than he was used to, and it needed a supreme effort to keep up the pace. However, he eventually got behind the wheel of the man in front. There he stayed mile after mile. Just occasionally the cyclist in front looked over his shoulder and smiled, but never said a word. After about five or six miles the stranger pulled in to the side of the road, glad of a rest, and dad stopped too.

His newly found cycling companion put his hand in his pocket and pulled out a packet of raisins. Emptying half in the palm of his hand, he gave them to dad. 'Take these son, and eat a couple now and then,' he said. 'It will help your stamina.' The stranger mounted his bike once more, and after a mile or so, with the wave of his hand, branched off the main road. Tired and frozen, it was dark when dad finally arrived home. So cold had it been that when he took his jacket and trousers off they stood up by themselves!

Some long time after the encounter on the Southend road with the stranger, looking through a magazine, dad saw a picture of him. It was only then he realised that he not only caught, but stayed, for mile upon mile, with the great Harry Green, who a few years earlier, had set a new record by cycling from Land's End to John o'Groats in two days, 19 hours and 52 minutes.

Dad had a fascination for anything mechanical, and at the first opportunity got behind the wheel of a lorry. Not content with driving one, he wanted to know how they worked. A self-taught mechanic, he was soon in demand. If a long-distance job came up the word would go out, 'Send Jim Ruston; if it breaks down he will fix it.' The first motors he drove had an open cab with only a canvas to keep out the elements. The solid tyres made them extremely uncomfortable to ride on, and with a 'crash' gearbox and heavy steering they really had to be driven. Dad took these primitive vehicles all over the country. He made many trips north up the famous Shap Fell in Cumbria, on route to Scotland. In winter it was a challenge. Dad would rest in the day and drive through the night. This was hazardous to say the least. The carbide lamps were poor and reduced visibility to a few yards ahead. However, if you parked up at night the extreme temperatures would cause the water in the radiator to freeze. More than one lorry driver cracked the cylinder block of an engine by starting it up in these conditions. The round trip to Scotland took a week.

When not on long-distance trips, my father expanded both his formal education and mechanical prowess. Evenings he played the piano in public houses. Firstly to amuse himself, then as his popularity grew, he would get 'poached' from one pub to the next, with ever-increasing rewards. In 1923 at St Saviours Church, Poplar, dad married Annie Elizabeth Miller. Things were fine at the outset. It was the 'Roaring Twenties', music and dance featured strongly in their recreation.

Between 1924 and 1928 they had three children Royston, Maud, and June. Dad was anything but domesticated, and continued his piano playing in the pubs. It was during this period that he met Alex Steel. They struck up an immediate friendship, and worked out songs they could sing together and comedy routines for a double act. They became inseparable. Dad spent more and more time on the 'act' and less on his day job. This led, quite naturally, to problems in the matrimonial home. Annie Miller was by nature highly-strung and quick to throw things in temper. It was not unusual for dad to arrive home late and find his clothes thrown onto the pavement. Sadly Annie contracted Tuberculosis and after a painful illness died in the Bancroft Lodge Annex of the Mile End Hospital. Widowed at the age of 30 with three children, the future didn't look too bright for Dad. He gave up the 'act' and slipped into melancholia. He truly loved Annie and was devastated by her death. He hadn't realised she was so ill. TB was common enough in those days and struck without warning, more often than not resulting in death. A cure had yet to be found. Pre-occupied with music and motors, dad hadn't fully realised the extent of her problem. He was a dreamer. A romancer.

My grandparents, Alfred and Hannah, looked after the children whilst dad came to terms with his situation. He renewed his partnership with Alex Steel. In 1932 dad met and married my mother. She had become engaged to David Jacobs, a violinist, who played in the Southern Syncopated Orchestra; he was of the Jewish faith. Whatever possessed Mum to think he would break with his religion and marry a gentile I cannot imagine, but he must have promised that he would. Finally, he broke off the engagement. This would not be as simple as I think he might have thought. Firstly there would be a case of breach of promise to answer, and secondly mum was pregnant. Mum took advice and brought an action through the court for compensation. This she won, and was summarily awarded £400, a considerable sum in those times. A terraced house in the East End could be purchased for about £100. Dad no doubt put the money to good use, in one of his many schemes! May Elizabeth was born in September 1932; her close family call her Maisie, and even she doesn't know why.

My father didn't hate the Jews, but neither was he enamoured of them. In his short lifetime, they had made considerable inroads into retail trade, and more importantly pawnbroking and money lending. Many East End families were in debt to them. Dad felt they were becoming too influential in the East End. Well read, my father had earned himself the label of 'poor man's lawyer'. If anyone had a demand for payment, or letter from the 'authorities' they would be advised to 'take it to Jim Ruston' because he could sort it out. He would represent the defendant, putting circumstances of mitigation to the bench. On one occasion, so eloquent was his plea it led to the Judge asking of him, 'What is your occupation?' 'Motor mechanic M'lud,' dad replied. The learned man responded 'Young man, you have missed your calling'. Dad saved many a home and its contents from the bailiffs. During this period he became friendly with the eminent lawyer Lewis Silkin (later created a Baron). It was an unlikely liaison. Silkin was a Jew, and a Labourite. He was Member of Parliament for Peckham 1936 – 50. Dad was staunch Tory. Both socially and politically they were 180 degrees out of sync. Dad learned a great deal from the lawyer, and coerced him into many a consultation on behalf of the needy, without fee. Dad thought the world of his legal friend, who often called upon him to do some legwork of behalf of his clients. My father was very proud of this. Dad helped Lewis with claims for compensation for the dependants of the infamous Bethnal Green Shelter disaster, which occurred on 3 March 1943. Dad said it was caused by too many people trying to get down the steps to the underground shelter at once. A lady carrying a bundle of clothes tripped, and people fell on top of each other. 173 were killed.

All of this however took time. There was always someone at the door. He never took a penny for his time or advice. Mostly it ended up costing him money. This annoyed mum a bit, but it was useless remonstrating with her 'rebel for the cause' husband.

With the Depression biting deep we were always short of money. It wasn't lack of opportunity that caused it; dad was multi-talented and ever resourceful. It was his concern for, and commitment to, others that engulfed him. What with raising funds for charities, and drumming up support for the newly formed BUF, little time was left for family matters. Thank goodness our mother was so independent and resourceful, else none of us would have survived.

Father Raven, the priest who had married dad to his first wife, was a remarkable man, and worked tirelessly for impoverished East-Enders, for whom he cared so passionately. Dad struggled with religion. If there was a god, why was there so much poverty and suffering? On the one hand he spent hours of his time, freely given, to the causes championed by his cassocked friend. On the other, he condemned the Church as a profiteering landowner. He thought the attitude of the Church towards the proletariat patronising, to say the least. Yet he had nothing but praise for Father Raven. And rarely refused a favour asked.

Meanwhile Ruston and Steel, who had started out as a pub act, were much in demand. They were playing the music halls and cinemas. Early 1935 a man named J.C. Cannell had stepped into their lives. He was a researcher for the popular radio series called *In Town Tonight,* which had started in 1933 and was now in its second series. The idea for the programme was the brainchild of Eric Maschwitz, who was Director of Variety at the BBC. He appointed the producer A.W. Hanson with a mandate to gather together a team to develop the concept. The programme proved immensely popular, and the listeners would rush home on Saturday nights to 'tune in'. J.C. Cannell invited Ruston and Steel to appear on the programme; they didn't need a second asking! After their first broadcast which took place at Broadcasting House on 24th May 1935, their appeal widened, and led to appearances on the same bill as many of the all time greats. To promote radio, the BBC had started an annual exhibition at Olympia. This event took place August/September and ran for 10 days. It was called Radiolympia.

In 1936, Ruston and Steel were invited to appear at Radiolympia. They broadcast each day for 10 days. Some of the programmes were being received in America. They were made. The tobacco company, Churchman's, issued a set of 50 cigarette cards featuring a selection of the people who had appeared on In Town Tonight (they are now collectors items). Also a book with the same title and written by J.C. Cannell was published in 1935.

Things seemed rosy until one fatal night at a meeting of the BUF when violence erupted. Dad had his left arm slashed down to his wrist damaging the tendons to his hand. Hospital and an emergency operation followed. Thereafter he was unable to span an octave with that hand. He adapted, but he wasn't the same. My father was furious, not because of his injury but at the level of violence caused by the antagonists, mainly Communists, who had infiltrated the meeting. They had hurled missiles at the platform on which Oswald Mosley was making his address. Particularly nasty devices included potatoes into which razor blades had been partly inserted; when thrown they were lethal. The constitution of the BUF promoted peaceful protest, the right to freedom of speech. It deplored violence. However more and more often incidents occurred, and it became necessary to defend both themselves and their right to assemble. Disillusioned, dad distanced himself from the movement.

The wearing of a black shirt was a bad idea. Confrontational. In his book My Life, published in 1968, Mosley himself agreed with the benefit of hindsight. Much has been much written about Mosley and Fascism in Britain in the 1930's. I have no need, even if I could, to expand on it. I think the most balanced view is that of Robert Skidelsky, in his book, *Oswald Mosley*, published in 1975. Fairness is all my father ever sought. Britain for the British. He was wrapped in a Union flag.

In 1952, after changing her religion to that of the Jewish faith, a prerequisite of proposal, my eldest sister, Maud, married Joe Travis. My father gave his blessing and attended the wedding. He even wore a black cap. Hardly an act of Anti-Semitism! It is however, a shame that my sister, having adopted her new faith, could not find compassion within her heart when called upon many years later to so.

The 'act' Ruston and Steel received an invitation to attend one of the famous Foyle's literary luncheons. They had met Christina Foyle at the BBC. She too had been an 'In Town Tonighter'. They were appearing 'up West' and were in top hat and tails. On leaving the luncheon and in good spirits (mostly liquid) they 'borrowed a bicycle'. Setting off towards the East End, dad riding and Alex on the crossbar, their vision, balance, and sense of direction became increasingly impaired. A bump followed by a crash, and the intrepid cyclists found themselves in a shop window, surrounded by glass, but otherwise unscathed. Needless to say, when one is not looking for a policeman two will surely appear. With apologies, and in mitigation, dad explained that his wife was due to give birth anytime and he was hurrying home to be with her. A likely story. The policemen bundled the 'act' into a van and drove them home.

When they arrived there, mum had just given birth to a girl, Evelyn. It was 17 June 1935. (69 years later a Foyle's lunch on this day and month would play a part in my life). The little house was full with family and friends, and of course two policemen. With congratulations and drinks all round, they had a party!

Annette Mills, the sister of John, composed a song, well more of a dance really, she called it *Hands, Knees and Bumps a Daisy*, and asked my Dad if he would perform it with her on stage at Collins Music Hall in Islington. When asked his opinion of the comical composition dad replied: 'I don't see it as being a record breaker, but it will stay with us for years to come'. It has. In the early 1950s Annette became a household name with a little puppet called Muffin the Mule who danced on the top of her piano. Sadly, and whilst still in her prime, she died from cancer. Dad was very fond of her.

I was the last to be born in Elsa Street. Temporarily better off, we moved briefly to Ship Street in Poplar, where Elizabeth Ann (Betty) was born, then to a much bigger house in Stepney Green.

EVACUATED TO SOMERSET

The train was crowded as we headed towards the West Country. The five of us and mum sat on one side of the carriage opposite another family of evacuees. Evacuees. This label would stick for years to come and would be uttered in many tones with as many meanings. A parent could stay with a child if under five. Betty was two and I three and a half. Thankfully, mum was to stay with us for the duration. It was about four hours before we got to Bristol where many of the children were to change trains for various destinations. We stayed on the train and watched the stations go by. We stopped at Nailsea, which meant nothing to us at the time. Quite a few got off here. The train lurched forward but didn't get up much speed before pulling in to Yatton Station. 'Come on kids this is where we get off,' said mum. The ladies in green were here once more, trying to organise some sense of order. The noise of the massive steam locomotive and the clouds of steam all added to the mild pandemonium that, as soon as the train pulled out, returned to normality. It was around 6pm in early October. It was dry but cold. We huddled together. In ones twos and threes the children were collected by the mostly kindly souls who would care for them during their stay. We were the last to leave.

After mum's protestations that in no way were we going to be split up finally accepted, a place was offered where we could stay together as a family. Mrs Kingcott, a well-dressed lady with a warm manner, introduced herself. She told mum she would take us to a farmworkers cottage, which was standing empty and belonged to Mr Griffin. Us kids were bundled into her little Austin Seven car. Mum thanked the WVS ladies who, after all, had much to put up with. They were doing their level best, not often appreciated or recognised. Not everyone would get a good billet, the quality of accommodation and hospitality would, quite naturally, vary. There were nitpickers on both sides. (Another variety of nitpickers would have to be suffered quite soon – Nitty Nora!)

We were glad to be off that draughty platform. The little car laboured under the strain of the load. The blackout was in force so there was very little light. We peered through the windows trying to make out the surroundings. Heading towards Clevedon we had just passed a pub called the Bridge Inn when suddenly we took a left turn. Up over a bridge we went and down the other side into a tiny village. As we passed the church and school Mrs Kingcott explained: 'This is Kingston Seymour'. The first we had heard of our eventual destination. We didn't stop right away, but carried on for another half mile. The car finally came to a halt in the middle of nowhere. Or at least that is how it felt to us London kids. Mrs Kingcott jumped out of her car and with a cheerful 'this way everyone' waved us towards the front door of a small detached cottage. 'This,' she said, 'is Rose Cottage.' As we stepped through the door, straight into the front room, the warmth hit us. A fire had been lit and there was a wonderful array of food on the table. More than we had seen at any one time in months. An oil lamp lit the room, adding to an atmosphere of security and friendliness. Mum started to cry, we all cried. The relief was enormous. This was to be our home for the next three years. Exhausted we ate what we could, then all piled into one big double bed with mum. This bond between us five kids would remain throughout our lives, and is something we still hold and cherish.

The next morning we got up, eager to look outside at our surroundings. The front door opened straight on to the road, which passed by the cottage. We looked first right then left and ahead. All we could see was fields. We really were in the middle of nowhere. 'Mum, come and see' we shouted. 'What's out there,' she cried. 'Nothing' said we. 'Well then, why do you want me to come and look!' We ventured outside and wandered cautiously around. Immediately opposite our cottage was a small stream – or rhyne, which we were soon to learn was the correct name. This rhyne and the many others in the vicinity held a fascination for me. I would challenge their superiority on a number of occasions in the coming months. 'What's that smell?' asked Eve 'That's cow shit,' Maisie replied. She never did mince her words!

Rose Cottage comprised two rooms down and two up. Also on the ground floor was a scullery. There was no electricity and no running water. Outside were a bucket lavatory and a wooden shed. Small gardens to both sides, with another rhyne running along the rear of the property. Cooking was by way of a cast iron kitchen range. This had two hotplates on which to heat saucepans kettles and flat irons; there was also an oven. Once mastered it would perform admirably, but it was essential to get a good fire going before asking too much of it. We fetched water in a metal milk churn from a farm about 200 yards up the lane back towards the village. The churn was placed on a set of old pram wheels, which we pushed to and from the farm to refill. This was a bit too close to nature for us Londoners!

The most noticeable thing was the stillness. It was so quiet it was noisy. Mrs Kingcott visited on our first morning to see how we were coping. 'We'll be alright thankyou,' said mum. 'What about school?' she inquired. 'Maisie, Stella and Evelyn are old enough to attend.' Much to my relief I never heard my name mentioned. 'Oh they can't go yet,' said Mrs Kingcott. 'Why not?' asked mum in a passive inquiring tone. 'You see Mrs Ruston, the school has suffered some damage to the roof, caused by enemy bombs, and we have had to close it.' We couldn't help laughing. We had come all this way to escape the bombs.

EVACUATED TO SOMERSET

This was not the first time the war had followed us, and it wouldn't be the last either. I reasoned as only a small boy can that Hitler was out to get me personally!

The district nurse paid as a visit. We all had a condition of the skin called scabies. This was highly contagious and common in wartime among those who had spent many hours in communal air raid shelters. The nurse said we would have to go to the Central Clinic in Bristol where we would receive treatment. The next day we walked into the village, about half a mile. The school and school house were next door to each other with the church and vicarage close by. A post office with shop, and another shop opposite. A cluster of houses from the modest to the quite grand, formed the heart of the village. A farming community, with an inordinate number of farms and holdings, given the acreage within the village boundary. We waited next to the war memorial erected to the memory of the fallen in the 1914--18 war. Before long, more names would be added from the current conflict. It's still like this today.

The WVS had arranged a car to take us to the Clinic in Old Market, Bristol. After checking our identity cards (everyone was issued with them in wartime, it was an offence not to be able to produce one on demand), we were ushered into a room and told to undress. We were put under the shower and washed with a liberal helping of carbolic soap. After this we were treated with a lotion that in time would rid us of the scabies. Thankfully it did. The irritation caused by scabies tends to make you itch, and scratching makes things worse. Panic set in when mum was taken off by a nurse to have a bath. I wondered what they were going to do to her, and started screaming and shouting. Stella assured me that not only would mum be OK, but she would really enjoy a good hot bath. I'm sure she did. We returned via the good offices of the WVS to Kingston Seymour smelling of carbolic soap, but healthier, for sure.

Maisie, Stella and Evelyn started school the next day. The head teacher was Mrs Coghill; school marmish, stern, but fair. Mum asked if there were any jobs going and was offered the cleaning of the school, and later the vicarage. She was very glad of the opportunity to earn a little money. Dad would send what he could, which wasn't much, and not at all regular. The farmer whose cottage we lived in was paid about 8s 6d (42p) per week for each of us for which he was to provide accommodation and food. The accommodation I have described; the food, never quite enough. We had to hand over the relevant ration coupons to cover this. Mum traded the rest for whatever she could get.

Needless to say, clothing coupons, completely useless when you don't even have enough money for food, were the first to get sold.

The black market in ration coupons was rife. Mum would, however, keep an odd sweet coupon, and if there were a few pennies left at the end of the week she would buy a bag of boiled sweets, which we would share. A real treat. To add to her already considerable burden, mum took in washing. Among the items she washed were the white coats worn by the farmworkers when milking cows. These would come in heavily stained with cow muck. In the scullery there was a brick-built zinc-lined copper. Filled with water and a fire lit underneath, it soon came to the boil. Everything white should be boiled in Persil, mum would advocate. She was very proud of her washing.

We had inherited a cat and we named him 'Kipper Licker'. A remarkable animal who found his own food, and often, after a 'hunt', brought back a small rabbit and left it by the back door. Mum was very grateful to her benefactor and treated him with a deal of affection. So you can imagine her distress when on lighting the fire beneath to copper one day, she saw a black smouldering creature fly out from under the boiler. Poor Kipper Licker had crept under there for a sleep. We didn't see him for days. He eventually returned; but never went in the scullery again.

We were always turned out spotlessly clean. 'Anyone can get hold of a bar of soap,' mum would say, 'even in wartime.' After a while and finding it almost impossible to make ends meet, mum took in a lodger. He was from Manchester and worked on a nearby farm. A lovely lad, miles from home and family, he was extremely kind to us. On dark winter evenings before bedtime he would summon us so: 'Come on kids, let's loook at a boook!'

The days passed by; Christmas was approaching. From Rose Cottage it was half a mile to the village. Weekdays we left home at 8.30am. Mum pushing the pram with Betty in, me hanging on the side half walking half running to keep up. Maisie, Stella and Eve, dawdling along, then having to run to catch up. When we reached the school the three eldest would go into the playground and wait for the bell to be rung. Mum would then go off to clean the vicarage, with Bet and me in tow. When finished there, we moved on to the schoolhouse. Once all the cleaning was finished, and mum had gone to the shop, if there was anything she needed-- or more likely if she had any money, there were always things she needed – the three of us would return to the cottage.

During those cold winter days I played outside for hours on end. Sometimes following the cows down the lane and back into their field, after morning milking. Other times mum would dump us in the pram and go off collecting wood for the fire. In the opposite direction to the village and a little over a mile from Rose Cottage lay the foreshore of the Bristol Channel. The rise and fall of the tide here is, I believe, the second highest in the world. At low tide driftwood accumulates along the shore. Mum, helped by me, bundled this up and tied it to the pram, with Betty still in it. I walked back hanging on to the handle and mumbling about it not being fair having to walk. Mum remonstrated with me, 'You big sissy, you'll be going to school after Christmas.' It shut me up. We pushed and dragged our load of firewood back to the cottage and placed in the shed. Trips to the seashore became a regular event and at weekends the three eldest all came to help.

Each weekday at 3.30pm mum, Betty and me, waited outside the school for my sisters to come out. Mum would send them off home with instructions of little jobs they had to do for her. Betty and I played with slateboards and chalks in the classroom, while mum cleaned the school. Often the three schoolgirls would meander along the lane homewards chatting away with friends, and become oblivious of time. Looking back towards the school they would see mum coming home already. Off they scooted, dashing into the cottage to begin their allotted tasks, just as though they had been home for ages. Mum was never fooled, but let it pass as long as they did their best with the jobs. She tried to let us have as much freedom as possible, but we had to help.

It was 1940 and we were in the middle of one of the worst winters in history. It was freezing and everything was frozen. At least we didn't have any plumbing to freeze up! Much as we all loved being outside, now we stayed in as much as possible huddled up around the fire, but wood still had to foraged for; and trips to the shop made. It was bleak, would we ever get used to it.

It would soon be Christmas. On the last day of school there was a carol service. With other parents, mum took Betty and me to hear the children sing. I could hear Stella and Eve above all the rest. They had beautiful voices and always sang together, unmistakable. Maisie could sing but was not really interested. Maisie was a scholar, always reading and studying. History and literature were her favourite subjects, and she knew them. In the few days before Christmas, mum let us make paper chains to hang up. These we cut from any waste paper we could find. I remember even a few pages from an old book were savaged by our scissors. Needs must! The farmer whose milking coats mum washed gave us a chicken. Helped by Stella, mum made a Christmas pudding. Just where she got the ingredients, I do not know. Probably ration coupons swap. If you have to be poor, I think it is a well to be poor in the country. Country folk are very resourceful, and farmers didn't go too short in wartime. Half the things we could buy with our coupons we couldn't afford anyway. Mum made sure we never went without essentials.

Christmas Eve. God knows from where she got the little presents that filled our stockings. A book, some crayons, an apple, nuts and a few sweets. And joy of joy, a small bar of chocolate! Betty had a little doll, me a lead soldier, the older girls a brush and comb with a mirror in a pretty bag. There was nothing for mum. Her reward was seeing the look on our faces when we woke on Christmas morning, excited and shouting 'Look what I've got.' She was a genius, was our mum, a bloody genius! We lit the fire in the range and got the dinner on. Maisie and Stella laid the table. Eve helped too. What a spread we had. Chicken with roast potatoes; Brussels sprouts, peas and carrots, and a Yorkshire pud. Mum loved a bit of Yorkshire. Then after, steaming hot Christmas pudding and custard. Addicted to it I became, and addicted I remain! We were so happy. No bombs, no going down the shelter. We loved our little cottage in the country, but most of all we loved each other.

6 January 1941. School re-opened after the holiday. It was a weary bunch of kids that made their way there that morning. Some 18 high explosive bombs plus many incendiaries had fallen in the village the night before. None of us had had much sleep. The following nights were interrupted by more barrage fire and the wailing siren warning of an air raid, then the 'all clear'. One night there was a knock on our door. On opening it mum was confronted by a most irate ARP warden exclaiming, 'Why aren't you taking cover; you could all be killed!' Mum laughed, 'Do you call this a raid,' she said. 'Do you think me and the kids are going to leave our warm beds for this?' The warden was none too pleased with mum's attitude, and it did little to endear us to the locals, scoffing at their war. If only they had been with us in London, I am sure they would have understood. We never took cover at any time during our stay there.

Early in June, and as a result of a night raid, police promptly announced that they had located an unexploded bomb, which due to its close proximity to the school, meant that the School would be closed until the bomb was made safe. Did I hear a mighty cheer? It was decided that those evacuee children billeted close to the school should move out at night and return in the mornings. Some stayed with us. Mum did find this amusing. 'What do they think it is,' she reasoned, 'A night-time only bomb? One that won't go off in the day?' Some strange decisions were made in wartime. With a good intention though.

In fact, despite numerous calls made by the head teacher, Mrs Coghill, to the authorities, demanding that something be done, the School remained closed for six weeks. Such was the heavy work load placed on the bomb disposal squads having to clear so many UXBs in Bristol and surrounding districts. Later that year a new teacher, Mrs Fountain arrived. She would teach me.

Mum had found a friend in a Canadian soldier, his name was Neld, and he came to stay with us on occasion. He knew how desperate I was to have a fort with soldiers in. One day, he turned up with it. I was so happy I promised to be good forever. I only had two lead soldiers. One had no head and the other no arms. I put them side by side and reasoned: the one with the head would tell the one with the arms which way to shoot. Like most small boys I had a vivid imagination.

If our mother found some comfort with Neld, and I think she liked him a lot, then I am pleased. She had little else. And dad had another woman, named Elsie, in London, with whom he lived throughout the war. Family folklore has it that we have half brothers or sisters, we have never met. I wouldn't be at all surprised if this is true.

After a brief visit one day, we waved Neld goodbye. And we never saw him again. However some months later mum got an elaborate card with pyramids on from the Middle East. Inside was written: 'I send my love to you and the Big Five. Neld.' I wonder what happened to him.

A new year dawned. The girls went back to school, and Betty and I played around the cottage. Betty enjoyed throwing the cutlery in the rhyne at the rear of the cottage, telling mum 'Bimmy done it'. I made a fishing rod (piece of stick with a length of parcel string and a safety pin!) and would sit for hours on end dangling my 'line' in the rhyne -- often nodding off to sleep and falling in the water. Mum did her chores. I longed for Saturdays when I could go to the seashore with my big sisters and collect wood. It made a change from going with mum and Betty. Stella, Eve and me had taken the pram intending to collect driftwood. We had just got beyond the lane and into the open approaches. It all happened so quickly, the throaty roar of an engine, Stella herding us towards a ditch, throwing ourselves on the floor and the rapid fire of a machine gun. As the rounds of ammunition struck the mud, little spurts of steam rose from the ground. We had been strafed, or so it seemed. What importance could three kids and a pram be to the might of the *Luftwaffe*! Needless to say, we hurried home without the wood. Mum had a job to believe it. 'No,' she said. 'It couldn't have happened.' 'It did,' we chorused. We soon got over it, although the memory of the incident lingered. I told you I thought that Hitler was after me!

A COCKNEY KID IN GREEN WELLIES

On another occasion a hard frost had caused the rhynes to become frozen. I thought it would be a good idea to walk on the ice. It looked alright, tried it with my foot, OK. Then crack, splash I was under. I grabbed the reeds growing on the bank-side as I went down, and managed somehow to pull myself out. Funny, I wasn't scared, only worried at what mum would say, or rather do. A fate worse than drowning! I was getting adventurous. Eve and I would explore the neighbourhood looking for anything that might amuse us. On one occasion we really did come a cropper. Stella spent much of her spare time playing with Mrs Kingcott's son David. The two of them had become inseparable. And Stella was always welcome at the farm his parents owned. One day Eve and I walked with Stella to Ham Farm, the home of the Kingcott family. We stayed by the gate as Stella went into the house.

Next to the gate was a wooden platform on which milk churns stood waiting to be collected. Eve and I climbed on and began jumping on and off. It was fun. Somehow we managed to knock a churn over. In our attempts to get it upright we got covered in milk. It was in our hair, our clothes, we were soaked. I had a pair of calf-length wellington boots on and as I walked they squelched. In panic we ran home. Mum was furious. 'I didn't do anything mum,' said I. 'What's all this then,' she said, shaking me by the scruff of the neck.

A knock at the door, it was Farmer Kingcott. He politely but firmly told our mother that whilst Stella would always be welcome at their farm, Jimmy and Evelyn were banned! Eve and I kept a low profile for a while, and apart from apple scrumping, and Eve's fascination with chicken's eggs and rusty frying pans, we didn't get into too many scrapes.

Spring arrived, and someone mentioned me and school. 'What me? I don't have to go till summer.' This presented no problem at all for my inventive mother. She took me to school after the Easter break, and just changed my birth date by a couple of months! None of us had any birth certificates; they were all lost during the Blitz.

A classroom in the school was used each night as an ARP post. This did nothing for cleanliness and hygiene. Mrs Coghill tried her best to improve conditions. There was always a shortage of coal for the stove and her assistant, Mrs Fountain, was often absent through illness. Not at all surprising this, seeing as she had to walk two miles from Yatton station every day in all weathers, and then walk another two miles back at the end of a full day. Some things were so absurd. For instance a physical education teacher called to give us a talk about the benefit of taking regular exercise. Most of the kids walked at least a half-mile each way to school every day, and with our diet, how much exercise did she think we needed? On discovering that almost none of us had any plimsolls, she suggested we ask our parents to buy them. What planet was she on! (The plimsolls eventually arrived in March 1945, nine months after we had left.)

Mrs Kingcott called at our cottage on Sunday mornings and took us to Sunday school. This was held in a chapel a few hundred yards further on from the church. Unchanged, it is still there. With summer in full swing, mum decided we would take a trip into Clevedon, a seaside resort with a heavy Victorian influence, about four miles along the coast from us. We walked, of course; there were no buses. We had a picnic, a few sandwiches of bread and jam, and a small cake each. We sat on the big field by the boating lake. Little did I know then that Clevedon would play such a major role in my life. We had had a wonderful day and didn't want to leave. 'Come on kids it's time to go, we can always come here again,' mum reassured. True to her word, we did, and often.

Dad's sister, our Aunt Emmy, came down from London, bringing her two friends Kathleen and Marjorie with her. The three young women were so pretty. But one of our aunt's friends kept crying. She had just received a telegram telling her that her husband had been killed in action. The other young women's husband was a prisoner of war. Aunt Emmy had brought them down to us for a few days to take their minds off things. My lovely aunt was kindness itself, and never spared a thought for herself. Her own husband, Alec, was fighting, she knew not where, with the 8th army.

With mum they walked to the Bridge Inn on the road to Yatton for a drink; a huge treat for mum, she more than deserved it. The two eldest took charge in their absence and bossed the three youngest around. We were perfectly safe in those days; we never locked a door during the whole of our time at K.S.

However there was one occasion when we did get a bit of a fright. It was about 8.30pm and we were about to go to bed. Mum always went with us at the same time. She was about to lower the oil lamp when there was a tap tap, on the window. It sounded particularly eerie because we had a broken windowpane, and DIY mum had stuck a piece of thick brown paper over the frame. On it went — tap, tap, tap. It was the first time any of us had seen mum with a look of fright on her face. Suddenly she pulled herself up to her five feet nothing, and with the iron frying pan in one hand, flung open the door with the other. The 'intruder' stood there. At first sight, clad in a leather suit and helmet, he looked to our eyes a German paratrooper. He was in fact an Army Dispatch Rider who had lost his way! It's as well he wasted no time in identifying himself; if Mum had 'clocked him' with the pan, and she would have make no mistake, he definitely wouldn't have known where he was!

Another hard winter and Christmas was upon us once more. There was a carol concert at school and a play. I can never forget seeing Stella and Evelyn on the stage dressed as trees. They had brown stockings on and Eve's kept falling down, much to her annoyance. Children dressed as elves peeked out from behind the 'trees'. I had to perform *Ring-a-Ring-a-Roses* with other infants in front of the stage. I was most reluctant to participate, but a 'shove' from Mum did the trick! Once again, as from nowhere and with nothing, mum produced a lovely Christmas for us.

We received a telegram. No one welcomed the telegram boy in those days, he usually bore bad news. It was from Granny Hare to say our Granddad was very ill. Mum decided at once that she must go to him. We were farmed out among the kindly villagers. Stella and I stayed with the Kingcotts, whilst mum, taking Betty with her, caught the train to London. I was threatened with my life not to go near a milk churn! After a few days, mum returned with the news that Granddad was over the worst, and would be OK. She loved him dearly.

Raymond Stuckey's mum had written to the authorities to complain about the standard of education at Kingston Seymour School. Indicating that her own son's reading was far below average. An investigation by the Chief Education Officer found not only was the general level of learning at the school as a whole above average, but the son of the complainant was himself above average, especially in reading! Poor Mrs Coghill was so hurt. Both she and Mrs Fountain, whom I adored, had flogged themselves to a standstill, in extreme conditions, to the detriment of their own health to do the best for the pupils in their care. Not only was she exonerated, but also given a written statement of the excellence found at her School. My family, and just about everyone else we knew, had nothing but praise for this remarkable woman.

Despite pleas from the County to stay, Mrs Coghill left in April 1943. She wrote in the school logbook of her 'appreciation to her colleague Mrs Fountain for her unswerving loyalty at a difficult time'. Mrs Coghill had been head teacher at K.S. school for six years, four of those under conditions of War.

A new Head Teacher, Mrs Eleanor Bate, arrived. Marjorie Baggs, the monitor (assistant teacher) for some reason or other took an instant dislike to Stella, and picked on her. Everyone loved Stella; she was extremely popular. Always first to put her hand up to help with anything. She was a very pretty girl with long blond hair. Although of diminutive stature, Stella had guts, and with a stern look on her face, said to Miss Baggs. 'If you don't stop picking on me, I will tell my dad when he next comes down, and he will come to see you. And you won't like that one bit!'

By the summer of 1943, we considered ourselves countrified, and had earned the label given us by our Cockney cousins, as 'carrot crunchers'. The name stuck for years after the war. We helped with the hay making, and later on potato picking. More family arrived from London for a holiday in the country. We would take them to our seashore and tell them to paddle in the mud. 'Dad says it's good for your corns'. With the queuing for food, and extra walking having to be done, most people suffered with their feet. There was a glut of blackberries. We picked and picked filling every receptacle we could lay our hands on. We even filled the tin tub that we had our weekly bath in. Mum sold them for a halfpenny per pound. We had a few more sweets that week, and mum bought Maisie the packet of seeds she had been asking for. Maisie scattered her seeds, and to her delight was rewarded with a magnificent show of marigolds.

Mum had grown vegetables since our first spring in Kingston Seymour, although she knew nothing of gardening. She just read what it said on packets. She found she had 'green fingers'; everything she planted came up. The plentiful crop may have been attributed to the fact that we dug a trench in which to empty the bucket lavatory. When full, it was covered over with earth, and a new trench dug. Eventually most of the garden was fertilised! Now Maisie too was hooked, she cultivated a piece of garden and tended it with care. This love of gardening has remained with her. Maisie worked in a garden centre for years and became very knowledgeable.

In the summer of 1943 a young child, Raymond Stuckey's sister, had fallen in a rhyne and drowned. It cast a shadow of sorrow over the whole community. The School children lined the path to the church as the tiny white coffin passed by.

Meanwhile daily life continued. Maisie won a prize for an essay she had written. She was presented with a religious picture, and about seven shillings (35p). She gave it to mum to help out. That's way it was; we shared everything. We hung the picture in the cottage. Where is it now?

Ron Wallis also won a prize; he was a great friend of Maisie's so she was delighted. Ron often let Maise ride his bike. They would go off together for hours on end.

Another cold winter, the lack of coal, the endless trips to the seashore collecting wood. Fingers numb, freezing feet, half pushing, half dragging the laden down pram, with mum encouraging, 'Come on kids, we'll soon be home. I will make some hot cocoa when we get there.' At times like this, she must have had a heavy heart, but she never showed it. Often, fog crept in from across the Bristol Channel and engulfed the village. It was extremely dangerous to go out in it for fear of falling into the rhynes that ran along each side of the road. Once, Stella leaned rather too far across the water to pick a flower, and in she went, splash. When she surfaced she still had her hat on! She always wore a hat. She loved them. She would buy one for a penny at a jumble sale and pretty it up with a piece of lace taken off of something else. She was amazing with a needle and thread.

It was early December, and dad came down. He was sitting just inside the open front door, when, suddenly, he shot up and said 'Liz, pass me my boots. I can hear a plane coming down'. It was pure instinct, he was right. The engines stuttered as it flew overhead, and then we could see it. Dad pulled on his boots and with mum shouting 'Do them up you soppy sod or you'll trip over the laces' ran across the road and leaped the rhyne on the other side. The plane came down on Mendip View Farm two fields away from the cottage, killing both crewmen. It wasn't until many years after the war I discovered that it was an RAF Martinet trainer, with instructor and pupil. Dad didn't say much, except that there was little he could do when he got there. He never spoke about his rescue work; he had seen such horrors. He tried to forget, but they haunted him for years.

It was Christmas week when Dick and Millie Miller, dad's friends from London arrived. They brought all sorts of things with them. Fruit, nuts, sweets and presents for our stockings. But the best present of all came in the person of our sister Maud. We absolutely adored her. She was like a vision from a fashion magazine. Black suit, white blouse and the highest of heels on her shoes. Her face made up with lipstick and eye shadow she looked like a film star. Stella and Eve would hang on her every word and ask countless questions about London. She was soon to be called up and would serve in the ATS. What a Christmas we had. The best yet. Us kids pretending to be asleep while mum aided by Millie, filled our stockings.

Christmas morning with a roaring fire we sat and listened to the grown-up conversation. Mostly about the prospect of when the war would end. Dad would tell a few jokes; we would all laugh. He was a marvellous storyteller. Millie Miller was a larger-than-life character with dyed hair and plenty of make-up. She was kind, very fond of dad, and I believe, quite wealthy. She fussed over all of us. We had our lunch with all the trimmings. The festivities were over all too soon. Dad and the Millers made ready to leave. It was Maud we would miss most, we hung onto her like glue, walking with her into the village, and out the other side then over the bridge on to the Yatton road. There we stood, waving until she was out of sight. It was three miles from Rose Cottage to the railway station. I remember crying because she was gone. I think we all did.

The days grew longer, the weather milder; it would soon be Easter. It seemed we had been in this village a very long time. Dad came down for a flying visit. He was worried about Roy. Our brother had joined up a long while since, and after training with the Royal Engineers volunteered for the Commandos. He was thought to be somewhere in the Adriatic. Try as he might, Dad could get no information or news of his son. When the war was over we found he had been at Sicily and Salerno. Fighting with Tito and his partisans, side by side with both Serbs and Croats. Based on Viz Island, No 2 Commando surrounded by the enemy caused havoc with hit and run raids. In Belgrade there is a picture in a museum of Field Marshall Tito, with Roy one side and Doug Fletcher, his closest friend, on the other. At the end of the war both they and their comrades were awarded the freedom of Yugoslavia.

My favourite teacher, Mrs Fountain, left school. I was miserable and didn't want to go anymore. One look from mum though, and off I went.

July 1944. School was about to break up for the summer holidays. With the end of the war in sight as some thought, our cottage would be needed for a farm worker. We were informed that we would be moving to Nailsea about 8 miles away; a much bigger village, with a much bigger school. When you are just a kid no one asks your opinion, or whether or not you mind. We had made many friends in Kingston Seymour, and had been shown much kindness and understanding. For sure we had learned a lot about country ways from the villagers, and I hope they learnt something from us. And so it was with a mixture of apprehension and hope that we loaded the things we had collected, much of which came via the WVS, on to the van that was to take us to our new home.

There was a clatter as the ramp of the van was lowered and for the first time I could see where we were. We were parked on a wide pavement. To our left was a row of stone grey cottages. The one we were to move into was in the middle – number 5. Access was via a gate in the wall, inside of which stood a tall Sycamore tree. The path to the front door was long with a narrow strip of garden to the left of it. This row of cottages, called New Rank, had been built in the 1820s to house glassworkers who had made the famous Nailsea Glass. The ruins of the old glassworks were immediately opposite. We had gotten used to being isolated. I soon found that this was a much bigger village than Kingston Seymour. In fact, it was described as the third biggest village in England, Coate's cider factory was here. There were two churches, chapels, several pubs and lots of shops. There would be much to explore. We spent the weekend settling in; it was summer, warm and pleasant. I encountered a few local boys who seemed friendly enough, but who laughed at my accent. They asked if I would like to play in the glassworks. We climbed the iron railings and walked among the remains of the old site. Overgrown with every species of grass and weeds imaginable it was a veritable haven for small boys. As an added bonus the American army had dumped two lorries there. Still painted in their national livery of khaki with a huge white star emblazoned on the bonnets they fascinated me. My new mates initiated me into their 'war games'; to start with I had to be the enemy, which involved getting 'killed' a lot. I didn't mind.

There were American servicemen stationed here. They had arrived in the build up to the D-Day invasion which had taken place the month before we arrived, there were quite a few still around. They used to park all manner of transport on the Drove road and start a smoke screen. My mates thought this was brilliant. It's a miracle none of us ever got seriously injured dodging in and out of the smoke, with so much equipment laying around.

A contingent of coloured troops were camped in Nissen huts in Nailsea Park, a short distance from where I now lived. I had been playing with some boys in Station Road. On the way home I had to pass the camp where the Yanks lived. Running (I rarely walked anywhere), I got about half way before I tripped over and cut my hand. Picking myself up I heard this deep voice booming out 'Hey son, come over here.' I looked up and there was the biggest American soldier imaginable. He was sitting on top of a wall, which ran the length of camp. I froze. Curiosity overcame fear, and I walked over and stood by the wall. As I did, he reached down and said 'Give me your hand.' With one jerk he swung me up and set me down on the wall beside him. With a huge smile, and amazing gentleness, he took my hand and wrapped a handkerchief around it. He gave me some chewing gum, the first I had ever seen. Perplexed, I just looked at it. 'You chew it like this,' he said and demonstrated. He was the first person I had encountered with black skin. Although I always looked for him whenever the Yanks passed by, I never saw him again.

There were still a few weeks left before the summer holidays started; we would have to go to school. At the outbreak of war the children from Wornington Road School, in North Kensington, London, had been evacuated, complete with teachers, to Nailsea. There was insufficient room in Christ Church School to accommodate so many, so after a period of classroom sharing in a shift system, it was decided that the evacuees were to use the village institute building as a school, retaining the name of their old London school. My sisters and I had been extremely happy at Kingston Seymour school, and got on well with the local children, never feeling like refugees. Now we were to be segregated, and so labelled once more evacuees. We certainly felt the difference in attitudes in Nailsea. There was a social stigma that surrounded us. 'Don't get too close dear, you might pick something up' was often heard. It was much harder for the girls than for me. In a recent book titled *Villages at War* by Peter Wright, one contributor had said of evacuees: 'They spoke a different language, were unruly, self-opinionated and not very well dressed!' Of course we had a different accent, and as to our opinion, that was mostly mistaken for pride. With regards our poor state of dress, when you lose everything, as many of us had, pride is all one has left. I have never met an East-Ender yet who took kindly to being patronised. Kids taking the 'Micky' were bad enough, but when adults joined in, it beggared belief. The 'Five' closed ranks, and stood up to all comers.

We didn't wait for school to break for the summer holidays. We packed our things, caught the bus to Bristol, got off at the City Centre and walked to Temple Meads railway station. We boarded the London train. Mum had received a letter from her sister suggesting once more that as nothing much was happening in London why didn't we go back, if not to stay, at least for a visit; why not? We were pretty fed up with Nailsea already. We got off the train at Paddington, and took the underground to Aldgate East. Walking up the Commercial road we turned into Salmon Lane, getting closer to Carr Street where our grandparents lived. They had remained in their flat throughout the Blitz, reasoning that at their age they had little to lose. They couldn't be argued with.

There was now far more damage than when we left. My cousins Terry and Tommy were excited to see me. 'Come on Jimmy, we'll take you to our den'. The bombed-out buildings were an adventure playground. It was great to be back, and they all talked like me! The sound of a heavy aircraft filled the air so I looked skywards. 'I can't see the plane,' I shouted. 'That's 'cos it ain't no plane,' said Tommy. 'What is it then?' I asked. 'Don't you know? Ain't you 'ad 'em in the country? It's a bleedin' doodlebug, that's what it is. You better get under here with us,' he beckoned. Suddenly the engine cut. 'That's it,' said Tommy, quite calmly, 'Now it will come down.' There was a huge explosion, as the flying bomb ploughed into buildings about half a mile away. When I got home I asked mum about the doodlebugs. She told me not to worry, if one falls on us we won't know nothing about it! Such was the courage of these Cockneys. Their attitude was: 'Sod Hitler, we're going down the pub!' We had had a lovely time. Half the family walked with us to the underground station, where with tears in our eyes, we said our goodbyes once more. 'He's after me, I know it.' 'Who?' asked Mum. 'Who's after you?' 'Bloody Hitler, that's who.' I replied. The last rocket to fall during the war was in March 1945 when a V2 fell on two blocks of flats in Vallance Road. Stepney, killing 124 people. Vallence Road, is a stone's throw away from my grandparent's flat.

Dad and Maud came down to spend that Christmas with us in the country. Maud, dressed in the uniform of the ATS, looked marvellous. She put her cap on my head. I wore it to bed. We were all so proud of her. From somewhere, dad had acquired a box of Christmas decorations. They were the most elaborate trimmings you could imagine, with gold and silver bells. We had them for years. Dad and our uniformed sister left soon after Christmas, and as we walked to the bus stop to see them off, as we always did, dad said: 'The war will soon be over kids. We'll have a party.' We so hoped he was right. We seemed always to be saying goodbye.

It was about the middle of January. I always rose early. Looking out of the window I couldn't believe my eyes. 'Mum come and look. It's snowing,' I shouted. There had been a heavy fall during the night, and now you couldn't see the front path, and there was a huge drift by the garden wall. Joyfully, I said 'No school today.' 'That's what you think,' retorted Mum. We got up and got ready as normal. It was about half a mile to school. We started out with not a few moans and complaints, greeted by deaf ears as usual. Slipping and sliding, throwing snowballs, we finally made it. Quite a few children had turned up, but there would be no school today. However, we did manage to get a few days' school in before the weather worsened, then everything froze solid. With no toilets in use, the teachers reluctantly submitted and closed the school until the thaw set in some weeks later. 'Hooray.' We had a marvellous time with snowball fights. We built a snowman and someone knocked it down. So we knocked theirs' down. The tit- for-tat battle lasted until the thaw. It was all great fun.

I had been to the shops for mum and saw a number of men clearing the snow. They had yellow patches on their trousers and on the back of their coats. By Hewett's shop on the corner of the Clevedon road stood two soldiers with rifles. They were watching the snow clearers. When I returned home and told mum what I had seen, she said, 'They are POWs [prisoners of war] I expect, probably Eyties [Italians]. Whew, I had been close to the enemy! They were here clearing our snow; my brother Roy was over there and had been fighting them! Perhaps he captured some of these. Yea, I bet he did. Probably about a hundred I expect!

One Sunday Mum said we had guests for lunch. It was a beautiful day, crisp and sunny with blue sky. Two men walked down the path, passed me with a nod of their heads, and knocked on the door. Mum opened the door and greeted the strangers. Then she called us. 'Kids, this is Hans and Geart; they have come for lunch.' She had only invited two German POWs to our house, that's all! What could she be thinking of, I wondered? Roy was still fighting the Germans, wasn't he? He had been wounded twice. Perhaps one of these might have shot him! Perhaps they might kill us! What would dad say? I had been brought up to hate Hitler. Everyone said he was evil. And he was a German, wasn't he? I vowed to keep my eye on these two. 'One move and I will get them with my bow and arrow.'

It turned out that Dad had met them in the village some weeks ago and struck up a conversation. Hans was proud and patriotic and couldn't understand why things had gone so bad for his mother country. Dad had spent hours over a beer explaining to him that Germany could never win the war. She had too many enemies; she was fighting on too many fronts. 'You will never overcome this country, Hans. Now that you have seen our way of life, you know what we are fighting for,' dad had told him. Geart, however, was glad his war was over and was more than content not to have to return to the conflict. It was bizarre, yet typically British. The most civilised race in the world entertaining the enemy at Sunday lunch! They came quite often. Geart gave me a boat he had carved out of a solid block of wood. He fixed two masts to it, and made sails out of fabric from an old shirt. I treasured it. They talked of their families and how they hoped the war would soon end and Europe would return to peace. Geart often said, 'How could we be at war with you? You are all so lovely.' I don't remember any of us kids mentioning Roy to them. Perhaps it was instinct. It would have been insensitive. I wonder what happened to them.

School was as miserable as ever. Still in the Institute, still segregated.

Then suddenly, the war was over. Everyone was excited. We quickly packed a few things. We were off to London for VE day, where else! The feeling of joy was overwhelming. Wait for us London, we're coming! The station was crowded, and people were hugging and kissing. Uniforms of all services mingled with civilians waiting for the incoming train. I could hear it before seeing it, then in it came, a magnificent sight. A mighty locomotive of the Castle class, pulling an endless line of carriages. With steam hissing from its pistons, it ground to a halt. The crowd surged forward. Thankfully somebody shouted, 'Steady now, make way for the lady with the children.' We piled into a carriage; mum and Maisie, lifted our bags onto the luggage rack. With a surge of power, and the clank of metal upon metal, the train pulled out.

We arrived just in time. The East End was a hive of activity. Bonfires had been built everywhere and were just about to be lit. 'Hey Jimmy'. It was Cousin Tommy. 'Over here mate.' You would have thought London had seen all the fire it could handle, but these were 'Ours'. Celebrations impossible to describe, it had to be witnessed to be believed. Pubs threw open their doors, and revellers went from street to street. Row upon row of people doing the Lambeth walk. Us kids were in among it all. Dad was playing the piano. Tommy, Terry and me drained the dregs from every glass that was put down. I hoped it would never end. The look on my mother's face was worth a king's ransom. One minute she was laughing, and the next crying; she and her contemporaries deserved medals. Our boys, fighting the enemy, knew they could count on the moral strength of those they had left behind on this island. Magnificent, they did not let each other down. We had survived. Hitler didn't get me after all!

The party lasted days. 'What now? Would we be staying here?' Stella and Maisie said that mum and dad were looking for a house. This was difficult. One-third of the East End had been completely destroyed. Given that the area had been overcrowded for years, there were now far too many people seeking too few houses. The East End would never be the same again. Nor would its people. Whole families took up residence in the new towns being built in Essex -- Harlow, and Debden to name two. Dagenham expanded. The spirit of old East End remains in these towns today.

After the celebrations, we travelled by train back to the west country. Feeling a bit flat we gazed out of the windows. Whilst there were still plenty of smiling faces, for us the future was uncertain. With the threat of war no longer uppermost in our thoughts, a void was left for other worries to fill.

The schools had been closed for a two-day holiday to celebrate VE Day. The Rustons had taken two weeks! We were not popular. On 2 July 1945 the head teacher of Christchurch School, Miss Morris, wrote in the School's log book:

To-day we have admitted 15 children, who for varying periods, have attended the Wornington Road Evacuee School, held at the Village Institute. All those evacuees wishing to return to London were taken back on 24 June and the Evacuee school closed on 29 June.

Among the 15 children admitted, were Evelyn, Betty and Me. Stella and Maisie were to attend the Senior School, known locally as Old Church, A few weeks later we broke up for the summer holidays. We were due to restart school on 2 September but Victory over Japan had been announced and another two days were added to the holiday. We had gone back to London for the last two weeks of our holidays, and so we stayed on. Although there was another round of celebrations, it wasn't the same as VE Day.

'So, just where do you think you have been,' said Miss Morris, as she confronted the three of us on our return to school. We tried to explain, but she was not interested. 'If you are to stay in this school, you will have to obey the rules. Oh yes, and I will see to it that you do,' she confirmed. I shook in my shoes. This was my first encounter with the redoubtable Miss C.H.L. Morris. Head teacher with a capital H.

The playground at Christchurch School was compacted earth, a reddish brown colour. When the bell rang we formed up in our respective lines, and on command, marched to our classrooms. Each morning a hymn was sung, and the Lord's Prayer recited. Evelyn and I were in Miss Morris' class. Betty was to be taught by Mrs Wookey, assisted by a student teacher. Once a week the vicar, the Rev J.H. Powell, conducted a short service during morning assembly. It was after one of these services that Miss Morris asked me to stay behind at the end of the school day, She wanted to 'talk' to me. Wondering what it was she wanted me for preoccupied my thoughts, and it didn't take much to distract me. I got a few very stern looks from Miss Morris and I thought, 'I'm for it!'

I waited by her tall desk. It had a sloping lift up lid, with a chair fixed to the bottom of the structure, making it one piece of furniture. The empty classroom echoed the sound of approaching footsteps. Striding right up to me, and with a big smile on her face, Miss Morris said: 'Jimmy; you can sing, can you not?' To which I replied 'I have never really thought about it Miss, but yes I do like singing.' I was somewhat relieved to observe the absence of the ruler she always carried and used in swift sharp retribution on any unruly pupil. 'You must join our church choir. Come along to practise this Thursday evening.' Now was this an invitation or an instruction?

And so began a relationship of mixed feelings between the two of us. During the week the daydreaming scholar would get an occasional 'reminder' from the ruler. Whilst in complete contrast on Thursday evenings and Sundays', there was an encouraging pat on the back and a 'well done'. This continued throughout my time at Christchurch. Even when I had left the school to go to Old Church, my loyalties remained with my former church choir. Raymond Llewellyn was head choirboy. He was extremely kind to me, and I liked him a lot. Many years later, if Ray saw Joyce and I waiting for a bus, he always gave us a lift. He had a beautiful Morris 10 car. It was black and always highly polished. We appreciated it so much. Especially during my national service days and when raining! Bless you, Ray. I felt so proud when Ray presented me with my first cassock and surplice. Every Monday, mum washed the latter in Persil; I was often complimented on it.

Miss Charlotte Helena Louise Morris was a remarkable woman. Totally dedicated to 'her' school and its pupils, she ran both in a disciplined fashion. She always wore dark sombre, yet practical clothes, and with her steel grey hair parted in the centre with two small plaits ending in whirls that covered each ear, her appearance would equally have suited a convent. She played the organ at Christ Church, and was much involved in church activities. On cold winter nights I hurried along to choir practice. Always first of the boys arrive, I would find Miss Morris standing just inside the door, warming herself by the radiator. She greeted me thus: 'Jimmy, come and stand by me, you must be freezing.' Our conversation was warm and friendly. I loved this side of her. As organist she wore a flowing black gown, adding to her mystery. A very private person, I don't think anyone knew her intimately. I learned much from this lady, not least of all loyalty and duty; she was the epitome of both. My one regret is that I lost all contact with her when in 1953 we moved to Wraxall. She is undoubtedly the one teacher with whom I had contact during my time in Nailsea who would have been interested in what became of 'her' pupils.

I hope I never let her down, and that she would have been proud of me. I owe her much. I am just sorry that I didn't realise it at the time. Miss Morris devoted her whole life to people like me.

I had made a few friends; the closest were Barrington Wright, Colin Luckwell and Mervyn Kitchen, and this was our 'gang'. Sometimes, not often though, we would allow girls along. These were Sonia White, Jennifer Colborn, and my sister Betty. There were many others, but those six plus me were the regulars.

After a severe winter in which everything froze, with ice forming on the inside of our bedroom windows and school closed for weeks, the thaw finally set in. A beautiful spring dawned, followed by a glorious summer. In winter we played endless football matches in Barrington Wright's back yard. With a tennis ball substituting for a football (none of us had one), we played out our fantasies. Arguments frequently broke out as to who would be Stanley Matthews. 'You were him yesterday' would be heard. 'No I wasn't, I was Tom Finney' would come back. One wet Saturday we went to watch Nailsea play. I was standing by the home goal post. Frank Newman, whose sister Ruth was in my class, was goalkeeper. A forward of the opposition fired a blistering shot towards our goal. Diving at full stretch, Frank pushed it round the post and straight into my face. Wallop! I went out like a light. It brought the game to a standstill, until the St John's Ambulance attendants brought me to my senses, proclaiming that I would live! I had a headache for a week.

Each year during the weeks before Christmas we went out carol singing. We walked mile upon mile. We all sang in the choir so didn't want to let ourselves down. We took it in turns to sing solo. If, when we knocked the door in the hope of a few coins for our rendition, the occupier praised the soloist, once we had thanked our benefactor and walked away, we often argued whose solo was being praised. Each of us was adamant that it was his. We were a competitive bunch. What we earned from carol singing, and we usually did quite well, was shared equally without fuss.

Some Saturday afternoon's finances permitting, my mates and I went to see Bristol City play at Ashton Gate. For 6d we sat in a row seats that were situated just a few feet from the touchline. We all had our favourite players. At the time, mine were Ivor Guy, Jimmy Rogers and Pat Beasley, who was also captain. Also, I liked the diminutive German winger Alec Eisentrager. The City attracted huge crowds in those days 20,000 – 25,000 was average. After the match it was a rush to get to the bus stop. Enormous crowds would be waiting for the buses for Clevedon the No. 25 which went through Nailsea and to Weston the

No. 24. One occasion indelible in my mind, Mervyn Kitchen, and me were waiting at the end of a very long queue for the Clevedon bus. It was beginning to get dark. A big black Austin car pulled up. In it was Mervyn's grandfather. He was landlord of the Friendship Inn in Nailsea, about 500yds from New Rank. Mervyn ran over to the car beckoning me to follow. Unfortunately there wasn't room in the car for me, and so I was left behind. I could see that Merv wasn't too happy about leaving his mate like this. It was an hour later before I got to the head of the bus queue.

Cold and tired, I boarded the bus and sat by a window. The bus jolted to a stop periodically and people got on and off. The warmth and rhythm of the bus as the journey continued caused me to doze. I thought surely by now we must be nearing Nailsea. I pressed my face to the window looking into the inky blackness of night, but could not recognise any familiar landmarks. I asked the conductor, Are we near Nailsea?' 'Nailsea. We don't go through Nailsea son, this is the Weston bus.' 'I had better get off at the next stop then,' I said.

The next stop was Brockley Coombe. Now, if you picture a scene from a Peter Cushing horror film, you are pretty close to Brockley Coombe at night and in winter. As I left the bus, two elderly ladies sitting on one of the long seats near the platform were remonstrating with the conductor as to the wisdom of letting this small boy alight alone in these surroundings. As the bus pulled away they were still arguing. I stood in the inky blackness and I wondered what I should do. It was a very long way to walk. I didn't have any money so couldn't catch a bus back towards Bristol, to where the Clevedon and Weston roads converged.

With the greatest of apprehension, and trying hard to look brave, I stood by the entrance to Brockley Coombe, a foreboding place, even in daytime. The eerie sounds made by the wind blowing through the tall trees sent a chill down my spine. I began to 'see things' that weren't there. I was beginning to get seriously worried when a car pulled up. I didn't know whether to hide or walk over see who it was. Before I had chance to make up my mind, the driver called to me. 'You alright son? I'm a schoolteacher.' Somewhat relieved I told him what had happened. He said he would take me home, and asked where I lived. Thankfully, I just said Nailsea, but not exactly where. I climbed into his car and off he drove.

We got into Backwell and turned left into Station Road. We were heading towards the station. As we got under the Railway Bridge he reached over and put his hand on my leg. I was still in short trousers then. Moving over in my seat, I tried to put my leg out of his reach. He persisted. We reached the top of Bucklands Batch with his hand still firmly on my leg. He was talking all the time, but I was not listening. My mind was going at 100 miles an hour thinking all sorts of horrors that may befall me.

Up ahead, I could see from the car's headlamps a man pushing a bike along the pathway of a house. I saw my chance of escape. 'Stop please, this is my house. That's my dad walking up the path with his bike.' I blurted out. To my relief the stranger stopped the car. I flung the door open and scrambled out. I ran through the gate of the house I said was mine, up the path, and hid in the shadows. My heart was pounding. By now the man with the bike had gone inside. I waited for the stranger in the car to pull away. Trembling I pressed myself against the wall of the house. It seemed like ages. Then slowly, the car drove off. I could feel a warm wet sensation down my leg. I was so frightened that I had wet myself. I ran and ran, with lungs bursting, and didn't stop until I was home. I didn't tell my parents. It was impossible to judge how dad would react. Mostly I never spoke to him or he to me. He would probably have blamed me for catching the wrong bus in the first place! I wasn't over bold, and this encounter made me even more timid. I guessed that the man in the car must have been one of the 'Nancy boys' I had overheard grown-ups talking of.

The woods about half a mile across the fields to the rear of New Rank were a picture in spring. A carpet of bluebells covered the ground. We picked armfuls and took them home, where they were always welcome. We built dens and made bows and arrows. Fierce battles were fought, often lasting all day. No one was ever seriously hurt, although sometimes blood was drawn. Somehow we remained friends, competing yet again with floating bits of wood in a river to see whose would go furthest downstream before getting caught in the weed. On the warmest days we gathered at Sandy Bottom, so called because of the sand on the riverbed. At a point where a footbridge crossed the stream the area was free from weed and the water about 3 feet deep, perfect for kids of our age. Endless summer days were spent in this location. There was a spring nearby we called 'Morning Spout'. It was years later and not until a new housing development was built nearby and one of the roads named Moorend Spout, that I realised our error of pronunciation. I have recently been informed that kids still swim at Sandy Bottom.

My dad's double act, Ruston and Steel had split up just after the start of the war. The bombing proved too much for Alex Steel; he lost his nerve and fled to the countryside. Dad, himself as brave as any man, couldn't understand this. An old-fashioned Cockney, he could not accept weakness in a bloke. Dad tried to continue on his own, but it was essentially a double act. Years later, dad saw Alex in Kent, working in a field picking potatoes. 'Look at you' dad said. 'We could have had it all.' It was the last time they met. Dad hardly ever mentioned him again. It's sad. Alex was much loved by us all, and Godfather to four of us. We are not all heroes. I wish I had tried to find him. I don't know why I never did. Dad broadcast a few times after that on the BBC from Whiteladies in Bristol, but it was short-lived.

Dad had now come to live with us. He had met Jim Fletcher, who like himself was a motor mechanic. Jim had a partnership in a garage close by named Small and Fletcher. He offered Dad a job, which he accepted. Jim Fletcher fancied himself as a bit of a drummer, so dad invited him to form a duo. They called themselves 'The Two Jims', and were quite popular.

Someone said a shop in the village were selling ice cream. 'Can't be,' I thought. Rationing was still in force and food in short supply. After nagging mum for a few pence we rushed up to the shop. There was a queue, for...yes, ice-cream! When I got mine, I looked at this small round block with a wrapper around its middle but nothing covering the ends. It was so hard it would have done serious damage if thrown at someone! But once it had softened with the warmth of my hands, and I had my first lick, it was delicious. A new experience, like the banana I had recently sampled. The first taste, unique, and remembered forever, but never equalled. I was 11 years old. The ice-cream was Eldorado.

To the disbelief of my brother and his comrades, at the end of the war it was announced that the army was to disband the Commandos. Roy, being a regular soldier would have to find another unit. His parent unit being the Royal Engineers, he went with 3rd Airborne Brigade to Palestine, mine clearing. Because of the troubles there, he got involved in much more. The conflict started following a joint Anglo-American report in favour of some kind of partition. The report recognised Palestine as a Jewish national home, but went on to say that it could never be purely Jewish land because it lies at the crossroads of the Arab world; and that the Arab population also looks upon Palestine as its homeland. The committee who produced the report recommended that 100.000 Jews be admitted to Palestine that year (1946). A dramatic increase over the 1500 or so already being admitted each month. The territorial dispute continues.

Roy was demobbed in 1947, and I heard that he was coming down to Nailsea. The day he was due to arrive, I rose early and went out on to the pavement to wait for him. Mum called out to me: 'Jimmy. Your brother won't be here for hours yet.' Unperturbed, I waited and waited.

A COCKNEY KID IN GREEN WELLIES

An open-back lorry approached. It pulled over, stopped right beside me, and out of the cab jumped a vision, like a film star straight from Hollywood. Dressed in khaki drill trousers and tropical shirt, he stood there with a smile that would melt an iceberg, and placing his hand on my head said 'All right son? You must be Jimmy. I'm your brother Roy.' Was this really the brother about whom I had heard so much.

I was so small when he left home, yet somehow I knew him. Roy leapt on to the back of the lorry and throwing a canvas bundle over the side said. 'I thought you might like this tent.' With a clatter he threw three billycans after it. I was made. I had told everyone at school about my commando brother. I had even written essays about him, and got top marks for one of them. Now he was here, and with a tent and billycans for me I thought, 'Right, follow that. From here on I am King.'

Roy stayed for the weekend, and I hardly left his side. Dad took him to the pub; I sat outside with a glass of lemonade. Dad was so proud of Roy; he was everything a father could hope for. Our dad, was very much a Man's Man, and his eldest son had been London schoolboys' lightweight boxing champion; had served in the elite No. 2 Commando in the Second World War, was a talented piano player, a terrific dancer, and handsome with a disarming manner. He would be a hard act to follow. He was my hero, and would remain so.

Sometime later dad had a phone call to say that his father had died. His parents now lived in Buckhurst Hill in Essex. I had only met my Ruston grandparents a couple of times. Dad went up to London by train taking Stella, dressed in her Girl Guides uniform, with him. She looked a picture. My sister was a dedicated Girl Guide and devoted to her Captain, Freda Vowles. Freda was a very popular leader and ran the Girl Guides in Nailsea for many years. Stella, with others, formed a guard of honour when Freda married. When dad and Stella returned from the funeral, my sister told me that as the family stood by the graveside, our brother Roy placed his coveted Green Beret on top of the coffin as it was lowered, so much respect did he have for our granddad.

Time was approaching when I would have to change schools. After another summer and the customary couple of weeks in London (would we stay this time?), I would have go to the secondary modern school at Old Church. The London trip was not without its dramas. Travelling up the A4 we had just left Newbury when we felt a bump, bump, bump. Dad pulled the car to a halt at the side of the road. 'Puncture,' he exclaimed. Unfortunately we didn't have a spare. To add to our problem it was Sunday and everything was closed. Dad lifted one side of the tyre from its rim and pulled out the inner tube (all car tyres had tubes in those days). Well it would be difficult to argue if there were more tube or patches! He sat and thought for a while, then said, 'Right kids, start pulling up grass, as much as you can.' Dad began stuffing the grass inside the cover of the tyre, then refitted the wheel to the car. 'Come on kids let's go,' he commanded. We moved off at about 10 miles an hour.

We had gone a couple of miles when we came upon a small garage. Although it was closed, dad stopped the car and went to look around. The garage owner, who had been watching from a window, took one look at the car full of kids, and opened up. A Good Samaritan, he found an inner tube with fewer patches on than ours (that wouldn't be difficult!). Dad took it with gratitude. I have travelled thousand of miles in cars driven by my father, but despite many breakdowns, he has never left a car on the side of the road. Somehow he always got them home.

I didn't like the look of Old Church School one bit, and it seemed to take a disliking to me. Eve had gone up to join Stella and Maisie two years earlier. Now I was joining them, leaving only Betty at Christ Church. The headmaster was Mr J. Gower. He had been there for years and was coming to the age of retirement.

I had sat the '11 plus' at my former school but must have failed otherwise I wouldn't be here. I don't remember being told the results. It has to be said that sadly our parents didn't take a great deal of interest in our school work. However, I was placed in the 'A' stream, so must have been of a reasonable standard.

The journey to school was always eventful. We had to walk the two and three quarter miles each way daily. It was great fun in summer kicking a ball along the road, or playing marbles in the gutter. But winter was a very different matter altogether. We arrived most days freezing cold and often soaking wet. Had we lived a quarter of a mile further we would have qualified for a lift on the coach which ran each school day from Long Ashton passing the door of 5 New Rank on its way to Old Church! 'Rules are rules. You live inside the three mile boundary,' a school official told Mum. And so in all weathers, we walked. We took sandwiches for lunch at the outset, then joined the majority for what was passed off as a 'school dinner'. I can see them now, potato the colour of shoe white, transparent gravy with solid lumps of cabbage, and a piece of something that at one time in its history had probably been either a cow or a sheep, we would never know. For 'afters' tapioca pudding that looked like frog's spawn with, if lucky, a dollop of jam plonked in the centre. The whole meal was usually cold, luke-warm at best. The dinner monitors would stand over anyone who needed 'encouragement' to eat, and make sure they did. One-third of a pint of milk was compulsory for each child daily. I loved milk, but sometimes even that was a challenge. Summer would see it curdle before we got it. Winter, and it would freeze, push its silver top off and protrude an inch or two from the bottle.

I spent an unremarkable four years at Old Church School generally written off as 'beyond redemption.' 'Asks too many, awkward and irrelevant questions,' said one teacher 'Doesn't pay attention; a daydreamer,' said another. How could I have been both? The facilities at the school were poor in the extreme. No library or science lab, and no gymnasium. The most contact I had with a gym shoe was when it was administered by the powerful Mr Mullens, on the seat of my pants, for guess what? Not paying attention. There was relief in the form of Miss Saar. Blond and beautiful, she took the girls for hockey. All the boys were in love with her. It was rumoured that there was something more than academia between her and Mr Mullens. I hope not, he wasn't worth it. He arrived at our school after my first year. A rugby-playing teacher, he tried to convert our football-playing school to his favoured sport. You can imagine how popular that made him.

A new class was created and they called it 4B. I was shifted into it from 2A. Promotion? Not on your life. They had in fact moved what they considered to be every no-hoper they had in the school into one class. But it was a boys only class, and there wasn't one similar for girls, so it defied reason. Did it mean that all the girls were scholars? Two afternoons a week we were marched off to the Vicarage garden, where we dug, raked and hoed. I swear it was this forced activity that put me off gardening for life. A new headmaster also arrived; his name was Secret. He used to get us cleaning his car, an Austin Seven. Secret was a jovial bespectacled character; a little overweight so there wasn't much room for him in the small car. On occasions when it wouldn't start he would instruct us to push him. We made sure we rocked it as we pushed! It was amusing watching our headmaster roll from side to side.

I was good at English though, could spell any word on demand, and write an essay on a wide range of subjects at the drop of a hat. We had an abundance of books at home and I was well read. After four years of woodworking classes, all I had made was a bundle of firewood! One boy had made an ashtray stand. I thought, my dad would like that; my mum would too. It would save all that ash being dropped on the carpet. I got the stand in a swap for something obscure, I can no longer remember. My philosophy: You don't have to be good at everything. As long as you are in a position to trade, most things are available!

I did have a talent for anything electrical, and could both wire and locate faults in simple circuits, without anyone ever having taught me how. These skills confused all of my teachers. I guess it was intuitive. English literature and science I favoured throughout my life.

PONIES, BOATS AND NEEDLES

The highlight of my senior school years came when one day fellow scholar Ruth Newman asked, 'Fancy going horse riding Jimmy?' 'I might,' said I. Sunday dawned, and Ruth and I walked to Dyer's Farm, which was situated at the bottom of Kingshill in Nailsea's west end. Three girls ran the riding school. Rachel and Barbara were most prominent with Betty helping out at times. Although up until now I had not had any proper contact with horses, I often observed them in the fields and admired their power and nobility.

'Rachel, this is Jimmy Ruston; he wants to have a ride' said Ruth. 'Oh does he now' Came the reply from a pretty girl in her early 20s, standing by a stable door. She was carrying a saddle and bridle, which she was about to put on a beautiful dark brown mare. She hesitated then said, 'You can ride Nobby.' I stuttered, 'I've never ridden before Miss.' 'Don't worry you'll be alright,' I was assured. 'I'll keep you on the lead rein.' 'By the way Jimmy, you can call me Rachel if you like.' And so began a friendship that would have a profound effect on my life. 'Ruth, Ruth, what about paying, I haven't got any money.' I confided in my friend. 'Seeing it's your first time they will let you pay next week; it's five shillings for an hour,' Ruth informed me.

I climbed on this mealy mouthed Exmoor pony, and with a rein attached to his bridle, the other end of which Rachel held in her hand, we set off across the moor. 'What's his name, your horse?' I asked. 'This is Beauty. The one my sister Barbara is riding is Melody, and the others out today are Mitsie, Lassie, Cleo, Ginger, and Cinnamon.' I couldn't have dreamed it if I tried, but in the coming years I would ride all these lovely creatures.

When I got home I told mum. She seemed pleased. Dad said, 'You will meet some nice people in the horse world Jim.' He wasn't wrong. I had one major problem, though; where was I going to get five shillings from, not just now, but every week? I was hooked. None of the boys at school rode, as far as I knew. I was so puny, small for my age. Nervous at first, I felt more comfortable as the ride went on. Anyway, I wasn't going to show it even if I was scared, as I have been many times since! Master this, and I felt I could rise above them all, not only in stature.

I got a paper round at 7s 6d each week. (37½ p) I thought lovely, after paying for my ride, I will still have some left. Blast, I would have to give up my Saturday morning cinema job. There wasn't any point in asking my mother or father for the money. It was not an option we enjoyed as children.

I had been going to The Maxime cinema (since re-named Curzon) in Clevedon on Saturday mornings for a couple of years. Roy Rogers and Trigger, Gene Autry and Hoppalong Cassidy were my favourite cowboys, whilst Laurel and Hardy remain my heroes of comedy. It started out with one visit; there was no way I could find the money to go every week. I got talking to a lady who was a cleaner there and I asked if I could help. 'Well my love, there isn't much you can do. That is, unless you don't mind cleaning out the ashtrays.' And so I became head ashtray emptier. About 300 of them! It meant leaving home at 6.30am. Whilst waiting for the bus, I used to lean against the wall of Parsons Bakery and feel the warmth from the ovens. Over the years they had caused a dark brown patch to appear on the concrete block wall, so it was easy to see where the best place to stand was. In exchange for ashtray emptying, the cleaning ladies paid my bus fare and fiddled me a ticket for the show! I was king. All the other kids had to queue. When the doors finally opened, and they all rushed in, who was already sitting in the prime spot? Me. Centre seat, front row of the Circle. I have always maintained that this job would cure for all time any latent ambition I may have harboured to smoke a cigarette! My father smoked a 100 a day; the opportunity was there.

Things were not going well at home. Although reconciled after dad's wartime affair, mum and dad were frequently rowing; which sometimes led to the hurling of missiles at each another. None of this helped when mum had one of her 'heads'. Maisie was suffering from epilepsy. So frequent were the fits that consumed her whole being that dad gave up his job at the garage to look after her. Mum got a job at Storey and Hale, a lemonade factory in Heath Road about a five-minute walk away. It was not long before Stella, too, got a part time job there, working in the office. She must have been about 13 when she first started work. Its funny, I can never remember Stella being a child. I think she must have been born an adult. She was always organised and responsible. She was my salvation, and I was devoted to her.

Dad was over-protective towards the girls, especially Stella and Eve. He wanted to know their every movement. Boyfriends didn't stand a chance. This caused a lot of ill feeling, with mum taking the girls' side. She wanted them to have a little freedom, and after the restraints of the war years, begin to enjoy themselves. Dad, of course, had one standard for himself and a completely different one for all of us. I did my best to keep a low profile. If I had played football on the way home, I would sneak in the back door and ask Stella to wipe my shoes over, and quickly put on some polish. I stayed out as much as possible and joined everything going, first Cubs, then Scouts and finally Army cadets. I still sang in the choir. Sadly my father put me down at every opportunity, and wouldn't listen to anything I had to say, calling me a 'chump'. Dad played the piano several nights a week, returning in the early hours of the morning. We were always short of money. Dad earned plenty, but spent it just as fast.

Our sister Maud came down from London, she was holding a baby in her arms. When she left, the baby stayed with us. I later discovered that it was hers, from a friendship that didn't work out. She had asked dad if he would consider looking after the child. 'Is it alright with you Liz?' asked dad. 'Of course it is,' our lovely mum replied. The baby was named June Ann. I couldn't possibly have imagined then how much I would grow to love this little pink faced bundle. I was to hear a command that would become all too familiar. 'Jimmy, take June for a walk in her pram' – 'Oh Mum!!!'

Maud came to live with us for a while and worked at the Grand Hotel in Weston-Super-Mare. It was during this period that she met Norman Silverthorn, whose parents were landlords of The White Lion at west-end Nailsea. A brief courtship followed by Norman asking Maud to marry him. She accepted, and dad and mum helped to make the arrangements. Maud bought a stunning outfit, and the wedding cake mum had ordered arrived. On the day of the wedding, Maud suddenly announced that she had had a change of heart. Dad said, 'If you are not sure you want this Maud, don't do it.' Much talk and tears ended with dad taking her to the rail station where she caught the London train. Maud had tried, but she hated the country. Poor Norman, such a gentle man, was literally left at the altar. This encounter did little to endear the Ruston family to the locals. I can't remember what happened to the wedding cake. I hope I had some!!

They must have been difficult times for Maud. She had had a hard enough life as it was, losing her mother in childhood, and then the war. Living alone in furnished rooms in London and working long hours as a waitress in one of the big hotels wasn't exactly glamorous. Yet she was a survivor, and we all loved her desperately. Each week without fail, a registered envelope arrived with money in to help towards June's upbringing. Maud kept this up until June left school.

To supplement my paper round money, I did every job on offer. In one of my many swap deals, I acquired a battery-powered 35mm slide projector. It had to be manually operated which required sliding by hand the film across the lens. To give a decent picture it was necessary to operate under almost total darkness. I suggested to Colin Luckwell, who lived in a bungalow opposite New Rank, that we start weekly film shows in his shed. We could charge the local kids 3d each. We made and pinned posters all over the village. We had quite a gathering at the first few performances, but inevitably we ran out of slides to show, so the Ruston and Luckwell Cinema Empire folded!

A COCKNEY KID IN GREEN WELLIES

Someone had said they were selling the paddleboats at Clevedon. The small ones were going for 10 shillings, and the larger ones for £1 more. It meant having to miss riding for a week or two, but if it were true, I was determined that I should get one of the boats. Saturday morning, off I went to Clevedon. There were only two small paddleboats left. I chose one and handed over my 10 bob (50p). Now to get it home, or rather how to! The boating attendant offered me the use of a set of pram wheels, and with the boat loaded on, I set off on the five-mile trek back to Nailsea. Thankfully, I met a number of good Samaritans on the way who helped me to push for a while. When one left off another would appear. I stood the boat up on its end against the garden shed. The next task was to scrounge some paint. Now painted a deep Georgian green, my purchase seemed worthwhile. I never even mentioned it to dad. He would have laughed at it. (Had I known then of my shipwright ancestors, I would have felt encouraged. I didn't even know the story of the jet-propelled boat at this time.)

With the help of a few mates I took my boat to the river. The sheer joy I felt when paddling down the river for the first time defies description. Especially with no one shouting 'Come in number five, your time is up'!!! With the tent that Roy had given me, and now a boat, the possibilities of escapism were endless.

I spent countless days with both boat and tent. I made a fire and brewed up in my billycans. Sometimes I took a few vegetables from our garden and made a stew. The site of the old Roman fort at Cadbury Camp was one of my favourite spots. High on a hill the views are spectacular. Colin Luckwell was my most regular camping buddy, but I was often alone. Sometimes during summer holidays we pitched the tent on his lawn and slept in it.

My riding was steadily improving. I had graduated to riding Lassie, a black pony with white socks, about 14hands high. She could really gallop. My best friends at Dyer's Farm were now Susan Davis, Juliet Salt and Helen Morris. But mostly I loved Susan. We became boy/girl friends and were teased mercilessly. She more than I. Susan was at school with the other two so the teasing continued there. We were devoted to each other. One year Susan saved all her pocket money to buy me the *Pony Club Annual* for Christmas. I treasured it. The pain of young love. For my birthday, she signed the card she had sent in her own blood! Mum opened everything that came through the door and this was no exception. She made a song and dance about it at first, but then made fun of me, which was even worse. She could be unbelievably insensitive at times.

PONIES, BOATS AND NEEDLES

Susan, Helen and Juliet went to a private school in Bristol, Redland High. Susan lived in a Bay-fronted Victorian house in Blenheim Road Bristol. Helen lived in an imposing period house on the Downs (her father was Sir Philip Morris, Chancellor of Bristol University), whilst Juliet lived in a large detached house in Nailsea. Her mother was a local Magistrate. I lived in a small terraced cottage, and went to a council secondary. Outside of our passion for ponies, we had very different lifestyles. I was envious of their education. They complained about having to do homework. I would have loved to have had some to complain about. At Old Church School we were never set any. I went with Susan to see Shakespeare's *Loves Labours Lost*. I loved it.

Susan writes from her home near Brisbane in Australia, where she has lived for many years with her husband Barry and son Tim:

Recalling memories from that era in our lives' is almost impossible. How do you recall in a meaningful way, such action packed, fun times? The 'Farm' was such a major feature of that adolescent period of my life. I was 13 when first introduced to Rachel Dyer. I had ridden little prior to that, my parents doing nothing to encourage it. I do know that I spent more time at the farm than I did at home over those years. I put in hundreds of miles a week on the pushbike, cycling backwards and forwards when we weren't using the bus. Sometimes on my own, but more often than not with Helen Morris picking up Anne Alexander who lived at Leigh Woods, and then, having reached Nailsea, calling for you on our way down to King's Hill. Other times I went alone after school. Others were no doubt dutifully studying, something that held no appeal or relevance for me. I was determined to work with horses, so why would I need all this bookwork? Jim, do you remember those endless letters we used to write to each other? I wrote those during exams, having run out of any further information to give to the examiners!

I recollect lunches in the garden or in the Barn if wet. Saddlery cleaning along the wall that bordered the farmhouse. Rachel getting Mitsie's harness out for us to clean. She was a hard taskmaster; everything had to be perfect. Lessons that have stood me in good stead ever since, which I now try to impose on my son! Vying with the other kids with the right to feed this horse or that, depending on who were our favourites at the time. Lining up outside the farm kitchen window, to get a saddle and bridle, and then struggling to get bridles on to horses I couldn't reach, but far too proud to admit defeat. The bareback rides as we returned the horses to their field on the moor. One summer, Helen Juliet and I went skinny-dipping in a rhyne. The water was so low down the bank that we had to use a halter from one of the horses to lower ourselves into it. One day while engaging in this pastime, we left Juliet in the rhyne taking the halter so she couldn't get out. She was not amused. We did rescue her eventually though!

My recollections of Rachel are very precious, and the older I get the more I appreciate what a special person she was. She would have all of us kids hanging around weekend after weekend, and all week in the holidays. I never saw her loose her cool. She could set us against each other in friendly competition without ever setting us against each other socially. She capitalised on this healthy competition to get work done around the place. Mucking out the stables. Who was the quickest? Who could saddle up the most horses for her in preparation for a ride? Who could survive the longest on the chaff cutter without pegging out? Who could run the most feeds out to the horses in winter?

Of course, there was also the competitive scene in the riding arena, but again that was healthy. You might win a jumping competition during a field ride, but then you had the best horse! The scene down there at the farm created for us an environment that would be hard to reproduce today, where us kids had pretty nearly everything we needed for healthy growth and development without the need to go outside for competition. Of course we did go to a few shows, and those were the high points.

There were times, though, when we weren't all that charitable. I remember being very scathing about your aspirations to be a jockey, when, shortly after you started riding and were still very much a green horn, you freaked out when we all went flat strap on Backwell Hill one day! The sheer speed and lack of control 'scared you shitless', as they say today (in Australia anyway!). We were unkind calling Miss Goodbody Miss Badcorpse when, if we didn't have our bikes, she would run us back to Bristol in her little Austin A30. We were less than charitable about some of the kids who came to ride, but who were not part of 'The Gang'. I think we were lucky that the era was one of comparatively hard times, and kids in general were not overindulged. Regardless of where we came from in the social scale of society, we were all very equal at the Farm. No one seemed to have more than anyone else did; including money to buy eats at Hewett's shop opposite the Queen's Head.

The experience I gained at the Farm enabled me to get a job with horses immediately on leaving school. This led to my attending Porlock Riding Centre on Exmoor, where I sat and gained a certificate from the British Horse Society qualifying me to teach. I came top of the course.

PONIES, BOATS AND NEEDLES

I feel all credit for this is due to Rachel Dyer. She showed me how to do so many things, and how to learn whilst still retaining the fun element.
(Don't forget your promise to send me a copy of your book Jim!)

With Maisie's epilepsy now under control, dad got a job at the Anglo American Asphalt plant, which was situated in Cole's quarry in Backwell about three miles away. He started out as foreman, but was very soon running things. The plant produced high-grade asphalt for government contractors, many of whom were engaged in re-surfacing the runways of airfields used during the Second World War.
It meant an early start, about 4.30am. It was a good job and extremely well paid. His salary was about twice the 'then' national average plus perks, which were many. Still earning money from playing the piano at weekends, things looked rosy, and dad seemed more settled than he had been since the end of the war. Who knows, perhaps we would stay in the west country.
Having left her job at Storey and Hale's lemonade works, Stella now worked in the offices at Cole's quarry. She would soon be 18. As with most things dad was ahead of the game. He hired the village Institute, a decent-sized hall with a stage, and organised a fabulous birthday party for her, complete with an eight-piece band. Suitably decorated, it certainly looked far more inviting than when it served as our 'evacuee' school. A considerable number of the villagers were invited, as well as our school friends. I asked Susan, Helen and Juliet. We had a wonderful time. Stella looked stunning in a long white evening gown with matching accessories. Maisie, Eve and Betty looked lovely, too. Despite a limited wardrobe, mum always managed to look smart, she was naturally a good dresser. She bought me my first suit, and for the first time I felt 'grown-up'.
I was burning the candle at both ends. Not content with the ponies, camping, swimming and boating, I had become quite involved with the Army cadets. A wooden hut had been erected in the lane beside New Rank. The newly formed Nailsea troop of the Somerset Light Infantry Army Cadet Force met there each week. I loved it, was very proud of my uniform, and in time joined the cadet band as a bugler. This of course meant extra practice and parades. There was to be a big parade in Clevedon we were given orders to be there at 10am on the Sunday morning. At the last minute it was discovered that the cadet who played the cymbals had not turned up. The bandmaster said 'Jim, will you play the cymbals? I'm sure you can do it.' Now it looks easy doesn't it? Anyone who has played them in a marching band will tell you that it isn't! The cymbal player takes his cue from the Mace, and striking the

cymbals together 'counts in' the rest of the band. Get it wrong – and disaster will surely follow.

We formed up by the clock tower in the Triangle, the town's centre, from where we marched to the Salthouse field on the seafront. I was a bit concerned about the condition of the cymbals, which were made of brass and were about 16 inches in diameter. I had noticed that the screw on one cymbal was quite loose, and tightened it up before starting off. It gradually worked its way loose again, so with the aid of a coin I dutifully re-tightened it. It was on our return march that it happened. I took the cue from the Mace, and began striking and counting, One, Two, Three, Four, Five, S-- then the right-hand cymbal spun from its position on its block and bouncing along the road came to rest with a clatter in the gutter. Amazingly the band came in on time. I struck the remaining cymbal in my left hand, with the block of wood I was still holding in my right, for six, and the crash of the cymbal that hit the road counted as seven! On reaching the clock tower once more, the band was dismissed. The officer in charge of the Nailsea detachment, Captain Harding, came over and said 'Well done, that was quick thinking.' I called it instinct. I played those old battered cymbals a number of times afterwards, but always kept a screwdriver in my pocket just in case!

Because he started work at 4.30am each morning, dad was usually home around 3pm. I remember the day very well; it was lovely and sunny. It was around 4.15pm. I was walking down the garden path and about to open the front door when there was a tap on my shoulder. On turning around I was confronted by a telegram boy. 'Ruston?' inquired the youth. 'Yes,' said I. With that he thrust an envelope into my hand, saying, 'Sign here please.' Clutching the telegram in one hand, and opening the door with the other, I proclaimed, 'Someone has sent us a telegram.' 'Jimmy, give that to me', demanded dad. He walked over to the window to read it. The blood drained from his face as he sat down on the sofa and looking straight at mum, he read aloud the message: 'Gone away. Love Stella.' 'No, no it can't be, let me see it mum said,' It was the first and only time I ever saw my father cry. With head in hands he wept. Stella was his Princess.

The days that followed were some of the worst in my memory. Dad frantically contacted everyone. 'Have you seen Stella?' It soon came to light that she had run away with a man she had met in the office where she worked. To add to dad's pain the man was married with two children and was someone he knew. It was rumoured they had gone to London. So off to London went dad. Summoning the family together, he gave all precise instructions. 'If you find them, give the fellow a good hiding, and bring Stella home.' Had they found them, that is exactly what would have been done. The law of the East End would have ruled! It wasn't to be. It must have been like looking for a needle in a haystack, trying to find one couple in among eight million people. In torment, night after night dad paced the floor of the bedroom. 'Come to bed Jim,' Mum would plead. I can't Liz. My little girl is missing and I don't know where she is.' My dad aged 10 years in as many weeks. As hard as he was on me, I felt deep compassion for him at that time.

Barrington Wright called for me to go to the swimming baths in Bristol. It was something we did as often as we could afford. Jacob's Well swimming pool is pretty ancient, but for us convenient, as the bus from Nailsea stopped just a few yards from it. Nearby was a shop that sold ice-lollies. Not the sort you buy today, though. These were literally blocks of ice, to which flavouring had been added. Delicious at first, but once you had sucked the orange or strawberry flavour away, you were left with a block of frozen water. I wasn't feeling all that special and told Barry so. 'You'll be alright, once we get in,' he said. The changing cubicles were situated all around edge of the pool, with a curtain pulled across while changing. Our clothes were left in the cubicle whilst we swam.

I suppose I must have been swimming for about half an hour, when the candle I had been burning at both ends met in the middle! I was on fire, I thought my head would explode. I got out of the water but found difficulty walking. The pain in my legs and feet was excruciating. The pool attendant came up to me and asked if I was alright. I said I was. He suggested I change and go home. I sat in the little cubicle with my towel around me. I didn't know what to do. I heard Barry calling me to get back in the water. 'I can't,' I shouted. The curtain went back and it was Barry. 'You're not getting out already are you,' he asked. I told him that I wanted to go home. 'Spoilsport,' he barked. Still complaining bitterly, Barry dried himself down and dressed. 'Come on then,' he remonstrated. 'I can't move mate,' I said. His face changed. 'What's wrong Jim?' he asked. I told him about my legs. 'Come on mate you can make it,' he said. Putting my clothes on was agony. Every touch felt like a burning iron and my head was banging away. The pool attendant and others watched me edge my way out of the building, using the wall for support. I didn't think it strange at the time, but on reflection, apart from Barry of course, why did no one offer to help me? It took forever to walk to the bus stop.

We got off the bus together and Barrington went home. The bus stop was right outside the house where he lived, opposite Dr Bown's. I still had a little way to walk. I finally arrived home, and sat down. By now I was feeling dreadful. My eyes were streaming, I couldn't keep my legs still and I was on fire. Mum said, 'If you don't feel well Jimmy, you had better go to bed.' Somehow, unaided, I crawled on my hands and knees up the stairs. I heard mum asking Maisie if she thought I was alright. 'Yes of course he is; just trying to get some sympathy I expect.' she replied. A few hours passed and Mum came up to see me. She looked worried and said, I think I will get Dr Bown to come and look at you.' Dr Naomi Bown, the kindly lady who had been our family doctor from the time we arrived in Nailsea, came up the stairs. It took her just a few minutes to decide that she was going to send me into hospital. The way I was feeling, I couldn't have cared less if she had sent me to the moon.

I was carried out of the house on a stretcher, the ambulance doors closed, shutting out the sunlight of a beautiful summer's day. Mum called out, 'Don't worry Jimmy, I will get daddy, and we will be right behind you.' I was taken to Ward 20 in Frenchay Hospital in Bristol, which had been built to treat American soldiers during the Second World War. The wards were identical, built in individual single-storey units, linked together by covered walkways sprawling out over several acres. Ward 20 was long, with about 20 beds, all of which were occupied, bar one waiting for me. The curtains were pulled around the bed. I was stripped and blanket bathed, and wearing a white theatre gown, which tied at the back, laid into bed flat on my back with no pillow. A wire cage had been placed over my legs to keep the covers from touching them. This contraption obscured my view to the extent I could see very little of the activities in the ward. The Americans had left a legacy, greatly welcomed I shouldn't wonder, of all manner of medical equipment. All the cutlery and utensils, even the dressings gowns, had USMC emblazoned on them. The latter were very posh indeed, beautiful material deep red in colour, only the best for the GIs. They certainly knew how to look after their servicemen. Now we were the beneficiaries.

Mum and dad arrived, and sat by my bed, they looked worried. One of the first things mum said was, 'Maisie is so sorry she was unkind, she didn't realise how ill you were.' Soon, accompanied by nurses, a doctor arrived. Mum and dad were sent out, and my examination began. I was wired up to a machine to check my heart, blood was taken, and limbs and joints inspected. This was all very distressing, as any movement was painful. The curtains were pulled back once more, and mum and dad returned with the news. They had been told that I had rheumatic fever, whatever that is, I thought. My parents had to go but said they would return when visiting was permitted. In those days visiting hours were confined to 2pm - 4pm Saturday, Sunday and Wednesday and

6pm - 7pm Tuesday evening. That was it. 'How long would I be here?' I asked. 'Oh, a week or two,' came the reply. I'm glad I didn't know then that I would remain flat on my back for five months, that my feet would never touch the floor of the ward, and that this illness would lay me low for a year.

My first night was uneasy. I was woken every four hours for temperature, pulse, and had to take four Disprin tablets. These had been dissolved in orange juice and tasted sickly. Six am arrived, and in walked an army of nurses and orderlies. They placed washing bowls in front of us and began preparing for the daily routine. I just lay there. I couldn't sit up. What did they expect me to do? As it turned out they didn't want me to do anything, quite the opposite in fact; they were going to make sure I had complete rest. A nurse washed my face, laid me over on my side and gave me a drink of tea from a small feeding cup, actually more like a small teapot with a spout. I was blanket bathed and fed. This routine changed little during my entire stay in Ward 20.

I heard the swish of her skirt before she came into view. I looked up and, towering over me, I saw for the first time the iron lady, Sister Sturgeon. An old-fashioned, no nonsense, matriarchal figure in a dark blue uniform, with stiff white cuffs and a hat placed on her head like a coronet. She was carrying a stainless steel kidney-shaped dish. I was soon to learn that these dishes invariably contained a syringe with a large needle fixed to it! 'Jimmy, your injection,' she pronounced. Quick as a flash, she pulled the curtain half round the bed, rolled me over on to one side, and with a smack from one hand, plunged the needle into my buttock with the other. It was over in seconds. 'There, that wasn't too bad, now was it,' she said. Not for you perhaps, I thought. It's me with the bum ache! And so it was to continue. Four injections daily, followed by four Disprin every four hours, and just for good measure, a further three vitamin tablets three times a day. I was beginning to rattle! The injections became fewer and after a couple of weeks stopped altogether. The tablets, though, continued for months. They also took blood samples regularly.

It was August and the weather glorious. I was bored beyond belief and watched the clock on visiting days. It could be very depressing. Ward 20 was Men's Medical. I was the youngest by far, at 15 too old for a children's ward, but barely old enough to be called, or treated as, an adult. I don't know how many people died in Ward 20 during my stay there. I just lost count, there were that many. I often wondered when my turn would come. Mr Robins, a neighbour from New Rank, was admitted. His family visited, and his daughter, Esme, walked over to my bed to ask how I was. She was there the day her dad died. She looked so desperately sad. He had been in the ward for just a few days. She was a friend of Stella's.

The worst experience for me was when Alan died. He was only 26 years old, and was in the next bed to me. Although not allowed to sit up, I laid on my right side to talk to him. He had a wasting condition, the cause of which (despite all their efforts) the doctors were unable to diagnose. They treated him for just about every known disease I think. Alan had a beautiful fiancée, who visited him unfailingly at every possible opportunity, as did his caring parents. Couldn't some concession have been made for additional visits, in view of his condition? In those days, hospitals were run under strict unbending rules. After his visitors had departed, using a snow-white handkerchief, Alan would wipe away the bright red lipstick left from the kiss his girl had placed on his mouth. He fought bravely, but lost the battle against whatever it was that was destroying him. Racked with pain, he never complained. We had been friends for such a short time, yet it seemed an eternity. It upset me so much that I had a relapse, and for a time was in crisis. It can't have been right for one so young to witness so much suffering and death.

It was difficult sleeping at night; catnapping during the day and no exercise made one anything but tired. There were also many distractions. Curtains being pulled around beds. Trolleys coming and going. I often lay awake for hours on end, my eyes fixed on the silhouette of the night-nurse, as she sat writing her notes by the light of a small table lamp on the desk situated at the far end of the ward. Pangs of loneliness and despair set in. Would I ever leave this place.

Still summer, I was hot, really hot, sweating profusely. I couldn't understand it. I wasn't feeling particularly sick or anything. Staff nurse McKay was passing the bottom of my bed when she suddenly stopped. 'My god Jimmy, your face is bright red,' she stammered. Pulling back the covers she discovered that someone had left the electric blanket, on top of which I was laying, switched on. It should have been switched off in the early hours of the morning; it was now about 11am! The practice with rheumatic fever was to sweat it out, and to that end I was always kept overly warm, but this was ridiculous. An inquisition was held, and I am sure someone got disciplined over the incident. Another occasion, bored with reading and listening to radio via headphones, I just lay there fidgeting with the bedcovers. Pulling one side out, I could see some red embroidery. With a bit of manipulation of the sheet, to my dismay I could now read the words 'Mortuary Use Only'. Well that was it, I thought. Just a matter of time now, they had put the sheets in ready!

It was Wednesday; mum was coming in to visit. She had to catch the bus from Nailsea to Bristol city centre, then from there get the number 26 to Frenchay – quite a journey. She never missed one of these mid-week visits and was always first through the doors of the ward at 2pm. As soon as she sat down I showed her the writing on the sheet. Startled by what she saw, she got up and stormed back down the ward to the Sister's office, returning almost immediately with the redoubtable Sister Sturgeon. 'What's the meaning of this?' demanded Mum. The embarrassment the Sister was obviously feeling manifested itself in the look on her face. I almost felt sorry for her. The offending sheets were removed in record breaking time, with nurses and orderlies flying in every direction. For the first time I saw another side of Sister Sturgeon. She bent over my bed and said in a comforting tone; 'Jimmy, I am so sorry this has happened.' She then went on to reassure both me and mum that I was, in fact, making quite good progress and all was well.

There were lighter times whilst I languished in that bed. One Sunday, my bed was pushed outside onto the grass for a few hours. It was a glorious day. There was a horse show taking place in the adjacent park, and I could here the shouts of encouragement as the kids on their ponies competed in the gymkhana. What I wouldn't have given to change places with any of them. Dyer's Farm seemed a million miles away. A few beds up from me in the ward was a Mr Williams. He had a greengrocer's shop on Lodge Causeway in Bristol. His son-in-law happened to be one of my footballing heroes, Ivor Guy, the Bristol City fullback. When Ivor came to visit his father-in-law, he always spent a while with me. When I was fully recovered I stayed with Mr Williams and his wife, and he very kindly loaned me his season ticket to the main stand at Ashton Gate. I felt like a king, sat up in the stand, a far cry from the 6d seat I was used to on the touchline.

A recorded delivery postal packet arrived for me. Any post was normally brought to my bed by a nurse but this time it was the postman himself, 'I got to bring it to you meself see, 'cause it's got to be signed for,' he said handing me a pen. I couldn't wait to open it. Inside was a lovely wristwatch. My sister Maud had sent it with a note, which read: 'Jimmy, hope you like the watch. Don't get any worse and expect a three-piece band!' I laughed and cried at the same time; homesick, I missed them all. Still no news of Stella. Had she known I was ill she would have come, regardless of the consequences. June was now three years old and nagged mum and dad to take her to see her Bimmy. Kids were not allowed in hospitals then. Still, dad brought her and let her stand by the French door, which fortunately, was near my bed. They would open the door a little so she could put her arm in, and I could hold her hand. She stood there for ages like that.

The nurses were, indeed, angels of mercy. Nurse Perks, very attractive with dark hair and an engaging smile. Nurse Matthews gliding down the ward with a mincing motion; never quite sure about him, kind and caring though. Reg, a nursing orderly, the 'salt of the earth'. Mrs Brown, she too an orderly in her late 40s, often blanket bathed me. When one of the nurses bathed me they always handed me a flannel saying, 'I'm sure you would prefer to wash your 'middle' yourself.' Not so Mrs Brown, who took particular interest in washing my 'middle' saying, 'I do this for my son Peter.' I thought nothing of it at the time, but with hindsight, the old cow was molesting me. To think mum used to bring her half a dozen eggs most weeks, thinking I might get favoured. I was, but with the wrong sort of 'favour'!

The occupational therapist came to see me to find out if there might be something I could do to help me while away the time. There are not too many things you can do when you are flat on your back. Anyway after some discussion, during which I told the therapist of my interest in radio, she managed to fix me up with a correspondence with the ICS (International Correspondence School). It was all theory work. I was not in a position to attempt anything practical. Whilst studying I made a conscious decision to pursue a career in radio and television.

Saturdays, Evelyn came to visit with her friend Olivia Colborn. This gave mum a break. The doctor's rounds were on Thursdays and every week I waited in anticipation of being told I could go home. If I could get my pulse rate down below 100 I was in with a chance. I'm sure that the anxiety I felt whilst waiting for the doctor fuelled the problem. My pulse was always higher at these times. Eventually all things come to an end. Sister Sturgeon brought the news saying, 'Jimmy, you're going home this afternoon if I can arrange transport.'

I was shown an immense amount of care and devotion at Frenchay Hospital, and have been ever conscious of it. I also owe a great deal to the many people who came to visit me, and a debt I can never repay to my loyal and loving family. Sister Sturgeon's parting words were. 'Good luck Jimmy, I hope we don't see you again under these circumstances.' I thought, I certainly won't miss that bloody needle!

My consultant Dr Nash said that I would need to stay in bed at home for at least another month, then gradually get up for a few hours each day for another couple of months. 'By the way Jimmy I don't wish to disappoint you, but it is extremely unlikely that you will be required to do National Service.' I replied, 'That's OK by me!'

I stayed in bed at home, and the nurse came in every day. Christmas 1952 came and went. Without Stella it was a quiet time. Dad had moderated his restrictions on Eve's social life, and seemed more tolerant. Spring was approaching and I was allowed to get up for a few hours each day. After six bedridden months, when my feet finally touched the floor the pain was excruciating, and I couldn't stand unaided. Thankfully, it was only a temporary condition brought about by so many months of inactivity. As the days passed I got stronger. Then one day the district nurse, who had been so patient and encouraging, announced that she would not need to attend me anymore. I was a free spirit once again. I started going for short walks, gradually building up to a few miles.

I went down to Sandy Bottom to find my boat. After some searching I found it up river in amongst the reeds at the bottom of the water. It looked so alone and abandoned, and with a gaping great hole in its stern. That little boat had been my first real possession bought with my own labours, and I felt a deep sense of loss. I dragged my feet back home and looked in the garden shed for my tent. It was nowhere to be found. It had just gone missing. No one knew or cared much what had happened to it. With Stella still missing and me in hospital, mum said she had had far more important things to worry about than the whereabouts of a tent. One Sunday morning I walked down to Dyer's Farm. Mounted, the string was just about to leave on a ride. I watched them go off with mixed feelings. Half of me wanted to join them, yet the other half was urging 'move on'.

There had been some talk of us moving house, but no details were imparted to the likes of us kids. One evening in April 1953 Dad announced 'This coming weekend we are moving to Wraxall. I have leased a lovely bungalow there.' I couldn't wait for Saturday to come. A moving van turned up, and we started loading our furniture and possessions in it. We had lived at New Rank, Nailsea for nine years, and had accumulated considerably more luggage than the few pathetic belongings we carried on arriving from Kingston Seymour. Without doubt, we were now far more affluent.

I sat beside dad in the big Humber van that he used for work. It had once been a Humber super-snipe saloon car, and now converted into a van was a veritable wolf in sheep's clothing. Incredibly fast, not much passed it, much to dad's delight and mum's annoyance. We drove for barely a mile when we swung into a driveway and pulled up in front of a pair of garage doors. Jumping out, dad shouted to me, 'This is it, Mij,' a name he only called me when he was in a good mood. 'Take a look around,' he said, waving his arms to indicate I should walk to the rear of the property. There were lawns, gardens and an orchard, about half an acre in total. A Victorian double bay fronted bungalow stood before me; very spacious, consisting of three large bedrooms three reception rooms, bathroom, plus a kitchen and a scullery. A half glass porch led to a hallway, which ran the length of the bungalow from where access to most rooms was gained. This was Allendale, and from here we would begin to shape our future.

It was Sunday morning and I had just got up. Eve and Betty were still in bed. I stood in the sitting room looking out of the window. Dad's car pulled up, and out of it climbed Stella. I couldn't believe my eyes. She had telephoned late the previous evening and dad had driven through the night to collect her from a flat in London's Knightsbridge area. The girl I once knew was now a woman, and looked a little sad, a lot tired and pregnant. I told her how much I had missed her. She went to see Eve and Betty, returning after a few minutes saying, 'They don't seem very pleased to see me.' To which mum replied, 'I'm sure they are, it's just that they have got used to you not being here. It will take time.' Tears were shed. Eve and Betty had faired worse than I with taunts of 'Your wicked sister, running off with a married man'. Eve also felt some guilt because she knew Stella was having an affair at the office, but was faced with the dilemma of loyalty to parents, or sister. The latter won; Stella and Eve were inseparable. I am sure Eve never thought the affair serious. And certainly harboured no thoughts that Stella might run away. In those day's 21 years was the age of consent.

Dad had bought a television set before we left Nailsea, a Phillips with a 12-inch screen. It would receive programmes from the BBC in black and white. At that time there was only one channel available. We all looked forward to watching the Coronation of Queen Elizabeth II, which was scheduled to take place in June 1953. It would be the biggest celebration since VE day and a national holiday was proclaimed. We invited some of our old friends and neighbours from Nailsea to watch the spectacle on our TV. The weather was glorious, so after the Coronation was over, mum laid on a wonderful tea outside on the lawn. With Stella back in the fold, everything was perfect. Dad poured the drinks, large ones, and everyone got merry. Happy and content, he talked of the days before the war and how he had watched the Coronation of King George VI on television in 1937. It's surprising how few people knew that it had been televised. It was also the first year that a scheduled TV service was made available to the public. My father was an accomplished raconteur who could hold an audience in the palm of his hand. But he needed a reason to perform, and sadly, less and less found one.

STEALING A GIRL'S BICYCLE

Although only a mile away from Nailsea, I made new friends at Wraxall, and the old ones drifted away. One girl I got friendly with lived on a farm, where I spent much of my recreation. She was a few years older than I was, and although I didn't realise it at the time, quite 'forward' as they would say. She pursued me quite relentlessly referring to me as 'My foolish heart', the title of a popular song. Then having got my attention, she would sing a line from it thus. 'Your lips are much too close to mine, beware my foolish heart.' After some coaching she got me into the hay loft. Kissing and fumbling followed by her asking if I would like to see her knickers. 'What for? I have got four sisters and there are always loads of knickers in our house. Why do I want to see yours?' I inquired. She dropped me soon afterwards. I guess she thought I was a hopeless case. Laughable by today's standards.

I was now 16 years old and the Maxime Cinema in Clevedon was advertising for a trainee projectionist. I applied and was engaged. The cinema took its name from the man who bought it just after war had ended; his name was Max Corne, a short tubby fellow and every inch a showman. Most of the staff there could remember me well from my ashtray cleaning days, which I began at the age of 10. They knew I was reliable so gave me the job. I was introduced to the massive BTH carbon arc projectors, but I was mistaken if I thought I was going to get my hands on the working bits. I was confined to cleaning the base on which they stood! My main job was rewinding the films once they had run through the projector. These were about 14 inches in diameter and very heavy. About five spools were necessary for a feature film. Two projectors were used in sequence, switching from one to the other as each spool emptied. This was done manually by two people. In the top right-hand corner of the picture a starburst would appear and this was the signal to run the standby projector. On the second starburst, the changeover was made by closing the lens on the projector in use, and opening the one about to take over. Perfection in the changeover was always sought, but not always achieved. If neither operator was alert, it would result in a momentarily blank screen or a double image. Stan Newton, the chief projectionist, was of the old school, and a stickler for discipline and performance. It was a career that once entered into, became a way of life for many. Stan worked at the cinema for 60 years.

We were showing *Trouble in Store* with Norman Wisdom. It was the film that made him not only a movie star but also a household name. The film had been a huge success all over the country and when it finally got to us in the provinces queues of people waited to see it. We retained it for four weeks. The morning after the last performance, I was told to take the reels of film down the stairs to the foyer. They were so heavy I could only carry one at a time. On the third trip I let a reel slip. It bounced stair by stair, the metal cover that protects the film came off and the celluloid spilled from the reel trailing behind as it descended. I had given the comic genius a rough ride. Thankfully I managed to retrieve and rewind it, without anyone finding out. The panic over, I smiled. I think Norman would have approved. Long hours, standing up most of the time, and late nights, brought on recurring rheumatism. As much as I loved the cinema, I left.

My brother Roy had married a lovely girl called Josie, an absolute beauty with blond hair. They came to live with us at Allendale, and it was here that Josie gave birth to their first child, a boy they named Roy. My brother and his wife only lived with us for a short time, during which Dad gave Roy a job at the asphalt plant where he was now manager. Of course, because Roy was the boss's son, dad expected him to out-load, out-drive, and tip his lorry faster and more times than anyone else. With ever- demanding requests to 'do one more, son,' I think Roy was glad to return to London for a rest!

A few days after leaving the Maxime Cinema, I caught a bus to Clevedon and called at the Labour Exchange. There was they said a vacancy for a boy at Marchant's Electrical at Six Ways. Marchant's was situated in a row of shops on a small promenade just down the road from where I was standing. Six Ways is so called because it is a junction where six roads converge, and is also the terminus for the Clevedon to Bristol bus. I walked down to the shop, and with a slip of paper given to me by the civil servant at the Exchange, approached the counter behind which a lady in her early 50s was standing. She was smartly dressed, and with blue rinsed grey hair and glasses looked every bit in command. 'I've come about the job,' I stated. She smiled, eyed me up and down and without uttering a word, walked from the counter to a door, which she opened revealing a flight of stairs to the basement. She stood at the top, and called in an autocratic voice, 'Wally.'

A well-built man also in his 50s, with grey hair and horn-rimmed spectacles appeared. 'You're the boy the Labour Exchange sent, are you?' he said. I said yes, I was he. In a firm yet friendly way he asked me to tell him a little about myself. I told him my name, and explained about my hospitalisation and my time in the cinema. 'What we really want is a lad who can learn about radio and later on television. That's the future son, television.' I had glanced around the shop whilst waiting, noticed a number of radio sets, all manner of electrical appliances, but didn't see any televisions. 'Come with me,' he said as he started down the stairs. We walked along a passage and entered a large storeroom. Sitting on the floor gathering plugs and switches about him was a man in a navy-blue boiler suit, slightly built with dark hair, aged about 40 I guessed.

'Jack, this is the new boy, you'll have to treat him gently though, he has just recovered from a long illness.' 'I'll give him bloody gentle,' came the gruff reply. 'Now Jack, Jack, I mean it, go easy on him,' Marchant urged. With that what I assumed was my new boss left the room. His name was Wally Marchant, an electrician, who had learned a little about radio during his wartime service in the Royal Air Force. He never introduced himself to me, and as far as I can recall, never asked if I wanted the job. I don't think a dozen words ever passed between us. He mostly referred to me as, 'the boy'. Relationships between employer and employee in those days were extremely formal. Everyone addressed him as Mr Marchant.

'You're not really delicate, are you?' asked Jack. 'No. True, I was ill for a long time, but I feel great now. It's just that everyone treats me like an invalid.' I responded enthusiastically. The man I had been talking to stood up. He wasn't much taller than me. Taking a fag from his mouth with one hand and extending the other he said, 'I'm Jack Cook, electrician. Do you want me to call you Jim or Jimmy?' 'Jim would be fine,' I replied. 'The lady upstairs,' I enquired. 'Who is she?' 'Oh that's the boss's misses, stuck up cow, she wants a good shagging,' Jack replied. I was a little shocked at this outburst. No one had ever confided in me so, not a grown-up that is. Jack told me he was a Londoner but came to live in Bristol after leaving the Army at the end of the war. When I told him I, too, was from London and had been evacuated, his face lit up. He said he travelled to Clevedon each day on his motor bike, and could pick me up on his way through Wraxall. So began one of those rare relationships. I looked up to him, and he made me his champion; telling everyone in the trade that 'his lad' could out-wire out-repair, out-fix anything electrical, better and quicker, than any other lad anyone had ever seen!

I was given a week's holiday, and went to London to stay with my sister Maud. It was my first major journey alone. When I arrived at Paddington station I felt at ease. I took the underground, changing lines from Bakerloo to Northern without a hitch. I walked carrying a heavy case, in which (besides my clothes) I had packed a few tools and bits and bobs, to the flat where Maud was living in Byrne Road in Balham. She was very pleased to see me and gave me a warm welcome. She has always been a marvellous host, and made me a wonderful meal. After I had eaten, we sat talking over a cup of tea then suddenly she began to cry. This upset me, so I asked what was wrong. She told me that she and her boyfriend Joe had taken this flat and were now living together.

Although she was not at all sure if it was what she wanted. Maud was working long hours as a waitress, and was too exhausted after work to do the many things that needed improving in the flat. Joe, of course, had helped and our brother Roy had turned up one day with a small television, which gave a lot of pleasure. I offered to do all the electrical jobs that needed doing and opening my case said, 'Look Maud, I have brought my tools in readiness.'

The sorrow seemed to pass as quickly as it had descended, and in traditional style we were soon telling jokes and collapsing helplessly with laughter. I had a lovely week, the highlight of which was undoubtedly when Maud's friends Peggy and Tex took us to the Savoy for afternoon tea. Tex had been an American GI and met Peggy during the war, after which he returned to continue the relationship. Tex had a Hillman Californian motor car, with a sunroof, the latest design. I admit to feeling superior as we coasted around the streets in the West End of London, with the windows down, radio blaring and people gaping. It wouldn't be so easy to impress anyone in the giant metropolis now that's for sure. Peggy and Tex were great fun to be with, and Maud was so happy when they were around. They married, and Tex took Peggy back to the States, where they still live.

On Saturday night, I called to see my Uncle Albert and Aunt Mary, they lived in Bow. Their daughters Renie and Sheila took me dancing up the Mile End. They were lovely girls and made me feel very special, telling me what a good dancer I was. I caught the tube to Aldgate East and walked up Commercial road. I was back in familiar territory. I went to see my Gran in Carr Street. The word went around 'Liz's son Jimmy is here.' Soon I was surrounded by relations. The feeling as always indescribable. These are not friends, they are family. The week ended all too soon, and I made my way to Paddington station with mixed feelings.

Within six months I could wire a house unaided. Each week I saved a little from my £1.17.6d (177p) wages, and bought tools. With my tool bag over the handlebars of the firm's bicycle, I was sent off to do minor repairs. After a year I was treated like the other electricians, but still paid as a boy, although I did get a raise of 5s (25p). When there were electric irons, kettles and the odd radio to repair, I stayed in the workshop and worked on the bench. I loved this best. The radio side of things was a challenge, and Wally Marchant didn't know much more than I. It was a bit like the blind leading the blind. We sold Phillips television sets, and the Marchant's had had a 'field day' leading up the Coronation, selling every set they could get their hands on. Little did I know then that the day would come when I too would enjoy a boom in TV sales, for my own benefit.

When it came to repairing television sets, our combined knowledge was basic, to say the least. Baffled, we called on the services of Syd Willis. He worked at the Phillips service department in Victoria Street Bristol. Television was in its infancy and few knew much about how it worked. I would take every opportunity I could to call Syd, and discuss the current problem. I learned a great deal from him for which I remain forever grateful. I think I was fortunate, to be given a more or less free hand in the workshop. On the other hand, the Marchants were charging their customers more for a couple of hours of my time in the workshop than I was earning in a week! Exploitation or what.

Three times each week, at the end of the working day, I took the bus to the College of Technology (now Brunel) in Bristol. I was studying Radio Engineering, and was in fact on the very first course held there dedicated to radio and television. The class was from 7pm to 9pm. By the time I got home it was 10pm. I plucked up courage and asked Mr Marchant if there was any chance I could attend a day release course. I was asking for just one day a week, as much for his benefit as for mine, there was nothing more he could teach me about radio or television. He looked down at me, and mumbled something about did I think he ran a charity. I never brought the subject up again.

His conscience pricked, Marchant did offer to pay my bus fare, which helped. Although he sometimes forgot, and I didn't have the guts to remind him. He also often forgot to pay my wages, full stop! This of course I had to mention. He would thrust his hand in his pocket, bringing out more money than I had ever seen, and hand over a couple of notes. I never had a proper pay packet the whole time I worked at Marchant's Electrical. With some of the proceeds from the television boom, the Marchants bought a brand new Ford Consul car and took themselves off to France for a holiday. Jack and I had a marvellous two weeks. We worked just as hard, but it was pleasant without the 'stuck up cow'.

My sister Evelyn also worked in Clevedon, in a grocery shop during the day. Then most evenings she took singing lessons. These were split between a lady in Clevedon and a male opera singer in Bristol. Eve had a lovely voice, and was singing with the Ken Lewis band, which was resident at the Victoria Rooms in Bristol. At that time, the place to be seen dancing on a Saturday night. The Victoria Rooms had a lovely ballroom with a good-size stage. Dancing was traditional ballroom with some Latin American, Samba and so on. Rock 'n' Roll hadn't as yet gripped the nation. Sadly, Eve's heart was never really in show business, much to the disappointment of dad, who had such dreams, and when she met the man she would eventually marry, she gave up singing in public.

One morning in Bonny's cafe, I was waiting for the tea I had ordered, when the lady owner, who I had come to know slightly asked, 'Do you ride, Jim? You see, I have this 13.2hh pony, and you being not over big, I thought she might suit you.' She must have seen the look of apprehension on my face, and reassuringly said, 'Oh, I don't expect you to pay anything, I just want her exercised regularly.' 'Her?' I queried. 'She's called Bonny,' came the reply. 'Named after your café,' I assumed. 'On the contrary, the cafe is named after her,' she corrected. I had bought myself a bicycle on HP, a Phillips Jaguar. That evening after work I cycled to the paddock where Bonny was turned out. There before me was this lovely pony. So much quality, she was like a small thoroughbred. Over the coming year we would become inseparable. I took Bonny home to Allendale for the weekend. It rained during the night, and when I went to see her in the orchard in the morning, I was greeted with a cloud of steam, rising between the trees. My Mum had only got up during the night and put a blanket over the pony to stop her getting wet. It was the middle of summer! My parents knew absolutely nothing about horses.

Bonny and I became familiar figures around Clevedon. I rode her everywhere. There was one problem, though; she didn't care for buses. When I saw one coming I rode her into the nearest gateway; even then she was frightened. One day on the way home to Wraxall, I just couldn't get out of the way in time, and the inconsiderate bus driver never even slowed his vehicle down, catching Bonny on the rump with a glancing blow as it thundered past. She went berserk. I don't know how I stayed on her back, but I did and she eventually calmed down. Thanks to Rachel Dyer, I had learnt enough to know it was safer for me to remain mounted if possible. It was a terrifying moment for both of us, not one I ever wish to experience again. I felt desperately sorry for Bonny. I shed tears for her. The bus didn't stop and there were no witnesses to what had happened. I kept the incident to myself. After a couple of days the swelling on Bonny's rump went down, but it made her even more nervous of buses.

I taught my niece June basic riding skills on Bonny, a perfect schoolmistress. It was one way of pacifying the dear child after one of her mother's visits. Maud visited as often as she could, and always showered June with presents and adoration. Fine, but when after a couple of days she had to leave, June sobbed for hours on end. She never got used to it. As she got older, on these occasions she sat on the stone steps at the rear of Allendale and became inconsolable. At times even Bonny couldn't help. It upset us all. There was nothing we wouldn't have done to take away the hurt and rejection she was feeling. I swore I would never ever let her down, no matter what lay ahead. I hope I never have.

I had made a new friend, Gordon Cullum. He lived with his mother and father, an RAF officer who was about to retire from the service, on a small residential caravan site in Tickenham which is about half way between Clevedon and Nailsea. Saturday and Sunday nights we rode our bikes to Clevedon and walked along the promenade. It was something that most teenagers in the area did. Starting by the marine lake we promenaded to the pier at the opposite end of the sea front, stopping off for coffee at Fortes Ice-Cream parlour before our return. Occasionally walking with one group of people, only to change direction to walk with another. Sometimes we went out on the pier where there was a juke-box in the Pagoda at the far end. These were simple times, full of laughter and fun. Gordon and I joined the Peggy West School of dancing. Unfortunately, Gordon had two left feet. After a determined effort to overcome his clumsiness he gave up. I could already dance; with a background like mine I could hardly fail. In a matter of months I was helping out with instruction. Peggy was clever; she gave me masses of praise and encouragement and so kept her unpaid assistant. I didn't mind one bit I loved to dance and was very fond of Peggy. I learned to teach the Waltz, Foxtrot and quickstep, which was to prove more than useful a couple of years on.

The summer of 1954 was wonderful, with many visits from our London family holidaying with their 'country cousins' or carrot crunchers, as they preferred to call us. It was marvellous for mum and dad, who still had not really adjusted to country life, to have so many relations to stay. Uncle Jack and Aunt Cissy, mum loved her, and their kids, Johnny, Ivy, and the terrible twins Colin and Clive, were particular favourites of ours. Mum made a big fuss of everyone and dad in particular was pleased to show them how well we were all doing. We had a big American car, a silver grey Studebaker Commander, and took our aunts, uncles and cousins for picnics on the beach at Weston-Super-Mare, stopping off on the return journey at the Star public house on Rhodyate Hill where dad played the piano in a duo, sometimes trio, in the big function room. Coach loads of day-trippers danced at weekends to dad's music. He played there for about 10 years.

'Jimmy, Maurice Radford is looking for an electrician and he wants to know if you might be interested,' my father inquired. Maurice had a small workshop at Backwell quite close to the Anglo American Asphalt

Co where my dad was manager. Maurice did most of the maintenance work at the plant. I had no tie to Marchant's; they had never offered me an apprenticeship, and this would be closer and with more money. I could carry on with my radio studies; I was doing that in my own time anyway so I had nothing to lose. I was sad to say goodbye to Jack Cook. He had been a bloody good mate, and I would miss him. As we parted Jack said, 'Take care Jim. You are much too good for this place, you're a bloody genius. Electronics are the future, and you know it. Stay in touch mate.' I never forgot Jack's praise, and tried to live up to his expectation. Mr and Mrs Marchant looked down their noses as if to say, 'How dare anyone leave us. What cheek.' A few years later I saw Jack Cook driving a van in Bristol. He too had left Marchant's and was working for a new electrical firm. It was a great reunion. Sadly, we never met again.

Dad's plant was full of heavy electric motors and the switchgear associated with them. I had made several calls with Maurice and knew pretty much what to expect. I was working on a piece of heavy switchgear immersed in oil. I had dropped the oil bath to get at the contacts that I had diagnosed would need replacing. The wizened-old maintenance engineer (I think his name was Robinson) employed at the plant, came around the corner, and on seeing me nearly expired on the spot. 'Where's Maurice,' he asked. 'He's not coming. I am here instead,' I said. He flew back around the corner, and into my dad's office shouting, 'There's a young kid here with the switchgear in pieces, he reckons Maurice sent him.' Seconds later he was back followed by my dad, who said, 'Don't worry, that's my son, he knows what he is doing; he is quite capable.' The first recognition I had ever received from my father, never to be forgotten.

Archie Mapstone, the blacksmith from Lower Claverham, came to shoe Bonny. 'Jim, you're an electrician, aren't you?' he enquired. 'They do say that the electric is coming to our village, and I suppose we will have to think about getting our cottage wired up ready for it,' he stated in a matter of fact way. 'I'll come and take a look at the weekend,' I offered. I started to wire my blacksmith's cottage in my spare time. The Mapstones were a lovely family, Mrs Mapstone taught piano. 'I teach syncopation, Jim,' she informed me. Archie used his skills to forge a set of decorative wall lights, which, once painted, I wired. He was like a kid at Christmas, so pleased with the result.

The electric came to Lower Claverham, and I was besieged with requests to wire houses. I did five of them, plus two farms, and the church! Then the salesman in me kicked in, and I sold the newly electrified villagers all manner of appliances. I ended up working for myself full time. I part-exchanged my bicycle for a brand new James Cadet motorcycle, a shiny red machine with telescopic suspension. I was sad to see my Phillips bicycle go but was glad to be rid of the aches and pains after endless miles of cycling on the daily journeys between home and work. Not made any easier by having to carry a tool bag and drums of cable strapped on the frame. Several times weekly I was also making round trips of about 35 miles to go dancing in Weston-Super-Mare. The candle was burning once more.

August Bank Holiday Monday 1955. The funfair had arrived at the Salthouse fields in Clevedon. It was a major event in our social calendar, looked forward to by children and adults alike. The colourful sideshows and rides, which included dodgems, roundabouts and the big wheel, were in full swing when I pulled up on my James Cadet. Very few teenagers had a motorbike in those days, so mine stood out among the pushbikes at the entrance to the field. National Service was in force, so most of the local lads disappeared at the age of 18, and when they returned two years later, they had changed and were now young men, pursuing activities of a more serious nature. They had a lot of catching up to do career wise, so most of the fairground 'Johnnies' were 18 and under. Standing with hands in pockets, I felt pretty superior, and strolled casually across to where the motor cycle roundabout was operating.

To start with I could only see the back of her, but as I got closer she turned around to talk to someone, and there was this lovely girl. I swear to God that it only took a split second for me to fall madly in love with her. She was wearing a white blouse and a full- length cotton skirt with a floral pattern. Her mid-brown hair danced around the back of her neck as she moved. She was watching the undulating roundabout with girls perched side-saddle on motorcycles fixed to its perimeter, and fellows standing with their backs against the safety rails. I guess it was a macho thing. Dangerous, it was considered cissy for a fellow to sit on the motorcycle.

Edging closer I said hello. She smiled and looked away. I waited for the ride to stop, and stepping on to the roundabout invited her to join me. She just shook her head. When the ride had finished she had vanished, so I set off in pursuit and found her standing by the dodgems. Once again when the session came to a halt I grabbed a car and invited her to ride with me. 'No thanks,' she replied, with a flashing smile that made me even more desperate. I drove round and round, and each time I passed her I beckoned her to get in the car. She just smiled and shook her head.

A COCKNEY KID IN GREEN WELLIES

This game of cat and mouse lasted well into the evening, by which time I had at least managed to start a dialogue with her. She told me her name was Joyce and she lived at Tyntesfield. I asked if I could take her home on my motorbike. She said, 'No, I have my own bicycle thankyou. I will be going home on that.' Her cycle just happened to be parked next to my motor bike. Fate, I thought. I had noticed that John 'Chicken' Port, a mate of mine, was at the fair, and he lived at Tyntesfield. I searched for him now and when I found him asked, 'Do me a favour Chicken, will you ride a bike home for me?' 'What for?' he inquired. I explained my dilemma. 'Who's the girl,' he asked. I told him. 'You've got no chance there, Jim. She's gorgeous but the trouble is she knows it.' 'I'll take my chances, will you ride it?' I said. 'Oh anything for a laugh I suppose,' he grinned. I have no idea where he got the nickname 'Chicken', because 'Chicken' he certainly wasn't. Later he made the Royal Navy his career.

I pointed out which bike was Joyce's, and bold as brass Chicken Port strolled over to it, and just rode off. This did not amuse Joyce. In fact she was furious, and I wondered had I gone too far. Sheepishly I said I could give her a lift home. Reluctantly, and exclaiming that I hadn't left her with much option, (the queues for the buses being horrendous), she accepted. We arrived at Tyntesfield before Chicken although I don't recall passing him on the way. By now she wasn't speaking to me. But as we stood there, I couldn't take my eyes off her. She had a lovely complexion, and wore deep red lipstick, and the fragrance of her perfume drove me wild. Chicken, with bike intact rode up. Joyce snatched it from him and disappeared into her house. 'Well done mate,' he said. 'That looked about as successful as the Titanic.' There was nothing left for me but to go home, but before leaving I thanked my good friend and asked, 'Do you know where Joyce goes in the evenings?' 'Yes, at least a couple of nights a week you'll find her in the youth club, just over there,' he said, pointing towards a building nearby. 'She plays table tennis.' 'But be warned, she's a bloody good player.'

I visited the youth club at Tyntesfield every night until I found her. Surprisingly, she didn't seem to bear a grudge. My offer to play her at table tennis was accepted. From here on my pursuit of her was relentless. She surprised me one day by asking me home for tea. I responded with an invitation to take her to the cinema to see *The Dambusters*, which was showing at the Kings, in Old Market. With hindsight, what made me think she would be remotely interested in a war film. We began to see each other six days out of seven every week. Joyce worked in the offices of Rowe Bros. Builders' merchants in Bristol, and lived at home with her parents, two brothers and a baby sister, Heather, who was just three months old. Joyce had longed for a sister, and doted on her.

The family had previously lived at Failand in a farm cottage, where Mr Goodlife, that was the family name, worked on a farm. Joyce's ancestors had been gardeners and farm workers for generations. She was a country girl; an English rose in every respect. Joyce's father had changed his occupation to work in a quarry, where wages and conditions far exceeded those offered by the agricultural industry at that time.

I took my new girlfriend home and introduced her to my family. Whereas Joyce's family were quiet and reserved, we were noisy and extrovert. Affluence had returned and we flaunted it. We had tried Poor, and hated it! All the things we had been denied throughout the war, and for some years after, we now had. Television. Telephone. A Radiogram. And a new piano for dad. Oh, and let's not forget the Studebaker Commander. The biggest car in the district. In the footsteps of their elder sisters, Maisie, Stella and Eve wore the latest London fashions, and set the pace in the locality. I was still among the few of my age that had a motor cycle, and not content with that, had my eye firmly fixed on the Studebaker. Catch me if you can. I was happy beyond belief, my little electrical business was thriving, I had a beautiful girlfriend whom I adored, and life was sweet.

A SUIT OF KHAKI

The buff-coloured envelope my mother handed to me had OHMS printed on the top left-hand corner. This was the first letter addressed to me she had ever handed over unopened! The letter was headed 'National Service Acts' and went on to inform and instruct me to attend a medical examination under the said act, at an address in Bristol. I wasn't unduly perturbed. I was expecting to be called upon, but thought it would be a formality, and that in view of my medical record, rheumatic fever and all, I wouldn't be passed fit for service.

I presented myself on the day stated in the letter at the reception desk of an imposing-looking building in Clifton Bristol. 'Name and initials,' inquired a civilian clerk. 'Ruston J.A.,' I replied. He took the letter I offered, and told me to go through the door on the right and wait. This I did, to find that I was not alone. The room was quite full, with boys of about my age sitting in chairs that had been placed around the room. An orderly in a white coat came in, and ordered: 'Strip to your underpants, and hang your clothes on the pegs behind you.' A shambolic five minutes followed. Eventually the room was quiet once more, with us back on our chairs, only now minus our outer garments.

The lad sitting next to me, even smaller than I for his age, had not hung up his jacket, but was using it to cover his legs. I thought this strange but said nothing. They had started to call out names. 'Andrews D.R. – next,' bellowed the orderly. The bearer of the name got up and was ushered through a door at the rear of the room. I began thinking, if this is going to be done in alphabetical order, I am going to be here all day. Suddenly, the lad I was sitting next to leaned towards me and whispered, 'I don't think they are going to want me.' 'Why ever not?' I asked. 'Look,' he said, carefully pulling to one side the jacket covering his legs. 'See, I haven't got any toes.' I looked down, and to my horror saw his deformed feet. I will never forget the look of embarrassment on his face as he covered his legs once more. I was outraged. How dare they put this lad through this humiliation. The fury was welling up inside me, and I thought if they don't handle this in a dignified way, I will make a scene. I thought of my mum, and what she would have done in this situation. Someone would have been in serious trouble from her. I reassured him saying everything would be OK, and that when he was called I would go in with him if he wanted me to. I just didn't know what else to do or say.

My new-found friend and I were talking about City and Rovers, and their chances of promotion, when the orderly called his name. He got up and shuffled across the room with everyone staring, because he was trying to walk with his jacket still covering his legs. I got up and immediately followed in his footsteps, keeping as close as I could to shield him from the curious looks he was attracting from around the room. I am sure no one meant him any harm, it was just plain old curiosity. I had moved too quickly for the orderly to stop me entering the room in which the examinations were taking place. We stood side by side before the doctor. The lad removed his coat, and when the doctor saw his feet, he went into orbit. 'Who sent this lad here?' he demanded to know. All hell broke loose. Clerks were running in with bits of paper, phone calls were being made, the doctor was berating everyone in sight. Turning to me he said 'Would you get this lads clothes, and bring them in here?' 'Certainly Sir,' I responded. Thankfully, he was a very caring man, and was not going to let this poor unfortunate lad suffer the humiliation of having to walk back across the room uncovered.

My turn came and after examining me the doctor exclaimed that despite the information contained in my medical notes, he could find absolutely no reason, why I shouldn't be passed A1, and fit for duty. Erring on the side of caution, he made an appointment for me to see the heart specialist that I was under during my time at Frenchay, Hospital to get a second opinion. So it was with mixed emotions when, two weeks later, I went to see Dr Naish, and his colleague Professor Parry. After several hours they pronounced me completely fit in every way.

As I left the hospital I thought 'You traitor, Naish. When I left Frenchay, you said I would never be called up!' One half of me was delighted, (everyone wants to be classed A1), but the other half was filled with trepidation. The thought of two years' service didn't bother me at all. It was the thought of being away from Joyce that filled me with horror.

I had to attend a selection centre, where I filled in numerous forms and had an interview with a selection officer. He asked me which of the services I preferred. I told him the RAF. He studied the form I had filled in and said, 'I see you are an electrician and studying radio. These skills certainly make you suitable for the RAF. However, the RAF have their quota of National Servicemen for this period, but if you would like to sign on for an additional year, three in all, I can guarantee you will be accepted.' He then went on to tell me about service life, and the courses available, whereby I could further my knowledge of radio and radar. Politely, I explained that I had no desire to serve a day longer than I had to. 'Right, so you'll go into the Army then,' said the S O brusquely, and with that he showed me the door!

Mum was worried about me having to go into the Army. Dad said it would do me good. He was never in the Army; how would he know? Two weeks before Christmas another buff envelope arrived again with OHMS printed on it. I held it for a while thinking, not before Christmas surely. 'You will report on the 5th day of January 1956 to No I Training Battalion REME Blandford Camp, Blandford, Dorset.' Enclosed was a list of instructions, a five-shilling postal order and a travel warrant to Blandford. One way! This letter had ruined my Christmas already.

Joyce was supportive and encouraging saying, 'It will soon pass.' 'But will you wait for me,' I asked, with not a little apprehension. 'Of course I will,' she reassured. We had a lovely Christmas. Joyce bought me a beautiful pair of kid leather gloves. I didn't know then just how grateful I would be for these in the coming months. We saw each other every minute of every day that was possible. A New Year dawned with the realisation that two more would have to, before life, for me, would return to normal. I finished off the outstanding electrical jobs that I had undertaken, and packed away my tools, together with the half-used drums of cable and accessories that I had accumulated. I polished my coveted James Cadet motorcycle, wheeled it into the garage and leaned it against the wall by the side of the Studebaker.

It was Thursday 5 January 1956. Call up was always on a Thursday. Mum and little June walked down to the gate with me. I had already said goodbye to Eve and my lovely Betty. The bus stop was just a few yards from Allendale. I caught the bus I knew Joyce would get on when it stopped at Tyntesfield. We sat together until the bus arrived at College Green in Bristol. I walked with Joyce to the building where she worked in Canons Marsh. A fleeting kiss goodbye, promises to write to each other every day and we went our separate ways. It was with a heavy heart that I walked across the city centre and up Baldwin Street, then along Victoria Street to Temple Meads station. It never occurred to me at the time that most of the young men waiting at the station were there in similar circumstances.

After changing trains, a crowd of us alighted at Blandford station. From here on we would no longer have to think for ourselves, at least not for the foreseeable future. Several 3-ton Army trucks were waiting in the station yard, and we were met by a Corporal and three Lance Corporals who ordered, 'All those for No I Battalion REME, line up here.' Once they had checked our names against the list they were holding, we were herded on to the trucks. Then the trucks rumbled off to the camp. As we swung through the main entrance of our new home, the Regimental Policeman on the gate closed the barrier. I recall thinking, I wonder what else they do besides manning that barrier. I would find the answer, to my chagrin. It was around 1.30pm; we were ushered into a hut where we were given a cup of tea and a cake. Our first Army meal!

The next few hours were not unlike an Ealing comedy. I felt sure that at any time someone would shout, 'Cut, it's a wrap, all come back tomorrow!' First stop was the barber. The lads who had long hair with side burns, very much in fashion at the time, were distraught as they glanced down to see their beautifully groomed hair in a heap on the floor. Each haircut took about three minutes. To keep the electric clippers cool during this marathon, the barber, a civvy, to add insult squirted three-in-one oil over the blades. With the customary short back and sides, and oily heads, we lined up outside once more. We were photographed; issued with our AB64 Part I record book and Part II pay book. An identity card followed with our photograph and details on. We were required to carry these 'bibles' at all times. We took an oath of allegiance to the Sovereign, then signed the Official Secrets Act.

We marched off in columns of three to the regimental stores, where we were issued with uniforms and equipment – three of almost everything. The Army reasoned thus: one wearing, one waiting, one washing. I have to admit it worked. Having collected the assortment of clobber, and stuffed it into the kit bag you had been given, the next stop was the company stores. Here we received blankets three, sheets two, pillows one, and a green bedspread. Added to this were two mess tins, knife, fork, spoon, and a large china mug. When once more we formed up outside on the road, the amount of merchandise we were expected to carry defied belief. With a bulging kit bag slung over my shoulder, a blue berry stuck on my head (which had more in common with a lean to shed than millinery) and the blankets piled up in my arms, it was impossible to see the man in front of me. (Oh yes, I have forgotten to mention, in less than two hours the Army had declared us all men; what a joke.) To shouts of 'Keep in step', 'What a bloody shambles' and 'I have seen better Girl Guides, than you shower of shit', we marched off to our barrack rooms.

The accommodation at Blandford Camp was a relic from the First World War. Spiders. These were wooden buildings, laid out with a central spine, leading off which were six barrack rooms, three either side of the spine, which housed the ablutions. Just inside the door of each hut there was a small room where the L/Corporal slept. The rest of us were divided down each side of the walls, 28 men to a barrack room. You were told to grab a bed, which would be yours for the duration of your stay. By the side of each bed stood a wooden locker. Bewildered and disorientated, we dumped our gear on our chosen beds. L/Cpl Scutt, a nasty little bastard, introduced us to our Platoon Sergeant. Sgt Foot, informed us, that we were No 9 Platoon and in A Company. We would wear a red flash on our epaulettes, which denoted this. On the wall he pinned a diagram of the way we should lay out our lockers. Then he demonstrated the novel art of making a blanket block. To achieve this, one blanket was folded long-ways, while the other two were made into squares; similarly so the sheets. The blanket squares and sheets were arranged blanket – sheet, blanket – sheet, the remaining blanket wrapped around all, so as to resemble a liquorice allsort. The green bedspread was stretched over the mattress and the blanket block placed at the far end of the bed with the pillow on top. Sgt Foot said, 'Don't worry too much at first; just make the best attempt you can. You will soon improve.' Very reasonable I thought. We were then told to change into our denims. Now denims, a tunic-style top and trousers, come in two sizes – big and bloody enormous. 'If they fit, you must be deformed,' was the saying. The khaki Army shirts felt rough to the skin. The socks were OK though, and then there were the boots. Two pairs, one for every day and one for best. The latter were sacred. Once changed into our denims, boots and gaiters, we looked an odd lot. As L/Cpl Scutt was quick to observe, 'You lot look like sacks of shit tied in the middle.' We were each issued with a large piece of brown paper and a length of string. This, we were informed, was for packing up our civilian clothes, in readiness for posting back to our homes the next day. We wouldn't be needing them at Blandford; we weren't going anywhere.

It was still only 6pm. We were told in which direction the cookhouse lay, and sent off with our eating irons and mugs to get some grub. We joined an endless queue of squaddies to jeers of 'get some in'. This was to become a boring, if not familiar, term, used to belittle anyone who had been in the Army less time than you. We were the latest recruits on the camp, so would have to suffer this abuse for a fortnight until the next intake arrived, and though we now swore we wouldn't, when the time came, we shouted as loud as anyone at the poor sods just arriving. When finally getting to the head of the queue what was on offer as an excuse for a meal defied identification. The tea was definitely an orangey colour. Bromide had been added to subdue any thoughts of naughties. Where did anyone think we would have the time or energy for anything other than soldiering in this god-forsaken hole? I could not eat the sickly mess before me. It had taken so long to get, and now it was congealing with the cold. On the way to the door I dumped the food in the pig bin and washed my plates with the tow mop, which swam in the luke-warm greasy water in the huge metal trough, marked 'Plate Wash'.

I took one step outside the door of the canteen, and a giant of a Regimental Policeman, who was screaming at me, confronted me, because I had committed a cardinal sin, by not putting my beret on properly before leaving the Mess Hall. He threatened me with everything he could think of and asked no, demanded my name and number. Now I had only been given my regimental service number a couple of hours before and wasn't sure of it, so faced the indignity of having to take my Army service book out of my breast pocket to remind me. The RP was not amused and wrote my name in his little book, telling me that if he had to take it again, he would 'put me on a charge'.

Getting lost on my return to our barrack room didn't help matters; the rest had already started getting their kit sorted out. This is where I blessed my time in the Army cadets. At this point I didn't need to ask any questions, and much to the dismay of many of my barrack room-mates, the assembly of webbing and cleaning brasses was second nature to me. I made nothing of it. Tomorrow, we would have to Blanco all of our webbing green. Most at first got into a terrible mess. I was used to Blanco. In the cadet band it had to be white, which is even harder to apply. But this is where any similarities between the Army and the cadets ended. The Army was definitely not playing at being soldiers; this whole experience was in deadly earnest.

The routine for tomorrow would follow a daily ritual. Reveille at 5.30am. Wash and shave in cold water, having waited your turn for the sink. No Plug. Go to the toilet. Dress. Make your blanket block. Do your best, but don't worry, the fatherly Sgt Foot said. Clean your bed space. Help clean the whole barrack room, including floors and windows. Do your Spider job. These were allocated by a corporal on a weekly basis. One week you may be cleaning the taps, another the basins and so on. Get down to the canteen for breakfast. It is an offence for any man to miss breakfast. The queue looked even longer than the first day. When finally I got to the counter and offered my plate to the Army Catering Corps private standing behind it, he plonked a fried egg, a spoon of tinned tomatoes and a fatty rasher of bacon on it.

With a mug of tea in the other hand I found a place to sit on and sat staring at this colourful collection of comestibles before me. The man next to me, whom I suspect had already 'got some in' turned towards me and with a pointing finger suggested that my breakfast reminded him of a miscarriage he had once witnessed. A sudden loss of appetite followed, and breakfast joined yesterday's dinner in the pig bin.

We hurried back to our bed spaces in readiness for room inspection. We could hear them coming down the Spider, the platoon commander, a 2nd Lieutenant, Sgt Foot, a corporal, and the sneaky Scutt. 'Stand by your beds,' screamed Scutt in a tone that would indicate someone had just shoved a red-hot poker up his arse. The fatherly Sgt Foot had taken on a somewhat different demeanour. Gone was the reasonable 'try your best.' 'Have you learned nothing?' he bellowed. 'Was I wasting my time last night?' With that he breezed down the room grabbing blanket blocks as he passed, hurling them to the floor and then fly- kicking them on his return. The young Platoon Commander stood by picking up points from the experienced regular NCO. A 2nd Lt, he wasn't much older than most of us, probably National Service too – many of them were. Most National Service commissioned officers never rose above Lt, and were generally resented by regular officers and NCOs alike, who saw to it that they got every shit job going. Most Regimental Sergeant Majors gave them a much harder time than they did us.

For the next few days at least, everything would be a 'first time' encounter. Our first muster parade at 08.15 hours was a shock to the system. There were about 1,500 men parading on a huge square of tarmac. I recall thinking, I wonder if dad's firm laid this. The men were formed up in Company's A, B, C and D, and a small contingent made up HQ. Each Company was divided into Platoons, with their Commander and NCOs standing in front. We were not called upon to take part in any drill movements, other than to stand at ease and then attention. We were on our first day of our first week of basic military training. No 9 Platoon A Company the newest recruits, bottom of the pile, the lowest of the low. As we would be reminded on a daily basis.

We were marched off the parade ground, to the command of 'Keep in step you bloody shower of shit' coming from the ever-present drill instructors, and kept going until we were halted outside the medical centre. Once inside we were lined up and told to strip to the waist. A medical officer walked down the line and placed his stethoscope briefly on the chest of each man in turn, pausing as he did just long enough to say 'Drop your trousers', whereupon he thrust his hand between your legs, and with a generous amount of your scrotum fighting to get between his fingers, commanded, 'Cough.' Behind him came two medical orderlies: one carrying a dreaded kidney-shape tray, the other a syringe that would hold a at least a half pint of fluid, attached to which was the biggest bloody needle I have ever seen! The medic gave each man an injection into the upper arm, using the same needle! He must have changed it at some point, but I never saw him do it. This deadly duo came around three times with different injections. The man in front of me, who I hadn't really noticed before was at least 6 feet 2inches tall and looked every bit an athlete. I saw him wobble slightly after the first jab, but on the third one he simply keeled over like a tree being felled.

With stiff right arms, and a feeling of nausea welling up, we were taken for a little gentle drill. 'It's good for you, keeps your arms from seizing up,' prophesied Sgt Foot. After the blanket blocks, we would believe him no more. In the first days of drill instruction all movements were done with the timing being called out by the whole squad. One, two three; one, two three; one... as you turn right, about, left and so on. 10.15 hours, joy, our first NAAFI break, a decent cup of tea and a sticky bun. You had to pay for it of course, but those few moments away from the purgatory inflicted by the drill instructors would be our salvation.

After a day of being bawled at during drill, 'Don't worry about your wives and girl friends, someone else is in their knickers now', 'I'll stick my bayonet up your arse, and bounce you around the square like a lollipop', 'You are 'orrible little men. What are you?' ('Orrible little men, Corporal,' we chorused), PT, lectures and endless queuing for meals, cleaning kit until 22.30 hours in the sanctuary of the barrack room now looked like a doddle. I managed to write a few lines to Joyce to say I was OK. I couldn't describe the misery I was feeling, so didn't try. I told her I missed her.

The days wore on. More drill now with rifles, often with bayonets fixed. Bloody dangerous I thought. Snow had fallen and it was becoming exceedingly difficult to keep your balance, especially on some of the Camp roads, which tended to incline. No tolerance was allowed for by the NCOs who continued with threats of charges and jankers for transgressors. We had been issued with gloves and warm they were. The problem was they were woollen, and so made it difficult to grip your rifle during arms movements. Drop a rifle, and guess what? You are put on a charge! Despite the freezing weather we left our gloves in our lockers. Some of the lads wore pyjamas under their uniform for extra warmth. This was OK as long as those in charge never found out. Occasionally, having dressed in a hurry, the leg of a pyjama bottom could be seen poking out over the top of a man's gaiter. This gave us all a well-needed laugh, except, that is, for the poor sod wearing them. A period of jankers was his reward.

A SUIT OF KHAKI

I can't remember too many names of those I did basic training with; there was never any time for socialising. One poor soul I do remember. His name was Hall (I can't recall his Christian name). The poor sod just could not march. The Army call it a 'tick toc' man. One who swings his arms and legs in unison instead of opposite. Poor Hall was tried at the back of the squad, in the middle, in front, but nothing worked. 'Hall, have you shit yourself?' a corporal demanded to know. 'No corporal, I have not.' The answer came with a lisp from the unfortunate soldier. 'Then why are you marching as if you have?' retorted the NCO. Hall also had a skin infection. Every time he shaved his face it would be covered with blood. After two weeks he was told to pack his kit and report to the guardroom. We never saw him again. I hope he was discharged. He was a smashing chap, quite religious. I never heard him complain.

Payday came around. This, in fact, was a parade that had to be practised. We were required to march up to a table where sat the Pay Officer, come to attention, salute, collect the 19s and 6d, and declare 'Pay and paybook correct, Sir', about turn and march off. The Army pay for a National Service recruit at the time was one pound a week. They kept 6d for barrack room damages. I had been earning good money in Civvy Street, and had left a growing business behind. I thought 'This is taking the piss.' It was, and they were. What's more, they would continue to do so for another two years!

We soon became a unit and looked more like soldiers. We were equal; class had no place in the barrack room. To survive we helped each other. Except, that is, if anyone stepped out of line on his own account, then he must take the punishment alone and not try to implicate others. I had already known upheaval and lived in both town and country, but for many of these lads, meeting people from different environments and various parts of the British Isles was an eye-opener. There were Geordies, Scousers, and Mancunians, Glaswegians, Taffies, Cockneys and country bumpkins, from public, private, grammar and comprehensive schools. Mostly we were all the same age, about 18 and a half years old. A few, though, had deferred their call-up to finish apprenticeships or college courses, and were now 21 years old. It proved much harder for them to accept the verbal bullying.

Three weeks had passed and we were given a 48-hour leave pass. Joyce and I had written to each other almost every day. Her letters kept me going in my blackest moments. When I arrived at Temple Meads station in Bristol, it seemed as though I had been away for years. It was about 7.30pm and Joyce had gone down to Allendale to wait for me. I walked to the city centre and waited for the Clevedon bus. I caught sight of my reflection in a shop window: 'Is that me,' I pondered. 'I look so different.' I had aged at least a year in three weeks! I got off the bus and with my little brown attaché case in my hand, ran up the drive and into the warmth of the bungalow. Back in civvies and re-united with my girlfriend and family, Blandford Camp seemed like a dream. Or should I say nightmare!

The weekend flashed by and I was back at Camp, preparing for the next morning when the whole merry-go-round would commence once more. We had become so proficient at our barrack room and Spider duties that each morning we could do everything that was required of us with time to spare. Even the blanket blocks looked great. So hungry had I become that I could eat the canteen meals and go back for seconds! More rifle drill and weapon training followed. Sgt Foot announced that we would be required to mount guard the coming weekend. I had heard rumours of the dreaded guard duty, but as in most things ignorance is bliss.

The rifle range was an experience. I had only ever used dummy ammunition in the cadets. Now it was live. We fired our .303 rifles, and both Bren and Sten guns. The latter are notoriously dangerous. They tend to jam and just fire away at will. It amazed me how good a shot some were, even though they had never fired anything other than a catapult before. Others were not just useless but bloody liabilities who could cause an accident. Weapons are a serious business. They have no place in the hands of the careless. Coming back from the range wearing our steel helmets, which were covered in a camouflage net, and bayonets hung from our belts, it was difficult to recognise one's former self.

The guard at Blandford Camp was made up of six men for main gate duty, and 12 men for piquet duty. The latter required that four men patrol the lines checking the security of buildings and so on. The duty was two hours on, four hours off. So each man did two shifts. Whatever shift you were landed with, one would be in the middle of the night. Mounting the guard is a ritual. Each man is turned out in his best uniform over which a greatcoat is worn, with boots highly polished and rifle by his side, he stands to attention in ranks of three ready for inspection. I was in the piquet squad and drew 20.00 – 22.00 and 02.00 – 04.00. There was still snow on the ground and everything was frozen. We went out in two pairs, and kept moving to keep warm. The time dragged by, but eventually we were called in.

A SUIT OF KHAKI

It was the second shift that was horrendous. By now the temperature had dropped well below freezing. I had never been so cold in my life, my face was numb and I couldn't feel my feet. If we had sat down for just a short while I am sure we would have died from hypothermia, I'm not joking. We got round the back of one of the buildings and finding a door open went inside. We found ourselves in a coke store that also housed a large boiler. It was lovely and warm. We sat on a pile of coke and began to doze. Suddenly the door swung open and a man in a boiler suit burst in shouting, 'What the bloody hell are you doing in here?' When he calmed down he told us he was a civvy employed to look after the boilers, and that we should think ourselves lucky he found us. Had we fallen asleep we would have been overcome by the coke fumes and probably died. I thought Christ, what a choice, hypothermia or suffocation. Another fate worse than death would have been to be caught asleep on guard duty, a Court Martial offence. I got main gate duty twice, and piquet once more whilst at Blandford. It didn't get any warmer.

On main gate you had a rifle but no ammo. If someone approached, you issued a challenge thus: 'Halt. Who goes there? friend or foe? If the answer was 'Friend' you replied 'Advance friend and be recognised.' When they were close enough you checked their Identity Card and said 'Pass friend.' Just who did they think was going to answer Foe? Then what would you do? Shout, 'Hang on a minute whilst I go and fetch some bullets for my gun?' It's ludicrous. Any sign of trouble and you were supposed to call out the guard. But they hadn't got any ammo either! I resigned myself not to try to understand the Army logic. And when they said 'Jump' just to reply 'How high, sir?'

We passed out of training and packed our kit bags. On our way to the main gate we passed the new intake and gave them an ear bashing. We said our goodbyes and swore to keep in touch. We never did. I was posted to Gosport in Hampshire. The railway station at Blandford was full of REME now out of basic training, and catching trains to all parts of the country. There was a bunch of us going to Gosport, although none from my old Platoon. At Portsmouth we were met by the customary 3-tonner the Army uses for just about everything that wants moving – furniture, rations, equipment or bodies!

The truck rolled through the gates of St George's Barracks Gosport. The sign by the main gate stated 10 Trg Bn REME. The colonial style barracks had been built here by mistake. Apparently the plans had got mixed up; they had been designed for construction in the Middle East. They were old but easier to keep clean than the Spiders. We each had a cupboard on the wall above our beds; our uniforms hung on pegs below them.

Things were much more relaxed here, and although there was a muster parade each morning it didn't last long. There was no drill as such, but you were expected to march to your duties in an orderly fashion. The training we received here would determine what we did for the rest of our service commitment.

With an electrical background, Army thinking decreed I should be taught to use a typewriter! With others I sat in a classroom, chattering whilst we waited and speculating as to what would be required of us. The atmosphere was congenial and things looked promising. The door flew open and in walked a Sergeant carrying a bundle of papers. He said his name was Priestly, and that he was our course instructor. The first couple of weeks were pretty uneventful. There was not nearly as much kit cleaning, and by and large when we finished classes at 17.00hours our time was our own until the next day. Guard duty came around infrequently, and when it did it was a case of marching up and down outside the main gate in between two sentry boxes, with your rifle at the 'slope'. When you got fed up with this, you came to a halt ordered arms and stood in one of the boxes. On cold nights we spent more time in the boxes than parading up and down. I think I only did two or three guard duties during my time at Gosport.

I had made friends with a Brummie; his name was Tony Fox. We became great mates and went everywhere together. The rest of the lads on the course were destined to work in an administrative capacity, and were an intelligent lot. Once passing out of here we could consign our boots and gaiters to the locker; we would be allowed to wear shoes, and as long as we were inside had no need to wear a web belt. Foxy told me he had heard that after three months' service, an application to keep a car or motorbike on camp could be made. I needed no second telling. I applied at once and permission was granted. I couldn't believe it was that easy. After all the bullshit and hassles, suddenly the Army had become reasonable.

With a 48-hour pass in one hand, and my motorbike permit in the other, I headed out of the main gate towards Wareham. Gosport wasn't an easy place to get to from Bristol. It was a case of train to Portsmouth, then catch the passenger ferry for Gosport. This route was slow and expensive. Or there was travelling by road if one had the means; if not you could thumb a lift, but again this was difficult. I chose the latter. Thumbing could take hours, but at least it was free. Eventually arriving home I jumped on my James Cadet, and shot off to see Joyce to tell her that I was now permanently mobile. The weekends were lovely but over too soon.

Sunday night, dressed in windcheater and helmet with a scarf pulled across my face, leaving just enough space to see, I set off towards Bath. It took about two hours to get to Camp. I made this journey many times in all weathers. On one occasion, so tired was I through lack of sleep having just finished a week of guard duties, that I dozed off on the bike. The next thing I knew, I was laying in a flowerbed with the bike on top of me. I had ridden straight up someone's driveway and crashed in his or her garden. Shaken and bruised, but otherwise none the worse for the experience, I continued on my way. I did demolish a few flowers though, but could find no one to say sorry to.

'Ruston, can I have a word.' It was Sgt Priestly. He had found me in the NAAFI, always my retreat in search of a cup of decent tea and a game of table tennis. 'Yes Sergeant,' I replied, giving him a cynical glance, complete with raised eyebrows. He paused then said, 'Can I borrow your motorbike this Wednesday?' Without a thought I said, 'Yes.' On the Thursday morning we were sitting in our classroom studying one of the Army's bible's – EMERs. *Electrical Mechanical Engineering Regulations.* (In the Army even repairs are done 'by the book'.) We waited and waited; the word went round 'Where is he?' Tony Fox said, 'Did he bring your bike back last night, Jim?' I said I didn't know, I hadn't looked. Why should I? I trusted him; he was our Sergeant instructor. After an hour or so a Corporal came in saying, 'You lot had better dismiss for today, your Sgt's had an accident and is in hospital.' And with a grin, added, 'It seems he fell off his motorbike.' 'My bloody motorbike, I hollered'. I couldn't contain myself. Foxy and me went to see Priestly in hospital. He looked a sorry sight and said that his girlfriend, she had been riding pillion, was also injured. Mad as I was I couldn't help feeling a little sorry for him lying there all plastered and bandaged up. And I certainly felt concern for his girlfriend.

The outcome of the accident was this: my bike was only insured for me to ride. I was fined for allowing another person to ride it and would have to pay for all the repairs myself. Priestly was fined for riding it without insurance. I had not noticed the clause Owner-Driver Only. Shit. A few weeks later Sgt Priestly promised to make recompense, if I didn't kick up any fuss. I was hardly in a position to, him being my senior. In fact, everyone was my senior! With hindsight, I should have made a formal complaint to the adjutant. Priestly would have been disciplined and made to compensate me for my loss. I was green, and since joining the Army had been constantly threatened with 'fates worse than death' if I opened my mouth without being asked.

Tony Fox and I went to the cycle shop to see the state of my bike. It was heartbreaking. The beautiful red and chrome machine, was now a tangled mess. The cycle shop owner informed me that it would cost about £20 repair. 'Bloody hell Jim, that's five months' pay mate,' Tony said. It was still on hire purchase and I had to pay the instalments. The owner of the cycle shop was very sympathetic and said he would repair and store it for me until I could afford to collect it. I couldn't ask for more. He was good to his word, but it was two years before I was in a position to redeem it. When I did, he greeted me warmly, saying he was confident that one day I would walk through his door to get my bike. He thought I had been badly treated and said that if he had been a bit better off he would have repaired it for free. As it was, he had kept the price to a minimum and didn't charge any storage. When I told my dad about it he just shrugged his shoulders saying, 'Soppy sod, I hope you learn from it.' He wasn't going to put his hand in his pocket. What's new! I was back on my feet, literally. Bollocks.

Meanwhile on the home front my sister Eve was marrying Don Waite. Having finished his National Service with the Duke of Cornwall's L.I., Don had joined the Police Force and was stationed in Clevedon. He had noticed Eve in the shop where she worked and had asked her to the Police Ball. I was due a few days' leave and took it to attend the wedding. Eve looked stunning, and the bridesmaids – Sister Betty, little June, Maisie's daughter Linda, sister June's daughter Teresa and Don's niece Nicola – did the happy couple proud. I carried out the duties of usher. Relations came from both sides and a reception for them was held at the Battle Axe Hotel. It really was a lovely day. Dad wanted Eve to sing Ivor Novello's 'This is my lovely day' – a song she had sung many times. Eve declined. I didn't blame her; it was her day and she should do as she pleased. Had she, dad, ever the showman, would have loved it. I don't doubt he had a few musicians lined up in readiness!

It was Joyce's 18th birthday; I had bought a small ring, at Parsons the Jeweller's in Bristol. I plucked up courage and in the traditional way asked her to marry me. She accepted, and I placed the ring on her finger saying, 'One day when I'm rich, I will buy you a much better ring' (years later when I offered to, she declined, asking for something else instead. The "something else" changed our lives considerably).Her reply was typical: 'I love this one, thankyou.' We were both as happy as a lark, that is until Joyce's father discovered she had got engaged to me. Her family thought the Rustons far too racy for one of theirs to contemplate marrying into. They made it obvious that I was no longer welcome at their house. From here on, we would have to continue our courtship in the great outdoors. The winter would be a problem.

I hoofed it up and down to Gosport until my course finished. I was summoned to the Company office and instructed to report to 116 Coy Amphibious Transport at the School of Amphibious Warfare in Fremington North Devon. Foxy and I said our farewells, and in time-honoured fashion promised to keep in touch. Despite everything, we had had a laugh. Evenings spent catching the ferry to Porstmouth dodging the Matlots (there were thousands of them and so few of us Pongos). Visiting the Union Jack Club for half of beer and a meat pie, living indeed! We were permanently skint and would pool a few coppers to escape to the cinema. I will never forget the ration truck incident. We were detailed to take rations from the store to the cookhouse. Tony and I were in the back handing a sack of flour to an ACC cook, when the driver lost concentration and pressed the accelerator pedal, followed by a stab at the brake. The violent jolt shot the bag out of the truck, emptying its contents all over the unfortunate cook. We were helpless with laughter exclaiming 'It wasn't our fault.' 'Bastards!' came the reply from an irate cook, now looking more like a snowman.   Tony was the only real friend I made in the Army. I had plenty of mates, but not close.

A single line ran from Barnstaple to Bideford, the engine pulling the train one way, then pushing back the other. Fremington was three miles down the track. A road leading past the parish church approached the entrance to the Camp. A single barrier blocked the entrance, to the left of which was the guardroom. As I approached, it looked deserted. Then a Corporal stepped out and asked me to identify myself. The NCO, quiet and relaxed, pointed me towards a stone-built barrack room. On entering I found that the showers and ablutions were inside the door on the right, with a couple of individual bunks on the left. There were about 20 beds with lockers, arranged 10 on each side, with the familiar coke stove in the centre of the floor about three-quarters of the way down the room. There was one empty bed space on the right-hand side. I dumped my kit on the bare springs and went off to find the company stores to draw some bedding. It was 14.30 hours and the whole camp seemed empty. At the stores I asked where everyone was and was told 'At Westward Ho!' 'What are they doing there?' I inquired. The storeman looked at me in disbelief and said, 'Taking DUKWs and LVTs (both are landing craft, the former a six-wheel amphibious truck, the latter small amphibious tank) out to sea. What do you think goes on here?' I felt a bit foolish and confessed that I really didn't know, no one had told me anything.

Back in the billet I packed away my kit and made my bed, on which I lay and continued reading the new book I had picked up at the station shop. A thoroughly good read with the title of '*Cockleshell Heroes*'. It wasn't until years later I discovered that Major Hasler, who led the Cockleshell raid, had founded the unit I was now about to join, and that Bill Sparks, his number two in the canoe on Operation Frankton, would become a dear and much-valued friend. My interest in escape stories had been kindled during my time in hospital when I was given *The Colditz Story* by Pat Reid, followed by *They have their Exits* By Airey Neave, the first man to escape from the infamous Colditz Castle during the Second World War. I eagerly read anything to do with capture, escape and evasion. It fascinated me and I wondered how I might fare in similar circumstances.

The peace of the barrack room was shattered when the door swung open and a crowd of soldiers hurried in. Taking no notice of me whatsoever, lockers were banged open from which eating irons and mugs were withdrawn, belts and berets left on beds followed by a mass exodus. The last soldier paused on his way passed my bed and stated, 'Canteen up mate'. Sitting in among as motley a crew as you would ever find, I soon found out that this was a daily routine. About 40 men travelled each morning to Westward Ho! Returning around 1730 hours. The sea air and the fact that most of the activity was in the open gave everyone a huge appetite that could hardly wait to be abated. This Camp was different to almost any you would find in the British Army. The bulk of the men were Royal Army Service Corps they provided drivers for trucks, DUKWs and LTVs. Then there was a sprinkling of REME, Signals, Medics, Sappers, Gunners and Intelligence Corps. These provided the technical expertise. 12 man Cadres made up of junior officers and NCOs from all regiments of the Army came here to learn about landing craft. All manner of things military took place here; this was a Combined Operations centre.

Next morning everyone got up without being called, and having whisked a broom over the floor and flipped a duster around, sallied forth to breakfast. On our return a Corporal entered our room to good-natured jeers from within, and addressed me so; 'I take it you are Craftsman Ruston, the new 'shiny?' (office bod). I confirmed that I was, and was told to follow the rest out to the waiting transport. Outside, half of us boarded 3-ton trucks and the rest climbed on a DUKW. I jumped on the latter. I didn't want to miss the chance of a new experience. We drove through Bideford and on to Westward Ho! It was a lovely day and we were in shirtsleeve order. It felt a million miles away from basic training. Perhaps National Service wouldn't be so bad after all.

Suddenly I could see the rolling waves of the Atlantic Ocean breaking on to the shore. The beach, along which runs a pebble ridge, stretches for several miles. It all looked blissful in the bright May sunshine.

'Ah – Ruston, welcome,' said a well-built man in greasy overalls. I could see from the leather strap, which held a brass badge to his right wrist, that he was a Warrant Officer Class 1. His cap badge was the same as mine. 'I've been waiting months for you, come with me.' We walked over to a wooden shed about 12 feet by 10' feet in size. Inside was a trestle table on which was piled hundreds of buff envelopes marked 'War Dept. Confidential'. On a shelf above was a row of volumes of EMERs. A pot of paste and a brush, covered in dust, stood at one end of the table. No one had been in this shed for a while. 'As you can see er, mm,' stammered the Sgt Major, 'I have made a start at the amendments but there are so many arriving weekly that I could not keep up to date.' 'Bloody hell, sir,' I exclaimed. 'I only have 18 months left to do.' 'That's the spirit. I like a sense of humour. You and me will get on well,' he responded. Sense of humour be buggered. I was being serious! I started to open the envelopes and take out the hundreds of amendments that would have to be pasted on the relevant pages of the EMER to which they referred. Sometimes the amendment slip contained just one word, often one letter, some only a full stop or comma! I was to languish unhindered in this shed for weeks. Apart from the Sgt Major, no one knew or cared what I did.

Some days I left my shed and went on sea trial with the courses; other times I wondered on the heath. When the sea became warmer, we swam most days. A lady called Jean provided NAAFI. She owned a small cafe by the slipway, and at 10.00 hours daily someone would be detailed to take a truck, or often as not, a DUKW to fetch her and the refreshments. Nothing would ever stop the Army taking its NAAFI break. Wednesday afternoons were reserved for sports. We played cricket, often challenging the locals. These games were always hotly contested. Lunchtimes were looked forward to. A small concrete building served as a canteen and a civilian cook came in daily to make our lunch. It was the best food I ever had in my two years of service. Lunch was served between 1230 and 1400 hours, and we wandered along in groups. If for any reason your work made you late, the civvy cook put your meal in the oven until you arrived.

A COCKNEY KID IN GREEN WELLIES

On finding out that in Civvy Street I was an electrician, the Sgt Major dragged me out of my shed on a number of occasions to look at things electrical. And so I became a bit of a dogsbody. A bit of technical admin, a bit of electrics, shunting a few vehicles around. I didn't mind what I did. Every day was one I wouldn't have to do again, that's all that counted with me. I was issued with a tank suit, a marvellous piece of kit, all zips and water and windproof too. This I thought will be great on the bike. A corporal instructor 'Smudger Smith' taught me to drive an LVT (landing vehicle tracked). I didn't much fancy them in the sea, though. They lay very low in the water, and with the Atlantic very rarely calm, it wasn't the most pleasant experience. Years later, my brother Roy told me of a near disaster experienced by the Commandos, caused by LVTs getting stuck in the mud at Lake Comacchio during the Second World War. They drew a lot of water for their size.

I had acquired an old Ariel 350cc motorbike. Not terribly reliable, but it was quite fast. 'Jim can I borrow your bike?' the request came from the MT Sgt. I thought, 'I've been down this road before.' 'I only want it on Wednesdays for a couple of hours, and in return I will fill the tank up with petrol,' he promised. I had made sure that the insurance covered any driver, also third party fire and theft. The promise of a full tank of fuel to go home with, was enough to persuade me. The arrangement worked out fine, with the bike going ever better and faster.

A sports and open day had been arranged. Joyce came down on the train and I met her at the station with the motorbike. I didn't take part in any of the activities. Instead I showed Joyce around the Camp, and took her to Westward Ho! Later that afternoon, with Joyce cuddled up behind me on the bike, we headed home. I craved for days like these, and hated being separated from her.

Sunday night came all too quickly and I motored back to camp. I was thinking, 'This is not a bad bike, a bit of a wreck, but it goes well.' Great thought I, until one day it blew up. True to his word the Sergeant had been filling the tank, not with petrol from the local garage, but with 100 octane tank fuel! The valves had burned out. Little wonder it went like a bleedin' rocket. Has anyone seen that pony? You know the one – Shanks!

President Nasser's decision to nationalise the Suez Canal Company on 26 July 1956, thereby forcing all users of the canal to pay tolls to his government rather than to the Anglo-French consortium that legally owned it, resulted in the invasion of Egypt by an Anglo-French force in November of that year. The conflict was over before it began so to speak, but not before causing chaos among the UK Armed forces.

A SUIT OF KHAKI

Some 20,000 'Z' reservists were called up; many of who were ex-National Servicemen. Down at Fremington we were 'invaded' by about 300 of these reservists, and a bolshi bloody lot they were. Although fully aware of the obligation being a reservist carried, few expected to be called upon to serve again. The reserves were formed into a new unit called 303 Company Amphibious Transport.

The peace of the Devon countryside was shattered. Vehicles were rushing about all over the place. The few landing vehicles we had in 116 Company would not nearly meet the demand, and so we made a request for additional DUKWs and LTVs to be brought down from the Army stores depot in Ashchurch, Worcestershire. I was dragged out of my wooden hut and 'asked' to work with an RASC Sergeant whose name was Griffith. Griff had been given the task of organising the logistics of the movement of transport. We pulled about 80 DUKWs out of the command depot at Ashchurch, and what a sorry state they were in. Perished tyres and electrical and mechanical faults were commonplace, and of course none of them were seaworthy.

Suddenly, gone was the low key no 'bull operation that I had got used to. With around 500 men now stationed hereabouts, a regime of discipline and parades returned in anger, bringing with it guard duties and bullshit. Our vehicles, currently in battleship grey, had to be re-painted desert yellow. A terrible mess ensued. 116 Company ceased to exist; we were now all 303 Company.

The reservists had an aversion to everything military. They didn't clean their kit or press their uniforms, and were invariably either late, or missing at parade times. This caused a great deal of ill feeling among 'us and them'. We didn't particularly want to soldier either, but we did want a quiet life. The disruption of our camp was total. By the middle of November and with the Suez crisis over, many of the reserves had been allowed to go home. Things never got back to normal, at least not whilst I was there.

The Army learned nothing about keeping landing craft in a state of readiness. More recently, in the Falklands crisis, the same problems we had experienced 25 years before were still there.

The letters I received from Joyce were getting 'cooler'. Darling Jim, had become Dear Jim. I was worried. With the Suez Flap' on, there had been no leave and I was anxious to get home to see her. On Saturday morning with a 36-hour pass in my hand, I hitchhiked up the A361. I went straight to Joyce's home and after knocking on the door waited outside for her. She came out and we walked and talked. Joyce told me that she had got a letter from her aunt telling her she should respect her mother's wishes and stop seeing me. I said something like 'Nosey old bag, what's it to do with her,' but I could tell Joyce was considering her mother's wishes. To say I was upset would be an understatement. Try as I might, I could not persuade her that it was her life, and at 18 she was capable of making her own judgement. She gave me back the engagement ring I had given her, saying, 'It is all too much for me. Everyone is against us. I can't take it alone. It's easier for you, you don't have to put up with it. You are not here all the time.' My world fell apart right there and then. I must admit I really didn't realise how bad things had got for her. Staying in every night of the week, unable to ever mention my name in front of her parents. She quite understandably got fed up with either having to visit my house all the time, or meet me in the great outdoors. No fun now; it was the middle of winter. We spent hours on end walking the lanes and standing in gateways. They were the hardest times of our relationship.

Over the weekend I managed to persuade Joyce to keep the ring, although she would not put it on. When Sunday night came, and it was time for me to return to camp, I was in tears. I couldn't leave things like this. I still had another year to do and I couldn't bear the thought of losing Joyce. I spent all night at the station, sleeping in the waiting room, then walked the streets of Bristol. On the Monday at 5pm I met Joyce from work. She was astonished to see me. I told her I had managed to wangle an extra few days' leave; she didn't look that convinced. I was AWOL.

I went home to Allendale. Mum and dad thought I was on leave. I never discussed the Army with them, so they didn't know where I was supposed to be. Towards the end of the week a knock on the door brought me sharply back to reality. A policeman had made the knock. In a voice that came straight from Dixon of Dock Green, he said, 'Hmm, we have er, been informed by the, um er, Military Police that 23272922 Craftsman Ruston J.A. of REME has failed to report back to barracks. Or to um er inform, his superiors as to why he hasn't done so.' I was always proficient with, 'It wasn't me, I wasn't there', reasons, and the Army had furthered my education in this direction. I looked the constable straight in the eye and said, 'I am catching a train back to Camp first thing in the morning, I will explain my absence when I get there'. 'I will inform the authorities,' said the constable and left without saying another word. 'What was that all about, Jimmy?' mum asked. 'Oh nothing much, just the Army can't seem to do without me,' I replied. Mum laughed.

A SUIT OF KHAKI

After saying goodbye once more to Joyce, she still wasn't wearing her engagement ring; I caught the train to Exeter where I changed for Barnstaple. Now everything would have been fine, I had made up my mind to return and face the music. As the train pulled in to Barnstaple station, I could see two MPs waiting on the platform. I thought, what a bloody cheek. I was returning voluntarily and they had sent two Redcaps to escort me back to Camp. I wasn't going to let those bastards humiliate me for their amusement. The escape and evasion plans I had been harbouring from books read on the subject kicked in. I opened the carriage door, jumped down on to the rails, and sprinted across the tracks and up on to the platform by a door marked 'Way – Out. I was so fit in those days; we all were. Calm and collected, I walked from the station and headed for the A361. The first car I thumbed stopped. Soon we were speeding up the road. The whole episode had taken just minutes. My mood swung. Anger turned to laughter, then concern. I was in the shit!

I had arranged to meet Joyce after work on the City centre. As she approached I felt a hand on my shoulder. 'You're under arrest,' said a policeman in plain clothes. 'But you can have a few minutes with your girlfriend though,' he said with a grin.

My escape was laudable, but evasion crap! The police had contacted Joyce at her office and asked her if she was meeting me. The poor girl was embarrassed and upset. I was behaving like a prat. Joyce being the wonderful girl she is, stood by me saying she would put the engagement ring back on her finger if I promised not to go AWOL again.

I was eventually escorted back to Fremington. The summary punishment meted out for my being AWOL was 14 days' C B (confined to barracks). I had got away light. The C B was a piece of cake. I served it with a fellow defaulter, 'Shug' Wilkie. Shug was from the Gorbals area of Glasgow. Shorter than me and twice as wide, he was a hard man. It was at a glance a most unlikely alliance, but we got on like a house on fire. Shug said 'With my brawn, and your brain, you'll do me Jimmy.' We skived just about everything we were asked to do. One look from Shug, and no one seemed to want to insist we do too much. One tedious regulation that is always enforced when serving a period of C B is that you have to 'Mount' and 'Dismount' with the guard detail. This means getting up at 05.00hours and in best uniform with rifle, report to the guardroom ready for the 06.00hours Dismount. Then repeat the exercise at 18.00hours in time for the evening Mount. You are inspected each time you parade. In basic training battalions, C B is fearsome. The level of turnout required being awesome. Of course,

Military Prison is much, much worse. One poor unfortunate lad was given 28 days in Colchester. When he returned to camp, he had lost a lot of weight, and with all the cleaning and pressing had virtually worn his kit out. The hardship he had experienced was so tough he became withdrawn, and wouldn't talk about it.

I applied for a transfer, and couldn't believe it when one was granted. I would have to wait to find out where though. Christmas was approaching and I found myself on guard duty both Christmas and Boxing Day. A few of the lads had been rehearsing for a concert they were planning to put on the week before Christmas. We all mucked in. I helped with the stage lighting and props. It was a typical Camp concert, with lots of bawdy humour aimed mostly at the officers and NCOs followed by fine singing from Sgt Griffith, with whom I had been working. Griff sang the Al Martino hit song 'Here in my Heart', the second line of which goes, 'I'm alone and so lonely'. You could hear a pin drop. Griff's fiancée had recently broken off their engagement. I felt for him.

I wasn't looking forward to being on guard duty over Christmas, but was resigning myself to it when my old C B mucker Shug offered me a swap. Shug had drawn New Year guard duty, and being from Scotland he was more inclined to be home for New Year than Xmas. On Christmas Eve I hitched home. It was easy getting lifts; everyone was in a festive spirit. Mum, dad, Betty and June had gone to stay in London with Stella for the holidays, so I had Allendale to myself. I didn't ring to tell them I was home. I knew it would upset them to think of me alone at Xmas. I called on Joyce of course. She was surprised to see me. 'No I'm not AWOL,' I assured her. 'I've just swapped my duty.' We kissed goodnight and arranged to meet the next afternoon. For my Christmas dinner, I had poached egg on toast followed by a pot of tea. Bliss. I was happy as Larry. Joyce and I spent Christmas afternoon and evening at Allendale. Boxing Day was equally pleasant, after which I headed back to Fremington.

It was approaching midnight on New Year's Eve. I was standing at ease on main gate duty, when the guard commander called out. 'Happy New Year Jim.' I reflected on the year that had past. Was it only one year? It seemed like more. I had changed. Things would never be the same again. A year from now and I would have only five days left to do. Everyone counted the days to de-mob. It didn't help, but everyone did it.

HAPPY DAYS ARE HERE AGAIN

After a period of leave I reported to 3 Training Battalion, at Arborfield near Reading in Berkshire. 3 Bn REME was a training establishment for wireless and telecommunication technicians. After basic training and selection those posted to this camp received between three and five months intensive training in communications. Together with Radar taught up the road at 5 Bn, these courses were the ultimate, in technical terms, then available in the Army. Those passing out from here would be X class tradesman. The highest regarded and paid of the Army trades. Anyone with anything to do with electronics in the army is generally referred to as a boffin. Few understood what they did. A, B and C were the training companies. HQ Company was responsible for the administration and general running of the Camp. I had been posted to HQ Company.

I presented myself at HQ Company office. Having left my kit on the wooden veranda outside, I entered the building and immediately saw, sitting at a big desk at the far end of the main office, a large amenable-looking NCO. On the desk in front of him was a name block. It read: CSM Rixon BEM. I stood and waited to be spoken to. Casually, with all the time in the world, the Sergeant Major looked up at me and said, 'Ruston, I've been expecting you. On time I see.' And with a huge grin he continued, 'Didn't take an extra few days' leave then?' I smiled back, 'No sir. 'I won't be doing that again.' I thought blimey, they know all about me already; better not give him any flannel. As the CSM got to his feet, a Corporal walked into the office. 'Corporal Price, this is a new bod. He's called Ruston, arrange for him to see the CO.' Rixon instructed. With that the CSM departed leaving me with Corporal Price. 'What's your Christian name? the Corporal asked. 'Jim.' I replied. 'I'm Terry, and National Service just like you. I'll arrange for you to see the CO tomorrow morning after Orders. Report here at 08. 30 hours.

Terry told me where the Company stores were, so I could draw my bedding, and pointed to the Camp layout displayed on the wall. I found where HQ Company billet was. I could see from the diagram that the accommodation was arranged in Spiders, identical to those at Blandford. There was, however, one subtle difference between these Spiders and the ones I had been familiar with. These were centrally heated. And I don't mean one coke stove in the middle of the room, which was Blandford's idea of central heating!

The Company office was a hive of activity when I reported there at 0830hours the following morning. CO's Orders took place each morning where anyone with anything to say or those who had been charged with an offence were marched before the Company Commander. HQ Company commander was Captain Wakeman.

A COCKNEY KID IN GREEN WELLIES

Normally Company Commanders are Majors. Wakeman wasn't promoted during my time there, though. I was at the very end of quite a long list, and when my turn came, the CSM marched me in and told me to halt and stand at ease. The officer sat at the desk in front of which I was now standing. I judged to be in his early forties. He may have been younger, but didn't look it. About my height but much heavier, he had a jovial look about him. 'Ahh, Ruston. What are we going to do with you?' He mused. He had my records before him and after a reference to my AWOL, said that the Company office was under pressure at the present time, and seeing that I had been on a typing course, perhaps I could help out temporarily. With that I was dismissed and told to report to Corporal Price.

On hearing I was to help him, at least for the present, Terry grinned saying, 'I have been asking for some help for weeks, but I didn't expect to get any. Now suddenly the Army's listening!' Terry Price was about six feet tall, a good-looking fellow with blond hair. Both coming from London, we got on famously from the start. He was due for de-mob about three months before me. Over a cup of tea in the NAAFI, Terry gave me the low-down on the way things operated in HQ Company. The CO, Captain Wakeman, liked a quiet life, and if you did your job, he would leave you alone. CSM Rixon was a gentleman, and having served 21 years he was due for de-mob early January 1958, and so really didn't want anything to disturb the peace. HQ Company ran things at 3 Battalion, the training companies are the nig-nogs, and we don't let them forget it, Terry informed me. I thought, this will do me fine, keep my head down, learn the wrinkles, and my second year could be easy.

I must say, and hopefully without sounding élitist, that the general level of education at 3 Bn was exceptionally high. In my billet there were draughtsman, accountants, chemists, plus quite a few of the specialists. Armourers, communications experts and the like. It made for intelligent conversation, a welcome change from the usual sex and football! I soon made friends, three of whom were special: Tom Stilwell whose task it was to duplicate all Company and Standing orders daily, and arrange distribution throughout the camp. Ron Poole, an armourer of outstanding skill, who could fashion from gunmetal almost any part he required; John. I am ashamed that I cannot remember the surname of this lovely guy. He was my table tennis opponent, with whom I had a running battle for the best part of a year. We spent hundreds of hours at the YMCA table, and immediately one of us had won, so the challenge of a return match would be insisted upon. John's comradeship was a great comfort to me during 1957. We went to

Reading to see a show billed as 'Fast and Furious'. However it turned out to be the most dull and pathetic variety show I have ever seen. It was so bad it reduced us to fits of laughter. If John was losing to me at table tennis, he only had to say 'Fast and Furious' and I would collapse helplessly on to the floor. I, of course, often used the same tactic.

I was walking down the road, which ran from 3 Bn down to 5 Bn and the REME depot, when I spotted a familiar figure. Hands in pockets...with a slightly swaying gait, the soldier got nearer. We were on opposite sides of the road when we drew level. Simultaneously, we stopped and turned toward each other. 'I don't bleedin' well believe it. Jim you old sod, what are you doing here?' It was the voice of my old mate from Gosport, Tony Fox. Tony said he had been posted to Depot Battalion, which was about half a mile away from where I was in 3 Battalion. The REME depot was a transit camp mainly for those being posted to, and returning from overseas. Those returning would sometimes languish there for months, waiting for a new posting in the UK. That night, Foxy and I met up in the NAAFI and told our stories of service life so far. His had been pretty mundane compared to mine. He was finding the whole experience a boring waste of time.

With summer approaching and my days left 'to do' diminishing, the lads in the drawing office had made me an elaborate de-mob chart, which I pinned inside my locker door. All was well. I was keeping my head down and not attracting any attention, the first rule of a skiver, when an unfortunate accident increased my workload considerably. I arrived at work at 0800 hours as usual, only to find the Sergeant Major in a sombre mood. 'Have you heard the news Jim?' (He always called me by my first name) 'What news?' I enquired. 'Terry Price has been in a car accident and is in hospital,' he replied. Terry had gone to Reading on a night out with two other Corporals. On their return their car collided with another. Corporal Beale who was in the car with Terry, was killed. I don't remember who was driving the car but it wasn't Terry. It would be some months before Corporal Price was fit enough to return to duty.

CSM Rixon informed me that Captain Wakeman wanted to see me. 'What now?' I thought. 'Right Ruston,' said the CO. 'Corporal Price won't be with us for some time. This is going to mean a lot of extra work for all of us. Do you think you can cope?' he asked in a typically Army mode, meaning too bad if you can't because you're going to have to. Realising I had been delivered a *fait accompli*, I replied with as much enthusiasm as befits, 'a never volunteer for anything conscript', 'Yes Sir, I can manage.' Giving the answer he wanted, I wondered what I was letting myself in for. For the next few months, I ran that office entirely on my own. It did, however, have its compensations. When an over officious Duty Sergeant tried to charge me with some minor misdemeanour, he got a flea in his ear from my CO, who informed him that 'If everyone worked as hard as this soldier, [me] the Army would be better for it'. From here on, I became a law unto myself, and led the life of Riley.

I was busily typing Company orders; these have to be posted on the notice board daily. First a 'skin' is typed, and then this is duplicated into however many copies are required. The duplicator was an old Gestetner, operated by hand by my mate Tom Stilwell. Tom's workroom was a tiny place with shelving from floor to ceiling, on which were stacked reams of duplicating paper. The increasing measures of black ink necessary to keep the old machine going led to Tom becoming almost as black as the copier. I don't thing I ever saw him without traces of his occupation adorning his uniform. Tom needed the 'skin' as soon after lunch as possible, if he were to get all the duplicating ready for first thing each morning. A big fuss was made if it was late. I was cursing the mistakes I was making, and using generous amounts of correcting ink, when in walked Tony Fox. Slightly out of breath, and red in the face, he blurted out, 'You'll never guess who is in the Depot?' 'Who?' I asked. 'Only bloody Priestly, that's who,' he said, in his broad Brummie accent. Well I was speechless. I really hadn't expected ever to clap eyes on him again. I arranged to see Tony at lunchtime, and together we would pay the erstwhile Sergeant Priestly a visit.

The look on Priestly's face when he saw Tony and me standing in front of him as he laboured over a typewriter in a small office down at the Depot was worth a million. He stuttered and blustered. In short he was flabbergasted. 'What happened about your bike, Jim?' he asked. 'You tell me,' I said. 'It's still in bloody Gosport where you left it.' I was furious. Foxy wanted to punch him. After a pathetic apology for not getting in touch and a hard luck story of his misfortune, I managed to get him to part with about £6, with the promise of more in a few weeks. I did get another three quid. But then he disappeared. So if you're out there Priestly, you still owe me 12 quid!

All leave passes had to be applied for at the Company office. Having first got permission from your head of department, you then needed the pass signed by the CO. I had the fortunate task of co-ordinating this operation. I say fortunate because he who actually has the pass in his possession could give it to the recipient a few hours before he was entitled to it. This meant that those with long train journeys could catch an early train. Or alternatively, I could make them wait until 1700 hours on the due day. I used this power to the full. From senior NCOs down, I pulled in favours galore for dishing out leave passes early. Not to mention the ones I slid through for signing for those not strictly entitled to them. Mostly, Captain Wakeman signed passes without more than a glance. A bit of a cynic, he often asked if there was one in amongst them for me. He never checked, but just raised his eyebrows with a knowing look. I hadn't the heart to tell him that I had so many favours owed, I didn't need a pass. Not even the Regimental Policeman would ask to see my pass as I walked in and out of the gate. The Provost Sergeant – we nicknamed him Froggy, on account of his bull-neck and frog like face – was the worst culprit for an 'extra' pass. I once got him five days' extra leave. I was flame proof.

The summer of '57 was marvellous. Each morning, together with a couple of mates, I swam in the huge freshwater lake near the Camp, which was called California. Captain Wakeman arranged for me to ride the horses in the Depot. Arborfield had once been the Army's remount depot. Currently the horses were at the disposal of officers attending the Training School, which was situated in the garrison. I exercised horses; and rode with the young subalterns offering them advice and encouragement. As horsemen, most were bloody useless. My CO also got the Motor Transport Sergeant to test me for a driving licence. I never did anything to reward this kindness. I was bitter in those times, and thought it a liberty to have been conscripted in peacetime. If there had been a war on, then I would have viewed things differently. Eighteen to 20 are supposed to be the best years of a fellow's life. The Army nicked mine.

Towards the end of the summer, Terry Price returned. He looked pale and had a scar running the length of his left cheek. I often saw him look in the mirror and run his fingers over the scar. His good looks spoiled, I felt for him. He was a lovely bloke. Terry had only two months left to do. I had five, and now I really didn't give a sod!

I had two weeks' leave in the summer, and got home most weekends. In charge of the guard duty roster, I made sure my name was never on it. Although on one occasion a group of people made a complaint to the CSM that 'Ruston has never done a guard duty since he has been here sir.' 'What are you going to do about it Jim?' asked the Sergeant major with a grin from ear to ear. 'I'll sort it, Sir.' I replied tersely. 'Now Jim, no revenge tactics,' he added. I thought, I'll find out who is doing the stirring, and I will fix them. I put myself down for weekend duty. Everyone knew how I loved to get away at weekends, so this surprised many. I, Of course, knew exactly what I was I was up to. I did the Friday night duty, and paid someone else to do Saturday and Sunday night. I also made it known that I knew who had dobbed me in, and would make sure that they got every shit duty going. Although I had my suspicions, I never did find out who the culprits were, but they didn't show their heads again. I kept a few passes back at random, and threw out a few duplicates. The rumour that Ruston was on the war path with the sacred leave passes had been enough.

With Corporal Price back at the Company office plus two new staff there wasn't a lot for me to do. Wednesday afternoons were reserved for sports. I played football for a while, but got bored with it. So instead I took the train from Wokingham station to Waterloo. Legging it along the Albert Embankment I called upon my sister Stella, who was living at Victoria Mansions with Don Shipway, the man she had run away with back in '52, and their two children Donny and Janine. Stella loved my Wednesday visits, which became quite regular. Together we went shopping and took the kids to the park. On a few occasions Don arranged tickets to see a farce with Brian Rix at the Whitehall Theatre, and afterwards we visited a top retaurant for a meal. Luxury indeed for a squaddie!

I will remember those days with affection, but also concern. Stella was beautiful, but so burdened with it all. She had had responsibility thrust upon her from childhood. When would someone come along and look after her. Stella always stood by the door and watched me walk with the parcel of goodies, cakes pies and so on that she had bought for me tucked under my arm,, back along South Lambeth Road, until I was out of sight. I loved seeing her, but hated the parting. I would arrive back a Wokingham station at around midnight and then walk the three miles back to Camp. A few times I got a lift with Tom Stilwell. Tom had a Ford Popular and lived in Shepherds Bush. I used to meet him in Hammersmith at midnight for the journey back to Camp. Happy days. Thanks, Tom.

The winter was on us, and in an effort to earn some extra cash, I organised a dance class in the NAAFI once weekly. I had posters made by my pals in the drawing office, and the Staff Sergeant in wireless workshops, whom I had helped on a number of occasions, supplied a record player and amplifier. Mainly regular soldiers, most of whom wouldn't have lasted long in a civvy workshop, manned the Wireless workshop. They took an age to find faults on equipment, and never knew the meaning of the words 'economic repair'. They just changed bits at random until things worked once more.

I brought my Victor Sylvester strict tempo ballroom dance records from home, and I was in business, so to speak. I had pinned the posters all over the place. Foxy took some for the Depot, and I paid a visit to the WRAF station nearby in the hope that the girls would be interested. Bingo, it hadn't occurred to me that so many of my contemporaries could not dance. About 8 or 10 girls came the first night, which brought more of the lads and so on. I charged a half crown each person. I did not pose any threat to the mighty Mecca Empire, but the extra money came in handy!

It was difficult getting lifts in winter, especially in the dark. If I could afford a ticket one way, and hitch the other, it was a great advantage. Many, many times, I walked from Bristol City centre in the dead of night, and headed up the A4 towards Bath. I often walked 20 to 30 miles. In the rain it was miserable. Joyce paid my fare countless times. She was, is, the most generous of souls. Ron Poole gave me a lift into Reading on many a Saturday morning. Ron had a Triumph Thunderbird, a lovely bike. I spent countless hours on railway platforms on benches and in waiting rooms. Arriving at Reading station at 01.00 hours on a Monday morning, there was still the six miles to Arborfield to face. It was rare to get a lift on this stretch of road at this time in the morning, so the journey was mostly walked.

I went home for Christmas. It was hard to believe that my two years National Service were almost over. I had been notified that my release date was Thursday 2 January 1958. Three days short of the two years. As with enlistment and de-mob was also always on a Thursday. Hopefully, for the last time in these circumstances, I said goodbye to Joyce. What could I say? No words could convey my gratitude for her love and support. I loved her more than ever, and knew that I would never fail her. Dad had asked if I would collect the Studebaker from the garage where it was being serviced on my way home. I said, 'Gladly.' It seemed unreal to think that very soon I would be able to decide for myself what to do each day.

The last couple of days in the Army were somewhat of an anti-climax. I played my last game of table tennis with John. 'Fast and Furious'. On the Thursday morning, after handing all of my kit in to the Stores, 'No I didn't want to keep any of it,' I replied when asked – I wandered around the camp saying my goodbyes. Ron in the Armoury, Tom, still covered in duplicating ink, and the lads in the drawing office. Captain Wakeman shook my hand, then shook his head. I don't think he knew quite what to make of me. I couldn't find CSM Rixon. His release date was the same as mine. I was walking towards the bus stop when I was joined by Foxy. 'Well mate, what was all that about?' he said. 'Buggered if I know Tone, but it was damned inconvenient!' As we approached the bus stop, I could see the familiar figure of CSM Rixon standing there. He too was in civvies. 'Well Jim, its all over, it wasn't that bad, was it?'

'From whose point of view, sir?' I replied. We all three laughed. He wished me well and I returned his compliment with sincerity. They didn't come much better than CSM Rixon BEM. I don't know what he got a BEM for, but I'm sure it was well-deserved.

Tony and I said our goodbyes. We had been together for most of our service. I had taken him home to Allendale for a week's holiday; he met Joyce. We all went dancing at the Salthouse in Clevedon. I never knew much about his home life, only that he was working class and came from Birmingham. We vowed to keep in touch. Regretfully, we never did. I have never seen anyone from those days since. Perhaps the memories belong together with the friends and faces I once shared so much with. Comradeship, the like of which one will never encounter again. Collectively, we shared one common desire: to 'get some in' and then bloody well get out. I can still see many of them in my mind's eye. They are all young men, about 20 years old.

I stood for a minute on Temple Meads station Bristol, and pondered. This station had played quite a part in my life already, what with evacuation and trips back to London, and now National Service. I wondered where I would be going when I next stand here. I collected the Studebaker from Clist and Rattle's garage in Flaxbourton. I wound down the driver's window, switched on the radio and drove off. I passed Tyntesfield where Joyce lived and shouted out loud 'see you later. With my right elbow sticking out of the window, I felt like a king as I drove down the hill to Allendale, and a million miles away from: 'That man there, you are bloody 'orrible. What are you?'

For some weeks, when waking in the morning and thinking I was still in the Army, I shot out of bed and scrabbled around for my uniform. It was strange being in a room alone. Periodically I dreamed of still being in the army; this went on for years. Slowly though, I settled back into civilian life. I missed my Army mates, but had no desire to go back and live with them!

I started work for a small television and radio servicing Company in Bristol called Electrolab. I was paid £10 a week and given a small Ford van to run around with. ITV had just become available from the new transmitter, which had been built at St Hilary in Wales. It opened on 10 January and was called TWW, Television Wales and West. This was the boost the television trade had been waiting so long for. The BBC transmitter in Wenvoe (also in South Wales) which had the monopoly since its commissioning in 1952, now had a rival. Most people had a television set that would only receive BBC programmes. These receivers would need converting to take the new commercial channel. This was a bonanza for the trade. Several electronic companies produced a converter that, when fitted, would enable the viewer to change channel by turning a knob. An additional aerial was also necessary to receive the ITV signal. Electrolab offered a package: converter and aerial for £15. We were inundated with orders. Credit terms were also on offer, so for a small down payment the deal was yours.

I was a 'new business engineer' sent out not only on enquiries for conversions to ITV, but also on all new breakdowns. My job was to sell the idea to customers that whilst their TV set was in for repair, why not have a converter fitted? After all, it only need cost a few coppers each week. I brought in more work than anyone did else on the whole firm. With my newly found wealth I made amends to Joyce for the past two years of austerity. I took her to work in my little van every day, and we went out most weekends. That is to say after work on Saturdays, and all day Sunday. The TV trade had imposed upon itself a service that was extremely difficult to maintain. Many firms offered a one-hour service. Some even extended their service to cover Sundays. Engineers were expected to complete every job they were given each day. This often meant working until... No overtime was paid. I don't know where these conditions sprang from, but they seemed universal.

Although competition was stiff, engineers were still in short supply, most being only partially trained (like me). The trained ones, few and far between that they were, had for various reasons not been called up to do National Service. This rankled with those of us who had. They were paid more than us – although it was preferable to sit with the ex-servicemen, and to promenade one's girlfriend along the seafront at Clevedon wearing a blazer sporting a badge of the regiment or corps in which one had served, than to be asked why one hadn't.

I had only been at Electrolab for three months when along with other members of staff I was summoned to a meeting. There, the service manager, Gerry English, informed us that the firm was closing with immediate effect. Apparently, they had over-traded and suffered a cash-flow crisis. Unable to pacify their creditors a decision had been taken to wind up the company. A bitter blow for us all. We had worked so hard, and things seemed to be going so well. I was sorry to leave. I had enjoyed working there and I had made two particularly good friends, John Holloway and Malcolm Lane. I had to give back my van. I missed it.

One of the girls in the Electrolab office approached me saying 'Why not go to see the firm that will be taking over our maintenance contracts.' These were the contracts that customers had signed with Electrolab in the event of their TV breaking down, for which they paid a monthly premium. Apparently, the official receiver who wound up the firm had sold the interest in the maintenance contracts to a small TV and electrical firm, just up the road in St George.

I caught a bus to Whiteway Road St George where, at No. 244 was the radio and electrical business of H.E. Curtis. I entered the shop and was greeted by a smart girl standing behind a counter busily unpacking a parcel containing pop records, 'Can I help you sir?' she asked. 'If possible, I would like to see the proprietor,' I replied. I gazed around the place thinking, 'This is much like Marchant's, only with a lot more television and radio sets on display.' 'What can I do for you then?' The voice came from behind me. As I turned I was confronted by the portly figure of a man shorter, and quite a few pounds heavier, than me. There was a resemblance of a smile, but strained, from the unopened face that greeted me. 'I understand that you have purchased the maintenance contracts from Electrolab, and wonder if you will be looking for an additional engineer to service them?' I replied. At this point, the man I took to be Curtis himself raised his voice saying, 'Maureen, there is a young man here who wants a job.' From a door behind the counter stepped an even shorter and more portly lady with a pretty face. She walked around the counter, and stood by the side of the man I had been addressing. 'This is Mrs Curtis and I am Harold. What's your name?'. Curtis asked. 'Jim Ruston,' I replied. From my viewpoint, the couple standing side by side, whom I hoped would be my new employers, looked much like a pair of Toby jugs. The respectful side of my nature kept control, and urged me not to laugh. After my army service, it was quite a long time before I could take anything seriously again.

The following morning I went back to see Mr Curtis as asked, and was introduced to a Mr Davidson, the television engineer. It was all Mr and Mrs in those days. I never did call them by their first names; it just wasn't done. Mr Davidson arranged a trade test by way of presenting me with three television sets with faults to diagnose. I found little difficulty in discovering the faults on two of the receivers, but the third eluded me. With a smile, Davidson said he was happy to recommend that I be employed as his assistant. It was agreed that I would start the following Monday morning at a wage of £12 per week and the use of a Ford 5cwt van.

As well as TV and radio, Curtis ran an electrical contracting business. He himself was an electrician, but with no knowledge whatsoever of electronics. The electrician employed to carry out the contracting side of the business was Ian Brown. An instant friendship sprung up between Ian and me. 'Jim, you're ex REME aren't you?' I said I was. 'I'm ex-Signals. What do you think of Harold then?' Ian questioned.

'Looks a bit of a cynic, with that 'what do you want to borrow approach,' I said. 'He's as tight as a duck's arse, make no mistake. Maureen's alright though,' Ian confirmed. A week later the TV set I was unable to repair on my trade test was still on the bench. Ian confided 'Davidson has been struggling with that set for weeks. He can't find the fault.' This was like showing a raging bull a red flag. I thought it a bit sneaky to give a fellow an obscure fault to find in a trade test. So I thought, I'll repair it before he does, and he won't have the nerve to ask what it was I found. I phoned my old colleague Syd Willis for some advice. On hearing my voice he laughed, and said, 'You survived all the bullshit and bully beef then Jim. What can I do for you mate?' With a few ideas from Syd, I stayed late one evening and effected a satisfactory repair on the belligerent TV set. I never offered an explanation and Davidson never asked. He was a nice enough man, but only an average engineer. He left not long after. Curtis was overjoyed to be saving a wage. I think he might even have given me an extra £1 a week.

My relationship with Joyce's parents was now becoming warmer. They had conceded that Joyce had stood by me, and there was little they could do to stop us marrying, other than to delay the inevitable. One evening, Joyce and I went to see Reverend Young at the rectory in Wraxall, and asked him if he would marry us in his church. The Reverend Young, a lovely man who loved fast cars, fine wines and antique clocks, had married my sister Eve to Don Waite at the same church two years earlier. Knowing both of our families, he said he would be delighted. We set the date for 4 October 1958. Scouring the classified ads in the *Bristol Evening Post*, we found a one bedroom furnished flat in Abbotswood Road Redland. It was on the top floor and a bit old fashioned, but we both decided it would do to start our married life in. Like any girl, although a little nervous, Joyce looked forward to her big day. There were no stag or hen nights for either of us. Together with her mum and aunts, Joyce helped prepare the buffet for the wedding. I got my things together, and on the morning I was to be married, caught the bus to Bristol to collect the flowers I had ordered. John Holloway, who had agreed to act as my best man called to collect me in his TV service van. We left Allendale and drove the few hundred yards up the hill to Wraxall church. I had ordered a car to collect Joyce and her father from Tyntesfield. There were no bridesmaids, Joyce had decided that as her sister Heather was not old enough to perform the duty, she would have none at all. This did cause a bit of a fuss, my mother being at the centre of it. She wanted her grandchildren to be Joyce's bridesmaids, and offered to pay all the expenses for them. It was

Joyce's day, and she could not be persuaded. It's a rare occasion when Rustons don't get their own way. This was one.

Joyce wore a white ballerina length dress in which she looked absolutely stunning. The service went off without a hitch, and soon we stood in the church doorway for the traditional photograph. The first words Joyce said to me once we were married were 'I've got a bone to pick with you.' 'Why?' I asked. 'You didn't order enough carnations for buttonholes,' she whispered. My first bollocking from my wife. Many would follow in the coming years, most justly deserved. Family and friends had gathered at the Battle Axe Hotel where, thanks to Joyce and her family, a wonderful reception was waiting.

A shower of confetti, and we were off to Temple Meads station. We were to spend our honeymoon with Stella and Don in Lambeth. As we stood waiting for the train, looking at my beautiful wife in her beige suit and peep-toe shoes in blue with matching handbag, I felt ecstatic. For me, surely nothing would surpass this moment.

It had been a simple wedding, but none the less a lovely day. A far cry from the thousands of pounds couples spend these days on lavish weddings. But will their marriages be anymore successful or indeed as happy as ours? Our relationship had already stood the trying years of separation and austerity. The promises we now shared would prove unshakeable.

We arrived at Victoria Mansions in South Lambeth Road at about 9pm and were warmly greeted by Stella and Don. I hadn't seen either of them since my Army days, so it was especially nice to be with them both once again. Stella and Don had met Joyce on a visit to Allendale one summer. Don had been suspended from his job, whilst an inquiry was in progress into missing funds to which he had access, so it was a particularly difficult time for my sister, who despite this had unselfishly invited us to spend our honeymoon with her. We had a marvellous week visiting all the tourist attractions, something that despite the many return visits made to my hometown, I had never done. Joyce had only been to London once before, on a day trip with her school. Stella's partner Don, they never married, was kind, going out of his way to make our holiday one to remember. We both liked him a lot.

I took Joyce over the East End to meet my Grandmother Hare. It was a different world altogether from the one she was used to. She doesn't like big cities, or any town for that matter. None the less she was interested to see where my roots lay. Although there was some building work being carried out, a great deal of the East End was still in ruins. Granny Hare welcomed us warmly saying, 'She's a lovely gel, Jimmy; but you don't look old enough to be married.' The tea was made, and whilst it was handed round aunts and cousins popped in and out to see 'Liz's boy and his wife'. My Aunt Lily and her sons Terry and Leon lived with my Gran, I never did know what happened to Lily's husband. Aunt Lily was also my Godmother, and always made a fuss of me. I never did ask Joyce what she thought of them all; I just took it for granted that she would love them as I did.

Having seen the sights and walked for mile upon mile around London, we took the underground to visit Maud in Balham. Then we walked all the way back to Lambeth with a tray she gave us as a wedding present. Our honeymoon at an end, we said our thanks and farewell to Stella and Don, and made our way to Paddington Station. Arriving back in Bristol, we caught the bus to Redland and walked to our new home in Abbotswood Road. Sunday, and Joyce cooked a wonderful roast beef lunch, with Yorkshire pudding – essential!

The following morning I arrived at Whiteway Road early, and was pleased to see my little Ford 5cwt van waiting for me. Wheels once more. The winter was upon us and the Curtis's told me that they had bought a bungalow so would be moving out of the house that joined the shop. Would Joyce and I like to move in? Harold Curtis said that he had intended on giving me a raise in salary anyway. But he offered the accommodation in lieu. I thought how thoughtful and generous the Curtis's were being, somewhat out of character with what I had been used to. Of course with experience and hindsight it was a better deal for them than for us. A 'tied' house gives no right of tenure, and the capital growth in the property benefits the employer/freeholder. Lessons to be learned, but not yet though.

Early in 1959, Joyce announced that she was pregnant and gave up work. We were delighted that we were to be parents, although I didn't feel all that capable of bringing up a child. My mother-in-law was a marvellous housewife and had passed her skills on to her daughter. Joyce was, is, an avid knitter and began knitting a selection of baby clothes. I was still working long hours and studying in my spare time. I had also made a number of friends in the TV trade, and visited their workshops where we shared knowledge and discussed new designs. TV technology was still all 'valve' and very much in its infancy, but moving rapidly forward. People were beginning to talk about a new device called a transistor, which would revolutionise the industry.

We had only been living in the house next to the shop for a few months when the Curtis's announced they had sold the recently purchased bungalow, and wanted to move back to their old home. After some deliberation they offered to buy a small terraced house in St George for Joyce and I to live in. We really didn't have a choice, another 'tied' house. Early summer, we moved into a two up two down house in Stanley Street, bought for £375! The vendors had wanted £400 but Harold knocked them down to £375. It was just after midnight and 22 July that year when Joyce went into labour. I drove her in my van to Southmead hospital, where once Joyce was settled in, I was told to go. I was advised to ring around lunchtime the next day. I drove home, not a little worried. Desperately lonely, I went to bed.

After work the next day, which was a Wednesday and my half-day, I drove down to Wraxall to see my parents. I rang the hospital just after 2.30pm to be told Joyce had given birth to a baby girl. Both were in fine health. I was overjoyed. Mum picked some flowers from the garden for me to take in to Joyce. Then I saw her, this tiny bundle of beauty, to whom I instantly lost my heart. 'Joyce darling, can we name her Jane Belinda?' I asked. 'Yes if you like, but why Belinda?' she questioned. 'There is a song that has playing on the radio and running around my brain for weeks. it is called "Jane Belinda". The singer is Jim Dale,' I explained. 'That's not much of a reason to name a child, but it's nice,' Joyce indulged. And so our firstborn came into our lives. I would be the best father I knew how, and she couldn't have a better mother.

Babies change your lives; the daily routine went out of the window. Stella and her two children were now living with our parents at Allendale. Ever caring and helpful, she came to stay with us for a few days to help with Jane. Sleepless nights became the norm and I went to work tired most days. Everyone made a huge fuss of our new baby, and even I took her for a walk in her posh new pram. This surprised everyone. Babies are not considered in the domain of Ruston males! For my father to have done this would have been unthinkable.

Don Shipway had been found guilty of embezzlement, and was in the open prison at Leyhill in Gloucestershire. He had committed the offence to feed his alcohol addiction, for which refused all offers of help. I went with Stella to see him on several occasions. One time it was the prison sports day, and the inmates were in the grounds with their visitors. The weather was fine and sunny. We sat together under a tree and chatted, just as we had done in Battersea Pleasure Gardens in better times. Apart from the blue prison trousers and shirt that Don was wearing, everything seemed so normal.

Stella was, quite naturally, feeling the stress, but trying hard not to show it. My emotions were confused. Don had shown me so much respect and kindness and had been so generous, but he deceived my sister. When they ran away together, all those years ago, it was an attempt on his part to evade facing the music regarding missing funds in the office where they both worked. Stella was an innocent party. She knew nothing of this. We had all forgiven him once, but now I wanted to hate him for doing it to her again. I decided that I would go along with whatever Stella wanted, and so tried to be as pleasant as possible. The whole occasion was surreal.

Don drank a great deal of whisky, which eventually led to his early demise. He died just after Christmas 1966. He was only 49 years old.

It was late one Friday afternoon that I hurried down Stapleton Road. I was hoping to get to KA Aerials before they closed at 5.30pm. Their premises were just under a railway bridge in the busy road. Pulling up at the nearside kerb opposite the aerial shop, and looking briefly in the rear view mirror, I flung open the driver's door. Bang! The collision wrenched the door from my grip and forced it back against the wing of the van. From my position in the driver's seat I still could not see what had happened. Then I looked down, and there to my horror on the ground clutching his chest was a policeman. I had knocked him off his bicycle as he was attempting to pass my stationary van. I scrambled out of the van just in time to see his helmet, which had rolled into the centre of the road, run over by a bus!

There was a new craze, go-karts. Basically trolleys fitted with lawn mower engines. Well, that's how they started out, but soon they became much more sophisticated. John Holloway (Lofty) and I bought a kart between us and practised on the disused runways at Lulsgate Airport.

In those days, the Airport was only used by a flying club. I had flown in gliders from there with John Bindon whom I had met whilst in Frenchay hospital. I think John was sweet on my sister Stella. She wasn't the least bit interested in him, but I got to fly! Another friend of those times, Tony Matthews, worked as a salesman for Clarke Bros., the Ford dealers in Muller Road. Tony was also keen on karting and his boss Tom Clarke, an engineer, had built a Kart. Together the four of us formed the South West Karting Association, and organised race meetings under RAC rules. We must have been one of the very first go-kart clubs to emerge. Competition licences were issued by the RAC. I still have mine.

We were returning from a go-kart race meeting in a brand new Standard Atlas van, which Harold Curtis had bought for me to use. The smart new van had H.E. Curtis Television emblazoned on its side. Harold was proud of this. The little Ford van I had been using was unlettered. John Holloway and Michael, Joyce's brother, were in the passenger seat, the kart was in the back. We were laughing and joking, when at a bend in the road, the van skidded out of control through a hedge and down a steep slope, landing upside down in a tree. The windscreen came out in one piece. I found myself on the ground looking up at the underside of the vehicle. Lofty was by my side, and somehow Michael had shot out of the passenger door. Apart from a few scratches and bruises we were none the worse for the experience. The kart came out of it with minimum damage, but the van? That was a different matter. It was a write-off. Harold was most upset to see his name desecrated on the side of the van.

My sister Betty was to marry. She had met a really nice fellow whilst staying in Kent during the hop-picking season. Roy Millen worked on the farm in Five Oak Green, where Mum Dad and Betty were staying. It was at the traditional Saturday night Dance in the grounds of the Hoppers Mission that Bet and Roy met. Roy, a very good-looking fellow with an engaging smile, was an instant hit with us all; and we remain as fond of him as ever. Roy's family had lived in the Paddock Wood area of Kent for generations, and had been farmers and landowners for generations.

The wedding was to take place at Wraxall church where Joyce and I had married two years earlier. Everything was planned, the big day approached. I was in a dilemma. The day Betty had chosen to marry was also the same day as the finals of the go-kart championship. It had taken our team months to qualify. I couldn't let the lads down, could I? I asked Betty if I could miss the ceremony, but I would make the reception. My little sister generously said she wouldn't mind, it was

OK. I turned up at the reception in greasy white overalls, disgraceful behaviour. I have never forgiven myself for it. What was I thinking of? We didn't win the kart race either. So I had alienated the family for sod all.

Bet's wedding had gone smoothly enough without me, although when it was time for the Bride to leave the house, dear Betty had locked herself in the bathroom and no end of gentle persuasion, then demands from dad, could get her out. It took some quiet reasoning from Stella, who promised to see her through everything, to get her to the church on time. With relations from London staying, Allendale was near to bursting, but miracle mum managed to put them all somewhere. On the Monday morning when everyone had departed, dad discovered a Beer Barrel still half full. Workmen from the local council were repainting the white lines on the road outside of our bungalow; dad called over to them saying: 'There is some beer here for you if you would like it, just pop in to the front porch and help yourself.' This they did throughout the day. By mid-afternoon the lines in the road were anything but straight, a couple of the workmen had fallen over and one was asleep in the ditch. Nothing was ever normal when dad was around!

Still working long hours selling and servicing television sets I came to the conclusion that there was little or no future remaining at the firm of H.E. Curtis. Impulsive as ever, I handed in my notice. Harold thought I was bluffing and wanting more money. He just couldn't understand that prospects meant far more to me than money. Anyone who has ever known me will tell you I am a workaholic. Money is important yes, but enjoying what you do is more so. The TV business is a way of life, a vocation, and in the right environment, thoroughly worthwhile. I wasn't happy, so I was moving on. This would not be the last time I would do this. Head down, working like a beaver, then snap, like a dead branch, I throw off the shackle and walk away without so much as a glance over my shoulder.

We lived for a short while with Joyce's mum and dad. I worked as a freelance engineer. I had built myself a bit of a reputation as a trouble-shooter, and was never short of work. I had bought, on HP of course, a Ford Anglia car to travel to and from Bristol. We had been allocated a local authority house in Nailsea. Money was tight but at least I could shape my own future, or at least that is what I thought I could do. Dad had a 30cwt van at the time and so moved our possessions, such as they were. The house had only just been built, and as yet did not sport a front path. Joyce had to negotiate the pram up a plank of wood, which was supported by two concrete blocks, being pregnant again didn't make it any easier. She was standing inside the front door when dad pulled up in the van. He flung open the driver's door and leapt on to what he thought looked like hard ground, only to find himself firmly stuck up to his knees in mud. Joyce laughed so much she almost gave birth there and then. Brother-in-law Roy had to pull dad out. This he found extremely difficult to do, on account of being in hysterics himself. Dad took it all in good spirits, and laughed with everyone else.

It was January 1961. We had spent a quiet but enjoyable Christmas in our new home. The winter was harsh but as yet no snow. Our only source of heating was from the coal fire in the sitting room. Joyce did all the washing by hand. The only 'appliance' she had was a Burco boiler. As practical as ever she reasoned, 'My Mum did the washing like this all her life. Why can't I?' But it was tough. And Jane was still giving her sleepless nights.

It must have been around 6pm when I reached the top of the hill by Wraxall church. As I descended I could see the welcoming lights of Allendale at the bottom. They seemed to be beckoning to me. I considered popping in to see mum, but thought if I did I would stay chatting and drinking tea and then be an hour or so late getting home. Joyce was due to give birth in a few weeks' time so I didn't like to leave her alone in the evenings. If only I had stopped at Allendale.

I drove through Nailsea High Street, and rounded the bend in the Clevedon road. The road curves left – handed, what you might call a slow bend. I was travelling at about 20 miles per hour when suddenly, a dark form appeared in front of me. A split second later, and simultaneous with me hitting the brakes, there came a loud bang. Then over the bonnet and through the windscreen he came almost at once bouncing back on to the road in front of me. By this time miraculously I had managed to stop. For a moment I sat in total disbelief. My hands felt sticky, and I soon discovered I was covered in blood. I was in shock, but controlled myself, got out of the car and ran around the front to see what I could do. I knelt beside the poor unfortunate man, feeling completely helpless. I tried to stop passing cars to get help. 'No I'm in a hurry,' said one. 'I don't know what to do,' said another. Both drove on, unbelievable. All I wanted them to do was phone for an ambulance.

As if from nowhere, people started to appear. Then an Ambulance arrived and soon after the police. An officer was talking to me and asking what had happened, when two ladies approached along the pavement. One was looking for her husband. The police officer spoke to one of the ladies, and it soon became evident that it was her husband lying in the road. The lady asked, 'Will he be alright?' Without hesitation the officer replied, 'I'm afraid he's dead.' With that the poor soul collapsed. A doctor administered an injection and they took her into a nearby house. Until that point I had no idea that the man had died. I obviously realised he was seriously injured. After I had made a statement the police arranged for my car to be towed away for them to examine for any defects. I had stopped in such a short distance, I knew there couldn't be anything wrong with the braking system.

I was asked to attend the police station the next day. Then, as mysteriously as they had arrived at the scene, everyone had gone. I stood alone on the pavement thinking was it real, or was I dreaming. Surely I would wake in a moment, and all would be normal. I was no more than half a mile from home, yet I felt a thousand miles away. The journey seemed endless. I opened the back door, and Joyce called out, 'You're late, where have you been?' On seeing the state I was in she went white. I explained what happened the best I could, then went upstairs to the bathroom to take off my clothes. I stood there shaking. My hair was full of Triplex glass from the shattered windscreen, and my clothes were covered in blood. I was in shock.

For weeks after the accident Joyce would not leave the house, fearing what people might say. I, in turn, could not get myself together, and moped around the house. I had no transport, no job, and we were broke. An inquest was held and I was exonerated from any blame. It transpired that the unfortunate man was a diabetic and had called at the Queen's Head public house for a drink. The conclusion was drawn that this probably impaired his judgement when crossing the road. We will never know for sure why he was on the side of the road where there was nothing more than a high hedge with a small grass verge, whilst on the other side was a proper pavement.

My Ford Anglia, practically a write off, was returned to me. Dad let me put it in the garage at Allendale, and there it languished. My third party insurance did not cover repairs, and the car was still subject to HP. Somehow I had to find the repayments. Echoes of my James Cadet motorcycle, but with far worse consequences. This tragedy haunted me for years. It stays with you. Somehow you have to get on with your life. Joyce was due to give birth to our second child any day.

Karen Louise was born in our modest house in Nailsea on 20 March 1961. Jane had gone to stay with Joyce's mum, and I paced the floor of the sitting room in anticipation of the event. A slap followed by a scream, and then we were four. In those days it was rare for a father to be at the bedside during the birth. Both doctors and midwives preferred the men out of the way. That suited me fine. I have never held a desire to witness the birth of a child. A thoroughly messy affair if you ask me, best left to the women! Once the nurse had attended mother and child I was allowed upstairs to see my new daughter. Looking at a newly born baby, emotions run wild. Is she like her mother, or like me? What will she inherit? What will she become? For the first time in weeks, my beautiful wife had a smile on her face. Jane now had a sister. And devoted as they would become, they were, ever remain, opposites.

I did a few electrical repairs around the village to earn a few bob to feed us. I walked everywhere with my tool bag thrown over my shoulder. I don't know why I never claimed unemployment benefit. After all I had always worked, paid my taxes, and given my country two years of my life for free! I have never been on the dole in my life. I haven't even considered it. Most of the villagers were both kind and sympathetic. (Some retained the old evacuee alienation and pointed a finger.) I started to look in the Situations Vacant in the Bristol papers. But it was Joyce who spotted the tiny advert. No more than a line in the classified column. It read: TV Engineer wanted. Apply Gardners Telemeter, 15, Perry Road Bristol. I had never heard of them, and almost dismissed it. Then again it might do as a stopgap, and we certainly needed the money.

I telephoned Gardners Telemeter and asked for an interview. I was surprised at their eagerness to see me. The following day I caught the bus to Bristol. No 15 Perry Road had a traditional shop front with a door at the right-hand side. The shop window had been painted out; on first impressions it looked closed. I stood on the opposite side of the road thinking, 'Do I want to even bother going over to try the door.' It looked so rundown, almost derelict. With negative vibes running through my body, I walked across the road and pushed open the door. Sitting at a desk on the right of the door was a huge man with a smile to match his presence. I said I had come for an interview for the engineer's job. 'Ah, splendid, but I'm afraid you will have to wait for half an hour. The service manager, Mr Payne, has got a little delayed on his way down from Gloucester. I hope this won't put you out at all?' Standing up, he leaned over his desk and offered me his hand. 'Claude Reid,' he stated. He was stock controller and receptionist. Over a cup of tea, Claude volunteered that the firm was quite new, but was expanding rapidly. He thought there could be a decent future for anyone joining at this stage. He himself had only recently joined the firm after having served 24 years in the Navy. We would become good friends, with a great deal of mutual respect.

Bob and John Joiner, who came from Cinderford (in the Forest of Dean) formed Gardners Telemeter in 1960. Whilst in America on holiday, the entrepreneurial brothers had somehow discovered a company that was renting out television sets with slot meters fixed to them as a method of collecting the rental payments. The meter would be set to suit the family's viewing habits, but also ensuring that a little over the weekly rental amount would accrue in the meter cash box. A collector called each month and took the rental payments due, handing the remaining cash back to the customer. A forced way of saving. The brothers returned from the States determined to set up a similar operation in the UK.

The company, whose trademark was Telesavers, now had its head office in Southgate Street Gloucester and eight branches in Wales and the West Country. A small fleet of Mini vans, painted bright yellow with a Piggybank Logo on both sides, gave them a corporate image. Their method of marketing was by direct selling, door to door.

Mr Harold Payne eventually arrived at Perry Road. He was of medium build, and just a little taller than me, with a quiet manner. Dressed in a quality tweed suit he looked every part management. But that is where it ended. I was soon to discover that he was no engineer. He asked me about myself, avoiding any technical conversation, which was a strange practice when interviewing an engineer. 'When could I start work?' I said, 'Tomorrow if you like.' 'Fine,' he replied. We shook hands, and he left. The whole encounter lasted no more than 15 mins. 'Got the job then,' said Claude beaming for ear to ear. 'I'll ring our transport manager and get you a van for tomorrow. Sorry Jim, but there is a bit of a backlog of work, and a few screamers,' [complaints] he apologised.

The branch at Perry Road had been relying on an engineer travelling down from the Gloucester workshop a couple of times a week to do the service calls. Inevitably, not all requests for service were dealt with. I was to be paid £12 per week and a bonus of 5s for every completed job, once 25 had been reached each week. I knew I could do at least 12 jobs a day, so would get to bonus by Wednesday each week, and with a back-log of jobs I would be in the money. I would also be allowed to use the van for private journeys. I said farewell to Claude and hurried to catch the Nailsea bus. Standing on the city centre, I thought, 'this could be a new beginning.' It was how I felt when I waited for the bus there on the day of my de-mob. Joyce was both pleased and relieved that I had returned to proper employment. The prospects looked good. We were not to know then just how good a job it would turn out to be. In due course our lives would change forever.

Stella and her two children were still living at Allendale with mum and dad. She had got a job with Bernard of Mayfair, a hairdressing establishment in Bristol. Bernard not only ran a successful salon, he also started a School of Hairdressing. Stella was his PA. Each morning I collected my sister from Allendale and dropped her off at her office in Whiteladies Road.

It seemed as though we were both starting out all over again. Life was difficult for Stella, although she hardly ever complained. We talked of all the things we would do, and reassured ourselves that things would get better. Stella would say: 'Don't worry Jim, it will never be as bad as the Blitz!' Bernard thought the world of her, and Stella grasped the opportunity to enter both of her children into the Bernard of Mayfair School of Hairdressing as soon as they became of age. She realised she would have to subsidise them, but she would find the money from somewhere. They wouldn't have a father to help them, so she was determined they should learn a skill. Her son Donny went on to become the artistic director at Vidal Sassoon in Bond Street, London. Eventually, Stella found herself a flat in an old Victorian house not far from the salon, and moved in. Sadly she would never be lucky in love, but she was to become an incredibly successful businesswoman. It was the start of the swinging 60s. I loved those days the opportunities seemed endless. We would both grab ours.

I had returned to my former self. Head down, blinkers on, totally focused. Gardners Telemeter was a progressive company and I wanted to climb the ladder. If anyone got in my way I was prepared to saw through the rung on which they were standing. The firm moved its operation from Perry Road to much larger premises in Temple Street. There was no branch manager as such, Brian Palmer ran sales, and I ran the service department, with the irrepressible Claude Reid looking after the stock. There was an army of meter collectors controlled by head office. The meters would accept two shillings or a sixpence. Collectors could be seen counting mountains of coins on Saturdays as they balanced their books.

The direct sales force were indeed a motley crew. They were paid £8 weekly basic, £4 commission for each rental agreement signed, and a car allowance of £7. Good money in those days, always supposing you were any good as a salesman. The best one I ever knew was Billy Parker. He could quite easily outsell anyone on the firm. I recall one time in Bath when a heated argument among salesman ended with Bill first laying down, then accepting, his own challenge. He bet a week's wages that he could put a TV into any house in any road. After consultation, a house was selected at random, and Bill went into action. Not only did he install a TV in the house selected, but also, for good measure, he put one in the house next door as well!

Bill Parker and I became great friends. When called up for National Service, Bill had signed on for the extra year, (for the money). Typical of Bill. He served with the Royal Engineers and was attached to the legendary Ghurkas at the time of the troubles in Malaya. Bill was going through a divorce, and had got behind with his maintenance payments. He was taken to court and the Judge asked him why he hadn't paid. 'I don't earn enough money, Your Worship,' stated Bill. 'But, I see from my notes that you sell television sets, surely this is highly paid,' replied the Judge. 'Yes,' agreed Bill, and with a hangdog look on his face continued. 'But you see, Your Honour, I am not a very good salesman.' 'Come, come,' exclaimed the learned man. 'It is a comfort to know that the last of Cavaliers is alive and well, and living in Bristol. Fined ten shillings!'

Generally sales and service got on pretty well, and often had a social drink together. It was at the Arena Club in Weston-Super-Mare on one such occasion that Bill met the girl whom he would marry, and stay with until death did them part. Bill was in charge of the 'pool' we had all contributed to for buying drinks throughout the evening. Bill was flaunting this bankroll in front of the girls at the bar, when he struck up a conversation with Irene. Rene has always said it was the size of the roll that attracted her; but I suspect she saw a little more than that in this loveable character.

The business at Temple Street. flourished. My service department had expanded. I now had three engineers: Malcolm Lane, whom I had worked with at Electrolab; Derek Morgan whom I had trained and taught to drive at H.E. Curtis; and Peter Kemp, a newly qualified engineer of exceptional ability. All three went on to become service managers. Technically, it was the best bunch of television engineers I ever worked with. Occasionally we were called upon to employ a ruse in order to repossess a TV set from a customer who was behind with the rental, but would not allow the collector to remove the receiver. It would go something like this: two of us would call at the house; one would knock at the door whilst the other one sat in the van, engine running, backdoor open, ready to roll. When the customer appeared, he/she would be advised that we were changing some of the older models for new. I know it sounds corny, but what threw them was engineers calling they were not suspicious of us; we were the 'good guys' always there to put their set right. We would walk in, pick up the TV and say 'The new TV is in the van I will remove this one to make space.' Once outside, with their TV in van, we drove off. Classic.

I have described how it is supposed to go; I will now tell you how it isn't! There was a customer in St Paul's who had had a TV on rental from us for more than a year without paying any money. The meter had obviously been by-passed. I thought I would go myself and take Derek

Morgan with me. I left Derek in the van and knocked on the door. After repeatedly knocking I tried the doorknob and ventured in. 'Is anyone in?' I called out. Emanating from somewhere in the bowels of the building came a deep voice saying, 'Down 'ere mate.' I descended to the basement and seeing a door slightly ajar poked my head around. There sitting up in bed was the biggest black man I have ever seen. By his side lay a white girl with peroxide blonde hair. 'Come in. What do you want?' said the incumbent. I explained the routine about updating his TV set. He looked puzzled, but nodded. I was about to walk over to where the TV set sat on top of a chest of drawers when the girl got out of bed, and with not a stitch of clothing on brushed passed me. She was big girl, top heavy, and as rough as a badger's bum in winter! Trying hard to stay calm, I stepped forward, picked up the TV, and slowly made my way out of the door and up the stairs. I couldn't believe my luck, it had been so easy. I had reached the front door and was about to step on to the pavement when I heard the pounding of feet coming up the stairs behind me. I ran, pushed the TV in the back of the van, and jumped in the passenger seat, shouting at the same time 'Go Derek, Go.' Morgan always drove as if he had lead in his shoes. Today was no exception. We shot off with tyres screeching. I thought, 'Yes, we've done it.' Well, not quite. In my panic I hadn't closed the back door of the van properly. The TV set shot out on to the road and shattered into many pieces. Looking behind I could see the big fellow completely naked and waving his fist at me. At least we had the satisfaction of knowing he would never watch our TV for free again.

The expanding Telesavers required a regional service manager to cover Wales and the West. I was offered the job and accepted it. The salary was good for those times: £1040 per annum with car allowance and expenses. I bought a Morris 1000 saloon car. Although a bit under-powered for the amount of miles I would cover, it was very economical. There was no Severn Bridge then, although one had been planned. The only way across the river was the Aust to Chepstow car ferry. When this was not running it meant my having to drive to Gloucester to get to Wales. I left home at 4am some mornings in order to be in Swansea for 8.30am when the Branch opened. I would then stay a couple of nights before returning home. I did this for years, and hardly saw the children grow up. Joyce coped extremely well on her own.

My wife had a great friend, Ann Norris, who lived opposite us in Nailsea. Ann's husband Norman was a struggling artist, and they had four kids. Ann herself had studied art and intended to return to it once the children were old enough for school. Norman went to Italy to study under a famous painter, so Joyce and Ann were in the same boat so to speak. I managed to get hold of a cheap second-hand TV and gave it to Ann. Eternally grateful she painted a marvellous portrait of Jane and Karen. We treasure it still. It also kindled in me a latent interest in art I never knew existed. One day, art would play a major role in my life. If someone had said this at the time I would have laughed. The Norris family later moved to Norfolk, and although Joyce exchanged letters with Ann for a number of years, we lost touch. What a pity.

My sister Maud and husband Joe needed some wiring looked at in a house they had bought in Cricklewood. I had some holiday due, so together with Joyce and the kids, drove to London. During our stay, Maud, Joyce and I, drove over to the East End to attend the funeral of my Aunt Mary. My Uncle Albert and Aunt Mary had lived in Bow for years. In my teens I visited them often, and laughed and danced with my cousins at a dance hall in Mile End. My dad was especially fond of Mary-Rose, Renee, Sheila, Dorothy, Valerie and little Sandra. He always referred to them as 'Albert's Girls'. I loved them too. Uncle Albert had died in 1957 from cancer of the throat. I remember the agony he was in when I last saw him, not long before his death. It upset me to see him in so much pain.

As if losing their father untimely was not enough, now their mother, my aunt, had been murdered. Aunt Mary was friendly for some years with a neighbour who for no good reason, strangled her. The neighbour was charged with her murder, and found guilty but insane. He was committed indefinitely to an asylum. I believe he died there.

After the funeral, the family sat in the parlour of their Victorian terrace home. The girls pale, yet stunning in smart black outfits. Maud looked a million dollars as usual. Rustons have a history of longevity but sadly it seems to have passed this family by. Now only Mary-Rose, Valerie and Sandra survive. I can still see them all now, sitting on chairs they had placed around the wall, to accommodate the number of relations and friends who had gathered to show their respect. They congratulated me on my marriage and welcomed Joyce unreservedly. This family have a great deal of heart, and in no way deserved the tragedy and sadness they have had to bear.

Having to go to Plymouth one week then Southampton the next, the little Morris was struggling. I exchanged her for a Triumph Herald Coupe. Lilac and white, flashy and anything but practical. It suited my image, or at least I thought it did.

My sister Evelyn and husband Don now had two lovely daughters, Susan and Julia. Joyce and I are Godparents to Susan. Don, in his pursuit of promotion in the police force, had been selected for a course at the Police Training College at Bramshill. The course would last for some weeks during which Eve would be alone. With me travelling around the countryside, Joyce was also spending many nights alone. We worked out an arrangement where Joyce would stay with Eve in Taunton one week, and then Eve would come to us the following one. This gave both Don and me a certain peace of mind, knowing that our wives and children were there for one another. Eve and Joyce have always got along well, and remain the very best of friends. As do Don and I. Over the years, Don rose from the rank of constable to Chief Superintendent and Commander of the City of Bath Police Force. Before he retired he was awarded the Queen's Police Medal.

Who will ever forget the winter of '63? We had had a marvellous Christmas. Our old friend Ian Brown had come over for Boxing Day. Ian was still working at H.E. Curtis and kept us informed of life with the Toby Jugs. It was just after lunch that the snow started to fall. It looked fairly steady at first, but unlikely to abate. Ian decided he had better make his way back to Bristol. We said our goodbyes. Jane and Karen never wanted Ian to leave; they loved him. As he drove away the snow began to fall in earnest. By morning there was a six-foot snowdrift against our back door. Roads were impassable and the nation had come to a standstill. We started to dig ourselves out. Betty's husband Roy and I cleared the snow around my car. We thought we would try to make it to Allendale to see if mum and dad needed any help. We got about a half a mile along what we thought was the road and got stuck in a drift. Roy, who was immensely strong, simply picked the rear of the car up and swung it round. I have never before or since witnessed anything like it. With a man like this, I would drive to the North Pole!

The snow hung around for three months, but like everything else, after a few days you get used to it. I still had to travel around the branches. I had planned a visit to our Branch in the Rhonda Valley, in South Wales. Intending to stay for a few days I booked in to the Castle Hotel in Bridgend. A colleague had recommended the Castle, saying the hotelier, whose name was Cliff, was a particularly good host. This proved to be correct in every way. Cliff was a mine of information. It was he who introduced me to Welsh culture, I made many friends. Bed and breakfast was £1 per night, so I stayed there frequently.

On my first morning I drove to Llantrisaint, at the mouth of the Rhonda, and started up the valley. The monochrome landscape (snow covered any colour there might have been) was stark yet beautiful. Huge slagheaps protruding through the fresh snow and iron winding towers at pitheads stared black at me. Row upon row of miners' houses nestled at the foot of the hills. Outside many of the houses, small piles of coal waited to be carried in. An allowance of coal was delivered by the colliery each month to miners working for them, and was simply dumped against the wall of the house. Having worked a long and arduous shift at the pit face, on reaching home exhausted and hungry the miners had to carry their own coal through the house to a shed at the rear.

The coalmines were in full production at the time; most of the families living in the valleys depended on them for their living. A hard life, a very close knit community. I really did not hear too many people complain about their lot; it was a way of life steeped in history and tradition. It seems incredible that this has all gone. The slagheaps have been covered in grass and industrial estates, producing and distributing high-tech products, replace pithead works. No one walks around in a flat cap with a black face anymore. A whole industry gone forever. Or is it? Maybe one-day ecology will force us to return to the natural resources on this planet, and the Boyos will dig again. I am both proud and privileged to have met and shared private moments with the miners of South Wales – none finer.

A sight I shall never forget occurred when driving into the small mining community of Tonyrefail in the Rhonda Valley. Snow was thick on the ground, and still falling lightly as I drove carefully down the sloping main street. In the distance I could see a tall, lone figure and a solitary sheep in the middle of the road. No attempt was made to move as I approached. I pulled up about six feet in front of a long-coated bearded figure, from where a wisp of smoke was rising. The flat cap adorning his head was collecting falling snow. Without removing his cigarette from his mouth, he said, 'No use going any further Butt, [mate] too dangerous.' 'I'm looking for the office of Gardner's Telemeter. Telesavers' I enquired. 'It's by yer,' the abominable snowman replied, followed by, 'Whom be you looking for?' 'Mr Checketts,' I replied. 'That's me, Butt. Who be you?' I told him who I was and so made the acquaintance of our service manager at the Tonyrefail branch. The Welsh are naturally friendly, and Checketts (I never did discover his first name, 'Everyone calls me Checketts,' he informed) was no exception. He invited me to his home for lunch.

Checketts lived with his wife and daughter at the rear of a cycle and electrical shop, which his wife looked after with help from her husband. 'Only part time d'you see, Butt,' he assured me, when I casually inquired as to how he found the time to look after our customers and run his own business. Back at the branch, which was no more than two small rooms, I found he had a staff of one. Himself! He said he was busy at the present repairing a number of coin-operated meters that had got jammed. 'It's amazing what people stuff in 'em Butt,' he mused. I was surprised to see that quite a few contained coins and asked why the cash box hadn't been emptied. Only collectors had meter keys, each one numbered and signed for. 'Well it saves time see, Butt. Instead of bothering the collector, I do both jobs at once, repair and empty them like.' 'How on earth do you unlock them without a key?' I asked. 'You haven't got a key?' 'No, no, Butt, not allowed to have a key see.' I open 'em like this.' He produced two pieces of copper wire about 40mm long by about 2mm thick, and before I could say 'You're kidding,' he opened the lock of the cash drawer of a meter. 'Well, saves all the paperwork, see Butt,' Checketts reasoned.

Before leaving I considered writing a report about the meter incident and his other employment. After some thought I came to a decision not to. If they told me to sack him, who ever would I find to replace him? They might tell me to stay up here and run things for a while. I left things as they were, promising myself to keep an eye on developments in Tonyrefail.

The manager of the Swansea branch was Ramon Ureutia, a small dark-haired man with a pleasing personality. I guess he was of Spanish origin, although I never thought to enquire. My interest in everything Spanish was still a long way off. Ramon was a talented musician, who played piano. Like my dad, he could play for anyone. He ran quite a good operation; at least that's how it looked on the surface. Nothing was very straightforward in Wales. 'We do things different 'ere d'you see, Butt.' I was learning to adapt. One could not apply the same management criterion in South Wales. The work ethic was different from what I had been used to. Also the strong sense of community, the Welsh are not afraid to be seen enjoying themselves – unlike we English who are always worrying about letting ourselves down in public. In many ways the Welsh are not unlike the Spanish.

In Newport, the sales manager was Jim Reardon, a hard -drinking hard-nosed salesman. Interested only in 'How many contracts have you signed today, Boyo?' Pity the poor fellow who hadn't turned in the results.

A major problem was discovered at the Newport branch involving both sales and the cash collection from meters. A decision was made at head office to suspend the senior staff at the branch. I was nominated as the bearer of the news. A daunting prospect for a 26 year-old. I was the youngest regional manager by years. All the Branch managers and many of the staff were older than me. My edict was to arrive at the branch by 8.30am, remove all keys to both the branch and the vehicles, leaving only the service department functioning. I did as I was instructed, and learned a great deal about myself in the process. I was a

L-R. Alfred James Ruston my grandfather. His mother's family, the Shirts, were the
musical influence in our family.   James Alfred Ruston my father.
Aunt Minnie Rose Wood (nee Shirt), in Sydney Australia 1934.   Joseph John Ruston
shipwright and engineer. In 1838 he built the first steamship in Austria. Audrey Ruston
age 10. She became the famous actress Audrey Hepburn. Like me, she is descended from
the London Ruston family of shipwrights.

L-R. Days before a bomb blew Dad's car to kingdom come.. Our home is under here somewhere. Elizabeth Hare, my mother, on her 21st birthday.
Sod Hitler we're going down the pub! Ruston and Steel. Dad ended up playing alone, in between working with heavy rescue.

L.R. Top: The Five arrive in the country Stella Eve Maisie Betty Jim.
Mum with Betty.
Mid: Maisie with the bike she loved to ride. Stella and Eve (on bike).
Rose cottage Kingston Seymour.

Top: New Rank Nailsea is on the left.
Mid: German POWs Hans and Geart come to lunch. Ted and Cousin Cissy Honeymooning
with us at New Rank (that's Maisie on the right of Cissy)
Bot: My brother Roy in Italy with No. 2 Commando. The old garage in Nailsea.
Mr. Small, Dad, Graham Williams, Jim Fletcher, Joyce Griffiths.
Jimmy Neate is in the front.

Top: Dyer's farm. Susan Davis is 2nd from left. Rachel Dyer is far right riding Melody.

Mid: L.R. Me and Cassim. Me with little June on Bonnie.

Bot: My first class at Old Church School. I am front row 2nd left. Jenny Colborn is on the far right of the same row. Sonia White is 3rd girl from right in the 2nd row. Ruth Newman is 3rd girl from left in the same row.

Top: Allendale. The following are my six sisters. L.R. Maud and her daughter June.
Mid: June and Teresa. Maisie and Linda. Betty.
Bot: Stella and Eve on the lawn at Allendale.

Top. Our wedding 1958 Best man John Holloway, Dad, Mum,
Me, Joyce, and her parents.
Middle. Joyce age 17. Together at Allendale on my first leave.
Bottom. Gosport 1956. Tony Fox is back row far left. I am middle
far right. Sgt (bike wrecker) Priestley is front row centre.

Top. Jane aged 4 and Karen aged 2, at Nailsea.
Mid: Rachel aged 5. Me, Joyce, Jane and Karen in Cornwall.
Bot: Alfresco on the terrace – early holidays in Cornwall.

100per cent Company Man, and never turned a hair when it came to the crunch. For the rest of my time with the firm I carried the label 'The Hatchet Man of Telesavers'. My moral stand has never changed. You give a 100 per cent effort, loyalty and honesty to he who pays. Or get out. It didn't make me too popular though.

Ken Buck had been a salesman in the Pontypool Branch. His manager, Tom Phillips had put Ken forward for promotion – a vacancy having occurred at the Bristol branch with Brian Palmer leaving for pastures new. I had always got along well with Brian though. A keen cricketer, he didn't take kindly to being bowled first ball by yours truly during an inter-department match we had organised between sales and service. Claude Reid was umpire and showed distinct pleasure when sending Palmer back to the Pavilion. I can't imagine what Brian had done to invoke such reaction in the otherwise genial Claude. Ken Buck was Welsh through and through. In a new three-piece suit, with briefcase and desk-set, (presented to him by his former colleagues in Wales) full of enthusiasm, he welcomed the salesmen to his first Morning Meeting at Temple Street.

The Bristol crowd, with Bill Parker to the forefront, were a challenge for any experienced sales manager. Poor Ken was a lamb waiting to be slaughtered. He didn't have long to wait before it happened. Invited out on his first evening in Bristol for a social drink with his new sales team, his chances of survival were zero. The next day he was nowhere to be found. He had got so drunk, by the time he had eventually found his way back to his hotel it was locked up, and he couldn't raise the porter. Wandering aimlessly around he fell in a ditch and ruined his new suit. I was summoned to try and find him. I eventually discovered him in one of the hotel toilets. He had locked the door and wouldn't open it for anyone. After some persuasion he finally opened it to me.

The sales team, feeling a little guilty, rallied around and produced good figures for his first week. Ken was a lovely man and became a valued friend. The turnover of salesmen was high, with many leaving after the first week when they found the going too tough. If you were new to selling, even after a period of training you didn't stand a chance against the Billy Parkers of this world. They would nick your customers from right under your nose.

Ken Buck settled in well at Bristol where he was much respected. He found a house to buy in Clevedon. Then without warning, Harry Payne, once my boss, but now on the same level, asked him take over the Newport branch where we had all the trouble. Ken was just the man to sort things out there. It also helped that he was Welsh!

A COCKNEY KID IN GREEN WELLIES

We rented ITT televisions exclusively – although in the early days the Joiner Brothers rented out a number of other mixed brands. A decision was taken to replace these early receivers with the ITT brand. I was given the task of disposing of them. They had very little value in the company's eyes.

Stella had met a TV engineer named Grahame Bond. Together they had started a small business in Kingswood, Bristol. It was a small shop and they lived above it. Their main business was repairs, and they sold the odd second-hand TV when they could get them. TV had still not been around for long, so second-hand sets were rare. I managed to secure a considerable number of our ex-rental receivers for Stella and Grahame for about £4 each. This was a huge amount of stock for a small trader. Stella's business acumen and credit standing with her bank produced the finance. They sold some of the sets to recover their outlay, and the remainder was rented out. This formed the basis of a business that became known as TeleBond, which grew into the largest independent TV rental company in the West of England. I don't recall Grahame even buying me a bottle of Scotch as a thank you, even though I had loaned him some of the money to buy the stock. Anyway, I always considered I did it for Stella. In those days I practically didn't drink either.

The giant ITT Corporation of America moved in on Telesavers and took it over. Both Bob and John Joiner were given golden handshakes. Things quite naturally changed. When I was asked to move north as regional manager, I declined. The Yanks are really tough. They made it clear that if I didn't take the move I would probably get looked over in future. I was in my fifth year with Telesavers and I had worked hard. They in turn had been good to me. But was it time to move on? I could have stayed. Many of my contemporaries continued for 20 years or more. The Joiner Brothers started a building company they later named Westbury Homes, which became nationally known.

I loved every minute of my time at Telesavers (since renamed Telebank) despite the long hours and thousands of miles I had to travel. I learned a great deal. And whilst I retained my interest in technology, I also learned a lot about management and selling, the hard way! I had spent two years in South Wales, and retain affection for the Welsh, their friendship and culture.

What of Checketts you might wonder? I last saw him in 1965; he was driving a brand new top-of-the-range Ford Zodiac, painted in cream and brown. He still sported the beard and flat cap, and had a roll-up dangling from the side of his mouth. On spotting me he shouted, 'Hello

Butt, there's good to see you.' On 26 October 1966 a disaster occurred in the Rhondda valley. At Aberfan a slag heap slid down the side of a hill burying school children and their teachers under thousands of slurry. 116 children and 28 adults lost their lives. I thought of my friends in the Welsh Valleys and wept for them.

I left Telsavers and joined Leech and Haines, an Oxford-based radio and TV retailer with a few shops. They had acquired premises in Northgate Street Gloucester and were looking for a manger to run the new shop. We sold radio TV and electrical appliances, a sort of small Currys. We also sold records. I needed someone to run this department, so engaged a young man who had experience in the field, Bernard Snowball. Bernie's main ambition was to work in the Cinema industry. This he later did, joining the giant Rank organisation. We remain friends.

Whilst I enjoyed the work and the people at the Gloucester shop, I felt I was in reverse. I had come a long way from my days with Curtis, yet now I was back in a similar situation, just bigger and posher that's all. Should I go it alone? It seemed pointless to be running a shop for someone when I could be doing it for myself. A few months later I left.

We had moved from Nailsea in 1963 to Yate on the north side of Bristol. This was a developing area with reasonably priced housing being built. Our first reason to move was to be nearer the proposed Severn Bridge, currently under construction. This would enable me to get to Wales much quicker, instead of having to rely on the unreliable ferry. A hint of bad weather and they stopped running. Frustrating, when one had queued for hours, only to be turned away. The second reason was a desire to own our own house. We made several visits to both Thornbury and Yate. Thornbury was our first choice, being situated much closer to the new Severn crossing. However Yate offered much better value in housing. We chose a traditional three bedroomed semi-detached bay-fronted house that was under construction. Big by today's standards, and built by a local builder with a very good reputation, it was on offer at £2,350. The price included a garage and central heating. The latter via a Parkray fire in the lounge. Such luxury.

In those days, a mortgage was far from taken for granted like it is now. Building societies allocated so much each month for lending, and could pick and chose to whom they would lend. It was common to wait weeks before knowing whether or not you had been accepted, and an offer made. Also it was necessary to find the house first and then apply. This not only delayed everything but also often caused the prospective buyer to lose out to another party. It was the beginning of a trend to buy instead of rent. Affordable homes were built, with the first-time buyer in mind. Yate would grow from a population of 7,000 to 70,000 in 30 years and average house prices would increase from £2,000 to 70,000.

Because of the distance travelled and long hours worked, I was never at home when the shops were open, relying on Joyce to keep me informed of local developments. Jane had started school at St Mary's; Karen would follow soon. It was 1966 and everyone was talking about the forthcoming World Cup competition, which England would host. On a rare week day off, I had asked Joyce if there was anywhere locally I could get some spare parts for our electric iron. She told me of a radio and electrical shop called Tily's. On entering the shop I felt I was stepping back in time. Having got used to my 'chromium-plated palace' in Gloucester (my old pal Mike Flook gave it this title; when someone was enquiring of my whereabouts he had replied, 'Ruston is in his chromium plated palace in Northgate Street.') The shop I was now standing in looked archaic.

If you want to know what is going on in an area, ask the local barber. I did. He told me of a shop in Station Road that might possibly become vacant. The present incumbent had traded there since before the war, and was considering retirement. I called into the shop he mentioned and found it was basically a haberdashery, but sold all manner of things. The brown wooden counter and shelving had been in position for 40 years or more, and most of the stock looked as elderly. The proprietor was a spinster by the name of Miss Redman. She ran the shop alone and lived on the ground floor. Above the shop lived her companion Miss, Bant, who had served for years in the Army. I was invited to call them Reddy and Bant. The two ladies were characters straight out of an Agatha Christie novel... sadly, rarely met these days. 'Yes,' Miss Redman said she would like to close the shop, but the task was too daunting for her. What would she do with all her stock? Taking the bull by the horns, I offered to organise a closing-down sale for her. I suspected a little push was all she was waiting for. I cleared the lot in two weeks. Reddy was amazed, and grateful. She readily (excuse the pun) agreed to granting me a 14-year lease on the shop, the first seven at a rental of £28 per month.

GOING IT ALONE

I took possession of the shop at 44 Station Road Yate on 14 February 1966. Valentine's Day. My first newspaper advert ran: 'Country districts TV sales and repairs.' I traded my car for a Morris Minor 1000 van, and my pinstripe suit for a pair of jeans and a sweater! Each morning after taking Jane to school, Joyce came to the shop with Karen to help me decorate. The premises consisted of a showroom, workshop and small storeroom. I wanted to make a plinth along one side of a wall on which to stand TV sets. Now you all know of my skill as a carpenter. I carefully measured the wood and took pains to saw it straight. Then was left with the task of finding a place that it would fit! Somehow I got it done, and once covered with a cord-type carpet it looked fine. I bought some green plastic letters and fixed them to the board above the shop window. It now read YATE TV. With a newly connected telephone I was in business.

The immediate problem I faced was getting stock to sell. I could not afford new and second-hand was difficult to come by. TV was still relatively in its infancy. People expected a set to last 12 to15 years, and had them repaired rather than buy new. I managed to get a few ex-rental sets and refurbish them. I now wish I had had the foresight to keep for myself some of those sets I let Stella and Grahame have. Colour TV was on the horizon but was not scheduled to appear for another two years. Even then initially it would only be available on BBC2. I would have to rely on repairs for a living, at least for a year or so. I got steadily busier. I worked in the workshop from 9am to 6pm daily. I did any service calls that came in, after 6pm offering a same-day service. I had a few TV sets, which I kept for loan to customers should I need to take their set in for repair. When things got tight, it became hard to resist selling my loan sets. I gave Joyce housekeeping money each Saturday, often borrowing half of it back the following week to buy spare parts with.

Advertising was costly, so I ran a couple of lines in the service and repair column of the *Evening Post* on a weekly basis. That little ad more than paid for itself. I was beginning to get known, and was recommended by satisfied customers. World Cup fever was upon us, so the demand for my service gathered momentum. I will never forget standing alone in my little shop watching Geoff Hurst score the winning goal. (Years later I was fortunate indeed to meet Geoff, and he relived the moment for me.) I ran around the shop and leapt in the air. That winter Brunel technical college in Bristol offered a two-year course on colour TV, aimed at existing engineers. Along with former colleagues, I enrolled. Brunel College backs on to Gloucestershire County Cricket Club ground, of no significance to me then.

A COCKNEY KID IN GREEN WELLIES

With my old employer, Harold Curtis closing his electrical business in favour of becoming a builder (bigger profit I expect), Ian Brown had come to work for us. I took on the existing sites Curtis was currently contracted to wire and so kept Ian in full employment. In between times, the electrician helped in the shop, and erected TV aerials. Pulling up on the forecourt of the shop one day I caught sight of a Parka-clad figure on a Vespa scooter. 'Looks to me like a Mod' said Ian. A young man walked in through the door, looked me straight in the eye and inquired, 'Got any jobs you want doing?' 'Who are you, and what exactly can you do?' I asked. 'The name's Logan, Keith that is; I can do anything,' he replied. Never was a truer word spoken by anyone I have ever known.

Keith's parents, now living in Yate, had recently returned from Australia where they had emigrated when Keith was 12 years old. Keith was devastated; he loved the outdoor life and the opportunities to sail in Australia. All Keith now wanted was to find a way to return to Oz. He said he intended to apply to join the Navy, qualify, and then offer himself to Australia. He was loading the van for me, when I asked him, 'What do you hope to do, in the Navy Keith'? 'Oh, fly helicopters,' he replied. 'But you have to be an officer to do that, and that will mean gaining entry to the Royal Naval College at Dartmouth,' I countered. In a matter of fact way, as though I had asked him not to forget to shut the van door, he grinned at me, then said, 'I know.'

Dad rang, and asked me to call and see him as a matter of urgency. I had recently purchased a car, a Vauxhall VX 490, quite a performer, so it didn't take me long to drive to Nailsea. 'Sit down son ... make a cup of tea Liz,' said dad, all in one breath. 'What's the problem?' I inquired. 'Its your niece, June. She has gone missing,' replied Dad. June had been attending a college of further education at Weston-Super-Mare. She was studying for a catering diploma. She had failed to return in the evening. After phoning the parents of a boy she was keen on, Dad discovered that he too had failed to return home. We came to the conclusion that they had gone off together. I said not to worry they would reappear in a day or so. Dad was fidgety, and mum kept crying. Having brought June up from a baby, they both worshipped her. I was immensely fond of June too.

The weeks went by and still no news of June. Dad was reproachful, and wondered what he had done to cause her to run away. I couldn't believe that it had happened a second time, first Stella and now June. For the next few months we spoke of little else. Then quite out of the blue a letter came from June saying she was in Scotland with her boyfriend Brian. Thinking June was pregnant they had run away, intending to marry. As it transpired, June wasn't pregnant after all, so it had all been for nothing. She had married in haste – or had she?

The morning the letter arrived, dad rang saying 'Jimmy, I want you to take me and your mother to Scotland, to bring June home.' Clearly he had made up his mind. The next day with Joyce by my side we collected mum and dad, and sister Maisie's daughter Linda, and drove the 400-odd miles to Edinburgh – with dad giving me instructions on the best route to take, and me arguing that things had changed since his lorry-driving days in the 30s! I was worn out when we arrived and suggested we book into a B&B first, then look for June. Dad said, 'No, lets get her first. I won't rest until we do,' Seeing the worried look in mum's eyes, I conceded. The address on the letter was Inverlieth Terrace. It was a Sunday and the streets were quiet. We eventually found the address, which turned out to be a four-storey building. We learnt that a young couple fitting a description we gave were living on the top floor. Still fit, I made nothing of the four flights of stairs. Anxious and angry, I pounded on the door of the flat I supposed was theirs.

Brian opened the door. June was standing behind him. Brushing her boyfriend aside, although I felt no malice toward him, I put my arms around her saying, 'What the bloody hell do you think you are playing at?' Haven't they [mum and dad] done enough for you,' I accused. Dad and mum were so pleased to see their beloved granddaughter, and embrace her once more, that any thoughts of recrimination were put to one side. The next day June returned with us; Brian followed days later. This wouldn't be the last 'Journey to rescue June' I would make. Sadly, her mother was less than interested in the affair. She would distance herself even further once she was told that her daughter had married a boy of mixed race.

The end of my first year in business, and I had made a profit. Joyce reminded me that I had always said when finances allowed I would buy her a new engagement ring. 'Yes,' I agreed. 'Well, instead of a ring for me, would you buy the kids a pony?' she implored. I admit that at first, I wasn't too keen on the idea. Ponies take a lot of looking after and they are costly creatures to keep, I reminded her. 'But you loved your days with ponies,' she reminded me. 'Don't be mean.' Now I have never been knowingly mean in my life.

I rented an acre paddock in North Road Yate. Then I began to look for a suitable pony for the kids. The first pony we bought was dark brown, 11.2hh and called Dandy. He was that all right; he thought more of himself than he did his passengers, and would dump them at will. I had gotten to know a man called Jim Warren who lived on a three-acre smallholding in Engine Common, no more than five minutes away from our shop. Jim, then in his early 70s, was somewhat of a country legend. He had traded in horses most of his life. A three-bedroomed cottage surrounded by an assortment of sheds was the home he shared with his wife Rose. Echoes of 'The Darling Buds of May'. Time had passed him by, and he did things his own way. Jim always had time for people, and was a great storyteller, many of his tales having a horse in them somewhere.

I asked Jim if he knew of a quiet pony, something for my children to enjoy and feel confident about. 'Well now,' he replied, adjusting his hat while he thought, 'My son Leonard has a little grey pony, no more 'n' 12 hands. A good little sort, might suit you.' 'Did I ever tell 'ee about the piebald pony I bought at Stow Fair one Bank Holiday?' Another story flowed, after which he said. 'Leonard lives in North Road, only just moved there. Give him a ring.' I rang Len Warren and he told me of the grey pony. 'He's the kindest pony you'll ever find. We call him Dopey,' advised Len. Well he was not wrong; the pony was Dopey, it had a job to get out of its own way. But the kids loved it, and felt safe when mounted. I think we paid £65 for him, quite a sum in those days. (This would prove to be a very expensive engagement ring indeed.) Joyce took Jane and Karen down to the field to see Dopey most evenings and at weekends. I joined them when I could.

Joyce passed her driving test first time, and could now drive the van, enabling her to get to Bristol to purchase spares for my repair work, which was a great help. The launch of colour TV was looming. I had been granted an agency to sell GEC televisions, and although sales were slow at first I was now shifting quite a few. When selling a new television set, more often than not, a part- exchange was involved. I re-conditioned these, and re-sold them with a three-month guarantee – often making as much profit out of the second-hand set as I did the new one. Profit margins on new sets were one third. This amounted to about £20. Before VAT was introduced a Purchase tax was levied. The unfairness of this tax was the point at which it became due. It was paid by us retailers when purchasing goods for sale. No matter how long you held stock, you only recovered the tax when selling. If, for instance, one held a sale and reduced prices, the tax already paid was unaffected. There were quite a number of rates too. TVs were in the luxury bracket.

Colour TV came in like a damp squib. Available at first on BBC 2 only, it had limited appeal. Consumers were interested enough, but would wait for it to be broadcast on ITV before making such a substantial purchase. I sold my first colour TV, a Phillips with a 25-inch screen, to and old farmer friend at Rangeworthy, Bob Bartlett. The set was an absolute monster, taking two men to carry it. It worked well enough though and was fairly reliable. It was some months before first BBC1 then ITV were to broadcast in colour. It was now 1969. By now I had two more agencies, Murphy and ITT/KB. Almost overnight the demand for colour exploded. The public were now in the mood. 'We want colour TV for Christmas' was at the root of every inquiry. The manufacturers were caught napping, with demand far outstripping supply. In our little shop we had a waiting list of customers wanting a colour set. Any make would do, just so long as it receives colour. Its seems difficult to believe it now. With a third profit, which in most cases was around £100, our little business was growing rapidly.

A grey-suited fair-haired young man walked into the shop one day and announced that he represented a Japanese company who sold hi-fi equipment and radios 'State of the art,' he informed me. 'And we will soon be bringing in colour TVs. In fact, we already have one model available.' My ears pricked. 'Unfortunately it only has a 13-inch screen,' he commiserated. Ears back in the normal position, I enquired as to the name of his company 'Oh, it's called SONY,' he responded enthusiastically. He urged me to sign up and become a dealer of what he quite emphatically stated would become a brand leader. 'Never heard of them,' I said. And anyway, not much good to me now,' I argued. 'I need 20-inch or 22-inch Colour TVs, as many as I can get'.

Due to import restrictions in force at the time, colour TVs coming from the Far East were limited not only by numbers, but also to a maximum screen size of 18inches. The Japanese manufactures Mitsubishi and Hitachi had an 18-inch colour set available now, and so stole a start on Sony, whose energetic rep, Andy Searle, had to wait passively in the background whilst his competitors did the business. Andy and I became good friends, and in a few years I would become a Pro Sony dealer.

Jim Warren had decided to sell his smallholding. 'I want £3,500 pounds for it, to include all the sheds,' he told me. He said he had bought a six-acre field close by in Tanhouse Lane, and intended moving a caravan on to it and living there. 'Can you get permission to do that?' I queried. 'Shan't ask no one. Shan't be 'urtin' no-one,' he replied. That was Jim's logic. Joyce was keen on the idea. I said I would approach the Bank.

Brian Palmer (not the Telesavers sales manager) was the manager of Lloyd's bank. I had a very good relationship with Lloyds, banking with them since our days in Nailsea.

With considerable confidence, I knocked on the door of the manager's office. 'Pleased to see you Jim.' What can I do for you?' Brian asked as he beckoned me sit down. Laying my last few years' accounts on the desk before him, I outlined my proposal to purchase Jim Warren's cottage and land (not forgetting the sheds!). Instead of the expected show of enthusiasm for my proposal, I received the following rebuff. 'No, no, too risky. Never know what you might have to spend on an old place like that.' I argued my case, but it was useless. I went back to the shop with my head lower than it had been for some long time. I didn't realise it then, but unwittingly, Brian Palmer had taught me a lesson from which in the future I would profit immensely.

A site manager from one of the new housing estates that were popping up everywhere, bought Jim Warren's property. He spent a couple of thousand on it, selling it two years later for £10,000. I was not amused. Meanwhile, Jim Warren had moved both in and out of the caravan on the land he had bought at Tanhouse Lane, selling the six-acre field to me for £1,500. I paid cash. Sod the bank! We had acquired another two ponies. Little Hiawatha 11.2hh and a 14.2hh chestnut gelding called Aston. The latter I bought from Bert Legg as a birthday present for Joyce, then rode him myself. Shameful!

The horse world is full of characters, and none less of one was Bert Legg. Bert lived with his wife in a council house in Kingswood, Bristol, and traded second-hand cars from a pitch in Warmley. Sporting a yellow waistcoat, on which hung a gold hunter watch and chain worn under a tweed jacket, Bert was every bit the country gent. He could often be seen, riding crop in hand, going through some imaginary chase whilst showing a prospective buyer a used car. Watching Bert's antics, they never looked too closely at the 'banger'.

Activities with the ponies began to hot up. Joyce's kid sister Heather came out every weekend to ride with Jane and Karen. 'What do you think about taking part in a gymkhana then, kids?' I asked. The response was a unanimous, 'Yes.' We now had a small trailer, which we pulled behind our 2.4 Jaguar saloon, and so really looked the part. In pouring rain we arrived at the showground eager to take part in the activities. Karen was too small to ride alone so I entered her and Hiawatha in the leading rein bending race. I would do the leading. The race required that you lead the pony and rider through a set of poles in a slalom fashion. There were usually about eight poles over a distance of 25 yards. On reaching the last pole you turned sharply, weaving in and out of the poles once more, on your return to the finish line. I have always had a nickname for Karen. I call her Oakley, or Oaks for short. No one else (*or almost no one else*) is allowed to use it. She was particularly small for her age, so I invented a name that would make her feel special. Jane was a natural on a horse, and also a talented musician, whereas Karen had to try so hard at everything. She even got thrown out of the recorder class at school as being a lost cause. But she had guts aplenty.

There were six of us in the race. I waited with bated breath, not wanting to let little Oakley down. Marks, Set, GO. I went off like a rocket. Little Hiawatha was very quick and had done it all before; I had a job to stay with him. 'Hold on tight, Oaks,' I encouraged, as we reached the bottom pole. Immediately I thought we were clear, I turned and headed back up the line like someone possessed. As we approached the last pole I could see Joyce and others frantically waving their arms and shouting at me. At first I thought they were cheering me on to win, then I looked back at Hiawatha, and to my horror realised that I had lost my rider. By now I had crossed the line a clear winner, but was, quite naturally, disqualified. You need to cross with both pony and rider! Looking back down the line I could see poor Karen on her hands and knees, crying in the mud. Her raincoat had caught on the pole as we turned, and literally hooked her out of the saddle. Upset, but none the worse for the experience, she went on to win a couple of rosettes. I was not popular for a while. 'Maniac,' Joyce retorted.

We went to show after show, with both our kids and Heather doing well. She now had her own pony called Prince. Karen was a great favourite among the gymkhana crowd. Being so small she was always at a disadvantage, but she made up for this with sheer determination. In cream jodhpurs and the yellow jumper that her mother had knitted for her, Oakley and Wathie were prepared to take on all comers. In a musical sack race, once a number of contestants had been eliminated and the last few places were being fought over, the crowd would get behind the tiny girl on the little bay pony. They became inseparable and were always in the rosettes. We had purchased Hiawatha from Fred Tuck, a lovely man who lived with his wife and children at Totteroak in Horton. He loved to see Karen do well, especially so because he had sold us the pony. Fred was the only person other than her dad, whom Karen allowed to call her Oakley. He only did this when she was competing, shouting from the top of his voice. 'Come on Oaks, you can beat them all.' Fred was very, very kind to us and a great help in our early days with ponies.

I bought Jane a pony called Shandy, from Bayham Sami, a young boy we had observed doing particularly well in the gymkhana events. Shandy was 12.2hh and strawberry roan in colour' He should have been named Houdini; he could get out of anywhere. If he got fed up in his paddock, he just popped to the one next door. This caused some embarrassment with our neighbours, and our 'sorry' wore thin after a while. When Jane outgrew Shandy we sold him to Fred Tuck. Fine, until one day Shandy decided to return home to us, brining two more of Fred's ponies with him!

Two outstanding kids from those gymkhana days were Johnny Francome, who rode a pony called Willie Wagtail, and a few years his junior, Paul Nicholls who had a little Haflinger pony called Little Miller. Both went on to become prolific winners under National Hunt rules. Johnny is now a regular commentator on Channel 4, and Paul a very successful trainer. Paul's father purchased Little Miller from Joyce's friend Nina Gerard, whose maiden name was Cave. Herself a great horsewoman, her brother Peter was even more successful. With a horse called Bronze Miller he won more than 20 races over the sticks. Chestnut with a flaxen mane and tail, Bronze Miller was quite flashy for a racehorse. When Nina bought the little Haflinger and saw he had the same colourings as her brother's horse, she named him Little Miller. Joyce and Nina spent endless hours at horse and pony sales, and also went to the annual Stow fair, famous for its characters and variety of horseflesh.

In the shop I now had two engineers, John French and Malcolm Charnock. John was ex-Radio Rentals and besides being a competent engineer was also an excellent pianist. We had much in common. At weekends John played in a trio around the various night-spots, and re-kindled in me a love of singing. On occasions, he invited me to sing with the trio, which I thoroughly enjoyed. John's ambition was to emigrate to Australia, something Joyce and I had considered. He thought to use his skill as an engineer to satisfy the Ten Quid Tourist syndrome. (A family could emigrate to Oz for £10 each the full fare being subsidised by the government.) Once settled he would ply his musical talent and hopefully turn Pro. Eventually he did all of this, and I admire him for it.

We were getting busier by the day and our customer base was growing. A new shop selling carpets had opened on the shopping centre. The proprietor, Reg Bain, had called on me, not to sell carpets, but to purchase a colour TV. In fact, he bought two! I didn't know then but this was typical Reg, never doing anything by half. Reg asked why I hadn't moved on to the shopping centre. 'Expensive, isn't it?' I reasoned. 'Do you know how much it costs?' he replied. Then it hit me; I hadn't even inquired as to the feasibility of a possible move up-market. Business was good, but could it be better?

By now Keith Logan had joined the Fleet Air Arm, and passed out of Dartmouth with the rank of Sub-Lieutenant. He was more determined than ever to get back to Australia, this time as a flyer. I would miss him terribly; we had become such good friends. When things were not going too well for him at home he moved into the shop, sleeping under the plinth I had made, mad fool. Even I wouldn't risk sleeping under something I had built! Often he stayed in our house. Joyce has a very special place in her heart for Keith Logan.

Keith had played for the local youth soccer team, which had since formed the nucleus of the newly formed Yate 'A' football team – the idea being to create a team through which to channel youth, bringing them on for the senior sides. A mixture of young and senior players worked well, plenty of jibing on both sides, not least of all from Logan. 'Come on you veterans,' he would holler. I was proud to play in Yate 'A', and even more so to be part of the side that played 17 games without defeat.

However there was a sad period, which all those with whom I played will never forget. A car travelling to a match in which Chris Tovey, Terry Witt and Dave Pearce were passengers, and which was being driven by Pete Jackson, crashed at Pye Corner, Hambrook, on the outskirts of Bristol, a notorious bend. Pete and Dave were injured. Chris and Terry were killed. Both having recently married, their families had lost husbands and sons, and Yate FC two loyal friends and players. A cloud, which lasted an awful long time, fell over the club. An image I will never forget as long as I live will be the look of sadness on the face of Dave Pearce at the funeral service. We were asked to wear our newly issued Club ties, the first the Club had ever had. The silence amid a sea of blue and white painted a thousand words.

Although I had played with Terry, I knew Chris Tovey and his family well. I recall playing in a match that we won against all the odds. It was during the run of 17 without defeat. Chris was in goal. In the last few minutes of the match, he dived to the bottom right-hand corner to push the ball away, only for it to be lobbed straight back in to his left. In one move he rose from the ground, and with arm outstretched, pushed the ball over the bar. Chris had kept our record unblemished. He was an athlete, full of life. Old men reminisce, and talk of golden days. You are part of them Chris.

It was suggested that a fund should be set up immediately to raise money for the dependants of the two men killed. It was then that the club paid me a compliment, of which I am justly proud, by asking me to be treasurer of the fund. I said I would be honoured to do it, on condition that money collected was paid out to the beneficiaries as quickly as possible and that the very minimum balance would be held over until more funds came in. I set up a bank account, my bank manager agreeing to waive any charges, and Roger Hawkins and I were joint signatories. Terry and Richard Jordan, Reg England, Terry Tansley, Micky Burns and many other club members worked hard to raise funds.

Although we all rallied around Pete with words of understanding and support, he was devastated. The accident affected him deeply. I've no doubt it still does. It brought back tragic memories for me, too. Pete and his wife Jean have always been, and remain, friends I value greatly.

As Christmas approached, we said farewell to Keith Logan. He had paid a visit to Australia House and convinced them that their country needed him. Although he had already been subsidised by the government with a £10 fare once, it wasn't his fault he was asking again; anyway now he would be such an asset. They wouldn't want to miss out on that now, would they?

As the '60s drew to a close, I reflected. For us, apart from the trauma of the first year, it had been a wonderful decade. We had enjoyed a great deal of success and had so much fun. Would the '70s be as kind?

GREEN WELLY BRIGADE

Jimmy Abrahams, the jeweller who traded from the new shopping centre, called to tell me of a shop unit to let. The unit in question was at No 9 South Parade. The present occupier, a hairdresser named Derek Hutchings, was quite a character. Good looking and flamboyant, with a liking for the ladies, he was ideally suited to his profession as a ladies, hairdresser. He had opened the salon about six months beforehand but with designs on pastures new, and decided to sell. Not prepared to wait for a buyer of a going concern, Derek was seeking to sell his interest in the leasehold property. We agreed terms of £500 for the lease to include fixtures and fittings. This was an incredibly good deal, for me that is. I had looked at the possibility of a new unit on the centre, and discovered that initially all one got was a shell. It would require plastering and decorating; even a ceiling had to be installed, plus expensive shop-front. Add carpets and furnishings, and the cost would be thousands.

The lease I had agreed to purchase from Derek was for a 21-year term of which less than one year had lapsed. Rent for the first 14 years was at £1,450 per annum without review, unheard of now. Already carpeted, we also managed to utilise many of the existing fittings. So with little money, and a lot of effort, we made the transition from Old Yate to the new expanding shopping centre. At last I had my very own chromium-plated palace! I saw a bit of Derek during the first couple of years at my new shop. He now drove a bright yellow sports car, and wore designer clothes to match! Evenings, more often than not, he could be found in Reeves night-club, in Bristol, where I had performed in cabaret. Then a trendy place to be seen. Somehow I lost all contact with him, although I became quite friendly with my new neighbour on South Parade, Derek's dad George, in the takeaway. I didn't hear from Derek again until 1994. The offer he made then proved irresistible.

The new shop would require 100 per cent of my time, so I decided this would be my last season playing football for Yate. I would hang up my boots for good. Demand for colour TV was still high, but supplies were short. There were never enough sets to make a decent display. I was making money, so couldn't complain. I kept the old shop on for a while, eventually selling the interest in the remainder of the lease for £500, exactly what I had paid for the new shop lease. No 44 Station Road, became a bicycle shop; it still is. I was sorry to say goodbye to Reddy and Bant, but would stay in touch.

A lady who worked part time in the takeaway next door to my new shop had called in on occasion. She said her name was Connie Vacher, and that she lived in Badminton with her husband Leslie, who was, and had been, Butler to His Grace the Duke of Beaufort for many years. The annual horse trials on the great estate were approaching, and Connie suggested that I offer a colour TV to the Duke on loan during the trials week. The Royal family always attended the trials on cross-country day. Connie said the Queen Mother was fond of TV, and might appreciate having a colour set to watch, especially if the weather was bad. If suitably impressed, the Duke might buy one, who knows? Although I still had more customers than colour sets, I still thought it a good idea.

I composed a letter to the Duke offering the loan of a colour TV. To my surprise the response was almost immediate. He thanked me most warmly and was 'delighted to accept the offer'. The second paragraph of the letter was a personal invitation to hunt with his hounds, an honour indeed. Come the day, I took Malcolm with me to help carry the 22-inch TV. I showed Connie's husband Leslie how to operate the receiver, and once satisfied all was well, I left.

It was around 4pm on Saturday when I got a phone call from a calm, but worried Leslie Vacher. I recognised the cultured voice at once: 'I am afraid to have to tell you that your television set has gone up in smoke.' Instant panic set in. I didn't have another set available to replace it with. I knew the cross-country finished at around 6pm, after which the Royal party would return to the house. I had also been reliably informed that the Queen Mother rarely missed *Dad's Army*. It was her favourite programme and was on at 6.30pm. I grabbed my tool kit, and motored to Badminton.

I had located and repaired the fault, and was just fixing the back cover in place, when Leslie, who had been watching me work, without warning moved quickly towards the French doors of the large sitting room, and opened them. I could now see a party of people approaching, headed by the Duke of Beaufort, who entered the room, then stood to one side allowing a little elegant lady wearing a huge smile to pass. Soon I was standing face to face with the Queen Mother. Speechless, I was rescued by Mary, Duchess of Beaufort, who introduced me to all present, saying 'This is our Mr Ruston. He hunts with us you know. [A trifle premature.] He has kindly provided this wonderful television machine for us all to watch.'

The Queen Mother was kindness itself and asked me if I watched *Dad's Army*. When I replied, quite genuinely, that it was a favourite of mine she countered. 'Then please don't miss it on my account.' Sitting herself down on a large sofa she invited; 'Sit by me, Mr Ruston'. And there I sat and watched the Walmington on Sea platoon, with our lovely Queen Mother. During the programme the Queen Mum asked about my family. Then inquired as to whether my children had ponies, and who was my favourite character in Dad's Army. I confessed to liking

Corporal Jones best. 'Me too, but I also enjoy Captain Mainwaring,' she replied.

Princess Margaret, who had just entered the room from another direction, first stood, then sat, with legs crossed, and clad in high black patent boots, with perspex heels. She was smoking through a long cigarette holder, and in between puffs demonstrated with her hands how she had leapt up to switch off the TV when the smoke appeared. 'Hadn't she herself had a television that had done the very same thing!' Prince Andrew who was then 10 years old asked intelligently what had caused the fault, and listened carefully as I tried to explain in as practical a way as possible. The Duke of Beaufort thanked me most profusely for my efforts. As I was leaving, the Duchess, who at that time was herself still riding to hounds, said 'If you see any antis about, ride them down!' The Queen Mother smiled, and the Duke laughed. But I think the Duchess was serious!

The summer was on us and we were doing the round of pony shows. I drove the car with the pony trailer behind, and Joyce drove my van. After helping to unload the ponies at the showground, I returned to the shop in the van, repeating the performance at the end of the day. A routine we had got into during the past few years.

One Saturday on returning to the shop, I saw the familiar boiler suit and wellington-booted figure of someone I had come to know, standing by the counter. It was Bill Washbourne, a local farmer who often called at the shop with something or other electrical that required repairing. Bill greeted me with his usual warm friendly smile, saying, 'Hello Jim. You might find this interesting. You know you often said that you would be interested in a smallholding if one came on the market around here...' 'I still am,' I replied. Bill continued. 'Now this is in the strictest confidence you understand. You must swear not to tell a soul.' He then went on to tell me of his neighbour Charlie Burgess.

Bill Washbourne owned Birdbush Farm, which is situated half way between Chipping Sodbury and Wickwar. It is approached from a turning off the Wickwar road, an area known as Mapleridge. Birdbush Farm is about 300 yards from the main road. Travelling past Bill's farm for about a half mile the road terminates at Shortwood Farm. This was the 56-acre holding that Charlie Burgess farmed. 'Charlie has been telling me that he can't face another winter on the farm,' Bill informed me. 'His wife has had a fall, and broken her arm. He's looking to sell'. My heart missed a beat, this sounded exactly what I had always dreamed of, a small farm of my own. I tried to stay calm. Taking a deep breath I said: 'I am very interested, Bill. Can you arrange a meting? 'He can be a bit of an awkward old cuss at times, but as genuine and honest as the day is long,' Bill informed. 'You would have to go at his convenience. He won't let anything interfere with his routine, especially milking. Only a small herd of Friesians, but some of the finest cattle you will ever see.' Pausing, Bill continued, 'Always buys the best, does Charlie.'

When I returned to the pony show to drive the car and trailer back, I said nothing to Joyce, but thought of little else until the Monday morning, when a telephone call came. 'Jim, It's Bill. Charlie says it's alright to call on him this afternoon at 2pm. Don't be late!' On my way past Birdbush Farm, I stopped to see Bill. In an almost fatherly way he advised, 'Now young Jim, Charlie Burgess was a policeman before he retired and took up farming, and before that in the Household Cavalry. Don't be put off by his formal manner, it's just his way. He's old-fashioned.' 'Nothing wrong with that Bill,' I said. 'At least I will know where I stand with someone like that. I like a straight talker.' Watching the broad grin spread across his weather-worn, generous face, I got the feeling Bill was loving every minute of it. He would like nothing more than to do a favour for both me and his loyal neighbour, buyer and seller. Chatting with friends at Market in later years, he would recall: 'I found young Ruston's farm for him.' And, 'I sold Charlie's farm for him.' This was all he wanted from the deal, nothing more. Bill would soon be my neighbour. I would never find better.

I pulled up in the concrete yard at Shortwood Farm and before me stood a grey unattractive farmhouse. It was obvious that at one time this had been a pair of farm labourers' cottages that had since been knocked together. The windows were the metal agricultural pattern, of various sizes, thus giving the front elevation an odd perspective. Joined to the right of the house was a row of calf-rearing buildings, with entry doors no more than 5 feet high. These led on to a cow shed and dairy. It looked as though very little had changed here for many years, although there was a newly erected three-bay Atcost barn with covered yard. I recall thinking, 'That must have cost a few bob.'

As I stepped from the car my first impression was one of silence. It was quite the most tranquil setting I had encountered since my days at Kingston Seymour, and aside from running water and electricity, almost as remote and primitive. However, there was a telephone. Wickwar 365.

I approached the front door of the house and was greeted by a tall man wearing thick corduroy trousers, stout leather boots and a check shirt with sleeves rolled up to the elbow. 'Charlie Burgess,' he announced, 'Jim Ruston,' I countered. Mr Burgess asked me in. We walked through a small entrance hall to a large sitting room. Sitting in an old armchair was a grey haired lady. Pointing to her plastered arm she explained. 'Slipped down on the path outside the back door. It had been raining, so it was wet and greasy. Don't fancy another winter here,' she said. 'Alright dear, Mr Ruston doesn't want to hear that. He's come to talk business with me.' Interrupted Burgess. With that, Charlie Burgess declared that he would make some tea. Sensing she wanted to talk, as soon as Burgess had left the room, I prompted his wife to continue. Good salesmen should first, and foremost, be good buyers too. First lesson in selling? 'Know your product.' Gently I led her to tell me everything she didn't like about Shortwood Farm. It was heavy ground. After rain, water hung around for months. A car was needed to go anywhere. There were no buses. Wonderful in summer, but bleak in winter. Charlie was well past retirement, and really could not continue to carry on much longer without help. But the farm was too small to support a farm worker.

Over tea we sat and talked. Outwardly stern, he appeared at first, but once the ice was broken, I found Charlie Burgess most agreeable. I got him to talk about himself, and his time in the police force. What had made him turn to farming? 'Something I always wanted to do, from a child,' he confided. I told him of my dreams as an evacuee. To have my own pony and one day own land. Then, with a face as straight as a poker, Charlie stated: 'There are two things worrying me. Firstly, can a young fellow like you find the money to purchase this farm? Secondly, it will take me months, maybe a year, to get it ready for sale. There is so much that needs doing, so much clearing up to do.' By now Charlie's demeanour had altered, his shoulders had dropped, his head bowed. I saw my chance; get in now, whatever he says go for it. I will never get another chance like this.

'Would you mind indicating the price you propose to ask for the farm, Mr Burgess?' I said. 'Well about a year ago an agent said it was worth £11,200. I suppose it might be worth a little more now,' he replied. I thought I had misheard him. I thought he would be asking much more, and had wondered how I would find the money. I knew I could raise £12,000. I had a job to contain myself. In my mind, I was already living there. I inwardly declared, 'This is mine,' I took a deep breath then made an offer. 'How about, I give you £12,000 for the farm, as seen. That is, for the house, land, and buildings only. You could move at your convenience, leaving everything just as it is. I will see to all the clearing up.' It was as though a cloud had been lifted from Burgess, although he queried, 'You have that kind of money available?' 'Don't you worry about a thing. I am good to my word,' I promised. 'Mr Washbourne will tell you that.' With a wry smile Burgess replied. 'He already has young man. That is why you are here.' For a second I was ecstatic, then

Burgess dropped a bombshell. 'I too am a man of my word Mr Ruston, and I have always promised the option of first refusal to buy my farm to my neighbour Mr Brown, whose land joins us over the back. I will go to see him this evening after milking, and if he is no longer interested, then I shall sell to you.' My heart sank. Surely no one in their right mind would turn down a 56-acre farm with four bed-roomed farmhouse, outbuildings a galvanised machine shed and a virtually brand new Atcost barn, for £12,000. Would they?

I went home and told Joyce what I had almost bought. Her emotions were mixed. Cautious about the money we would have to raise, yet excited at the prospect of owning our own farm. We waited for the phone call. It didn't come. The next morning, as I was about to leave for work, the phone rang. 'Mr Ruston, this is Burgess speaking. Shortwood Farm is yours, if you still want it,' he declared. 'Thank you. Yes Mr Burgess, I still want it,' I replied. 'Can I bring my wife down this afternoon to meet you and Mrs Burgess? Then you and I can exchange the names of our respective solicitors and get things moving,' I suggested. 'Fine, fine. See you at say, 2pm?' he replied. I turned to Joyce and almost screamed with joy, 'It's ours.' Not yet it isn't. You have to raise the money first,' reasoned my ever cautious wife.

There's an old adage I recalled at the time: 'The best laid plans of mice and men.' Joyce and I had been talking for some time about increasing our family. Loving our daughters as much as we did, we would have liked a boy. We tried to adopt. We were told that because we were still capable of producing a child of our own, we couldn't be considered. I felt strongly about wanting to give a loving home to a needy child, of whatever sex, so was naturally bitter at being turned down. My bitterness was exacerbated by not being told the reason for rejection until after Joyce and I had gone through all the tests and interviews. Thankfully things have changed. Having decided to have a baby of our own, Joyce was now pregnant. The baby was due late November. I had also made plans to go to Germany with Reg Bain. Since being a close neighbour of his on the shopping centre we had become good friends, sharing the many tales of woe of the retailer. Joyce knew I had always wanted to visit Germany, so didn't object to my going. Now, in the middle of all this, I had gone and bought a farm!

I helped Joyce from the car, and she stood gazing around the scene before her. 'Takes me back Jim,' she said, referring to her childhood as she spoke. I sallied forth, and knocked on the door of the farmhouse. Looking over my shoulder, as I waited for a reply, I could see Joyce walking around the farmyard. She walked in a way that looked as though she belonged here, part of it, as though she had been here all her life. Joyce is country, I am city, and it shows. The Burgess's took us on a conducted tour of the land. Although I had already struck a deal to buy the place, I hadn't looked around the fields. Something I wouldn't overlook now, of course. The old couple expressed their concern about Joyce walking up and down the hilly fields in latter stages of pregnancy. Joyce reassured them she was OK, and got on extremely well with the delightful pair. The farm was virtually in a ring fence. In other words, the buildings were more or less central to it. Ideal, in as much as no field is too far from the house.

That evening we held a council of war. Joyce sat pen at the ready to calculate our financial position. The very best deals rarely come along at the most convenient time. It is this syndrome that sets apart those who want it badly enough from those who merely think they do. I am definitely of the former group.

Our house in Celestine Road was now worth £3,200. After agent's fees and paying off the mortgage we would realise £1,800. The six-acre field at Tanhouse lane would fetch £1,800. Again there would be solicitors fees and so on, so we could expect to be left with £1,600 from the sale. I calculated that I would need to raise £4,000 the amount being one third of the purchase price of Shortwood Farm. We were £600 short. 'We will have to sell the pony trailer,' I announced. Joyce agreed. It would be the end of the show season anyway, and with all the extra work at the farm there wouldn't be any time to take ponies anywhere. In fact we sold everything we felt we could do without. We could not risk taking any money out of the television business; it needed its capital to survive. It was an expensive business stocking a retail television shop. £1,000 went practically nowhere. Our target was in sight. We had potential buyers for both the field and the house.

Armed with my latest accounts, and proposals for the purchase of Shortwood Farm, I made an appointment to see Brian Palmer at Lloyds Bank. I thought, 'This time I have all the answers.' The business is in its fifth year, and profits have increased substantially. The TV trade was booming, and the future looked bright. 'Hello Jim, what can I do for you?' Brian asked in his usually friendly manner. I outlined the proposal, backing it up with facts and figures. I would put one-third in cash, and would ask to borrow the remaining two thirds from the Bank. This proposal was classic lending. Or so I thought. 'No no, can't consider it.' And shaking his head still further, the bank manager gasped, 'Oh no.' Instead of accepting that he knew best, as I had done once before, I asked 'Why not?' To my amazement he just waffled, and could not give me one good reason why he was rejecting my proposal. I snatched up my paperwork and walked out of the bank.

A COCKNEY KID IN GREEN WELLIES

Looking across the precinct, I could see the recently opened branch of Barclays Bank on the corner of North Parade. Someone had said the manager was a forward-thinking man. His name was Mr Jenkins. I walked across to Barclays and strode up to the counter. A smart and extremely pleasant man greeted me. 'Come in,' he said beckoning towards his office door. We sat down, and I relayed to him my encounter with Palmer at Lloyds. Having studied my proposals and accounts, Mr Jenkins, with head shaking slowly, said, 'I fail to see anything wrong at all with this. I should have thought any bank would be interested in this.' He went on to say that he had just been promoted to manager and this was his first branch, a brand new one at that. Whilst it was expected that one day it would be quite big, given that the area was expanding so rapidly, for the time being it came under Chipping Sodbury branch, and the jurisdiction of its manager Brian Harding. With enthusiasm Mr Jenkins said, 'I will phone Brian. He'll love this.' I fixed an appointment for the following day and met Brian Harding. 'Jim come in and sit down,' he said all in one breath. 'Lloyds are mad turning this down it's a classic banking deal.' 'That's what I thought,' I replied with some relief.' 'As far as I am concerned we'll do it. I will have to write it up, and get it ratified by head office, but that's a formality. They won't turn this down.' He assured me.

I was due to leave for Germany the next day, so didn't have much time to reflect on the last few hectic days. It would mean transferring my business and private accounts to Barclays, which I organised with 'Please call me David,' Jenkins. I thought of cancelling my trip to Germany, but on the other hand thought it might give me time to relax, and consider of the extra responsibilities I was about to embrace.

Looking back on the White Cliffs of Dover, from the stern of the Dover-to-Ostende ferry, I reflected on how the troops returning after so many years of war must have felt, coming home to these wonderful shores. Reg Bain had just bought a new Ford Capri motor car. He would drive us down the Rhine and show us some sights. Us, meaning Billy Parker and me. This could get interesting. Reg, an ex-Sergeant Major in the Royal Army Medical Corps, and Parker and Ruston two ex-squaddies. Reg had had a distinguished career in the Army, in which he served for 22 years. It was whilst serving in Germany just after the war that he met and married his wife Ottie. (I'm sure it's short for something, but I don't know what.) We motored down through Germany, stopping at the Mohne Dam, the scene of the famous Dambusters raid. Looking over into a lake, which in fact was once a valley with a village community living there, one feels the total absurdity of war. You are friends, then you fall out. For a period of time you rain terror down upon each other, until one party gains the upper hand by asserting far more force than the other. Then you become friends again.

We stayed in a little guesthouse, close by the dam. I was keen to see the dam at night and walk over the road between the towers, stand in the middle, and try to imagine what must have gone through the minds of the crew in the approaching Lancasters, as under heavy fire they levelled out on their bombing run. Also to imagine the terror in the minds of the helpless civilians on the ground, who witnessed the bouncing bomb strike and breach of the dam, flooding the valley below, drowning thousands of people. Many of them women and children like us in the East End of London. The weak and meek suffer most in war. It was a moving experience for me. Time had lessened the hatred I had for the Germans. Reg gave us a good history lesson on what happened in Germany during the war, the suffering unimaginable. The fire storm in Dresden, where people caught fire even though they were nowhere near any flames. With temperature at 1,000 degrees centigrade they simply combusted. House bricks exploded. There was so little of Dresden left that after the war when re-building was planned, it made more sense to ignore the original demography, and build it in a different place. Modern-day maps of Dresden are fundamentally different when compared to those of the pre-war era.

Reg had a pal, Len Harvey, still serving in the Army, and stationed at Munster. He took us over to see Len and his wife Sylvia. Len was a Warrant Officer in the Royal Corps of Transport, previously called RASC. Their drivers had driven our DUKWs in 1956. We were made very welcome in the Sergeant's Mess and couldn't believe the low price of drinks, subsidised of course. Everyone was in a party mood, and the ladies were dancing the Schloss, a form of line dance that later became very popular in the UK. I liked Len and his vivacious wife instantly; they seemed great fun. Len said he was looking forward to de-mob, now just two years away. He had already served 20. We all went for a meal, after which Len and Sylvia invited us back to their married quarter. It transpired that Sylvia's parents lived in Yate, and quite coincidentally happened to be customers of mine. Just as we were leaving, a blond-haired teenager rushed in said, 'Hello,' and rushed out again. 'That was our son Gerald,' said Len 'Always in a hurry.' He reminded me a little of myself at that age. I said if I could be of any help to them when they returned to civilian life, to give me a call. Len said they had in mind running a fast-food business of some kind. He had recently attended a catering course with a view to a change of direction once back in Civvy Street.

A COCKNEY KID IN GREEN WELLIES

We visited Dortmund and called to see Ottie's grandmother, who later came to live, and die, with Ottie and Reg in England. She was a sweet old lady, and reminded me of my Granny Hare. Reg told the story how during the war, Ottie, then just 16 years of age and working as a nurse in a hospital five miles away from where she lived with her mother, had walked home carrying a packet of wall paper paste with her. They mixed the paste with water, heated it, and with a little black bread, ate it. It was all the food they had. I had long harboured anti-Germanic feelings, but it was impossible to feel any animosity towards this fragile little lady. Reg, speaking fluent German translated for us. It was good to listen to her war. When we left she squeezed my hand saying. 'Jimmy, you're a nice boy. I hope you will come again.' At least that's what Reg said she had said!

We had a marvellous 10 days. We drove up one side of the Rhine, down the other, and for good measure took a boat trip up the middle! Consuming vast quantities of wine as we did so. Billy kept us entertained with jokes the whole way. My ribs were aching with so much mirth, but I do have one regret. Just before we started out on our trip, I bought a brand new pair of Chelsea boots. I left them in the guesthouse on the Mohnsee. Whenever I hear the Song 'I left my heart in San Fransisco' I think of my Chelsea boots!

Despite having had a marvellous time, I was glad to be home. We spent the weekend discussing Shortwood Farm. 'Have you heard from the Bank?' I asked Joyce. 'No, not a word from either Bank.' I thought this strange and became concerned. Monday morning came around and I drove to work as normal. I unlocked the back door of the shop and could see a figure standing by the shop front as if waiting for us to open. Taking a better look I could now see it was Brian Palmer, so I let him in. Before I could get a word in he burst out, 'I didn't turn your proposal for a loan down. I merely indicated it would have to be considered.' This made me angry. 'Are you trying to tell me that I misunderstood you saying NO, out of the question!' I responded. 'You turned down a perfectly good proposition I put to you once before. I was not going to take it lying down twice.' 'This morning I have received a letter asking me to transfer all your accounts to Barclays,' he stuttered. 'They say they have your authority to do so. I tried to contact you but you have been away,' he said. 'Went on holiday,' I replied. 'Needed a break.' Poor Brian didn't know what to say next. I later found out I was one of his best accounts.

We had agreed to take possession of Shortwood Farm on 29 September 1970. It was Charlie Burgess's choice and typically traditional. Michaelmas Day. The local agricultural auctioneers had arranged a farm sale for Charlie. There were quite a number of items we would liked to have bought, especially the tractor, but we could not afford any of them. We intended to go to the sale, but wouldn't be tempted to bid.

As David Jenkins and Brian Harding were having lunch together, they talked of me and Shortwood Farm. 'What's Jim's farm like then David?' inquired Brian. 'Can't say. Haven't seen it yet. I thought you had Brian?' David replied. The two bank managers came to realise that neither of them had actually seen the property they had agreed to loan the money against, and I was about to take possession. 'Good god,' said Brian 'It might be a shed in a field.' In fairness they hardly knew me. They rushed round to the shop. 'Jim, can we see Shortwood Farm,' they asked. 'Of course you can,' I confirmed, and arranged it. The two intrepid managers were more than suitably impressed with my purchase and the bank's equity in it. We became firm friends.

Joyce and I went to Charlie Burgess's farm sale the week before we were to take possession. The machinery and implements were laid out in rows on the 15-acre field that is situated to the left of the approach road to Shortwood Farm. Each piece of equipment had a large label attached with a lot number on. Everything necessary was there to run a small farm. Tractor, roller, mower, trailer, plough, harrows and any amount of hand tools. 'Let's start with the cattle then,' said the auctioneer standing on his rostrum in the covered yard. 'What'll you bid me? Who'll put 'im in? It's not where we start, its where we finish up as counts.' His sharp voice echoed around the high walled barn, as systematically, and without emotion, he knocked Charlie's prized cattle down to the highest bidder. This lovingly cared for herd of Friesian dairy cows made top prices, no more than was deserved. After the cattle came the implements. I had to keep my hands in my pockets. The fields would need trimming soon and harrowing. How would I do that without machinery?

Once everything had been sold and the buyers and lookers – there are always plenty of those, dispersed, Charlie asked me inside for a cup of tea. He looked sad, but Mrs Burgess had a smile on her face. She knew there would be no more winter for her at Shortwood. We made arrangements for the hand-over to take place on the 29th. As I was leaving, I reminded Charlie to leave everything he didn't want, junk and all, behind. I would deal with it. 'I don't think I would have ever got around to selling, if you hadn't made it so easy for me,' Charlie said as he shook my hand.

On the 29th, Joyce and I arrived just in time to see the Burgesses leave. We stood in the middle of the yard waving until the couple had disappeared from view. For a while we were silent, each with our own private thoughts. I had the farm I had dreamed of, and our horses would be here at any moment. Could this be real? The Sunday morning rides at Dyer's in Nailsea seemed such a long time ago. I was now in my 34th year. 'Not bad,' I thought, 'Not bad!' And Joyce, a farmer's wife, and not a farm worker's daughter living in a tied cottage. For her, too, this was beyond anything she had ever dreamed of.

Our peace was shattered by the clatter of the lowering of the ramp on Roger Jones's cattle truck. 'Where d'you want these 'osses then Jim,' 'Put them in the covered yard Rog,' I replied. That would do as a temporary measure. The furniture van arrived, and soon there was chaos. Joyce, now heavily pregnant, and doing more than she should; Jane and Karen, who had come to help, but seemed more interested in exploring than being useful, and me getting agitated with everyone, what's new!

Somehow we moved in. Joyce, ever the caring mother, set about finding the linen to make up beds. It was an exhausted family that crashed out that night. Our first morning dawned; the early sun shone through the window. I strolled around the cowsheds and barn. No horses. Where were the horses? I soon found out. Walking towards me from across the Homefield Joyce called out, 'A fine farmer you'll make. What time of day do you call this?' She had been up for hours, put the horses out, and walked the fields to check all was well with our land. A country girl born and bred, she got into a routine on the first day. Not many days went by, and in all weathers, that she didn't walk the boundary of that farm. Back in the house, Jane and Karen were getting ready for school. Joyce had collected eggs from a few chickens that Charlie left, (another *Charlie* wouldn't be as generous) and set about making breakfast.

The kitchen was a single-storey lean-to, none-too-weather- proof affair, attached to the back of the house. It housed a sink, a Rayburn solid fuel cooker, and not much else. I had 'riddled' this antique, and poked it around in the hope of getting it to function. And although there was a glimmer of a fire, hot, the cooker plate was not. The kids had to make do with cereals before leaving for school. The eggs finally fried at 11.30am, with Joyce feeling guilty as she ate them. I had many battles with this mind-of-its -own stove. 'I was an evacuee you know,' I told it. 'I've handled worse than you.' I swear it was grinning at me. I eventually gave up on it, and replaced it with electric, but it hadn't finished with me yet.

Len Warren had kindly offered to put some in heating. I would purchase the materials and do some labouring, he would do the plumbing. He also convinced me it was time for the Rayburn to go. Len had dismantled the relic, and with me on one end of the main body of the thing, we were struggling through the back door when I stepped on a nail that was protruding through a plank someone had left on the ground outside. The nail went straight through my foot. With me lying prostrate on the floor, Len had to prise the plank off the sole of my shoe. I felt decidedly sick and limped around for a week. The bloody cooker had won. I took a hammer to it, and smashed its cast iron body to pieces. Ha! Only to find sometime later that these old antique cookers are just that. Antique – and valuable! Rayburn Two – Ruston Nil.

I took the kids to school each morning. Jane was now at Chipping Sodbury Grammar, which was in transition to a comprehensive. She looked so lovely in her uniform, complete with a black beret that had a red tassel fixed to the crown. Karen was still at St Mary's. After dropping the kids off I went to the shop, returning to the farm for lunch. Joyce collected Jane and Karen from school in the afternoons, with me getting home as early as possible once the shop had closed. And so we got into a routine. There was so much to do, and the nights were drawing in. Luckily the weather was beautiful and we prayed it would remain so, at least for a few weeks.

Mr James, a farmer who had been my neighbour at Tanhouse Lane, rang ask if I had any grass keep to sell. We couldn't possibly use all 56 acres in the immediate future, so I let him have 40 acres. He would take off the hay the following June, and then graze cattle on it until September. This suited me fine, and the cheque for £300, paid in advance, came in very handy. Mrs James ran a gymkhana on her farm for a few years. I fixed up the PA system and did the announcing for her. The Jameses are good farmers, and exceptionally nice people.

The phone rang. It was my sister Maud. 'Jimmy, I am in a police station near London Bridge, and I want you to come right away.' I thought, 'I need this now, don't I?' 'Why Maud, what's the panic?' I asked 'It's my daughter June. She was about to throw herself off London Bridge when a policeman spotted her and managed to talk her out of it. Now she will only talk to you.' How could I refuse? Joyce shook her head in dismay as I jumped into my car and shot off up the lane.

I arrived at the police station and with my sister Maud pacing around saying, 'What is she doing with her life?', I tried to console my niece. 'I'll be alright once I am out of here, and with you Jimmy,' June confided. The policeman raised his eyebrows, and with an expression of 'There's another one' on his face, opened the door for June and me to pass into the night air. 'You take her Jimmy. I just don't understand her anymore,' my sister said as we drove away. Maud had been less than pleased with June's marriage to Brian, and now she had a granddaughter she was not exactly enamoured of. One half of Maud was pleased that June had left Brian, whilst the other half was fed up because her daughter wouldn't conform to her mother's principals. Or should I say prejudices?

We hardly spoke on the journey back. I knew my niece would tell me everything, but in her own time. She also knew that neither Joyce nor I would question her. Back at Shortwood Farm, Joyce had got the spare room ready for June and had left us some supper. We sat across the table just looking at each other. Half of me wanted to smack her around the ear; the other half had promised never to let her down. I couldn't fail her now. June was still in bed when I left for work the next morning. Joyce let her sleep on. When she did finally surface, it was lunchtime, and I was home. Reassuringly, I told June that we expected nothing of her. She could help with the horses, or just laze around the house, it was up to her.

June was 24 years old. I can see her now, as if it were yesterday, wheeling the muck barrow up the lane to the manure heap alongside the old galvanised Nissen Hut. After a few days she described the chain of events leading up to her standing on London Bridge, intent on jumping off. She and Brian had a child, a daughter, Claire, after which they had separated. Claire was currently living with her grandma. June went to London to find work. There she fell in love with a Greek musician named Costas, who together with fellow countrymen was touring with a band. Greek Taverna-style bands featuring a Bouzouki were very fashionable in the 70s. Because of the problem with work permits, the band had to return to Greece. June had made up her mind to follow Costas, and was working like crazy to earn the fare money.

A girl June was working with told her of some slimming pills she was using that had a side effect of keeping her awake. She seemed to have plenty of energy and needed very little sleep. June, wanting to lose a little weight (she always felt chubby anyway), thought she would try some. A prescription was needed so she went to see the doctor recommended by the friend. For a fee, he duly supplied the 'slimming' pills. June was now able to work double shifts. Without realising it, the pills were affecting her mental health. And when Costas left with the band for home, she flipped. She hadn't saved enough for the fare, and thinking life wasn't worth living, decided to throw herself in the Thames.

It later transpired that the 'slimming' pills were, in fact, amphetamines, now more commonly known as 'speed'. June had no idea. The result could have led to tragedy. A few years later, after investigation, the doctor who had prescribed them was struck off.

June stayed with us for a month or so. I told her if she was still determined to go to Greece, when she thought the time right, I would give her the fare. She worked hard on the farm during the day, and spent the evenings studying Greek. Eventually Joyce and I drove her to Heathrow, where she took off for Athens, and Costas. What would become of her?

It was dark as I drove down the lane to the farm. The lights were flickering in the stable yard and it looked so welcoming. I could hear the sound of a hammer on metal, and as I got closer the chink, chink, got louder. I got out of the car and detected that the noise was coming from the long cowshed and to my alarm saw my heavily pregnant wife swinging a sledgehammer in an attempt to knock the metal cow ties from the concrete floor. 'Joyce, don't do that love, you could have the baby here and now,' said I in panic. She stopped banging, and with one hand pressing on the small of her back, whilst the other held on to the metal tie she was wrestling with, she straightened herself up, and looking the very picture of health explained 'Someone has to do it, and you don't have time. The horses need to be in at night. Anyway it's not a bad place for a baby to be born. It was good enough for little Jesus, wasn't it?' There was no arguing with her. She carried on swinging the hammer, until she had removed all the ties, about 10 of them. In a few days, with the help of Brian Gilborson, we had converted the cowshed into four stables.

Brian, was a builder during the day, but at night he played piano in a trio called The Same Three later becoming much better known as Chantilly Lace. At one time their bass player was Pete Budd, who later came to fame as the leader of The Wurzels who had a number one hit with 'Combine Harvester'. Adge Cutler founded the Wurzels, but was tragically killed in his MG sports car on the way home from a gig one night. Adge came from Nailsea. I knew him well. His father Jack owned a cycle shop in the village. Reg Chant played accordion in the original line up, and told me he was the only member of the band who could read music. I hadn't realised it at the time, but the monster that is showbiz, was spreading its tentacles and stinging me every once in a while.

It was Sunday and everything was normal. Joyce's sister Heather was helping the kids with the ponies, and I was sweeping the yard. Joyce was in the house. Suddenly the porch door opened, and Joyce, in a quiet controlled voice, called to me, 'Jim, can you ring for an ambulance?' I dropped the brush and ran to her. 'Is it the baby?' I stupidly inquired.

'Well what do you think it is?' she replied. I must be the most hopeless husband anyone could be unlucky enough to get lumbered with. I know nothing of housekeeping or children, let alone babies. But I am good in emergencies. Resourceful, I stay calm. I made the phone call. Joyce had everything else organised. Heather went with Joyce in the ambulance whilst I stayed with Jane and Karen, promising to follow later. Our new baby daughter was born on 22 November 1970.

'You know I'm not much good looking after kids, so I have taken them to Ann and Len Warrens,' I told Joyce when visiting her and the baby for the first time. Ann had kindly agreed to look after our children for a few days. Joyce offered Jane and Karen three names from which to choose for their little sister: Victoria, Charlotte or Rachel. They chose Rachel, to which Joyce and I added Anne, after Ann Warren, as a token of our regard for a true friend. When Len and Ann had their first child, a girl they named Joanne, Joyce and I were delighted to be her Godparents. A beautiful girl she is too.

The winter set in. Gone was the wonderful mass of colour, as leaves on the many different varieties of trees in both Lady and Lower Woods, having gone through gold to brown, now lay rotting on the ground returning the goodness to the earth, thereby funding nature's cycle. The woods, standing stark against a grey winter sky, took on a new role. They would be hunting in them soon. '*Charlie*' had visited his vixen. Young cubs would be getting adventurous.

A Land Rover was being driven across our 15-acre field. I waited in anticipation as it approached ready to berate whoever it was who had the cheek to drive across MY land. The vehicle pulled up a few yards in front of me, and out stepped a weather-beaten gentleman, who, having seen Joyce approaching, immediately doffed his cap. With a huge smile on his face he said, 'Hello, I'm Major Gundry, joint Master of the Duke of Beaufort's Hunt. I've come to see if I can be of any help, and to ask if our hounds will still be welcome across your land?'

I had heard of the Major. He looked like a character from the pages of *Punch*. His face by cheek and jowl resembling that of a bloodhound, as keen and interested too. 'Well Major, I have been invited by the Duke to hunt, but as yet, don't have a horse.' 'Splendid, splendid. You will have to come out at least twice a week, nothing less d'you hear,' he commanded. I could see that he was sincere. Then came the sting. 'If you have time, perhaps you could cut back some of the brambles that are growing across the hunting gates in Lady Wood. They are a hindrance to the huntsman.' I had made my intention clear regarding the hunt. He was now gently informing me of my responsibility. The Major was an absolute past master at PR. He could calm, and persuade, the most irate of landowners to consider his point of view. Even those not akin to the sport of fox hunting. The hunting fraternity could certainly do with him as their spokesman now.

The ponies were in by night and, weather permitting turned out during the hours of daylight. The continuous rain was making everything so muddy, especially gateways, where in places a wellington boot could get so bogged in that it often got left behind. A muddy foot followed! Joyce continued to muck out stables and brush both ponies and yard, whilst dragging a pram with Rachel in behind her. This kid really did grow up with horses.

Joyce's family came for Boxing Day, and her brothers Mike and Chris brought their guns. After lunch the boys and I went across the fields rough shooting, bagging a number of wood pigeons in the process. Michael, to his delight, shot a woodcock, quite rare. If you ever shot a brace, you became a member of an exclusive group with the same distinction. (Caroline Beaufort's mother, Mrs Fielding, loved a woodcock for her lunch) My father-in-law, whom had worked the greater part of his life on a farm, pointed out a few things that needed doing, but understood that machinery was needed to accomplish the tasks. I told him that anything that couldn't be done with either a shovel, fork, rake, shears, or hammer, would have to wait. Those were the only 'implements' we had right now.

Fred Tuck came to ask if I was interested in a three year old 13.2hh bay mare. She was called Pippa Dee. He had no use for her at the time and was also short of somewhere to keep her. 'I'm not asking a lot for the mare. I thought she might come on for one of your girls', he said. Joyce was in favour, so I bought her. I think I paid £80 for her. A week passed and Joyce said, 'Jim come and look at Pippa.' I went out into the yard, where the mare was tied to the rails. I looked but I didn't see anything untoward. My wife is amazing with animals of any kind. She has the eye and instinct to see that which others miss. 'Can't you see she's in foal?' she asked. Truthfully, no I couldn't. I also thought that Fred surely would have noticed. He grew up with horses and his family are all very knowledgeable. Fred would have known if the mare was carrying a foal, and asked me for more for her. I shook my head and went off to work.

It was 15 February 1971 – the day the nation was to go decimal. As I got up, my mind was on the changes we would have to make at the shop. All price tickets would have to be exchanged for new ones, showing the price in decimal. The old 240 pence to the pound had been replaced by 100 new pence. The government had, quite skilfully, relieved us all of 140 pence for our pound without a murmur! I had given the task of changeover to Jeff Badman. Jeff was my shop floor salesman. He had previously worked in the Yate branch of Curry's until I walked in to their shop one day and offered him a job. I had observed him from a distance, and liked what I saw. He had a quiet manner and his product knowledge was excellent. They call it head-hunting nowadays. Like Telesales, nothing new about that either. We were doing it in 1970. Using a commercial directory, we targeted business people, offering free home demonstrations of colour TV. Very successful it was too.

As I got to the bottom of the stairs, Joyce was walking in through the front door. 'Come with me,' she beckoned. Bleary eyed – I'm never good first thing – I followed her across the yard. I looked over the door into the stable and standing beside his mother was a lovely grey colt foal. 'Now do you believe me? You men know nothing of females,' said my wife waving her hand in a dismissive way as she walked back in the house. She was right of course. Despite a mother and six sisters, a wife and three daughters, I still knew sod all about the opposite sex.

I got in touch with Fred Tuck. He was flabbergasted, and not a little embarrassed, saying; 'Good luck to you Jim, two for the price of one.' In the future we would have many more deals, and things would even out. We thought we should call the foal Decimal something or other, but ended up calling him Blue Boy. We would certainly never forget his birthday!

I bought Joyce a 14hh grey part bred Arab filly from Audrey Petty, known affectionately to all as Aunt P. Audrey has a lovely sense of humour, and erupts into raucous laughter at anything remotely funny, whilst slapping her hands in unison on her Harris Tweed skirt. Joyce's filly was named Paradise and was by Aunt P's Anglo Arab stallion Moulton Khalifa. A 15hh grey, with the lovely kind temperament one comes to expect from Arab horses.

We were looking for a young colt we could eventually stand at stud. Aunt P told us of a three-year old 14.1hh bright chestnut colt she had bred, and was now for sale. His current owner, Mrs Bailey, hoped someone would want him for breeding. His name was Carnaby Street. We arranged to see him and were in no way disappointed. He certainly lived up to his name. Bright eyed with a 'Look at me' air about him. We paid £200 for Carnaby, and took him home.

We named our stud Maple, after the area in which we lived. Mapleridge. From now on the names of all foals born at our farm would be prefixed by Maple. Most of the horses we bred we registered. Some of their names live on in the pedigrees of those who came after.

I bought a 14.2hh chestnut mare from a lady name Scott. The mare was Ataka Kimari and she had a foal at foot by the thoroughbred stallion My Lord. The Scotts now lived in Devon, but had lived for many years in South Africa at the foot of the Ataka Mountains. Kimari was an orange chestnut, not red as in 'a chestnut mare, is one to beware'. Red chestnut mares have a reputation of having a bad temper. Sadly this is generally true. Of course there are exceptions. I thought she would make an ideal first 'wife' for Carnaby, him being a complete novice. Hopefully Kimy would stand quietly for him. Mares usually come into season 10 days after foaling, and then every three weeks through spring to early summer. It is quite easy to tell if a mare is in season. They lift their tail and 'flash' the vagina showing pink with liquid oozing from it. Some will still come into season up to late autumn. It is not unknown for mares to conceive in winter. The gestation period for a mare is 11 months. Like people, though, they are all different, with many exceptions to all rules. One has to learn by experience.

Before taking the mare to the stallion the general practice is to 'try' them. This involves taking the mare you want to cover to a trying gate. This is a stout door on which one side is the stallion; you present the mare on the other side of the door. The stallion will put his head over and explore the hindquarters of the mare. If she is ready, she will 'flash' like mad. If not, she will often kick seven bells out of the door. In the big studs 'teasers' are used. These are usually young stallions of no great consequence that are only going to have a couple of mares themselves, and so are used for the purpose of teasing. When a top stallion is fully booked, it would be unwise to make him tease as well. The stress would be too great. I think all men can identify with the teaser. Poor sod!

So having 'tried' Kimari, and got everything as ready as I knew how, it was still with apprehension, and not a few nerves jangling, that I led Carnaby Street from his box, and walked him down to the covered yard where Kimari was waiting. Joyce had fixed a twitch on Kimy's nose, in case she had a mind to kick. A twitch is a rather necessary, although barbaric, piece of kit. It consists of a stout stick about 3 feet long through which a hole is bored at one end. A cord is passed through the hole to form a loop, which is then tied off. The loop is passed over the horse's nose, and the stick twisted round and round causing the loop to get smaller and smaller, until it has a firm grip on the flesh. It is also as well to have a bridle on the mare, and a bit in her mouth.

I led Carnaby into the yard, stopping him just behind Kimy. She lifted her tail and flashed. He was already drawn. Gently lifting his forelegs over her back, whilst moving his back feet forward he closed on her, pushing her forward. Joyce leaned against Kimy's chest to help her balance. Concerned for Joyce, I thought, 'It's a bloody sight more dangerous down that end than it is back here.' Carnaby lay for a moment on Kimy's back, and then slid off the side. With a glazed look in his eyes (like pissholes in the snow), he stood perfectly still. I led him back to his box, removed his bridle, and patted him on the neck. It had been too easy. Surely there was more to it? There was much more. You'll see!

Joyce's brothers had set up a clay trap in the bottom field adjacent to Lady Wood. This field had quite a slope, and Mike (Joyce's brother) thought it ideally suitable for clay shooting. He said if I organised a shoot, he would act as safety officer, the most important job on the day. No matter how casual and informal the day was to be, safety was paramount. And Mike was very professional. He had followed me into the television trade as an engineer, but his heart was in the countryside. His one ambition was to be a gamekeeper. I'm pleased to say it was fulfilled. I invited a few friends including, Billy Parker, Mike Fuller and Roger Bennett.

Roger, never does anything by half. He arrived in the yard and climbing out of his brand new Mercedes saloon, hailed, 'Morning all.' Standing by his limousine, dressed in a tweed shooting jacket and wearing buckskin britches topped off with knee high boots, he looked every bit a model for Harry Hall. From the boot of his car he drew a gun. No ordinary gun of course, nothing less than a precision-made double-barrelled side-by-side, from the Royal gun maker Purdie. With a cigar clenched between his teeth and a bandoleer that held his cartridges slung over his shoulder, he sauntered through the yard. He looked a true aristocrat. As Billy Parker said, 'You don't have to be one to act like one!'

The shoot was going well. Most of us had had a turn. It was now time for Roger to show us. Mike placed him at the bottom of the slope, with his back toward the wood. Roger said he was ready, then shouted 'Pull'. The clay released and was over Roger's head, before he could get his gun up. Mike had a word. Roger declared readiness, 'Pull'. This time he got his gun up in time, but when following through, stepped back against a strand of wire Mr James had erected to keep his cows from straying in to the wood, overbalanced, and disappeared down the bank into the ditch. He emerged with bits of bramble stuck to his Harris tweed, mud on his shiny boots and suffering a complete sense of humour failure. He threw the valuable Purdie to the ground, saying. 'I'd be better off fishing!' The whole shooting party was in hysterics.

Later I heard that he had traded the shooting gear for fishing tackle. I would loved to have seen him on the water!

I was walking in Chipping Sodbury High Street near where the present-day gallery stands. A man was running toward me, he looked familiar. It was Brian Palmer, my erstwhile ex-Lloyds bank manager. As he got level, pausing, he shouted, 'Have you heard? We have just sold a 66-acre farm at Yate Rocks for £29,000! He barely got to the end of the sentence when his expression of excitement turned to one of anxiety. He had just realised who he was addressing. I could barely wait to respond 'That makes my farm look bloody cheap, doesn't it Brian? He had no answer, and mustering a weak smile, replied, 'You must be pleased?' 'No thanks to you though'. I countered, with vitriol. With a spring in my step I continued on down the high street, passing The Bell Inn as I walked. Shortwood Farm must now be worth at least £25,000. It had doubled in price in one year.

The television business was going at a cracking pace. The UK manufacturers, aware of the threat from Japan, were going all out to ensure their market share. But they still had problems with production and more importantly, reliability. A television set made in the UK was breaking down at an average of four times during the first year, whereas a set made by the Japanese had a failure rate of less than a half of 1 per cent during the same period. Whilst parts were guaranteed for one year, the retailer had to supply labour free. I experienced UK-made TVs breaking down as many as 12 times in one year. Expensive, and embarrassing. About 25 per cent were failing whilst on display in our showroom. This situation improved with time, but not before the Japanese had a foothold so strong they would eventually dominate the market. As they did with the motorcycle industry. We can have no complaints. In the early 70s, in a state of apathy we just stood around watched them do it.

Christmas approached and I was rather hoping that as much as I had loved every minute of the past year, perhaps it could slip quietly into history without too many more events or surprises. Frankly, I was knackered! Connie Vacher, who was still working at the takeaway next door to my shop, said that the Duke of Beaufort's stable manager, Brian Higham, was interested in buying a colour TV. There started a friendship that endures to this day. Brian and his wife Audrey are originally from Yorkshire. Brian had first come to Badminton during his National service in the RAF. He was a driver and often stopped at Badminton to visit his uncle, Bert. Bert Pateman was kennel huntsman to the Duke of Beaufort at that time. Brian started work at Badminton in 1959 as second horseman to the Duke. His duties were as groom and to ride out with the second horse for the Duke on a hunting day. On a full hunting day the Master of Hounds, huntsman and whippers in (usually two men 1st and 2nd whose task it is to assist the huntsman with hound control) would all require two horses. They would cover far more ground than the field (followers). It was nice to have a fresh horse for the second half of the day if you could afford it! Many could, but few did.

Whilst I was installing a colour TV for Brian at Badminton he said, 'You should hunt with us. Have you thought about it?' 'Yes I have,' I replied. 'In fact I have an invitation to hunt from the Duke himself. 'Well then, when are you starting?' asked Brian. 'Well I don't have a horse suitable at the moment, but I would like to find one,' I replied. 'Now then, I might just have the very horse for you, not too big, about 15.3hh, a real tough little sort. He was bred at a place called Saxmundham. We call him Sax, Brian informed.

The stables at Badminton are really something to see. The present buildings are formed in a square around a gravelled yard. They have been there since 1878. The 9th Duke sold his commission in the Blues to raise the funds in order to modernise those that existed previously. No wonder officers of the armed forces in those days were considered élitist, if having money could buy membership to what must have been an exclusive 'club'. In today's forces, having the 'right background' is still a huge advantage, if one aspires to get to the top. Merit alone is rarely enough.

The long buildings are entered by a door at each end, and one can walk down the corridor, which runs the entire length of the buildings, passing row upon row of loose boxes, each measuring no less than 12 feet by 10 feet, without walking one foot without cover. Ceilings are high; so air circulation is good. Sliding doors made of oak give access to each box. In one corner of the yard the Stable manager's office is situated, through which access is gained to the magnificent tack room. Saddles and bridles from days of yore adorn the walls. Military, sidesaddle and driving harness are all there. The room is heated by large iron water pipes, running at waist height along each wall. Extremely useful for drying wet saddles as they come off the horses on hunting days. Polished wooden racks are provided on which to hang the tack. The smell of saddle soap and leather lingers in the air. Light pours in through a Victorian sash window, under which stands a table bearing the scars from generations of use. As old as the room itself, and creating a timeless atmosphere. I doubt there is a better tack room in all England. Perhaps the one at the Royal Mews? I don't know.

'Here he is. This is Sax. Brian had slid back the door of one of the boxes, and there, standing bright eyed and ears forward, was this lovely bay hunter. I didn't need a second look. 'Do you want to try him?' asked Brian. 'I'm not really dressed for it,' I answered. I was in a suit, and on my feet were smart black leather shoes. Brian urged. 'You'll be alright. Just trot him around the yard, get the feel, see if you like him,' I didn't want to appear whimpish. Brian summoned one of the girl grooms to put a saddle and bridle on Sax, and lead him into the yard. I jumped on and trotted him round. He felt great under me, and I had no hesitation in telling Brian so and that he would suit me. There were many more pressing purchases needed for the farm than a hunter. But with horses, if they feel right, they usually are. Try looking for one that suits you. It can take months, even a year.

Back at Brian's house we discussed price. The television I had just sold him, a Sony 18 inch, was £350. He wanted £500 for Sax. I gave him back the £350, and would give him the balance when I collected the horse. It was Christmas week and Brain suggested I accompany him to the Boxing Day Meet at Worcester Lodge. I wouldn't get the chance to ride Sax before, so was apprehensive to say the least about taking him hunting for the first time. I hadn't followed hounds since I was a teenager on the Mendips. But it didn't look like I had too many options. The Duke had invited me, and now his stud groom had found me what certainly looked to be a super horse. 'See you Boxing Day then Brian,' I said gingerly as I left. 'You'll be alright,' assured Brian. See that 'oss, whoa, that 'oss, can he jump. And ditches too, he'll make nothing of 'em. Come from the Cambridgeshire see, plenty of ditches there, big 'edges too.' I thought, bloody hell, what do they go like, the Beaufort I mean. I would find out on Boxing Day!

Brian had kept Sax at the stables. On Boxing Day, I could ride out from there. I already owned britches, boots and a hat, but not a hunt coat. I immediately thought of Bert Legg. Bert talked of good hunting days, but I doubt his black coat had seen many of them! He was happy to sell me his coat. But not until I had listened to the story surrounding it! 'It's alright Bert, you don't have to *sell* it to me!' I assured. I struggled with the hunting tie, more commonly called a stock, a term abhorred by the Duke of Beaufort. Winding it twice around the neck it is tied in a double knot at the throat, a tiepin is fixed, and the ends are tucked in your waistcoat. I looked the part, but could I live up to it? A hive of activity greeted me as I arrived at stables at 10am in good time for the 11 o'clock Meet at Worcester Lodge. Brian was busy organising everything. He had just got hunt horses away, and was preparing to mount the Duke and Duchess. Catching my eye, he told me to wait in his office. The Duke rode off and then the Duchess appeared. Climbing on to the mounting block she looked so frail, but none the less elegant. Sidesaddle, she rode off through the archway into the yard behind the big house, and out into the park.

'Right Jim, let' go,' said Brian. I mounted Saxmundham and felt him quiver under me. A feeling I would come to love. Horses seem to know instinctively that they are going hunting. The quiet docile hack that anyone can ride is a completely different kettle of fish in the hunting field. We rode through the yard and out into the park, and we could see the Duchess up ahead. We cantered on past the lake and into the avenue. The Duchess was riding on the right-hand side of the wide grassy avenue that runs for three miles from the north front of Badminton House, to Worcester Lodge. 'Don't overtake the Duchess Jim,' advised Brian. 'It wouldn't be right.' I thought, 'I'll try not to,' but Sax was taking quite a hold. I tucked myself in behind Brian and Sax seemed to settle. On reaching Worcester Lodge the scene was electric. Traditionally, people turn out in force on Boxing Day to see the spectacle. We had to thread our way through to where Huntsman Brian Gupwell had the hounds gathered. As protocol demands, I doffed my hat and said good morning to the Master, The Duke of Beaufort. Had I been female my hat would have remained on my head whilst the Master raised his. That's sex discrimination isn't it?

Members, those who have paid a full fee to hunt for the season, are normally, given time, invited to wear the colours of the Duke's family livery, the coveted blue and buff. That is a royal blue coat with buff-coloured reveres. Farmers are invited to wear the Hunt Button. Not just one of course, a whole set, worn on a black jacket. It was quiet some years before I got mine. Hunt staff – I prefer to talk of them in those terms rather than as servants, although by tradition many people still refer to them as the latter – are dressed as follows. The huntsman and both first and second whippers in wear green coats, white britches, a black hard hat, and black boots with brown tops. The stud groom and those bringing up second horses wear a black coat with plain buttons. I think the latter outdated. It seems to me absurd that the stud groom (the traditional title for the stable manager) is not allowed to wear, at the very least the hunt button. As I write, Brian Higham in his 41st year at Badminton, yet when he rides to hounds he wears nothing of the livery of the famous hunt he represents. Tradition you see.

The joint Masters, the Duke of Beaufort and Major Gundry, wore the blue and buff, as do the hunt officials. To day the Major was wearing a green coat. He was hunting the hounds, as he had done on Mondays and Thursdays for the past few years. The Beaufort hounds hunt four days each week, from early September until April. The bitch pack hunt Wednesdays and Saturdays; whilst a mixed pack hunt Mondays and Thursdays. Brian Gupwell was now hunting the bitches and the Major the mixed pack. The Duke, regarded by all in hunting circles as the greatest huntsman of them all, had given up hunting the hounds himself some years before I started. I was lucky enough to see him hunt the hounds on an occasion when Brian Gupwell was injured. The Duke, now in his 71st year, was still riding to hounds four days a week.

The huntsman took the hounds to draw Swangrove wood, adjacent to Worcester Lodge. The field followed at a distance, where the field master, Mr David Somerset, a cousin of the Duke, kept them in check. Encouraged by the huntsman, hounds cast through the wood. Finding nothing, they re-entered and cast back. The field had ridden from clearing to road, then back along the wide grassy tracks to the field where they had started. I thought, 'This is fun,' and Sax was loving it. Brian smiled and said 'We won't find [a fox] in here, there are too many people about. Charlie's long gone. But we like to buzz around a bit. The spectators love to see the hounds work, and His Grace won't disappoint them. We'll move off soon and find elsewhere.' I thought, this gives me a bit of time to get used to my new horse.

The Major declared Swangrove 'blank' and we moved on. Finding a fox in Bodkin Wood the huntsman blew 'Gone away', and we were off.

'Keep behind me called Brian in his warm Yorkshire brogue.' I will, I will, if can hold this half ton of vibrant muscle. We came to a medium-sized hedge 'How are you for a bit of jumping Jim?' Brian shouted over his shoulder. Before I could answer he was over the hedge and had disappeared from view. Here we go. Sax took off, and with grace and ease landed well into the field, on the lea side. There were horses all around me now; it was like a cavalry charge. A wall came up, and Sax popped over it. I was no more than a passenger. If I could sit tight and steer him I might be OK. My heart was pounding, the excitement akin to first sex. I hope I would enjoy it as much! By the time hounds checked we had travelled quite a distance and jumped a number of obstacles. A few had fallen, so there were loose horses that needed catching, and friends of those on the ground, gathered their mounts. Sax was breathing heavily, almost as heavy as me! We neither of us were hunting fit. We hacked around, moving from one covert to another, and suddenly it was 2pm. Time to bring up the second horses for the Masters and their staff. Brian beckoned to me. 'Had enough for one day Jim?' he asked. Breathless, I answered, 'Yes I have Brian. But it has all gone so quickly. There is not much time to think, is there?' 'You'll get used to it. Then you'll find all the time in the world to study what's happening, and take your own line,' advised my newly found friend.

As we walked back to the stables, I thanked Brian, telling him how pleased I was with the horse he had sold to me. He said I could leave Sax with him for a few days until I could arrange transport to move him to Shortwood Farm. The next time I went hunting the Major introduced me to Tom Smith and Jack Windell, both of whom farmed at Badminton and hunted regularly. Respected tenants of the Duke of Beaufort, and expert horsemen, the pair also judged hunter classes at county shows through the summer. I could not be in better hands. The Major instructed Tom and Jack, 'Look after this man, he's an electronics wizard, and has a farm near Lower Woods.' And with a big grin added 'He might be useful!' The Major had his PR hat on.

Both Jack and Tom had racehorses in training. Tom always rode a thoroughbred, and went as quick as any one I ever saw. Jack was more cautious. In his black coat, hunt button of course, and battered hat with a spare stirrup leather, which lay across his shoulders and hung down the front of him, Tom Smith was the epitome of a hunting farmer. Some time later, Brian told me that Tom had said, 'That man you sold the horse to, from Lower Woods way. Brave fellow, always up the front you know.' Kind words indeed, from 'one as knows', as Brian would say.

Whilst I would never profess to be an expert on either subject, I learned everything I know about horses and stable management, from Rachel Dyer with whom I had come into contact so many years earlier, and Brian Higham. And what I know about hunting comes from Tom Smith and Brian Gupwell.

I bought a TK Bedford lorry chassis from my neighbour Bill Washbourne, and Fred Tuck found a suitable cattle container to fit it. This we converted into a horse box, which, when finished, looked quite smart. Aunt P asked if I would drive up to Norfolk and collect an Arab stallion named El Santo, whom she hoped to stand at her Wotlands Pony stud. It was a long and tiresome journey, and I couldn't seem to get more than 50 miles an hour from the lorry so was averaging about 30. I thought of dad and those long journeys he made to Scotland in the 30s. The heater wasn't working, and it was freezing. Despite the cold I had the window down for most of the return journey.

We eventually got back to Aunt P's and unloaded the horse. He had travelled really well. Anxious to get back to Shortwood Farm I loaded up her own stallion, Moulton Khalifa, whom we had agreed to have for a season to show and perhaps cover the odd mare. I could also ride him. As I drove into our yard Joyce was waiting to help me unload. The round trip was 600 miles, and had felt like 6000! Exhausted, I was pleased to get to bed.

The following day I harrowed the Homefield with the tractor and chain harrows I had bought at a farm sale. I taught Jane to drive it, and she spent hours working the fields. The tractor a Ferguson T30 was painted grey. Jane thought this a bit dull, so one weekend she and her friend Sheila re-painted it red and christened it Ernie. They made a splendid job of it too. Fred Tuck managed to find a grass cutter to fit Ernie, so I was able to coppice the paddocks. When I climbed off the tractor I felt a numbing sensation in one side of my face. For a few minutes I took little notice, and put it down to the effects of recoil from my shotgun. It was cold, and my right eye began to weep. I kept wiping it. I was getting annoyed because the tears were blurring my vision. I put my hand up to my face, but there was very little feeling. I thought of the shotgun theory, then realised I hadn't used a gun for a couple of weeks. What was it? I went into the house and looked in the mirror. The whole right side of my face had dropped. I couldn't drink properly, and my right eye wouldn't blink. Joyce looked at me, and suggested I visit the doctors. 'It will be alright by morning,' I said, unconvincingly.

Next morning I went to see my doctor, also my client, and friend. Dr Carr examined me saying, 'Bell's Palsy, that's what it is.' You will recover, but your face may never be quite the same again.' 'What do you think has caused it?' I asked. I went on to tell him what I had been doing for the past couple of months, and he deduced that long working hours, pressure of business, and leaving the window down in the lorry causing a draught for such a sustained period of time, had all contributed. The candle again. It had been burning at both ends. By now you would have thought I might have noticed! Although after a few weeks it improved greatly, the right side of my face never did fully return to its former self. My right eye does not blink naturally, unless I make it, and my smile is one-sided.

I grew to accept things as they were. Small price to pay for the success I have enjoyed. I think there is a price to pay for us all. If some loss of looks was my price, I would settle for that. (I was a conceited bastard anyway.) Nature dealt the cards, 'Take that! Now let's see how you deal with it.' Instead of hiding away, which was my first thought, I went out singing with a band.

It was 2 May and Joyce's birthday. It dawned with a surprise for us all. 'Jim, Jim, come and look,' my wife called. Looking at the clock I could see it was 7.30am. Pulling on some clothes, and still only half awake, I dragged myself out into the yard. It was a beautiful morning. I peeped over the door of the stable where Kimari was kept. There with the most beautiful chestnut filly foal stood the proud mother. Joyce was gently patting Kimy on the neck whilst Rachel, now 18 months old, was stroking the foal. Joyce was overjoyed. 'What a birthday present darling,' I said. It was a just tribute to my wife, who for so long had struggled alone. Although we now had a groom, Pauline Smith, Joyce still did the Lion's share of work. Jane was next out; like her mother she has always been an early bird. Karen is a different kettle of fish, and won't get up until she has to. Looking at the three girls standing in the stable with their mother, admiring the mare and foal, was a beautiful sight. I felt immensely proud. It was a happy family that eventually went into the farmhouse for breakfast – on the way opening an envelope the postman had just delivered to find that Joyce had won £25 on the premium bonds. Halcyon days.

Pauline Smith, or 'Biff' as she preferred to be called, had been recommended to us by Bert Legg, she was everything Bert had said. Dedicated, honest, hard working, and a natural with horses. We employed her as a groom. This she did, and much more during the years she was with us. I never like to think of people working 'for me'. I would much rather, 'with me'. You could set your clock by Biff. Each morning at 8am sharp, she drove into the farmyard, in her little grey mini van. With her faithful Alsatian dog Shane close at heel, she walked across the yard to check around the horses. Joyce was usually in the yard to greet her, and discuss anything that needed adding to the daily routine.

In summer only the stallion and mares who were about to, or had just, foaled were kept in at night. The rest were in the paddocks. Usually no more than three or four stables needed mucking out. In winter it was much harder with 11 stables and the covered yard to attend to. Joyce often coped with the whole lot on her own. Amazing! The days we were to attend horse shows were hectic. Showing classes at the big shows start at 9am so this means being on the show ground by 8.30am. For instance, Devon County Show is in Exeter. Surrey County is in Guildford. It meant leaving Shortwood Farm at 6.30am, latest. Which in turn means rising at 5am. Biff would stay overnight and next morning, together with Joyce, prepare the horses to be shown. This takes quite a time. Cross bred ponies are plaited; pure bred Arab and Mountain and Moorland are not.

Joyce is brilliant at producing horses for the show ring, and is as adept as anyone at plaiting manes and tails. It is wise to prepare manes in advance of intending plaiting. The hair is 'pulled' until even, never cut. 'Pulling' tails is an art, and the best person I know at this is Brian Higham. He taught Joyce – say no more. One also needs to be bold; whilst most horse don't mind having their hair pulled, some object strongly. Enter the twitch!

On show days I generally made a special effort to get up and help, not at 5am though! Once the horses were loaded, and the kids bundled, with their sleeping bags, into the Luton (the space above the driver's cab, an integral part of the horsebox) with Joyce and Biff sitting next to me, I drove out of the yard. No more memorable time can I recall than the Arab Horse Society Show at Kempton Park. Not wishing to seem unkind, but those in the AHS are a bit on the snobby side. Arab horses are expensive, and most people own them reflect this. We had entered Kimari with her foal Rebecca, by Carnaby, at foot (not yet weaned). The entry for the part bred Arab mare and foal class was huge. Joyce led Kimari, Biff led Rebecca.

I leaned on the rails of the show ring, with Jane and Karen by my side. Rachel, sitting in her pushchair, was close by. We all watched in silence. The judges observed the whole class walk around the ring, then called them into line at random. At this stage one shouldn't take too much notice of the placing. The judges need a much closer look before making any decisions – although some Judges will notice horses they have seen at previous shows, and often pre judge them accordingly. There were two lines of mares and foals, and Kimari and Rebecca had been called in at the bottom of the first line. Joyce and Biff had spent a great deal of time at home with their charges, and it showed. I was so proud of them.

Then suddenly the moment of truth. The Judge asked the competitors to walk once more around the ring. A lovely chestnut mare with a gorgeous colt foal I much admired was called in first. It seemed like forever before the Judge signalled his second choice. He beckoned, but Joyce and Biff kept on walking. The steward had to run after them, 'He means you, Miss,' he said waving his clipboard at Joyce. I couldn't believe my eyes. There they were, standing second at the premier Arab show in the country. The show everyone connected with Arab horses dreams of winning. Even more remarkable for us, it was Carnaby's first foal. Joyce had been dreaming of this moment for four years, since I bought Paradise for her, and her love of Arab horses was born. Little Rachel was so excited. 'Wasn't Kimy and Becky clever daddy,' rightfully praising the animals most. We headed for home, singing all the way. 'Sing, Doh, a deer dad,' the girls chorused. From the *Sound of Music,* the first movie I ever took Jane and Karen to see, this was one of their favourite songs. The film ran at the Odeon cinema in Bristol for almost two years. My old mate Bernard Snowball was assistant manager there during this period.

We had a marvellous summer. Our old friend Keith Logan was visiting from Australia, and helped us out for a few months. We needed some additional stables and had decided to buy four timber built boxes measuring 12 feet by 12 feet. First a concrete base measuring 48 feet by 12 feet had to be laid to accommodate the boxes. 'No worries mate. Dad and I built our own house in Australia on rock, so this is a piece of cake.' Keith prepared the base and I ordered the concrete. A readymix lorry arrived at 9am. I don't know how this happened, but only Joyce and I were there to lay it. A base of 48 feet by 12 feet is an awful lot of concrete. The sun was up, it was hot, and the concrete was beginning to set. We used a hosepipe to keep it wet, and somehow we got it down. We both had blisters on our hands, and poor Joyce was suffering from cement burns on her arms. The things I have asked my wife to do! Where the bloody hell was Logan? 'What me boss? I didn't know you meant today. Never mind, think of the fun you had doing it yourself.' Cheeky sod, but we love you!

The hunting season was in full swing and I was enjoying marvellous days in the saddle. John and Ann Jefferson lived in Bitton in Bristol, where they ran a riding school. Ann, a qualified instructor, was extremely nervous in the saddle, so barely rode. Odd really. John urged Ann to hunt with the Beaufort, thinking it would be good for the riding school. Poor Ann was horrified at the prospect of galloping across fields and jumping hedges, but compromised by joining the Hunt supporters' club. She did quite a lot to raise funds for the Hunt. On one such occasion, Ann and John organised a party at their home in Bristol, a lovely Victorian house with a huge cellar, ideally suited for entertaining.

With the party in full swing, I was greeted on arrival by John Jefferson, who told me that Major Gundry had been asking after me, and in not a particularly friendly tone. I thought little of it, and entered into small talk with John. I was standing in the entrance hall near the foot of the stairs when the unmistakable figure of the Major approached me. Holding a glass of whisky in one hand, and pointing a finger of the other, he said, 'You promised to do something for me and you haven't done it. You said you would introduce clients to my company, and you haven't.' He was referring to a request he had made that I might channel HP agreements through a finance company he had formed,

Dryfield Finance – DRY being the last three letters of his name, and field taken from the name of his home at Shipton Moyne, Clayfield.

Whilst I had shown an interest in his finance facilities, when the paperwork came through it was of the old-style HP documents, now consigned to history by the trade. I had no intention of going backwards, and informed him so.

The Major continued, 'You're not a man of your word.' My immediate response was to say, 'I don't think this is the time or place to discuss business matters.' 'Your salesmen run your business, not you he,' blared. This he followed with, 'Next season you can pay double to hunt with The Beaufort, and I don't care if hounds never cross your land again.' When threatened, the East-Ender in me makes a swift appearance. I stood my ground, telling him his behaviour was disgraceful. And was he suggesting that his views, were those held by the Duke himself, whom I knew coveted the freedom for his hounds to cross land granted by those who owned it. However small the holding might be. At this point, I think the Major realised he had gone too far. He sat down on the stairs, with his head bowed. Was this the man who had greeted me so warmly on my first hunting day? I said quietly, 'Major Gundry, I see the officer, but not the gentleman.' With that I walked out of the house.

My feelings were a mixture of anger and disappointment. How dare he threaten me? Everything I have, I earned. I owe nothing to any man. I considered going to see the Duke of Beaufort and laying all before him ask, 'Would my status in the Beaufort Hunt depend on commercial favour?' After much thought I decided to let it go. Many people witnessed the contumely behaviour of their joint Master, even more heard about it. Some rang me to say they had had confrontations with the Major, and that it all blows over. Whilst I thanked them for their support, most had hunted for years. I was a new boy. Major Gundry didn't spoke to me for many years, and was heard to make a number of snide remarks at my expense. Although both horses and hounds hunted across my land on a number of occasions, I waited 14 years to be invited to wear the hunt button.

My neighbour on the shopping centre, George Hutchings, had intimated that he was considering selling his takeaway business. I knew that Len Harvey, whom I had met in Germany, was about to be de-mobbed, and that he wanted to acquire such a business. Len's wife Sylvia had already returned from Germany with the children, and her son Gerald (Ged) was now employed in my workshop as a trainee engineer. I arranged for Len to meet George and a deal was struck. Once Len was released from the military, he would take over George's takeaway. Len Harvey was a lovely man, generous to a fault. He commuted his Army pension, and with the lump sum bought himself a fast food business.

Connie Vacher, who had previously worked for George Hutchings, now worked with me at Yate Television Centre. Connie, an excellent bookeeper and personable saleswoman, soon adapted to the TV business, 'Jim, Lady Caroline Somerset has asked if we could install a colour TV for her, at the cottage.' 'Of course, but I am surprised she hasn't already got one,' I answered. In fact the Somersets did already have a colour TV, on rental from one of the national companies. The reception was very poor, and despite many requests and subsequent visits from engineers, little improvement was achieved. Lady Caroline had since learned, through Connie, that Yate TV were getting stunning picture quality in Badminton. I called at The Cottage and met for the first time the elegant and charming Lady Caroline Somerset.

She was born Lady Caroline Jane Thynne, the daughter of Lord Bath and his first wife Daphne. Lord Bath became a household name when he opened up to the public, first with his stately home, and then with the help of the Chipperfield family, creating a safari park at Longleat.

Caroline married David Somerset in the 50s. A cousin of the 10th Duke of Beaufort, he became heir to the title and family seat at Badminton on the untimely and tragic death, the result of a yachting accident, of his father. They lived with their children, Harry, Eddie, Johnny and Anne, in the Dower cottage at Badminton. David hunted on Wednesdays and Saturdays, performing the duties of field master. He was an accomplished and brave horseman. One year he finished in second place at the Badminton Horse Trials, no mean achievement I assure you. Good looking with an engaging smile, he appears a man of few words, unless you get in the way that is. Or alternatively give him bad advice!

The one TV installed at the Cottage soon became three, then four. When video recorders first appeared on the domestic market, the first one I got my hands on went to Caroline Somerset. Made by Philips, very expensive and with a maximum recording time of one hour, there wasn't a huge demand for these machines. Reproduction was superb, but it weighed a ton! With four colour TVs and a video recorder, more followed in the ensuing years, Lady Caroline was my single biggest customer, remaining so for 25 years.

With so much electronic equipment in the house, quite naturally, frequent service calls were necessary. I often called myself to attend to faults, even scrabbling over the roof in the rain on one occasion to repair the aerial! Caroline was a lovely person, of whom I was immensely fond. We had many, many, long conversations over a glass of Scotch. Confidences I will never disclose. But there were some amusing moments, like the time I called when Caroline had just returned from fishing on the Duke's water (she would smile at the double entendre here). She had caught a huge salmon; I believe it was a record catch at the time for that stretch of the Wye. She had managed to put it in the bottom of her quite large refrigerator. Greeting me at the door with, 'Come and see what I caught today.' I followed her into the kitchen where with much aplomb she threw open the fridge door to reveal her prize fish. It stared at me for a second, then slid majestically on to the kitchen floor. Together, on our hands and knees, we struggled, pushing and shoving, trying to get the giant salmon back in the fridge. We were in fits of laughter. The phone rang. Caroline got up, saying with a huge grin, 'I've got to answer that, can you manage?' I was now soaking wet and smelling fishy. I got the tail end of the huge fish in first, and using my feet shoved the rest in after it. I shared a lot of laughs, and some sadness, with that wonderful lady. A Lady indeed, in every sense of the meaning.

Carnaby Street was beginning to make his mark. We had had a particularly good crop of foals by him, and as a result demand for his services were on the up. When foals were expected, it was an anxious time for everyone at the farm. When close to foaling, our mares were brought in at night, except for the mountain and moorland breeds. These are best left outside, but of course still need constant monitoring. Checking the mares last thing at night, then again as early in the morning as possible, is a job Joyce loved to do herself.

One particular morning whilst still in bed (where else), I could hear Joyce shouting for me, 'Jim get down here fast.' I leapt out of bed and pulled on a pair of jeans and a jumper. I dressed in a hurry, and as I ran out of the house, caught sight of Joyce disappearing into the tack room. I followed her in and got a mighty shock. She was soaking wet, muddy and blood stained. 'My god. What has happened. Are you alright?' 'I'm OK, it's Raffia. She has had her foal but it has slipped under the wire down the bank into the stream. I have managed to it get out of the water and back up the bank, but need a hand to check he is not injured. It's a colt by the way.' With the 12hh, strawberry roan Welsh pony mare going frantic with worry, my indefatigable wife had managed to gather the newly born foal in her arms, and on hands and knees managed to claw her way up a steep bank. All the while calling out words of reassurance to the foal's mother.

Carrying a bucket with a few aids in we ran across the fields, rounding a hedge. There standing in the morning sunlight was the proud mother with her son. We named him Magic. Joyce carried out many such missions of mercy during our stud farm days. Dozens of foals were born at Shortwood, and we never lost one.

One night just after we had retired, Joyce said she could hear the sound of horses in the yard. She got out of bed and went to investigate. About 20 minutes passed and she hadn't returned, so I got up to see what was keeping her. It was pouring with rain; I grabbed my wellies, pulled on a coat over my pyjamas, and went out into the yard. There was no sign of Joyce. I could here a faint rustling sound coming far over to my right. As I followed the sound it got louder. I walked up the lane and through a gap in the hedge and saw my wife, dressed in a short nightie and wellington boots, running through a field of corn rounding up two horses. Joyce led the culprits back into the yard. Soaking wet, we just stood there laughing at each other.

Having increased trade no end at the Takeaway, Len Harvey had begun to expand into outside catering. Looking for new business he called at a recently converted country house at Yate Rocks. Formerly a small manor house, it had been bought by an entrepreneurial couple by the name of Francis and Joan Milner. They got consent from the local authority for a change of use from residential to commercial, obtained a licence to sell beers and spirits, and opened for business. They named the venue The Randolph. Joan and Francis had never before been involved in such a venture, and were green in every respect. Len struck up an agreement with the couple to run the catering side of things. Trade was extremely slow at first. A wedding reception or two and an odd anniversary celebration was about all the business they had managed to attract. Len approached me and asked if I would consider putting on some entertainment on a Sunday evening at The Randolph. Although I had heard about a new night-spot in Yate' I had yet to see it.

The many arms of octopus, masquerading as the entertainment world, had spread its tentacles, giving me a flick every once in a while, to remind me of my heritage. I had taken to go, on a fairly regular basis, to The Chequers at Hanham, on the outskirts of Bristol. The Chequers had become famous locally as a meeting place for musicians and entertainers. Most popular were Sunday nights when the place would be packed. The resident duo at the time was Don Stevens on piano and Ted Hooper on drums. With guest musicians joining in throughout the evening, this could grow to a six or seven piece band.

Recalling just a few of the names that appeared on those magical evenings; Ivor Smith saxaphone, Pete McQuade guitar, Syd Johns Vibes, Trevor Ottolang drums, Fred Benbrow banjo, Ron Tricky Uke. And singers, Pete 'Dino' Summers, Diane Bell, Mike Lines, Robbie

Romero, and myself. The drag artist Adrian Varcoe, the gay duo Harrigan and Shallard, another duo The Tones, who were also gay. Angelo the Italian who played a number of stringed instruments, including a mandolin which he played with both hands held above his head.

There was big Frank Oliver, a tenor with a wonderful voice. Frank was also compere at The Sandringham, a dancehall in Downend. Each night he wound up proceedings with the song called, 'The Last Goodbye' from the musical *The White Horse Inn*. Building the crescendo by stamping his feet and banging a tin tray on his knee, also often hitting himself over the head with it, whilst waving to the audience, who waved back with handkerchiefs in the air, he brought the song to its climax. Then bowing deeply walked out backwards. What a character. I always thought he looked a little 'punch drunk'; perhaps it was banging the tray on his head that did it.

A special mention is deserved for the wonderful David Evans who had shared fame at one time with his partner Tony Fayne. Both men were born in Bristol. Their impressions, delivered simultaneously, were unmistakable. They were big on radio in the 40s, and in 1949 went into Variety. When Fayne and Evans parted company, Tony Fayne continued in the business, becoming a straight man and feed for Norman Wisdom. A job he was still doing until recently. David Evans, by now an alcoholic, died completely alone in a shed at the bottom of a garden. Totally broke, it wasn't even his shed or garden. He was a lovely man with whom I was privileged to share a stage. I will never forget his impression of Winston Churchill delivering his stirring wartime speeches: 'We will fight them on the beaches' and so on. I don't think anyone ever did it better. Show business takes its toll. Perhaps the most rewarding, but the hardest for sure.

Just about everyone on the Bristol music scene in the 60s and 70s appeared at one time or another at The Chequers. Sadly in the mid 70's, Don Stevens died quite suddenly. Syd Johns, as well as being an accomplished vibes player, played piano and took over from Don, but it would never be the same. Fewer and fewer musicians frequented the Chequers, with the public following the trend. Don Stevens was the heart of the place; he was a great pianist. It was his magic they came for.

Maybe I could recreate The Chequers appeal, at The Randolph? I agreed to get a band together, compere the evening, and invite guest musicians and singers. I started off with Syd Johns on piano and Ted Hooper on drums. The first Sunday, with help from Dino and the old Chequers followers, we had a good response from the public. Bearing in mind, apart from a few faithful from Bristol the audience would have to come from the immediate area. Not too many people would travel out from Bristol in winter. And in those days the bar closed at 10.30pm. By the third week, if you didn't get in by 7pm, you would not get a seat. Week after week we packed them in.

Syd Johns couldn't make it one week, and recommended a keyboard player named Cliff Stock. Cliff had a trio he called the Checkmates, and agreed to stand in for just one Sunday, but ended up playing more often. Later I would join The Checkmates. In the meantime I alternated Syd with another keyboard player named Mary Gay. Mary, Ted Hooper and myself did a lot of gigs as The Moonlighters. We could have been out every night of the week if we had wanted it. Sadly Ted Hooper died quite suddenly, like his close colleague Don Stevens had done. They were both in their early 50s.

Britain joined the common market on 1 January 1993. On the 22nd day of the same month share values fell by 4 billion in one day. It became known as Black Monday. In April, along with other measures Value Added Tax was introduced. Firstly it allowed us to claim back all the purchase tax we had paid on stock we were holding. The VAT rate was initially set at 8% of the selling price; retail price maintenance was still in force then. The previous iniquitous purchase tax, had been 25% on electrical goods, so prices fell. This was a welcome move, but didn't last long. The manufacturers' saw a window to increase their price, and VAT rose to 12%, putting prices very much where they were before the new tax was instituted.

Another change came from the commercial banks, who for years under the guise of a finance company, had offered hire purchase facilities to customers through the retail trade. Ridiculous though it may seem, we small dealers were subject to recourse. In other words we were expected to underwrite the agreements our customers had with the finance company. If the customer failed to make payments under the agreement, we had to reimburse the lender. With the colour TV explosion, the average loan was now £300, much more attractive to a lender than the previous average of £60. The commercial banks grasped the nettle and offered a simple personal loan agreement, of which the goods were not a part. Effectively it could be used for any purpose.

As competition among the banks for this lucrative credit business rose, they even started to offer us commission on finance deals. What a turn around! This was perhaps the watershed of consumer credit. Barclays had introduced the Barclaycard, Britain's first credit card, in 1966. But it had been painfully slow to catch on. I well remember thinking 'What use is this!'

A COCKNEY KID IN GREEN WELLIES

Farrier Mike Strickland had shod our horses for some time, so it was not unusual for me to see him cranking up his forge in the stable yard on arriving home for lunch. Except that on this day although his van was in the yard, I could see he was with Karen and her pony Gina in the homefield. Karen now had a skewbald pony that she loved, and wanted to do all sorts of things with. First she wanted to breed from her, and when I said no, she turned her attention to driving the pony in long reins with a view to getting a small cart for the pony to pull. She was in the homefield practising the art when Mike arrived. The farrier, known to all as Stricky had a lot of time for Karen. He admired her guts. 'Let me show you the proper way to do that, young lady,' he had said, whereupon my daughter passed the reins to him saying, 'Go on then Stricky, show me.' Stricky took the reins, and with the command 'Walk on' set off around the field. All was fine for a while until Gina started to trot, getting faster and faster by the minute. Stricky was having a job to keep up, and urged the pony to slow, with the command of 'Whoa' coming in ever-increasing volume and not without a trace of panic. Then Gina broke into a canter.

By now Joyce and Biff had joined me, and we stood grinning at the performance. The inevitable happened. Unable to keep up the pace, Stricky fell over, but refusing to let go of the reins, he was dragged around the field with Karen in hot pursuit. We all thought it was hilarious, except Stricky that is, he had an instant sense of humour failure!

Mike Strickland told me of a thoroughbred mare that Monty Stevens had for sale at his Lucknam Park Stud in Colerne. Monty's claim to fame was that he owned Raffingora, a prolific winner on the flat over a short distance, now standing at stud. The mare Monty had on offer was bay and about 15.2hh. named Weybridge Lass. By The Bosun, who himself was by Crepello, she was nicely bred. She had had a few races over Five furlongs, but the best she had managed was fourth at Bath. She was really too kind an animal for the racetrack, and bottled it when it came to the shake up. She had good conformation and moved well. I thought she might breed a nice show hack, and with this in mind bought her for Joyce. Running her hands over our new acquisition, in the loose box where I had installed her, Joyce smiled approvingly, saying, 'I shall call her Bridget. She should breed something nice.' Initially, our new mare did pose a bit of a challenge. She hated being brushed around the hindquarters, and on one occasion kicked the brush right out of Joyce's hand.

Neither Joyce nor I had any thoughts of using Carnaby on Bridget instead we had in mind a former winner of the Champion Hurdle at

Cheltenham, Saucy Kit. Roy Edwards, who had ridden him to glory in the race all National Hunt jockeys hope one day to win, now stood the horse at his Shropshire stud. I had booked Bridget in to him, and looked forward to what might be. However, Carnaby Street had ideas of his own; he fancied this attractive mare for himself. In good weather we let Carnaby have a gallop around the field close the Dutch barn. The hedge in this field was particularly high and so he was unable to see horses in the adjoining paddock. But there was absolutely nothing wrong with his nose! Unbeknown to us, Bridget had come into season. Biff, noticing Carnaby had got into the paddock with Bridget, called for help. Joyce ran to her assistance and the two of them chased around the field with a bucket, trying either to get his attention or warn him off. They finally caught him, but not before he caught Bridget! Saucy Kit would have to wait. In the autumn, Bridget gave birth to a gorgeous chestnut colt foal. We named him Mayfair.

The following year I took Bridget to Saucy Kit. I had discussed Saucy Kit with my friend Brian Higham, who informed me that David Somerset was considering using the same stallion on his mare Cuddle Up, already a proven brood mare of good stock. I offered to take their mare up with ours. Six weeks later I drove to Shropshire and collected the two mares. Both had conceived. As I made ready to leave, Roy Edwards thanked me for the business, and gave me a brown envelope. Inside the envelope was a bill for service by the stallion, and 'keep' for the period our mare was in his care. I gulped as I read the bottom line thinking, 'Its not just the horses who are Thorougbred, the prices are too!'

It was December 1973 and the Prime Minister Edward Heath was in conflict with the miners over pay. As a result they had come out on strike. Shortages of coal meant reduced output of power from the electricity generating plants. This was causing havoc to businesss both small and large. In our shop at Yate, we only had electricity for four hours during normal opening times: two hours mid-morning, and another two mid-afternoon. I bought a generator to give us power during the rest of the day. With only 3kw output from the generator our activities were restricted to say the least. Our entire business depended on electricity. Everything we sold plugged in to the mains. The generator meant that we could keep the workshop going and have one or two sets working in the showroom. The latter certainly sorted the wheat from the chaff. The more sophisticated power supplies, employed in the better-class receiver, coped adequately with the fluctuating power from the generator. Others, not so well designed or built, often lost vision; some packed up completely. You get what you pay for in electronics. The crisis lasted for three months, during which time the miners lost the sympathy of the public. This would herald the beginning of the end for the coal industry.

Inflation had reached 25 per cent and interest rates were 15 per cent. This meant overdrafts were costing 18%. Three times what I was paying when I first bought Shortwood Farm. On the one hand the value of the farm had quadrupled, whereas on the other I had to find substantially more money to service the loan on it. Everyone felt the squeeze and nothing was selling.

My niece June wrote from Greece and suggested that mum and Dad join her in Athens for a holiday. I thought this a splendid idea, and telephoned my sister Stella to ask her opinion. Stella concurred. Splitting the cost between us, Stella and I sent our parents on their first trip abroad. Mum and dad were really excited at the prospect of flying, and of course visiting with their treasure, June. They had a wonderful holiday, June saw to that; it was the first they had taken together in their lives. Dad in particular got so much from his stay in Greece. He returned an authority on everything Greek. It was the first thing I had given my father that he couldn't either lose or give away. There was to be one more. Stella and I often reflect on the happiness the holiday in Greece gave to our dear mum and dad.

June returned from Greece with Costas and his band, and asked if I could possibly help in some way with work permits for them. She thought that as I knew the Greek band Odyssey, I might be able to find out how they got permission to work here. Odyssey were managed by a friend of mine named Brian Mannering. He did a good job for them, getting them on the TV talent show *New Faces*, the result of which led to a record deal. I saw them for the first time at Tito's nightspot in Cardiff, where they were resident.

The first night I watched Odyssey perform, there was a young, although not that young, illusionist on the bill. I was more impressed with him than with the band. I had never seen an act quite like his, and wondered why we hadn't seen him on the telly. After the show we all went for a meal, and ended up sitting around a large table getting steadily worse for drink, whilst the illusionist or rather 'unusualist', as he described himself, performed feats of magic right under our noses. He told me he had been treading the boards all over the country for 10 years without recognition, and at times despaired for his future in show business. Unanimously, we assured him that it was only a matter of time before he shoved the ageing David Nixon, out of his seemingly impregnable slot with the Beeb. When the opportunity did eventually come he grabbed it, and was an overnight success. It had taken 15 years around the clubs to get noticed. Television made him a star in 24 hours such is the power of the beast. Paul Daniels is now a household name.

I couldn't help June with the work permit problem of her Greek musicians. Brian's band Odyssey were facing similar difficulties. June's band returned to Greece, but this time she didn't follow them. Odyssey split up.

I installed closed circuit television in one of the loose boxes in readiness for Weybridge Lass to foal. Very few had CCTV in those days, so I was somewhat of a pioneer. When Bridget went into labour, Joyce and I watched the monitor into the night. The front feet and head of the foal presented itself, but nothing more was happening. Not wishing to panic, we waited, until we could stand the suspense no more. 'Come on,' I beckoned to Joyce. 'Let's get out there, I think Bridget's in trouble.' The mare was sweating heavily and breathing very hard. Joyce and I got down beside her. We pulled on the legs of the foal, and uttered words of encouragement. The bag had not yet broken from around the foal's head, and there was no sign of life. We pulled the soft sticky tissue away from its mouth and nostrils. 'Breathe you idle bastard,' I shouted. 'Breathe!' Time passed, it seemed like an age, and we were getting anxious. It was warm work so I removed my jumper and shirt, and was down to bare skin. 'Pull Joyce, pull!' I urged. 'I'm doing my very best,' she replied trembling with the exertion.

Eventually we had most of the foal out, then with hands and feet and one final pull he left his mother and lay beside us. I tied off, then severed the umbilical cord, got rid of the placenta and cleared up. The foal had done absolutely nothing to help himself. Then emotion took over, near to tears we had done it.

Thank god for the CCTV. If we hadn't been there I am sure we would have lost the foal, and maybe the mare too. Who knows? It also helped that I had attended a special course at Royal College of Veterinary Science, at Langford in Somerset, designed in conjunction with the British Horse Society for small stud owners. I had been nervous during the birth of Bridget's foal, but confident with the knowledge I gained from that wonderful institution.

Bridget got up and Joyce rubbed her down gently, telling her how special she was to us. With some help the foal, a big chestnut colt, struggled to his feet. Idle he may have been, but he was gorgeous. 'What shall we call him?' I asked my wife. She paused before answering, then with conviction replied, 'Young Kit.' Joyce got Bridget a feed from the tack room, and reluctant to leave as we were, we returned to the house for a well-earned hot drink. We just couldn't resist sitting for a while in front of the TV monitor watching the proud mother, now content, with her son nuzzling up to her. We collapsed exhausted for a couple of hours shuteye.

I put the TV camera to good use on a number of occasions. One memorable time was at the surgery of my friend veterinary surgeon Bill Walter. Bill's practice was at Bury Hill, Didmarton, right in the middle of Beaufort country. The house, yard and operating theatre had been custom built for the purpose. Bill had a new partner in the practice, Lawrence, his former colleague Phil Janaway, having left to set up on his own a mile down the road. Bill was a loveable 'Soldier of Fortune' a man's man, with an air of *bonhomie*.

Bill was ready to perform an operation on a horse that had a soft palette. This is a piece of skin that grows across the windpipe, causing respiratory problems. The condition had been confirmed by passing an endoscope down the horse's throat, enabling one to see what was going on. To the viewing end of the endoscope I attached a television camera, which in turn was connected to a monitor we could all view. The remedy for the ailment is to make an incision in the throat and remove the blockage. It's obviously not quite as simple as this sounds, but then I'm not a vet! The horse, now under anaesthetic, lay prostrate on the floor of the theatre. Bill was to make the incision using an instrument powered by Radio Frequency coil. The advantage of using RF to make an incision is that you are able to work in a clear field, with very little blood to impede one's path, the blood vessels having been cauterised. Bill switched on the RF generator machine and made to cut. Nothing happened. He adjusted a few knobs. Still nothing happened.

'Jim, what do you make of this?' he asked. I replied saying that I would have to remove the cover of the machine before I could see what was going on. I had never seen one of these before, and to add to my dilemma this machine was not only ancient, as medical equipment goes, but also ex-military and built like a tank. 'How long can we keep the horse down?' Bill asked Lawrence, who replied, 'About another 45 minutes.' 'Right Jim, see what you can do,' said Bill. I found the fault was caused by a short circuit capacitor in the oscillator circuit. I soldered in a new one and Bill went ahead.

I don't remember Bill being impressed in any way. I know he had a high opinion of my ability as an engineer, he had voiced it to many. I guess he thought it routine for me. I accompanied Bill on many occasions, once using a radio microphone strapped to a horse to monitor the heartbeat. Another time, electronically monitoring the temperature of a horse undergoing cryo surgery (using liquid nitrogen to freeze the area to be operated on. The case in question was to remove warts). I repaired all manner of equipment for him. We often talked into the early hours of how electronics was being utilised more and more in the service of the horse.

The TV business was tailing off. Supplies were now plentiful, and discount houses had opened offering lower prices. With interest rates high, the public were looking for keener deals. Retail prices in the trade were not keeping pace with other commodities. In 1970, I was delivering a £300 TV set in a van costing £600 brand new. By 1978, I would be delivering a £250 TV in a similar van costing £5,000. The overheads for running the business quadrupled, but the profit margins halved. The trend would continue. But I was too caught up with other things to spot it.

Young Kit, now about nine months old, was growing into a lovely animal. He was running in a paddock with a filly foal named Chelsea Girl. The two looked a picture as they played together in the lazy summer sunshine. We didn't like leaving youngsters out at night, whatever the weather, especially not valuable ones like this pair. When it got dusk we put them in the covered yard, letting them out again first thing next morning. I noticed that Young Kit seemed to bump into things, and always followed another rather than taking the lead. Joyce said that at first she had thought him awkward, but was becoming increasingly concerned at his behaviour. We put him in the loose box with the TV camera in, monitoring his behaviour closely.

After a day or so, Young Kit's breathing became laboured and he was unsteady on his feet. Joyce went out to see soon calling me to join her. He had got down on the floor and was clearly in trouble.

Joyce phoned her vet, who said he would come at once. I got down with Kit and cradled him in my arms; he was shivering, so we put a thick blanket around him. I was at a loss to know what it was that was causing the poor animal such distress. Phil Janaway arrived and coming into the box said, 'He looks poorly Jim, I'll see what I can do.' We talked with Phil, asking all the normal routine questions about the foal. After some time Phil decided to give Kit an injection in an attempt to relax him and hopefully ease his respiration. He looked in Kit's eyes through an optical device and proclaimed 'He's blind, Jim.' 'How could that be, what could have caused it?' I asked. 'There is only one cause that I know of, and that's lead poisoning,' Phil replied. 'Lead poisoning, how could he have got that?' I said shaking my head. Phil answered, 'I don't know, but it is so severe it is causing paralysis of his larynx, that's why he can't breath.' 'What can be done Phil. Can you treat him?' Almost as soon as I uttered the words I knew instinctively that it was hopeless.

Kneeling beside me, with one hand on Young Kit's head, and the other on my shoulder, Phil delivered the dreaded verdict. 'Sorry, so sorry mate, but he won't survive,' he quietly proclaimed. I looked up at Joyce. She had her back to me, and as she walked toward the door I could hear her sobbing gently. 'Do what's best for Kit, Phil, ' I said with my head bowed. Phil left the stable and went out to his car. I sat alone with my arms around Young Kit. Phil returned and gave the final injection. Young Kit was at peace now. Joyce came back in and we stood together looking down at what might have been.

We talked of the night when, in this very same box, we had struggled so hard to bring Young Kit into the world. And the elation when it was all over, and our lovely Bridget, so proud with her son by her side. We had such hopes, such dreams. Animals, mostly so rewarding, can also break your heart. I wept uncontrollably. Then got thoroughly drunk.

After a while the guilt creeps in. We should have noticed earlier that something was wrong, why didn't we? Why didn't I? Perhaps it we had… It's all too late. We searched the farm for a source from which Kit might have come into contact with an old paint tin or a painted gate perhaps. There was none. What about Chelsea Girl? She had been with him all summer. Phil gave her a thorough examination and discovered that she was virtually blind in one eye. She too had contracted lead poisoning, albeit a mild dose. She probably ate some of whatever had killed Young Kit. Lead poisoning in horses is remarkably rare, and virtually the only cause of equine blindness.

We have wonderful photos of Bridget with Young Kit in our album of equine memories. Chelsea Girl went on become an excellent riding pony. Len Harvey bought her from us for his daughter Tracy, who was ever mindful of her poor sight. The two gave each other a great deal of pleasure for a number of years.

We seemed to have more horses than ever on the farm. Many of them were mares visiting our stallions.' As well as Carnaby we now had a 13.2hh Palomino stallion called Shergolds Morning Mischief. He was name Morning Mischief on account of him being an orphan foal that had to be bottle fed, which produced a number of traits in the fledgling. A lot of a character, he was lovely to ride but had to be watched when mares in season were around. On one such occasion I was passing the door of his box when I paused and turned towards him. In an instant he grabbed my jumper between his teeth and lifted me off the ground. I was carrying two buckets; one had water in the other had feed. It took quite an effort to bring the buckets up around each side of his head, but the shock of it caused the stallion to drop me. Shaken and bleeding from the chest, I took a pitchfork handle from the tack room and had a 'word' with the delinquent!

A beautiful bay mare, about 16hh, had come to visit Carnaby. Try as we might we could not get her to 'show' to him. We thought this odd indeed. Every time we took her near Carnaby she kicked seven bells out of his door, but she would stand and 'flash' like mad to a filly. We were on the verge of giving up when Stricky appeared in the yard on a routine visit. I explained our dilemma and asked if he had ever countenanced such behaviour in a mare. Screwing his face up he replied, 'As a matter of fact I have. What you have here mate is a Wildew.' 'A what?' I asked. 'A Wildew, a lesbian,' he explained. 'Didn't know there was such a thing.' I replied. 'Many don't, but if I'm not mistaken, you've got one here,' He advised.

I asked Stricky what he thought we should do. 'If she's in season now I'll help you to cover her,' he offered. 'I'm sure she is in season,' I replied. Biff took the mare down to the covered yard in readiness. We hobbled her, for her own, and our stallion's safety. Hobbles are a pair of leather straps that tie the hind legs just above the fetlocks. The customary twitch was also employed. I brought Carnaby into the yard where Biff and Stricky held the mare. As soon as I got Carnaby close to her hindquarters she let fly. Hobbles or no hobbles, she kicked with such ferocity that she not only broke the leather straps but also broke free from the twitch and from Biff and Stricky who were holding on to her. It's a miracle that none of us were injured. I took Carnaby back to his box; he was shaking, and must have been thinking 'Get me out of here, she's a bloody nut case.' 'We could always sedate, then rape her' Stricky suggested with a big grin on his face. He didn't like being defeated by a horse. 'I don't think so Mike, Joyce would never go along with that,' I advised. The mare's name was Holly. We will never forget her.

Joyce and Biff held countless mares whilst Carnaby covered them. It's nothing short of a miracle that neither horses nor humans came to any harm. It's a dodgy old business I can assure you. Without doubt the girls were up the sharp end!

COME TO THE CABARET

Joan Milner wanted to start a Georgian banquet evening, with entertainment, at The Randolph. She asked Len Harvey and me to travel with her across the Severn Bridge to Chepstow, to take a look at a banquet already up and running in a castle there. We did, and we were suitably impressed with what we saw.

Joan organised the costumes. I was dressed in a gold three-quarter-length coat with brown satin britches, white stockings, and black shoes with a big silver buckle on. With a fop like wig, jabo and gold brooch, I looked as big a nancy as you will ever see! Mary Gay, my keyboard player was dressed in a green crinoline dress, and comedian Dave Pitt, in a swashbuckling outfit resembling a Cavalier. Dave had only recently started out. In fact, it was me who gave him his first spot in front of an audience. Dressed in a black velvet jacket with bow tie, he used to come to my Sunday nights at The Randolph. Dave always stood by the bar and was very supportive of everyone who performed. It was me who approached him and asked if he had any thoughts of performing himself. He said that he certainly did but was shy to ask me to give him a go. He was terrible at first, but persevered, and got better and better. Dave Pitt has worked in cabaret all over the country, and still makes me laugh 30 years on.

Len Harvey, with help from a menu researched by my niece June, put on the banquet. Our first night did not go without incident. There were teething problems with the food, and also the entertainment. Not least with the script I had written for the 'host' whose duties were performed by a singer called Colin. Classically trained, he found it difficult to ad lib, essential with live shows of an ad hoc nature. We muddled through but it still felt flat. Len Harvey came into the room and, failing to get my attention, banged a big serving spoon on the table. I ignored him, so he banged again. Simultaneously, we noticed a flicker of amusement from the punters. I shouted to two of the waiters, 'Throw him out.' Len, catching on at once, protested loudly, getting many of the guests, now on his side, to chant 'Let Benny stay.' Len, realising this could run, shouted, 'Poor Benny, it's not fair. He, [pointing at me] is always picking on me.' The audience warmed to Len, and booed me. To curry favour, I got the idea of leading a conga around the room. During which, for reasons I cannot explain, I led them up on to the tables, which stretched the length of the room, then off at the far end. They went wild.

Later I asked Len why he was banging the spoon on the table. 'Oh, just to ask if you were ready for the coffee to be served,' he replied. Completely by accident, we had created a winning finale for the banquets that was to last long after I had moved on. Years later people were still heard talking 'of the time we danced on the tables at The Randolph'.

I considered buying The Randolph, but could not come to an agreement with Joan Milner. I always keep my cards close to my chest, and she is a shrewd businesswoman who negotiated with a poker face. As Len Harvey once said: 'Lovely woman, but wears an expression like someone has just shit in her handbag!' Had there been an agent involved, who knows, we might have reached agreement.

I was restless and wanted a change. I had been approached by Radio Rentals, a national television rental company, expressing an interest in my shop premises on the shopping centre. They offered £15,000 for my interest in the lease I was holding. It still had 14 years to run and the rent was very reasonable. I was considering their offer when the Entertainment Centre, (then called Stirling Suite) which was and still is situated in the middle of the shopping centre at Yate, went into receivership. It was huge, a two-story building with capacity for around 1,000 people.

I arranged with a director of Sterling Promotions who held the lease (and in fact had run the business as a night-club, restaurant and discotheque for a number of years) to view the premises. The local papers reported me as saying when I first walked into the place, 'It's big, I'll take it.' I can't remember if I did or not. But I do remember thinking what great potential it had. I knew the present business had failed, but I could, and would, do much better. Not for one moment did I consider, at what cost, at what pain.

I told Joyce what I was thinking of doing. At first she was horrified, but she knew if I had made up my mind it would be useless arguing. 'What about the TV business, it has been so good to us. Will you keep that going?' Another bombshell from me. 'No, it has run its course. From here it will only go downhill. I'll sell the lease and dispose of the business piecemeal. It won't be easy and will take time, but it will work out,' I answered bristling with enthusiasm. The press were all over the place, anxious to find out what was happening to the town's only major place of entertainment. When word leaked that I might take it over, they pestered me for an answer: I could give them none. But they wouldn't go away.

Jane and Karen, now teenagers, were delighted at the prospect of a night-club to play with. They had become bored with horses. I think this was partly my fault. With so much work I hadn't taken them to many shows lately, and they seemed always to have to help on the farm. With a record number of mares visiting Carnaby, and our own mares with their new crop of foals, there were more horses at Shortwood than ever before. It was early in 1976 and a warm summer was promised. Sitting here all these years later I honestly don't know what possessed me to make so many changes, in such a short space of time. They would irreversibly have an effect our lives and not necessarily for the good at least not in the short term.

Sitting in my tiny office (I never believed in large posh offices, still don't), I opened the post as usual. There was a letter from Radio Rentals withdrawing their offer to purchase the lease of my shop on South Parade. No explanation, just 'we are not going ahead with the purchase.' This was a mighty blow and I should have read the signs. The economy was running down, inflation and interest rates were high. One cannot live with both at the same time. What do I do now? I was due to sign the contract for the Entertainment Centre the following day. I could borrow the money I needed for the shortfall from the bank; there was adequate equity in Shortwood Farm. But this would push me to the limit. It would also mean that I would have to get the new venture up and running in record time, to generate the income necessary to service and pay back the loan.

I talked it over with Joyce; she was not at all keen on the venture anyway, but said whatever I decided she would support. She also said that she had never before seen me so apprehensive about a project. Another sign I chose to ignore. I went along to the bank. By now David Jenkins had moved to Calne in Wiltshire, and Brian Harding to Clevedon. The new manager at Barclays on the shopping centre was Bruce Egan, a charming man, extremely friendly but weak. His main hobby was collecting tortoises. He invited me to his home for a social drink. There were tortoise ornaments everywhere. One in the shape of a footstool, another a door stop. Their little heads poked out from behind chairs and curtains. Even the teapot had a tortoise design on it. Bruce informed me that he had collected more than a hundred. 'I like them, because they don't do anything,' he explained, leaving me none the wiser. He agreed to advance the money I needed to purchase the Centre.

I would still be tight for working capital. So I took up an offer my brother-in-law Joe Travis (Maud's husband) had made when I discussed my new business venture with him earlier. Joe loaned me £5,000. I agreed to pay him interest at £50 per month and return the capital sum on demand. The terms favoured him more than me. I repaid half the sum invested after two and a half years, and the balance 18 months later. During this period I paid Joe £1,750 in interest. He didn't do me any favours.

I signed a contract to buy the lease and fixtures and fittings of the business known as the Sterling Suite. I re-named the Centre Stars and

Stripes. The ground floor would be Stripes Disco and the first floor Stars Cabaret Club. I set myself a target to open the cabaret club after one month, with the disco following a month later. Mistake number one, I should have done it the other way around. The disco would generate far more, and much quicker than the cabaret club, but it was the club business that I knew best, so I threw everything into opening it.

Nineteen seventy-six was the American bi-centeneary year and there was a lot of publicity material around with Stars and Stripes emblazoned on. I purchased a whole load of sweatshirts for the bar staff to wear, and they looked great in them. A graphic designer friend of mine created a stars theme with hanging mobiles that looked terrific. I designed, built and installed the sound and lighting equipment myself. I was working 18 hours a day. The candle was burning at one end.

Cliff Stock, with his band The Checkmates, agreed to play for me on Sunday nights, but he was booked already most Saturdays, so could only fit in a few of these nights for me. John Mills, who ran JME entertainment agency, offered me a few acts suggesting one that I might open with called Mouth and Trousers, a husband and wife act. John Mills said they were the best live cabaret act he had seen for some time. To provide backing for the cabaret then later play for dancing, I engaged a band called Fresh Pages.

The scene was set. The Bristol papers led with 'Local business man and cabaret artiste Jim Ruston, saves town's entertainment centre'. They went on to recount my family's previous involvement in the world of show business. My idea was first to establish a Sunday night with guest acts similar to those I had started at The Randolph, and follow with the opening of the disco. We opened on a Sunday, four weeks after taking over the venue, with 'Jim Ruston, The Checkmates and Guests, at Stars Cabaret Club, Yate'. The doors opened at 7pm. By half-past there wasn't a seat to be had. The first night was a huge success and I thought, 'This is easy.' What a fool!

I now concentrated on getting the disco ready. This was an enormous task. The venue had a very high ceiling, which I thought needed lowering to create the effect I had in mind. Quotes for the work were terrifying, and it was all going to take too long. I hit on the idea of creating the illusion of a lowered ceiling. I had a false ceiling specialist erect a metal frame that would normally hold ceiling tiles, without the tiles. Imagine a giant chessboard, only one that you could see through. I cut pieces of ply and fixed them randomly in the frame, and to these I fitted downlighters.

Calling again on my electrical experience, I assembled, out of plastic slip tube, 10 pieces each about 20 feet long. To these I fitted spotlights at intervals of one foot, I then fixed the 'arms' I had assembled to the overhead frame. I added a few more effects, such as strobes, and projectors, which threw multi-coloured patterns on the walls. I connected the whole frame to a sound to light generator. The effects were marvellous. My graphic designer pal made mobiles once more, this time creating a striped effect. Instead of the months I had been quoted to lower the ceiling, I had the effect I was looking for in a week. Later, others copied my idea of using a suspended ceiling frame.

I was in the office at the club preparing for our first Saturday night at Stars Cabaret. I was hoping it would be as successful as the previous Sunday nights when there was a knock at the door. It opened, and standing there was a slim-built good looking young man, about 5 feet 10 inches with dark brown hair. 'Hello. The names Tom, Tom Kiethley. Is this Stars and Stripes club?' he inquired. 'Yes, can I help?' I offered. He continued 'I am appearing here tonight, and wonder if its OK to park my caravan in the car park overnight. D'you think it will be alright like?' 'From the north?' I asked. 'Yes, is my accent that obvious? he replied. I am one half of Mouth and Trousers. I am the Trousers. You'll know the Mouth when you hear her,' he jested. 'I can do better than the car park for you, you can leave your caravan at my farm which is nearby,' I responded. 'Thanks mate, brilliant. I will go and tell Sue, she loves animals. She has a horse herself,' He replied excitedly.

John Mills had not exaggerated the talent of the act he had sent me. Mouth and Trousers went down a storm. You don't see many standing ovations on the club circuit, but they got one. We became firm friends and they stayed with us on the farm for a couple of weeks, from where they travelled to their engagements throughout the West Country. Tom and Sue later changed their management and subsequently their stage name to Bright and Breeze. Tom is a brilliant musician, singer and comic. Sue can sing dance and play the bagpipes! Although she didn't actually know she could play the pipes until Tom wanted to introduce 'Mull of Kintyre' into the finale of their act and he gave her a week to learn! A multi-talented pair. Although appearing on TV a number of times, their act never seemed to quite suit the box' Inexplicable. Tom, however, found a spot for himself on TV, appearing in several series as a straight man on the Russ Abbot show.

Bright and Breeze appeared at Stars Cabaret many times, and I went to see them work at a number of other venues. Tom and I founded The Straight Arm Club. After 25 years it still has just two members, him and me. When we get together we have our AGM and annual dinner. It has become customary to complain bitterly at the AGM, about the crap organisation of the previous function – whereby he or I resign, then after drinks, get re-elected. We have a secret handshake and a motto: SAND. (Straightus armus never dieus). Our club uniform is a beige double-breasted raincoat with belt and a blue beret. We once did a double Frank Spencer impersonation on stage, which brought the house down. Frank is our patron, although we have never asked him to be. I have not seen Tom or Sue in recent years, but know that when we next meet, we will exchange signs. Nothing will have changed.

To alleviate both work and financial pressure, we decided to sell some of the horses. An auction was planned to take place on the farm. We would put most of the horses on sale, although putting extra high reserves on those we didn't really want to part with. That way it wouldn't look as though we were just trying to dump the horses we no longer wanted. We also had far too much tack, and so included much of this. Although without doubt it was a wise move, it did provide one or two shocks. My hunter Saxmundham, who had given me so much pleasure, went under the hammer. I still had April Chimes, and the way it was looking I wouldn't have much time for hunting anyway.

A Dutchman named Jan Wiersema had approached me at shows on several occasions asking if I would sell Carnaby Street. At first I replied with an indignant, 'No, he is not for sale.' When Jan turned up a couple of years later, I listened to what he had to say. He told of the good home, in a very professional stud that Carnaby would go to, and how they would show him and so on. I said I would consider it, but he would have to bring the people he talked of over from Holland to see me. He agreed. And so it was that I came to part with a horse I always said money wouldn't buy. 'Never say never.' I asked a huge sum, and they paid it. I let them have his show bridle, too. Much as I would like to have kept it, somehow it didn't seem right. It was Carnaby's. Together Jan and I arranged the export details, and I felt happy enough. I had a lot on my mind, so didn't dwell on the prospect of life without Carnaby.

Carnaby and I had become practically inseparable. With a little help from me, Biff had broken him in to ride, and he loved it. I spent hours on end galloping over the fields, and up through Lady Wood, accompanied more often than not by my daughter Jane riding April Chimes. Whenever I left the farm Carnaby would call to me from his stable, repeating the performance when I returned. He wouldn't shut up until I went to see him. If I was in a hurry and ignored him, Joyce sent me back out saying, 'For goodness sake Jim, go and speak to Carnaby. You know he won't rest until you do.' I suppose it was quite natural for me to have this relationship with him. It was me who provided him with his girlfriends!

We had had so many magical moments, some in the show ring, others on the farm. He loved life, and had the most wonderful temperament of any horse I ever owned. After a couple of years at stud he got into not only bad but a dangerous habit. He started to rear long before required, as I led him down to the yard to cover a mare. It is said that if a horse rears, and you pull him over, it will cure him of it. Now this is an extremely dodgy practice. You could severely injure the animal's back. I reasoned that the floor in the covered yard was so deep in straw that if I could pull him more or less sideways, he would come down without the risk of injury.

I chose exactly the wrong moment to discipline Carnaby. Leading him down to the yard one day he reared. I asked him to stop and he wouldn't so when we got inside the covered yard I pulled him over. He came down with such a thump that it winded him. So incensed was I at having to resort to such tactics, and blaming him for it, I leaped on to him as he lay on the ground, and proceeded to beat him up with my fists. So busy was I meting out such an injustice to the poor creature that I hadn't noticed the two ladies who had entered the yard behind me, one of whom yelled, 'Is this really necessary?' Without looking, I answered 'Yes, it bloody well is, and if you don't wish to see it, piss off.' Silence followed. I got to my feet and turning about could see my accuser. It was none other than the redoubtable Aunt P, accompanied by close friend and devoted horse lover, Jilly Rolands. The two women stood red faced, as I first greeted them, then left them for Joyce to pacify. Everyone except Karen was horrified at my behaviour. She was all in favour. 'You gonna beat him up again dad?' she would ask.' To which I would reply 'No, no, it's not a good idea.' Although smallest and skinniest, mentally she was the toughest. I certainly would not recommended you do likewise to a horse, but it worked for me. Carnaby never reared again.

We arrived at Southampton Docks, and I led Carnaby from the horsebox. He had travelled well and looked about him with interest. I reported to the Customs shed and was shown where to put my horse. Having checked all the export papers, the Custom's Officer said I could go, and that Customs would look after the horse from here on. I went over to the stable to see Carnaby for the last time. I put my arms around his neck and kissed him on the nose. As I walked away he whickered after me as he had always done. I climbed into the lorry and drove off. I was numb. After a while I stopped in a lay-by and poured a cup of tea from the flask Joyce had made for me. I asked myself 'What have I done? How could I?' He was my soulmate, and I had deserted him.

A COCKNEY KID IN GREEN WELLIES

It was a very sorry me that arrived back at Shortwood. I couldn't look as I walked passed the empty stable that still bore the name Carnaby Street on its door. A couple of weeks later my pain was eased when I received a letter from the Dutchman postmarked Gronigen Holland. He wrote that Carnaby had arrived in excellent condition, giving us due credit for that. Carnaby had settled in well, and already had many admirers.' A few years later, we received a letter to say that Carnaby had won a national championship. Delighted, I wrote back congratulating them all on their achievement. We have a pencil portrait of Carnaby drawn in 1971 by Ros Goodwin, hanging in our sitting room. A striking likeness.

I booked Dave Lee Travis to open Stripes Disco. I never rated disc jockey's at all, but was assured by John Mills that they 'packed 'em in.' 'People will pay good money to watch and listen to someone playing records to them?' I needed convincing. It was a Saturday and we were all wound up in great expectation of a full house in our newly refurbished disco. DLT, as he is universally known, arrived at around 5pm driving a luxury camper van. I met him as he pulled into the car park, and offered him the same hospitality as I had shown to Mouth and Trousers when we first met. He said, 'Thanks, but no thanks. I will be fine parked at the rear of your club.' 'Won't you get pestered by fans when they realise that this is your camper van?' I asked. 'I can take care of that,' he assured me.

Once again, John Mills had not exaggerated and the kids flocked in. By the time DLT was due to appear on stage we were at capacity. The cabaret club was also in full swing. I swear I could feel the whole building jumping. DLT employed a guy called Froggy as his warm-up man. Froggy also supplied and erected the massive sound system that was part of the DLT roadshow.

Froggy wound up his audience, then using pyrotechnics and strobe lights introduced the star of the show 'From Radio One, the man himself, Mr Dave Lee Travis.' The kids went wild. From behind the stage, a large 'Gorilla' appeared and began stomping up and down the boards. More flashes, more strobes. Then the 'Gorilla' reached above his head and in one swift movement pulled off his false mask, and DLT shouted, 'Hello everybody, it's great to be in Yate.' His fans were ecstatic. He 'killed' the music, and began talking at the same time dishing out obscure records, ones that had never made it. The record companies give these away like confetti. The kids loved it. Then he made a sign to Froggy, and the music blared out once more.

At first, I must admit I was impressed. DLT had made a great entrance, which had captured the imagination of everyone, including me. What will he do next? I wondered. I waited, thinking what can he do next? 'Nothing' was the answer to that. His act was over. For 50 minutes he played, or rather Froggy played requests and DLT signed autographs. With a few more flashes and strobes, he left the stage and went back to his camper. Later he came up to the cabaret club for a meal, and played drums for a few numbers. He wasn't a bad drummer.

During the next few years I re-booked DLT three times. In between I engaged David Hamilton, Paul Burnett, Simon Bates, Kid Jenson and Paul Gambaccini. The last two were practically unknown here at the time, having only recently arrived in England. DLT was always the most expensive, his last appearance for me in 1998 costing £900. The rest were all in the region of £400 to 450. Yet once more I have to concede they were excellent value – for me that is. I still can't understand anyone paying to listen to someone play records!

Keen to introduce live groups at my venue, I embarked on a self-destruct mission. I took the good, the bad and the 'What the bloody hell did I promote them for,' bands. Among the good were the 'Real Thing'. With their hit record, 'You to me are everything', they had moved up to number one in the charts on the Tuesday, appearing for me the following Saturday. You can't get it more right than that. But it was the only time I did.

The Motown era was at its height. We prospered with bands such as Sweet Sensation, with their biggest hit 'Sad sweet dreamer'. The Fantastics were all that their name suggests – a lovely bunch of guys. The Detroit Emeralds went down a storm with the audience. The Crystals were ever-popular with their chart topper 'Da Dooh Ron Ron'.

I promoted Bob Geldof and The Boom town Rats. They had only made one record, 'She's so Modern', which flopped. I was very impressed with Bob though. Quiet, intelligent and thoughtful off stage. He had an energy and presentation when performing that reminded me of Mick Jagger when he first started out. Of course, Bob did not have the exaggerated gyrations of Mick. None the less, it was who he reminded me of. It was early days for Bob and the Rats, and the punters were indifferent. (They would pay to listen to records though!) We were only half-full and lost money. I was confident that they would make it, and was delighted for them when they did.

Then came the New Wave and Punk Rock scene, bringing with it head-bangers and air guitars. Johnny Rotten and Co. Slaughter on the Dogs. Siouxsie and the Banshees. Siouxsie and I fell out big time. One of her band, I never found out which one, had sprayed the name of their group with an aerosol can on the freshly painted toilet walls. I told them to clean it off or I would throw them out. They tried to call my bluff.

It got to about an hour before we were due to open the doors before they relented. No way would I have backed down. Not my kind of band, or music, but the punters loved them.

There was a series on TV called *Rock Follies* with Judy Covington. A group calling themselves Brandy were aping the band in the series. Early 'girl power' and long before the Spice Girls who suggest they invented it! The writing was on the wall the moment they walked through the door. They linked arms and paraded around the dance floor singing 'Rock Follies'. I don't know what they were on, but something was firing them up, it was still only 4.30 the afternoon. I opened my office door to a sneaky pressman. 'I'm from the *News of the World*,' he announced. Then he went on to say that he had been following this particular girl band around the country in order to do an article for his paper. As this was the biggest venue they had played, he would base it on their performance here, if it was OK? 'Be my guest,' I said.

Brandy were so bad that even the kids booed. I told Eddie Gardiner who was one of my doormen (bouncers) to tell them to stop playing. The girls in the band ignored him, turned their amps up, and carried on. I was fuming. 'Eddie, go on stage and pull the plugs out' I ordered. Eddie looked at me and said 'It might cause a riot boss.' I replied, 'I'll risk it, Ed, they are taking the piss.' Eddie is a 6 feet 5 inch rugby player. If he says it's Xmas, we all start singing carols! Alone, he calmly climbed on to the stage and pulled out the plugs. The punters cheered. Brandy went wild. They pulled down the glitter curtains that formed the backdrop to the stage and started to wreck the place. They punched holes in false partitions and threw everything they could lay their hands on across the stage. With a little help, although still kicking and screaming, Eddie pushed them and their gear out through the side door.

The News of the World reporter had got far more than he had bargained for. But how would he write it up? He had been pro Girl Power and that was his angle, the reason he had followed them. He said they hadn't been that bad on the previous occasions he had seen them. Dino, my friend from the Chequers days, and now my bar manager he also performed in cabaret – and had witnessed the furore, and went outside to pacify the girls. He came back after a few minutes with a message from them saying they were very sorry, and would I at least pay their expenses because they were skint. With my background, needless to say I am usually a soft touch for a lame dog. But the girls had behaved appallingly, causing alarm and damage to property, mine! I sent Dino back with the answer 'Not a penny, and I'm going to sue for the damaged caused.'

COME TO THE CABARET

'When the *News of the World* reporter asked my opinion of Brandy, I said: 'They can't sing, they can't play, they are bloody awful. So I should think that the way pop music is heading, they will probably become stars!' (They didn't last long).

The next day the Sunday paper ran an article covering the progress of the all girl band and printed my comments.

Stars Cabaret was going well enough, but the older audience were more fickle than the disco kids. John Mills phoned offering me a young comedian who had recently been a winner on the popular TV talent show *New Faces*. He was fresh to the club circuit, and John thought he had a future. 'He is asking £175, but I told him you wouldn't pay that, but that you might give him a ton. What do you think Jim?' I agreed to take him.

Confident and cocky Jim Davidson gave a 'money for value' performance. Suggestive but not blue, the punters loved him. After the public had gone, Jim stayed on and told me how he became inspired to tell jokes about the police from his brother who had been in the force. Nick, Nick, and the Talking broach had come from there. A Londoner himself, most of the characters he spoke of were modelled on people he knew.

The next time Jim Davidson appeared on TV, he told of how he had lost his driving licence on his way home from a night-club. After leaving us he had been stopped in Coalpit Heath, a notorious stretch for getting nicked for speeding. I don't think he was amused by it! Jim did not exactly endear himself to the Bristol public by his treatment of their much-loved local TV news presenter Alison Holloway. He met Alison while in Panto at the Hippodrome, Bristol's premier theatre. A whirlwind courtship led to them marrying. Jim wasn't exactly a one women guy, so the marriage didn't last long. He also became unreasonably 'blue' in cabaret. He has talent and is naturally funny. He doesn't need to be filthy. Now I am told he has cleaned up his live act considerably, and wants to encourage family entertainment. I applaud that.

Whilst I am on the subject of 'blue' comics, how times have changed. In my early days at The Randolph, I gave a young man a spot in front of my Sunday night crowd. He was going quite well until his final joke when he used the 'F' word. I have never heard an audience go so quiet so suddenly in my life. A few days later Joan Milner received several letters of complaint. Most blamed me for allowing him to say it! I had no idea he was going to, and was as surprised as anyone. The culprit was Martin Connors, whose father was the legendary Shag Connors, who with his band the Carrot Crunchers were widely loved and respected.

Mick 'Shag' Connors died prematurely. He was the 'salt of the earth'. A committed animal lover, he had a small holding and reared the cockerels he used on stage. They were only there for effect, and were well cared for. A singer songwriter, an all-round entertainer, who created a niche for himself and his band, one that his son Martin is still enjoying to this day. Martin plays guitar and sings, leading the Carrot Crunchers in his own inimitable style. A smashing bloke, but he will never be Mick. God rest you mate.

Who will ever forget the drought during the summer of 76? There was not a blade of grass to be seen at Shortwood Farm, and our worries were twofold. Firstly we were having to feed hay to the horses, which is virtually unheard of in summer. Secondly because the grass had not grown there would be a poor harvest. The coming winter would see prices for hay at a premium, and we would be in the unfortunate position of having to buy in. The government had issued warnings of severe restrictions on water supplies, and watering the lawn or car washing with a hosepipe was illegal. Standpipes were erected in some areas, and people queued with buckets to fill. It lasted four months. But the effect on the farming economy lasted much longer.

Stella's daughter Janine, who now worked for me at Stars and Stripes, came rushing in breathless early one evening. Her mother and father had fallen out big time, and Stella had left her husband taking their son Grahame with her. Could her mother stay overnight with us at Shortwood Farm, until Janine could 'sort something out?' Naturally we agreed. Stella arrived distressed, and was greeted with sympathy by Joyce. My sister waited up for me until I got back from the club in the early hours. We sat for an hour chatting, during which she confided that her relationship with her husband and been turbulent for some time. This time he was more belligerent than usual, so she left. She had had enough of his manic behaviour. Her one night stay with us lasted for three months!

Stella and Grahame's television business had gone from success to success over the past eleven years, yet they still did not have a decent home in which to live. For the first few years they lived above their shop in Kingswood, Bristol, 'open all hours'. Then Stella found a nice Victorian detached house in Beacon Lea Kingswood, not far from their shop. The people that owned the house immediately took to Stella, as most people do, and sold her the property at very reasonable price.

Having moved in at Beacon Lea, Grahame embarked upon a trail of DIY projects that he simply never completed. The house was a wreck.

The central heating system resembled something from the early days of steam! To add insult to injury, he laid concrete over the pretty garden situated on one side of the house, and set up a second-hand car lot! Potential customers knocked on the door at all hours to inquire about the cars for sale. One Sunday morning whilst they were still living above the shop, Grahame led a customer upstairs to the bedroom where he and Stella slept, to show a radiogram he had stored there. Stella was still in bed! She hid under the covers in embarrassment. Grahame made no apology. Typical of him. He attended a different charm school to the rest of us!

Everything was getting too much for me, so after much soul searching, and not a little pressure from the bank, I decided to sell Shortwood Farm. Neither Jane nor Karen was any longer interested in the ponies. Jane had a new boyfriend, Eddie Gardiner, who worked part time for me at the Club. Not to be outdone and although still only 15 years old, Karen had struck up a friendship with Gordon Stephenson. Gordon had approached me one day asking for a job at the club. I sent him on his way, telling him 'put on a suit and get a hair cut'. I didn't expect him to return, but to my surprise he did. What could I say? And that's how Karen met him. Gordon had a small car, which was freedom for Karen. I didn't begrudge my girls anything. After all I was doing what I wanted. And anyway, I felt happy in the knowledge that I both knew with whom and where they were, the majority of the time. I think most parents these days would settle for that.

Of course one has ideas and expectations for one's children's future. But you must not try to live your life through them. I have seen many relationships crumble through this ideal. They have to find their own way, however painful. And it often is. Be there for them, and in support of them. When they realise that you will always listen, however cross you may be with them at the time, it's surprising just how often they will confide their anxieties. My children are now parents themselves. I am as proud as a peacock when they are heard to say, 'I'll ask my Dad for his advice about that.' That'll do me for an epitaph!

We had two flats with the club; one at each end of the shopping centre. I let Jane have one, and she moved in with Eddie. If it worked out, they would marry. I remember at the time thinking, 'What if I had made that suggestion to Joyce's parents when she was 18?' Joyce's sister Heather and her husband Ian both now worked at Stars and Stripes occupied the second flat. These flats were very spacious. Once the farm had been sold, if we couldn't find a suitable house, we could always camp out with our family for a short time.

A COCKNEY KID IN GREEN WELLIES

My dad hadn't been well of late and was showing signs of frailty. He had been to the club but had not stayed for a show. One of my Mum's favourite singers was Emile Ford, so I engaged him especially for her. Emile arrived quite early on the Saturday he was to appear, and was in the dressing room doing press-ups when I knocked on his door. Although well past his youth he was in superb physical shape, and quite one of the nicest people I have ever had the pleasure of working with. We sat, and over a cold soft drink Emile never touches alcohol – we discussed, as I always did with cabaret acts, the format for the evening.

I didn't hear mum and dad enter the club, so when I left Emile and walked back into the cabaret room, I was surprised to see them sitting by the edge of the dance floor. Mum greeted me as always, with a smile only a mother can give. 'Hello Jim love. Are we a bit early?' she wondered. 'No it's alright mum, I'll get you a drink,' I replied. 'Is he here yet? Emile Ford?' she asked. I told her he was, and I would get him to come and say hello. You should have seen my mum's face when Emile came around the corner from the dressing room. It was a picture. 'Are you going to sing, 'What d'ya wanna make those eyes at me for?' she asked of the star. 'Right now if you like, lady,' he offered. 'Please,' mum encouraged. So it was, that the talented Emile not only sang his big hit for my mum, but continued to perform the rest of his act. He sang for an hour with just mum and dad for an audience. He was magnificent, and they clapped loudly in appreciation. Soon after Emile had finished, mum asked me if I minded if they left. Dad was not feeling so good. I kissed mum, and catching hold of dad's arm led them to the lift, and took them down to their car. 'Don't wear yourself out in this business, Jim. Stay on the farm with your horses,' Dad said as he slid into the seat of his little silver grey Vauxhall Viva. A couple of years later those words came back to haunt me.

I thanked Emile and told him, 'You didn't have to do that.' He replied, 'Your parents made the effort to come here just to see me. I assure you, the honour is all mine.' Emile Ford was a class act. He used a quality PA system with pre-recorded tape to provide musical backing for his songs – common now, but innovative then. We opened at 8pm to a capacity crowd. I sang a couple of numbers, then introduced Emile, saying: 'Ladies and gentlemen please welcome a real star, at Stars Cabaret Club, Mr Emile Ford. Emile, beautifully dressed and with a massive smile, greeted his fans, then proceeded to entertain them for more than an hour. As fresh and with as much enthusiasm as he had done so for my mum and dad two hours earlier. He was, is, talented, charismatic, a great performer. He possesses the most important of all ingredients, humility. That's why he's a true star.

COME TO THE CABARET

I had leased my TV shop on South Parade to my old mate Billy Parker. Bill together with a colleague named Mike Fuller (with whom he had worked at a TV retail firm called Atkinson's) had started a TV business in Kingswood, Bristol. They were now the proprietors of Vision On, with retail premises in Staple Hill. There were not too many Saturday nights that I can remember when Bill Parker and his lovely wife Rene were *not* at their usual table in my Club. Bill supported me enthusiastically in everything I ever did. Rene was also very popular with my family, especially so with my daughter Karen, who adores her. Rene's brother Larry McNess was probably the most enduring of punters. He still reminds me that during the 70s he earned a fortune, but spent it all at Stars and Stripes. That I can believe. And he was helped I'm sure, by the female entourage who followed him everywhere!

We sold the remaining horses and found good homes for our two Jack Russell terriers, Meggy and Sam. Duke the Doberman Pincher, we would take with us. Doberman's are one-family dogs and rarely change their alliance. It is very risky to try. I had bought Duke as a guard dog for the farm. We were a bit isolated and it brought a great deal of comfort to Joyce having him around. They are wonderful companions, quiet, they rarely bark, and in the case of a dog, gentlemanly. We had several farm cats living outside in the barns. One of them gave birth to a litter in an empty stable. Duke had watched the mother carrying the kittens around in her mouth. In his wisdom, he thought they should be in the house. So without harming a hair on their tiny bodies, one by one he carried them in his mouth setting them gently down inside the porch! Horses, cats and dogs all got along famously together. I honestly cannot remember an altercation.

We bought Duke through an advert in the *Western Daily Press*. The kennel advertising dobermans for sale was situated a few miles over the Severn Bridge in Wales. Joyce and I made the trip and arrived in the yard of a large, old country house. All seemed very quiet and a toot on the horn didn't produce anyone, so I ventured out of the car to take a look around. I had gone no more than four or five yards, when the biggest Doberman bitch you ever did see bounded around a corner and stopped in front of me. She then arrested me by placing her mouth around my thigh! Rightly or wrongly, I froze. What now, I wondered? Joyce, still sitting in the car, looked on in terror. I beckoned to her whispering 'drive as close as possible, and position the car so I can jump into the passenger seat.' How I thought I would achieve this without the doberman closing her jaws on me I will never know.

Thank god I didn't get to find out. The owner came into view and called to the bitch, who immediately released me. I was in shock but furious, and remonstrated with the owner about not having a sign that warned people to stay in their cars until attended to. He didn't bat an eyelid, saying 'You wanted a guard dog didn't you? That's what we sell here.'

Once the sale of our home had gone through, we put our furniture and effects into storage and carrying a few personal items in our hands, Joyce and I climbed into separate cars. We drove slowly up the lane, and as we rounded the corner I glanced back. That was the last time any of us saw Shortwood Farm. Although we have many photographs, including one lovely aerial picture of the farm (reproduced on the front cover of this book) and live no more than four miles away, none of us have ever returned. It would be too painful to contemplate. It isn't the house or land that we miss. It's the horses, for us, the place would never be the same without them.

People have often asked if Shortwood Farm came back on the market would I buy it back? I have always said no. You can't relive what's in the past, so don't try. The risk of disappointment is too high. I always said I would buy Allendale if ever it came up for sale. It has more than once, and I have known about it, but resisted.

Having paid off all my loans with the proceeds of the sale of Shortwood Farm, and not having to worry about the TV business, I was now lean and mean, and able to concentrate fully on making a success of the wild animal I had named Stars and Stripes. Joyce took over the financial accounting, something she is well qualified to do, and will do when required. Joyce is extremely efficient, and is always in a position at the drop of a hat to tell me how we stand. Crucial, when you have so many balls in the air!

I set about attracting more private functions to the club. We already had the local branch of Lions annual do, as well as the Police ball. There were also a number of wedding receptions, and 18th birthday parties. I would not allow either stag, or hen nights; they can get out of hand.

Wednesday nights were reserved for the authentic Rock 'n' Roll crowd. It's funny how the image has changed over the years. They were perceived in the 50s as 'bovver boys' dressed in Edwardian suits with the odd bicycle chain hanging from their coat pockets. Now that image could not be further from the truth. The 70s Teddy Boys were no trouble at all. They still dressed in the classic Drapes, with suede shoes (brothel creepers) but dedicated their time to keeping Rock 'n' Roll music alive. Mostly men (very few girls used to support these nights), they would linger around the bar talking of Elvis, while others danced alone, or together. That might sound a contradiction, but that is what they did. With the thumb of one hand tucked in their belts, whilst a fag kept the other occupied, they performed their own peculiar brand of Rock 'n' Roll. As one who was there first time around, it was alien to me. Mates I had that followed the Teddy Boy code when we were young had one thing on their minds; 'Birds'. It was cool to be a Ted, or at least some girls thought so. I couldn't make this modern day lot out. They were only interested in the music, or who had the best drape and record collection, which they referred to as 'wax'.

There were two memorable nights that I remember during my association with the 70s Rock 'n' Roll crowd. I was approached by an agent saying he was bringing the Rock-a-Billy legend Charlie Feathers over from Memphis, and asking me if I would be interested in promoting him at Stars and Stripes. I had to confess that I had never heard of him. When I mentioned the possibility of Charlie Feathers coming here to the Wednesday-night crowd, they looked at me in total disbelief. 'Charlie coming here?' Apparently he was their hero, a legend, who was responsible more than any one else for the birth of Rock ' n' Roll. A name in America well before Elvis, who himself admired Charlie.

I agreed to take Charlie Feathers and friends and promote a night of Rock 'a' Billy. They arrived mid-afternoon on a Saturday, tired and somewhat despondent. So far their tour had been a flop. Everything that could go wrong had. The agent who booked them had pretty much let them down; he had arranged for them to play in some pretty crummy places and, with virtually no publicity, fans were few on the ground. Our local cult followers had drummed up quite a few, so a respectable crowd turned up to see the great man, but we could have attracted many more. My advert in the *Bristol Evening Post*, which could normally be relied upon to get things right, had read 'Charles Feather'.
The many fans on the edge of the scene did not think for one moment that this referred to their legendary hero Charlie, so ignored it.

Those who came witnessed an evening of Rock 'a' Billy and country music they will never forget. Also on tour with Charlie Feathers were Matt Curtis, Ray Campi and his Rock 'a' Billy Rebels, Colin Winsky, Jerry Sikorsky, John Blair and Drummer Steve Clark. After the show I entertained the guys in our restaurant, making sure that they were well fed and watered. One O'clock in the morning, Charlie picked up his guitar to play some early stuff for me that he had written. First one, then two got up; suddenly there were five of the guys jamming with Charlie. They played until 4am, then one by one put down their guitars and stretched out on the leather benches that ran around the room of the Stars Cabaret Club.

We locked them in to sleep where they lay. Next morning, with eyes still only half-open, I helped them pack their gear and load it in their van. Over coffee Charlie Feathers said, 'Thanks for everything Jim, this is the best venue we have played since we arrived here.' I felt embarrassed. Was this the best that England could offer the father of rock? I apologised for the lack of publicity he had received, assuring him he deserved much more. Making me feel worse than I already did, he added, 'This is my first time in your beautiful country. I have been meaning to come over for such a long time, but heck, never did seem to make it.' Sometimes our hospitality, or lack of it, is unreal, but this took the biscuit. He should have been on national TV and radio. I could have done so much more, but the agent who phoned me to say he was bringing Charlie over was economic with the truth. In fact Charlie was already here and had few bookings. There simply wasn't time for me to intervene. Otherwise I would have, no question, no matter whose toes I trod on.

As we parted Charlie said, 'Jim my friend, come over to Memphis for a visit some time. We can go shoot 'n fish 'n or sump'n. I don't know, but we will get up to sump'n that's for sure.' Sadly I never did. I don't have too many regrets in life, but that's one of them. If Charlie Feathers did ever set foot on these shores again, then I'm not aware of it.

A week after the Rock 'a' Billy show, word got around that Charlie and Co. had been at Stars and Stripes, disappointed fans rang asking about their heroes. Some even paid us a visit just to stand on the spot where Charlie stood.

Elvis Presley died in August 77. My Rock 'n' Rollers went into mourning. Paradoxically it was a Wednesday and all the pop radio stations were playing tributes to Elvis. My regular Teddy Boys turned up with black arm bands on their drapes. One of them got on the mike, and paid tribute to The King. It was quite moving. They were genuinely distressed. Wednesday nights at the Stars and Stripes were never the same. Attendances got lower and lower, and when the stalwarts drifted away, I brought it to an end. I had got on tremendously well with the West Country Rock 'n' Roll scene. They were a genuine, caring group of society. I wonder if any of those that I knew then are still in drapes?

My dad had been feeling very poorly for some time. 'You can tell how bad I feel Jim, I haven't had a fag for a week'. (His method of determining his level of infirmity.) 'What does the doctor say?' I asked. 'Doctors, what do they know?' he replied in his usual authoritarian manner. 'Got to see a specialist,' he added. A few days passed and mum phoned to say dad was much worse, and that she had called in the doctor, who in turn had told her he could no longer cope with Dad's illness, and that he would have to get him admitted to hospital. 'Will you come and take your dad to the hospital Jim?' Mum asked. 'Of course, I will come right away,' I responded. 'No son, it's late. You don't have to rush down now. The doctor says tomorrow morning will be OK,' She replied.

'Cup of tea Jim?' Mum asked. 'Please,' I replied. Mum went into the kitchen and I sat beside my father. 'What do they say is wrong, dad?' I questioned. 'I don't know son. I have a terrible pain at the bottom of my stomach and it won't go away,' he replied. Two years before he had been admitted to Ham Green hospital in an emergency. He had suffered a 'bleed' on that occasion. They let him home after a week. I asked my sister Maisie's daughter, Suzanne, who was a staff nurse then at the Bristol Royal Infirmary, (she now has a Master of Science degree and is a lecturer at Exeter University) the significance of the diagnoses. But she was reluctant to tell me, although suggested it might re-occur. I thought, cancer?

Dad sat, ashen faced, whilst mum and I drank our tea. He didn't want any. No tea, and no fag – both normally his priorities. Dad sat in my car beside me, and Mum sat in the back. It was a quiet journey with few words exchanged. We pulled into the car park at Frenchay hospital and alighted from our vehicle. Looking along the line of wards, which are end on to the car park with their respective numbers painted in white, it was easy to spot Ward 20, which had once been my 'home'. 'Hasn't changed much dad, has it?' I said. 'Not a lot son. I wouldn't mind a shilling for every hour I spent sitting out here, whilst your mum sat with you. It was the only way I could have a fag you see.' 'Thanks for all the times you drove out here to see me dad, you too mum,' I said with feeling. 'Soppy sod, it was nothing,' Dad assured me.

Once the admission paperwork was complete, the hospital staff asked mum and me to leave. 'There would be a number of tests, and they would take time' a nurse informed, then added 'You can visit this evening.' I took mum back home. She could have gone to stay with Stella who was now living in a beautiful period house in Cold Ashton in Wiltshire, but she preferred to be in her own home.

A COCKNEY KID IN GREEN WELLIES

The specialists announced they planned to operate on my dad, not explaining either to him or us why, only that they wanted to 'open him up'. I asked Dad how he felt about it. He said he had nothing to lose, he felt dreadful and couldn't feel any worse. I think had he known exactly what was wrong with him, he would have declined the operation. I would certainly have encouraged him to, if I too had known. When my sister Maud, who had been phoning every day, heard of the impending surgery, she declared her intention to be with dad and see him through it. She duly arrived and stayed with mum, and was a great comfort to us all. One morning mum couldn't sleep, and rose extra early. On her way down the stairs, she could hear a muffled sound coming from the lounge. Opening the door quietly, she found Maud, sitting on the floor in the middle of the room, surrounded by old family photos, sobbing.

Dad was born on Trafalgar Day, 21 October. His birthday came around a few days after he was admitted to hospital, and before his op. The whole family descended on Frenchay. My sisters each took a small gift, and I took a bottle of the best champagne we had in the club. 'Thanks Jim. I'll share this with some of the fellows after you've all gone home. It's a pity they haven't got a piano here; we could have a real party!' he said. He meant it, too.

I was spending my time between the club, the hospital, mum's, and Stella's, where half the Ruston family were in residence. It was the first time we had all been together in years. It's sad that it takes desperate times to bring families together. Ours, I'm sure is always there in spirit, but not often in the flesh. Dad had the op, and much to our relief, recovered from it as well as we could hope. Then, when all seemed to being going quite well, and most of the family had returned to London, dad had a relapse. His condition became critical.

It wasn't until then, that we found out dad had cancer. Even though we now knew what the problem was the hospital seemed reluctant to discuss it. Thank goodness things are much changed nowadays. The London contingent hurried back to the West Country. Most of us were at Stella's when the hospital phoned to say we should come at once. My sister Betty, with husband Roy, brought mum up from Nailsea, whilst we, in convoy, tore off to Frenchay. We arrived to be told that our father had just passed away. Not one of us was there with him when he died. We were upset beyond words.

I was standing, exhausted and completely numb, in the corridor leading to Ward 6, where dad lay, when, accompanied by Betty and Roy, mum came through the side door. She looked straight at me. I shook my head. Then Mum said with her voice in a tremor, 'No, he's not dead is he? Not my Jim, he can't be. I didn't say goodbye to him.'

My mum was petite and looked so vulnerable. I thought; 'How dare they. How dare they take her husband from her' I wanted to smash the place up, and scream, 'That's my mother you're hurting'. I wanted someone to blame. My parent's relationship was rarely smooth, especially in the early years. But they were devoted to each other.

The family left the ward in sombre mood. My brother Roy put his hand on my shoulder and saying, 'We don't have a dad no more.' and walked away. But before he could drive off we had to give his car a shove. It wouldn't start. Puzzled, Roy said, 'I don't understand it. It has never let me down before.' Then we all looked at one another and laughed. We had spent half our lives pushing old cars that belonged to our father. 'He's reminding us that he's still around,' I said. Mum, with tears still flowing down her cheeks, grinned from ear to ear.

We went to a local pub and had a drink. Then it was all back to Stella's for some food and more drink, lots more. The night before my dad died, after closing the club, I went out to Frenchay. It was 2.30am when I got there. I walked quietly into Ward 6. The night nurse was sitting alone at her desk filling in reports. Seeing me, she rose to her feet and asked if she could help. I told her who I was, and asked if I could sit by my dad for a while. I sat there listening to the breathing and murmurs of the patients. I gazed around reflecting on the months I had languished in a bed similar to the one I was now sitting by, dad was being my visitor then. Apart from its number, Ward 6 was identical to my old Ward 20, even the nurse at her desk and the shadows cast from the small table lamp she needed to read by were familiar. I remembered the hot summer nights when I couldn't sleep, and a nurse would come and wipe my brow with a cold flannel.

Speaking in a whisper I told the young nurse who my dad was, and the incredible life that he had led. To my surprise she answered, 'I think your dad is a bit of a celebrity here. Everyone seems to know him. On his birthday he walked around the ward giving champagne to those whom could drink it. Before he could be stopped, the bottle was empty. He won the hearts of us all. He doesn't conform much does he?' I looked down at dad, his breathing laboured, and his eyes opened. I'm not sure he knew who I was, the effects of morphine distort everything. He beckoned me closer. Then with difficulty said:
'There were these two tramps walking in the park...' Would you believe it? He was only trying to tell me a joke!

A couple of days later I collected dad's possessions from the ward where he died. There was the wristwatch Maud had brought, a hip flask from June, a cigarette lighter and other presents that he had been given. But there was no sign of the champagne from me! The second gift I had given him that could not be lost nor given away (although even this he shared).

I wouldn't miss our relationship, because there really was none. But I would miss what he was. A complex man, there were moments of wisdom, eloquence and a tolerance that could only emanate from one who had lived through much change in fortune. I came to realise what an influence he has been on me. I quote him often. It's a shame I could never bring myself to tell him how much I loved him. He was a Victorian, and we never got beyond a handshake.

I organised dad's funeral, hiring 10 black limousines to carry the family in mourning. I had a floral tribute made in the shape of a grand piano. We dressed for the occasion. The girls looked stunning in black suits, wearing their finest jewellery; the men also sombre, in dark apparel. The entourage filled the road outside mum and dad's house. In the style befitting a showman, the cavalcade moved off through Nailsea pausing at New Rank, where we lived towards the end of the war. Then slowly on past Allendale and up the hill turning left by Wraxall church, where three of us had married. I held mum's hand as she whispered 'I can't take it Jim,' Reassuring her I replied, 'You can mum, you must. Dad's counting on you.' She stiffened, and pulled her shoulders back, asserting her presence as head of the family. I was so proud of her.

The day was calm, and autumn leaves were deep on the ground as we pulled up outside the church at Failand. We couldn't bury dad at Wraxall; there is a covenant at that church which says you can only be buried there if you are living in the parish at the time of your death. It caused us a deal of grief, but there was nothing we could do. We offered money, but even this would not change their minds! The cars came to a halt in stillness. Then, as from nowhere, a mighty gust of wind got up and for a few seconds it almost took us off our feet. After that, complete calm was restored. It was eerie, unforgettable.

After the internment I invited everyone to the club, where I had laid on a buffet and, of course, plenty of booze. Roy played the piano, and talk was of nothing but dad. I had also invited my friends Bill and Rene Parker. I knew it would be difficult for me, and thought if I had someone from outside of the family present, I would not break down. Those two friends are precious to me. The family mingled. Teresa sat on my lap and ruffled my hair, as she has done since she was a child. I love all my nieces, it's just that some are closer than others.

Mum was lost without dad. Betty and husband Roy would take care of her from now on. Although, mum would not move from her own house; she valued her independence. It was fortunate for us all that Betty lived just a few doors away from her.

THE CANDLE BURNS OUT

The Stars and Stripes club had now completely taken over our lives. We even had our Christmas dinner there in between preparing for the next event. I saw Joyce and Rachel each morning, but then only briefly. A typical weekend went something like this. Friday night, Stripes disco, with a private function in Stars cabaret room. Saturday, all-day darts competition. Saturday night, Stripes Disco and Stars cabaret. At 2am on Sunday morning, one lot of revellers left, to be replaced by another. We held a Northern Soul disco until 7am. Sunday, all- day darts. If not darts then some other event. Sunday night, Stars cabaret. In reality, we opened at 7pm on Friday and did not close again until midnight on Sunday. The candle was burning at both ends again.

Northern Soul is so named because it started in the north of the country, in Wigan. People danced all night, some were spectacular, to nothing but soul music, much of which was imported and unavailable here on general sale. Coach loads of fans of the soul scene descended upon us, bringing with them their own DJ, who in turn brought his personal record collection of the very best soul music. No alcohol was consumed, only soft drinks were served.

But there was a sting in the tail. I hadn't noticed it at first, but I did wonder where the dancers got the energy to leap around all night. After a while I began to catch on, and found a very discreet use of soft drugs among some of the supporters. I contacted the local drug squad who had made routine visits to the club previously and were already aware of the drug abuse this seemingly innocent music club generated. The under-cover officers were brilliant. They rarely came into the club, preferring instead to do random searches of punters as they got off the coaches. Also searching the cars of those who had travelled independently. The officers were far more concerned with seeking out those actually dealing in illegal substances, rather than those who of their own volition popped pills and smoked pot.

There was never any violence at Northern Soul discos. In fact two doormen were more than adequate to keep order, whereas on a normal Saturday night disco at least six were required. On conventional nights, the odd fracas, that if not quickly contained, would turn into a scene competing with a John Wayne movie. There were a few of these incidents, and it amazes me still that no one was ever seriously injured. A fat lip, a black eye, but rarely anything broken. Surprisingly, very little of the furniture got damaged. When things looked as if they could get out of hand, I ordered all the lights up and everyone out of the club, bringing the entertainment to an end, no matter what time it was. This had a sobering effect on the punters. They quickly learned that I would not tolerate bad behaviour, no matter what it cost me. My relationship with the local Police was good. In spite of my brother-in-law Don Waite being the Commander of the division in which my business was located. I never sought, nor was I ever offered, any concession. My sister Eve's husband Don, a Chief Superintendent, was the consummate professional. We allowed each other space, and got along very well.

When I took over the Entertainment Centre at Yate, I inherited the police ball. It meant closing the venue to the public on the night of the ball, which was never popular with my punters. The policemen organised the band, but we did the catering for the buffet.

One year I was approached by one of the officers who was on the police ball committee, who informed me that in future the police would arrange the food side of things themselves. They had no complaints with what we had done in the past, but thought it would be more economic for them. 'So it may be,' I replied. 'But I don't allow people to do that.' I was already upsetting my regulars by shutting their disco for the night. Losing the revenue from their entrance fees into the bargain was not funny. I was making no charge to the police for the hire of the club, and did not intend to make more concessions. The policeman went off in a huff. A few days later I heard they had moved the police ball to another venue.

One night, I think it was around 9pm, the cavalry arrived in the guise of 15 police officers, led by Inspector Gerald Hodder. The boys and girls in blue walked straight past my doorman and into Stripes disco. They were checking for under-age drinkers. Unbeknown to us, the police had already 'planted' two plain-clothes officers in the club – one male, one female. They were standing by the bar drinking when their colleagues arrived. The police officers' interviewed a number of teenagers, a few of whom were under 18.   Under age drinking is a nightmare for licensees, and unless identity cards are introduced it will remain so. You try guessing the age of girls between 16 and 18 when they are dressed and made up. Some are younger than that. It's much easier with fellows.

I was taken to court and charged with serving alcohol to three under-age girls, who now, dressed down in court, still looked iffy. Funny how the police never produced any fellows. I was fined £400. The chairman of the bench, Howard Lewis, whom I knew very well, looked at me with sympathy, but he and I both knew it was cut and dried. The police had the evidence. I had to admit I was at fault, or rather my bar staff had been. I didn't work behind the bar myself, so hadn't actually served anyone. The licensee carries the responsibility, even if he is not actually present at the time the law is broken, as I wasn't. I was gradually turning the club around from loss to profit. I had cut down drastically on live pop bands. For every band I promoted that made us money, there were two that didn't. I thought. 'I can't get away with it. Surely the punters won't continue to support a disco, with no live music?' They did. The absence of live groups didn't make a scrap of difference. We packed them in just the same. I booked the odd celebrity DJ once in a while, but nothing more. My judgement had been wrong. 'They won't pay for someone to play records to them, will they?' They bloody well will. They did, and still do! Although it lost money, I missed the live scene. I would sooner listen to a third- rate live band than a first rate disco any day. On reflection, I remember when dad first came to see my new night-club. He looked around, liked the Stars cabaret club, but when he saw Stripes disco heaving, he turned to me saying, 'Jim, this is the future for dancehalls, whether we like it or not.' He was always ahead of the game. I should have listened.

My intake of alcohol was on the increase. It had started with the occasional whisky, and it grew. I was drinking at least a half a bottle a day. Gone was the one shot of spirit to 10 shots of dry ginger; it was now the other was around. If we were out of dry ginger, who cared! I drank scotch like lemonade, in a tall glass with ice, with little, if any effect.

My daughter Jane was getting married to Eddie Gardiner. They were to marry in St Mary's Church Yate, with a reception afterwards at the Stars and Stripes club. Everything was arranged. We were still living in the flat at the Centre, which wasn't a very suitable place for the bride to leave for the church. Our friends Brian and Sue Mannering, who lived in a nice bungalow a couple of miles from us, offered Jane the use of their home in which to dress and prepare for her big day. It was a kind gesture. Brian was still at his factory in Wickwar. Sue, a hairdresser, had a business in nearby Fishponds. All set. (Excuse the pun!)

After a hectic weekend at the club, I was feeling more exhausted than usual, and irritated by a dull pain in my stomach. The pain intensified until it was uncontrollable. It could not be abated, even with the usual dose of paracetamol. (Those I ate like smarties.) It became so excruciating that I asked Joyce to send for a doctor. One came examined me and, realising the distress I was in, gave me a pain killing-injection saying 'This will help you sleep. If you are no better when you wake, let me know.' The relief from the jab relaxed me almost at once, and I fell into a deep sleep. However, on waking I felt even worse. Joyce called the doctor once more who after a cursory glance at me, rang for an ambulance. The ambulance took me to Southmead Hospital, not Frenchay as I had expected.

I was in so much pain that I got irritable when bombarded with so many questions. All I wanted was an injection to ease the pain. It seemed like an age before a doctor finally appeared and said he would give me something for the pain. Before he did so, a nurse shoved a tube down my throat, and attached it to a plastic bag, which, in turn, she pinned to my pyjama jacket. Then a doctor inserted a needle in my arm to which a drip was connected. Trussed up like a turkey, the relief I felt when the needle with the morphine went into the top of my leg was heaven sent.

When I awoke, a doctor informed me that I was suffering from acute pancreatitis. 'Probably caused by too much alcohol,' he said casually. 'We will leave the tube down, to rest your organs, and the drip will give you all the nourishment you need during the next few days. 'Few days. How long are a few days, my daughter is getting married on Saturday?' I pleaded. The physician replied, 'Can't say right now, but I'll keep an eye on you.' He smiled, then left. The candle, burning at both ends, had now met in the middle.

I could have an injection every four hours, but the relief from pain was only lasting for three. The following hour was purgatory. After a few days, once one's system becomes accustomed to the drug, the period of relief begins to decrease. The problem a doctor faces is that morphine is addictive. He dare not over prescribe it. I have suffered varying degrees of pain during my life, none of which comes anywhere near that caused by an inflamed pancreas. It goes right through you, and no matter how you position yourself, there is no respite from it. Joyce came in to see me; she was wearing a dark red velvet suit and looked stunning. I said how sorry I was for all the fuss I was causing. She just smiled saying, 'Don't worry love, we will manage. Just get better, please.' No recriminations, just words of comfort. What a woman.

A few days lapsed. I was still in serious pain. I woke from my injection to face a period of acute discomfort, and to my surprise, sitting by my bed was my old mate Billy Parker, with his partner Mike Fuller. By now they had been in business together for five years, but it had aged them ten. They had been sitting beside me whilst I slept. 'Thanks for coming to see me.' The stock greeting for all who visit one in hospital. I confided to Bill, 'I'm worried about Saturday. I won't be there to give Jane away. God what a mess I've made of things. Would you honour me, by walking Jane up the aisle?' I asked my dearest friend. 'Jim, this is your old mate you are talking to. I would do anything for you, and the honour would be all mine. But anyway, it won't be necessary, you will be there – wait and see. I know you!' With this assurance from Bill, I responded, 'Thanks for the confidence mate, but right now I couldn't walk the length of this ward.'

Friday came, and the pain, once unrelenting, had subsided. I had a good night's sleep. The day sister came on duty and I asked her what the chances were of my going to my daughter's wedding. 'And what do you propose to do about these?' shaking the tubes from my drip and catheter she admonished, in a manner reminiscent of the matriarchal Sister Sturgeon, I had encountered as a boy. Undaunted by her reply, I asked what time the doctor would be around. 'Can't say,' she said. 'Well can you get him for me; I need to talk to him,' I insisted. The Sister went away, muttering as she did so. I could hear her talking to others in her office about the man who thinks he is going to a wedding, 'Huh, some chance of that.' She informed her colleagues.

It wasn't the doctor whom I had expected, but a consultant surgeon who came along and sat on my bed. He was Canadian. 'They tell me you want to go to your daughter's wedding. Do you think you can do it?' he asked. 'I am prepared to give it a very good try,' I replied with enthusiasm. With an almost distant look on his face, the surgeon replied, 'If it were my daughter, I know I'd give it a go.' I wondered if he was thinking of his family back home. Reluctantly the ward sister telephoned Joyce who, although pleased, was worried I might have a relapse. Bill Parker arrived with my wedding suit. The sister, still shaking her head, removed the tubes, and looking straight at Bill said, 'Get him back here, immediately after the service. Do not give him any champagne either.' Helped by my pal, I slid into the passenger seat of his car. I felt just about as dreadful as I looked.

I walked Jane up the aisle. I was wobbly, so the vicar suggested that I sit rather than stand throughout the service. I really can't remember much more than that. I was drifting in and out of consciousness, trying hard to concentrate, and not wishing to alarm my already overburdened wife. The service over we all went across to the Stars and Stripes, which was just a few hundred yards away from St Mary's Church. My brother-in-law Don Waite had kindly offered to take me back into hospital. I thanked the guests and left. I climbed into bed, where a doctor shoved the tubes back in. I was content, though. A few days later, my friendly Canadian consultant, before discharging me, said, 'It's up to you Jim. You can leave the booze alone, or I can open you up when next we meet, because for sure we will, and it will be mutilaltive.' I still have the odd drink. But after one or two, the word 'mutilative' flashes before me. It's the only deterrent I need!

Joyce took me to Cornwall for a few days to convalesce, and we stayed in the old Victorian Carlyon Bay Hotel near St Austell. They had a dancehall with a live band playing for traditional ballroom dancing. We sat and talked of the future. Joyce's face lit up when I told her I had decided to get out of the entertainment business. 'I don't honestly think I could take much more of it,' she said. 'This had been the final straw.' The next few days we visited some of the places where we had stayed in the 60s. When, as a family, accompanied by Joyce's mum and dad, we rented a house or cottage each year for our annual summer holiday. There are not too many places on the south coast of Cornwall, where we have not stayed. We have travelled the world since, but they remain the best holidays of our lives.

I contacted an agent and put Stars and Stripes on the market. We had run the club for four years but it felt like 14.

When word got around that I was selling up, I got a call from my old friend Alan Wells. Alan had owned and run the Webbington Country Club at Loxton, near Bridgewater, for many years. It had been a successful family business, but was now ailing. I guess you could say that just about every entertainer, you could name, had at one time or another appeared at The Webby. In its heyday, it boasted a gambling casino, which in turn provided a great deal of revenue. On occasion that the odd act flopped, economically it didn't much matter. The Webby was a 1,000-seater, the biggest cabaret club by far in the West Country. Coach-loads descended at weekends, when the venue was mostly at capacity.

Alan Wells, a lovely bloke, but very much a ladies' man, had a few liaisons with beautiful women. The most famous of all was Jayne Mansfield, whom he hoped to marry. The film star returned briefly to the States, intending to become engaged to Alan when she got back. A few days after arriving in America, she was tragically killed in a car accident. Alan was devastated. Divorced from his wife Julie, who had supported him through thick and thin, he married Penny Chisholm, a stunning *Playboy* centrefold model.

After the war, fed up from years of austerity we Brits let our hair down. Clubs sprung up all over the place to accommodate demand from a new wave of people determined to enjoy themselves at last. A few pints for the man, a couple of shorts for the lady, 'chicken in a basket', a good comic, and everyone was happy. It was affordable. From the mid 50s on, the cabaret scene grew. By the mid-60s it was at its peak, then it levelled out and disco reared its ugly head. They were much cheaper than bands, or live acts. First to go were the dance bands; a disco would play for dancing, leaving a bit more in the pot to pay for a decent 'turn'.

Gambling had become popular, and casinos were opening everywhere; it was running wild. Something had to be done to control it. A gaming act was passed in 1968, the effect of which strictly limited the activity. New gaming laws came in, and with them a restriction on how many gaming licences would be allowed in a given region per capita. To this day there have never been more than 121 licences held at any one time; on average there are around 115. Whilst venues have not increased in number, the revenue from them has, dramatically. One of the criteria that had to be met was that there was to be 'un-stimulated demand'. In other words, no advertising, and 48-hrs lapse before membership was granted and so on. Casinos were to be tucked away, and appear uninviting. You would have to make a determined effort to join one.

Sadly, the Webbington could not meet any of these conditions, so was not granted one of the coveted licences. Nevertheless, Alan Wells, undaunted, carried on booking live bands and cabaret. Then the new M5 motorway swept south, bypassing the Webbington completely. Alan tried to persuade the planners to build a slip road to Loxton, even offering to pay the costs. He failed. Things started to slide. Alan did what he could to attract new business. The strippers, now a regular feature, were no longer a novelty; people were far more liberal minded. 'You've seen one, you've seen 'em all' was the opinion. Alan had a penchant for striptease artistes, and kept faith with them until the end. The big acts got more expensive, and with the introduction of tougher drink-driving laws, the punters got fewer. You don't have to be Einstein to work it out.

The day had come when the Webbington was to go under the auctioneer's hammer. I was standing with Alan Wells in the main room of the venue and thinking of all the famous acts that had appeared on the stage we were now standing by. Many had made their debuts here. And some, not that much later, returned as TV stars at highly inflated fees. The Webbington, now empty, echoed with the voices of Bob Monkhouse, Shirley Bassey, Des O'Connor, Georgie Fame, Freddie Starr, Tom Jones, plus super stars like Roy Orbison and Neil Diamond, to list but a few of the household names who played there. The Webby reigned supreme in the West for more than 25 years.

The auctioneer had set up his portable rostrum in readiness to conduct the auction. Soon the Webby would have a new owner. Bob Potter, who owned Lakeside Country Club, was the highest bidder, and Alan's castle, his chromium-plated palace, was knocked down to his rival. 'End of an era mate,' I said to Alan. 'A little birdie tells me you might be interested in buying my Stars and Stripes club at Yate,' I added.

Yes, Alan was interested in buying my business, but right now was not in a position to do so. With the Webby in liquidation, it could be some time before he would know how he stood financially.

The last time I saw him, I was standing by the bar in a seedy little strip club, just around the corner from Bridewell police station in Bristol. The air was heavy with smoke and the music loud. A girl in a state of semi-undress was gyrating on the stage, and the majority of the punters, few though they were, were facing her way. I was aware of someone staring at me from the far end of the bar. It made me feel uncomfortable, and even that I might have an enemy, I probably do, more than one! The stranger started to walk over to where I was standing. Suddenly I could see the unmistakable grin that is exclusive to Wellsy. Shaking my hand warmly, Alan told me he was now in the catering equipment business, and doing OK. I think it was the only time I ever saw him without a bird on his arm! I bet one wasn't far away. It was great to see him. Alan Wells is a legend in his field, and gave a great deal to showbiz at considerable cost to himself. Wherever he is now, I hope he is happy and content. He certainly deserves to be. He should write his memoirs. 'If you fancy it Al, I would love to be your agent!'

I found a buyer for Stars and Stripes. An ex-Mecca executive called John Payne who, after leaving Mecca, started out on his own, purchasing a small bingo hall down south. All went to plan at first, and we exchanged contracts. He was anxious to get possession, was a man of substance, so I saw no harm in letting him in. The day came to finalise the deal, but he refused to complete, saying that he thought the goodwill, included in the contract of sale, did not exist. However, he was prepared to complete, but at a reduced figure. I couldn't believe it. The day following completion we were due to go to court to transfer the various licences attached to the club. To add insult to injury, Mr Payne went abroad on holiday for a couple of weeks.

Over the years, many people have misjudged how I might react in a given situation. When my back is against the wall, I am at my very best, so look out! I stood in the dock of the Magistrates Court in Chipping Sodbury, and stated my objection to allow the transfer of licences I held to a third party on the grounds that Stars and Stripes was still in my ownership; thereby asserting my discretionary rights. I listened, whilst learned council for Payne told the bench how, even without his client here, it would be quite in order for the court to transfer the licences of the Stars and Stripes club, to Mr Payne's appointed agent and manager, Mr Aldous. It was when the lawyer acting for Payne said 'You can,' to the bench, that I thought, 'I've won'. The chairman of the bench was

Howard Lewis. I knew him well enough to anticipate that no city lawyer could come into his court and tell him what he could and could not do!

The chairman of the Magistrates consulted his legal clerk, then looking at me, and with a wry smile, said. 'Mr Ruston, you can keep your licences.' On leaving the court I was approached by Aldous, who with his lawyer by his side was asking, 'What do I do now?' The legal man suggested, 'Why don't you ask Mr Ruston for a job!' I responded with, 'Go right away and make sure my premises are secure, and do not attempt to open them for business. If you do I will inform the police.' Payne came back from holiday and was flabbergasted. His new club, his mini-Mecca was closed. I wouldn't budge on the contract terms, so ended up back in Stars and Stripes. Payne lost what he had spent on the place, plus the deposit he had paid me – not very clever of him. Later I was offered a much better deal, and at a much better price.

I was having a drink (orange squash) at the Park Tavern opposite Victoria Park in Bath. The Landlord and Lady, were Don and Margaret Collins (the first time I met them was whist they were working at the Webbington a few years previously). Don ran the bar and was as proud as a peacock of his real ale. The selection of bar meals on offer had the most variety of any pub in Bath. Pizzas with everything, devilled kidneys, chicken livers in garlic, the list was almost endless. It was the only pub in Bath to be listed by Egon Ronay. The place was always full, and attracted nightmare entrepreneurs, and high flyers. (There could be a book on this place alone!) Don was the perfect host, and made everyone welcome. 'Jim my old mate, I want you to meet Sacha. I have told him you may be able to help him with a new venture,' Don said with enthusiasm.

He introduced me to Sacha Zehran, a Frenchman who once had a restaurant in Bath, but who was now living in Charleroi in Belgium. Sacha told me he was going to open a new gambling casino and night-club. His main concern was that the only knowledge he had of casinos was as a punter! Don had told him that I had a niece in the casino business. He was right; it was June who, on returning from Greece, took a job in the Victoria sporting club in London where she learned the rules and laws that apply to gambling casinos in England. I warmed to Sacha immediately, and invited him to have a meal in my restaurant at Stars and Stripes. I would invite June, and he could tell her what he had in mind, then ask if she was interested in becoming involved.

Sacha was suitably impressed with June – most are; she is confident and pragmatic. His opening gambit still makes her smile to this day. It went: 'Jun, I am Sacha Zehran. I 'ave a casino, but I knoe nozzing about gamleng. Will you run it for me?' It's the shortest interview she ever faced! June agreed to recruit dealers and take them to Belgium to work in Sacha's casino. She did a fantastic job, even providing the beautiful dresses for the girls to wear whilst dealing. I went over for the opening night, where the champagne flowed like water.) It was hard to stay on '*juice l'orange.*') Gambling was neither illegal nor legal in Belgium. They allowed it, but there is no licence to apply or pay for. They have inspectors who monitor casinos, but as long as there is no trouble, play goes on. That country missed out on a huge amount of revenue. The government's cut on gaming here in the UK is worth millions each year. The Belgians' play a different game of roulette to the one we have here. It's called 'Opta', the main difference being the wheel is static and the ball much bigger. They play 36 numbers, with two zeros, whilst we play 36 with one. The odds are also more in favour of the house.

For accommodation, Sacha had provided a house out of town for June and her colleagues to stay in. It was in a secluded spot, and luxuriously furnished. Naïvely, I asked June why the lighting and décor reminded me of the hostess bars in Germany. 'You mean why does it look like a brothel? That's because it was one!' she laughed. A spade is a spade to June! Before I left to fly home, Sacha said how impressed he had been with Stars and Stripes, and asked whether I would consider designing the lighting and sound equipment for a new discotheque he planned opening. I thought, why not? I now had a manager running the club, and was about to enter into an agreement to sell it.

I checked all was well at home, then catching the ferry at Dover, headed once more to Belgium. My Datsun Coupe, quite a large car, was packed to the roof with sound equipment and lighting gear. I could not believe it when, with no more than a glance, the Custom's Officers waved me straight through. Had I been stopped, I had nothing I couldn't explain, but it must have looked a suspicious load. Arriving in Charleroi, I found Sacha in his office. He welcomed me saying; 'You must be hungry, we go to dinner.' I am not a food person, but I do admire the way continentals take time to have their meals. It is a social occasion for them, whereas we shovel it down and leave in a hurry. Why, I can't explain. Can you? How many times have you been in a restaurant where the waiter hovers around as you drink your coffee, and having given you the bill a course ago, he now wants you to pay, so he can be rid of you.

I had a lot of fun installing the sound and lighting equipment for Sacha's 'New Jimmy's discotheque (so called 'New' because there was already one named Jimmy's. I think the similarity later caused problems for Sacha). The opening night was even bigger than the previous one at the casino. Bouquet upon bouquet of flowers kept arriving, with messages of congratulations, and wishing luck and success. Everyone bought champagne at £28 per bottle. Imagine that happening here. 'Jim, got any Champers?' my punters would inquire at an anniversary do. 'Yes we have Moet or ...' I would reply. 'No, not that. You know, that sparkling stuff, three quid a bottle. It all tastes the same to us,' they confessed. It did surprise me that the French would stand for such prices, even in a nigh-tclub. Champagne is cheaper in their shops than ours.

The discotheque in Charleroi was my first technical venture in a foreign country. I learned fast to get along with the French tradesmen. I was a guest in their country; they would not change to suit me so I would have to adapt. They had electricians and electronic engineers, so why had Sacha brought in an Englishman? I would have to show them my worth, but not before assuring them of theirs; this I did at every opportunity. I have always worked openly, with no secrets. I will explain what I am doing to anyone who cares to listen. If you know your job, you should have no fears.

Although I didn't know it then, I was to face a far more technically challenging project, but in a different country. Next time it would be in Spain.

BACK TO BASICS

Jane and Eddie had their first child, whom they named Rebecca. I was 42 years old, and a grandfather. Rebecca was born in Southmead Hospital, after which, mother and baby were transferred to Chipping Sodbury maternity hospital. A wonderful place, which sadly no longer exists – a victim of NHS cutbacks. Joyce was quite naturally delighted, although she really didn't look old enough to be a grandmother.

Brian Mannering had become involved in the re-building of Cathode Ray Tubes for the television trade. His involvement came through an electronics company that rented part of his factory at Wickwar, where Brian and his partner Roger Elliot ran a firm making signs. The electronics firm folded. Brian, ever the entrepreneur and seeing a chance to make some money, put forward a proposal that was accepted, and took over the tube rebuilding plant.

He approached me offering a job as a consultant. Whilst one is always pleased to be offered work, I was not sure that I wanted to go back into the electronics industry. Anyway, I still had the responsibility of the Stars and Stripes and was considering continuing with the design of lighting and sound systems for Discotheques. Then Brian said something that fired my imagination. 'Jim, how would you fancy helping me to set up a factory in the south of Spain?' 'Why Spain?' I enquired. 'Well, firstly I have a very close friend there, and would like to do something for him. He would make an excellent business partner. Secondly there is only one plant in Spain currently re-building tubes, and new CRTs are often difficult to get and very expensive.' Brian continued: 'We have already bought a piece of land on a small industrial site at Campello, about half-way between Alicante and Benidorm on the Costa Blanca.' I said I would think it over, but that it would depend largely on the sale of my club.

A few days after seeing Brian, he rang me saying, 'Jim can you come up and see me? I have a proposition to make.' Brian had spoken to the financial investment firm who were backing his CRT project here, and the proposed one in Spain. They would agree, in principal, to buy Stars and Stripes from me, if in turn I agreed to act as consultant to Supervision, the name they had given the new tube re-building company and lend the electronic expertise necessary to start up the plant in Spain. That was the deal.

I went each day to the factory in Wickwar and familiarised myself with their way of working. They were a super bunch of blokes, but without sounding unkind, it was very much a case of the blind leading the blind. The factory foreman, Gordon Shutt, was the salt of the earth. Mechanically quite capable, but electronically clueless. On reflection, it was amazing how the plant was running, and with quite good results too.

I spent time with each operator, and tried, to explain in lay terms, how a cathode ray tube works. Not easy. It proved most enlightening; each having their version of how they thought it worked, which differed quite considerably. Later I would employ the same technique when training the Spanish operators. But this time, with no pre-conceived ideas, it would be easier.

Joyce and I were shopping in Bath, a city we both love very much. Pausing for a moment to browse in the window of an estate agent, I spotted an advert for a house for sale in Acton Turville. My first thought was, 'Funny place to advertise a house for sale in Acton Turville. Chipping Sodbury, Chippenham, perhaps, but why Bath?' The house looked attractive in the photograph, and was ideally situated, Acton Turville being just one mile from Badminton. We went inside and asked a few questions. The agent gave us printed details of the property, but advised 'I don't think we can arrange for you to view for a while. The owner is going on holiday, quite soon.'

As we left Bath I said to Joyce, 'Lets go to Acton Turville and have a quick look at the outside of this property; it can't do any harm.' We found the house described in the agent's details as Wisteria, quite easily and stopped outside. Detached and set in a half acre, to the front was a large lawn on which grew a number of cherry trees, some ornamental, others fruit bearing. The rear was mainly cultivated, with row upon row of vegetables, leading to a small orchard where a dozen or more apple and plum trees stood, laden with fruit. With blue flowers growing from the plant from which it took its name, climbing up the front of it, it looked like a picture postcard. Turning to Joyce I said, 'I want this house.' 'You can't just go bustling in without an appointment. They might not like it,' she replied in consideration. 'If I wait for the owners to return, from wherever it is they are going, someone might get it before us,' I argued.

With caution, I walked up the path passing beneath the cherry trees, and gently knocked on the door. An elderly man answered. I apologised for the impromptu visit, and explained that I was interested in his house. Luckily, he received me well. Within 10 minutes, Joyce and I were inside looking around. I told the gentleman whom I had been addressing of my connections with Badminton, and he said he had heard of me. He then told me his name was Eddy Hayes, and that his daughter Ann kept the village shop. He was a builder, and had built Wisteria himself back in the 30s in readiness to move into when he got married. He then confided that he had a daughter living in Canada and was anxious to see her again, before time ran out.

BACK TO BASICS

As we all walked up the back garden, Eddy told me how he had bought the land from the Duke of Beaufort's Estate. Then later, finding he could do with a larger garden bought more, which doubled the size of the plot. 'When are you going to Canada?' I asked. 'In a few days' time,' he replied. I continued. 'Mr Hayes, I want to buy your house, and if you will sell it to me, I will shake your hand on it right now, and at the asking price'. A smile spread across his face as he shook my hand warmly.

Two days later, Eddy Hayes rang me asking if I would go to see him. I panicked, thinking, 'He hasn't changed his mind, has he?' No fear of that. In fact, quite the reverse. When I called upon him he handed me the keys to Wisteria saying, 'You had better have these. I won't be here to look after it. My solicitor won't like it, but I know I can trust you. You come well recommended.' I would never have let him down, and he knew it. To be trusted means everything to me.

Life at the factory was going at a pace. The production line was flat out and we were preparing equipment for the Spanish venture. I had encountered some technical problems with the electron guns that we were using in our rebuilt CRTs. They were made by South West Vacuum Devices in their plant in Tucson Arizona, and were supplied through their UK partner Ray Westwood, who lived in Stratford-upon-Avon. Ray suggested that I make a trip to Arizona to see operation there and meet the principal of his firm, John McQueen.

Bill Parker's TV business folded. It had started in the colour boom days, but by the time Bill and Mike had established themselves enough to attract the top agencies needed to compete in a competitive market – Sony Hitachi and so on – the bubble had burst, and they struggled. Their matching E-Type Jaguars were the first to go. Bill's was bright red and he loved it. Despite cutbacks, and a supreme effort from both partners, they were made bankrupt. Vision On was now Vision Off!

I got Bill a job working in the office, at Supervision. Although it wasn't really his thing, he settled to it and gave his best. But he had lost the sparkle he once had, and would never be the same again. He was devastated by the bankruptcy, and although reassured by friends and family, who stood steadfastly by him, felt the pain of failure acutely.

The closure of Vision On quite naturally affected me. I now had my old TV shop in South Parade back on my hands, and with it the service commitments for the rental sets still owned by me. I wrote to my old customers explaining the situation, and called upon my friend Lady Caroline Somerset, to tell her I was back on the scene. I hadn't seen much of her during past the few years, although I had seen a bit of her youngest son Johnny who frequented the Stars and Stripes disco. He once got into a fight there. Unperturbed by this incident, he returned often. I always had someone looking out for him, although he never knew it. Had he known, he wouldn't have thanked me for it. I like him a lot.

I didn't hunt much during my night-club days; there was never much time. After I came out of hospital, in an attempt to reassure myself that I was going to be OK, I bought a horse, and quite by co-incidence kept it at livery with Yvonne Fowler at Acton Turville, where I was later to live. The horse was a 16hh dark brown gelding, a good sort of hunter who pulled a bit. The first time I took him hunting the meet was at Hawkesbury Upton. I left Acton Turville and hacked on through Badminton.

I was approaching Little Badminton when I saw two riders coming out of the park gates at the top of Well Lane. I soon realised that it was David Somerset and Miranda Morley. On seeing me they waited, and greeting me warmly asked, 'Where have you been all this time?' We hacked on to the meet, during which I brought them up to date with my activities. It was interesting to observe the expression on their faces whilst I talked. Changing from one of astonishment, then quizzical, and finally, amusement.

I barely knew Miranda then, but I did get to know her much better in the mid-80s. Slim and attractive, with dark hair, she looks a picture on a horse. I knew David Somerset, heir presumptive to the Duke of Beaufort, as an astute businessman and owner of one of the best-known art galleries in the world, Marlborough Fine Art, with galleries in London's Bond Street and New York. An excellent horseman who rides horses that complement his ability. He is immaculate too. I don't think I have ever seen him even slightly ruffled, no matter how hard the day. A civil man, who most definitely does not suffer fools!

It was my first trip in a Boeing 747 Jumbo Jet. We landed at JFK, New York a scruffy airport, I thought, which wouldn't hold a candle to Heathrow, from where Ray Westwood and I had flown. We were to stop overnight in New York, travelling across the US to San Francisco, then ultimately fly to Tucson, in Arizona. We could have flown straight to San Francisco, but Ray thought I might like to see New York. Typical of him, he is one of the most thoughtful people I have ever met; his hospitality is second to none. I was suitably impressed with the Big Apple, as I guess most tourists are. The view from the top of the Empire State Building is awesome.

In the evening we strolled the streets, stopping for a few beers in a bar which had a live band playing jazz. I began thinking I could get to like it here. I really think I would have fitted in, I felt at home there. I sat looking at the musicians, and with my feet tapping felt empathy with their style. Without a word being spoken the guy on piano nodded to me, I walked over. He pointed towards the mike, I said, 'Lady is a Tramp? He smiled, and went straight into it. It was the best piano, bass, and drums, trio, I ever sang with. It was so easy; they were that good.

San Francisco: 'the morning fog fills the air' as it rises up from the bay, engulfing the Golden Gate bridge. Alcatraz, although closed as a penitentiary in the 60s, sits out there menacing. My mind went to the early Cagney and Bogart films when they talked of The Rock. Ultimate incarceration. We had a drink in Di Maggios on Fisherman's Wharf, and rode the cable cars. Hired a car and drove out to San Jose. Every place seen is either featured in a film or captured in song. Memories from the Maxime Cinema!

As we headed down to Tucson in a Boeing 727, we hit a little turbulence. The captain came over the intercom saying, 'Not to worry, this is quite normal in these parts at this time of year. It's due to the extremely dry climate.' 'Might be bloody normal for him, but my bum is opening and shutting like an effing revolving door,' exclaimed Ray. The turbulence worsened, then we entered an electrical storm. Now this is not funny. It was like being in the middle of a spectacular firework display, pretty, but frightening. The plane dropped, then climbed. When we finally made our approach it was pitch dark, and the runway was a kaleidoscope of colour. The wheels of our aircraft made contact with a screech of burning rubber and the plane slewed sideways, wing tip first, down the runway. When we finally came to a halt, there was a round of applause from the passengers. I looked for Ray; he had almost slid under the seat! White faced, he shook his finger at me saying; 'Don't ever let me do that again!' I told him, I hadn't planned on repeating it myself.

Once in a while, if you are extremely fortunate, you meet a person who will leave a lasting impression on you. John McQueen was around 6ft tall with blond hair. I think he was 70 yrs of age when first I met him. Wearing spectacles and a hearing aid in no way spoiled the image of a man in excellent physical shape. I spent some time with John in his laboratory, discussing the problems I had encountered using the electron guns he manufactured. It was a fascinating experience, especially the process of forming cathodes. Cathode rays are an everyday term familiar to anyone who owns a television set. But how may people do you know who understand exactly what they are?

The cathode employed in a television picture tube is barium carbonate, which when processed in a high vacuum and heated to 1000 degrees centigrade, freely emits electrons. There are three cathodes in a colour TV tube. Only one is needed for monochrome. After years of valve manufacture (during steam radio days), further developments proved that electrons of sufficient quantity and velocity will ignite phosphor, causing it glow. Cathode rays. The electron gun is the device that controls and focuses the electron stream.

Ray Westwood had told me that John McQueen was responsible for showing the first colour picture on a television set to the world. I asked John about it. He was reluctant to make any claims, but the facts are undisputed. John not only demonstrated a TV with a colour picture but also had built the cathode ray tube on which it was displayed. He actually glass-welded the faceplate to the main body of the tube with a hand-held blowtorch, quite an achievement in itself. He showed me a photo, taken during the process.

The colour TV tube was developed by RCA, the film giant. Rather surprising, considering at the time that television was closing cinemas left and right. I suppose they took a 'if you can't beat 'em join 'em' line. With the emergence of colour TV, they also saw the potential for the production of low cost TV movies. (And bloody awful a lot of them turned out to be.)

Working in the office of South West Vacuum in Tucson, was a Mexican, Jose Fernandez, who asked, 'Jim, Ray tells me you ride. Wanna come up to my ranch and see some horses?' 'Does a bear shit in the woods!' I replied. Jose took me to his ranch, and introduced his wife Rita and daughter Kimberley, both fine horsewomen. Rita rode High School in county shows. She looked amazing in her western outfit, like a movie star from the Roy Rogers era. Jose roped steers. They mounted me on a 15hh brown gelding, a horse trained for cutting cattle from a herd.

Tucson is situated on the edge of the Sonora Desert. A cow town where cowboys still walk around with spurs on their boots, and guns in holsters. Wide-brimmed Stetsons adorn the coat hooks in the bars. Pick-up trucks have a rifle in a rack behind the driver's head. Yet there is a feeling of friendliness and safety.

We rode out into the desert towards the foot of 'A' mountain, from the top of which Indians used to watch for wagon trains to ambush. We rode between the giant Cactus, most of which are hundreds of years old. 'They don't get their first arm until they are 100 years old,' Jose informed me. We were at a 'lope', a slow canter. My mind flashed back to those early Saturday mornings at the Maxime Cinema in Clevedon. Small boys with eyes glued to the screen watching our idols, Hopalong Cassidy, Roy Rogers and Gene Autrey – shoot down the baddies. Then, my wildest dreams would not have extended this far, and now here I was, riding a western trail, with a genuine Mexican for a 'pardner', and thinking, 'If there is a heaven on earth, this must be it.' I hoped it would last forever. I was beginning to feel a bit light-headed; we had been out for quite a while, and it is such a huge country it takes ages to get anywhere.

Back in the UK our idea of a long ride would make them laugh in Tucson. They take a bedroll and go off for days, sleeping under the stars. I wouldn't fancy my chances out here on a horse on my own. In 100 degrees Fahrenheit you dehydrate quickly. Jose could find water anywhere; it's just amazing. He came to Tucson when he was 16 years old by simply walking across the border from Mexico, only 70 miles away. Others did the same. Suddenly, Jose pulled up in front of me saying, 'We are taking a rest, you look a little hot Jim.' 'Do I?' I replied. He said he had been observing me for some while, and knew I was getting near the point when I would pass out. He was quite casual, and smiled when he said it. I thought right mate, wait until you come to England and you're out with me, and there's a bloody great hedge in front of us, let's see who faints! They don't leave the ground too often in Tucson! Seriously, I will never be able to repay Jose for the experience. To ride with great horsemen, on their terms, in their environment, on the very best horses, is a privilege very few people get the opportunity to enjoy.

San Xavier Mission in Tucson is just about the oldest building they have in the USA. Built by monks in the 17th century, and now a major tourist attraction. People come from all over the States and the rest of the world for that matter, to see it. It is a lovely structure, but looks a bit lop-sided. It was designed to have a dome at each end of the front elevation. However, only one, on the left-hand side, was ever built. The Indians, from the local tribe of Papagos, sell their wares on stalls close by. Papago Indians have incredibly flat faces – not, though, unattractive. Folklore suggests that when born, they are hit in the face with a shovel! The reason I mention the mission is that some years after my visit I discovered that Caroline Somerset's mother Daphne Fielding (Lord Bath's first wife and a writer), had lived in Tucson for many years, and knew the mission well. Caroline Walter's (Bill, my vet's wife) mother, Mrs Stevens, whom I had met on a number of occasions, had also lived in Tucson and frequented the mission. I have two pictures of San Xavier that were once owned by these ladies. Neither one knew the other.

I had had a wonderful first visit to the US of A. On the evening before our departure, we were invited out to dinner. We sat around a huge table with John and Peggy McQueen, Lenny Minutello, his lovely wife Rosa, Gerry Tumarkin and his wife, (Gerry and Lenny were co-directors of John's), and Jose and Rita Fernandez. Americans place a great importance on their evening meal. They don't bother too much with lunch, a sandwich will do, but the evening meal is mostly planned. The portions are enormous. I ordered a prawn cocktail; it could quite easily have eaten me! When we got to the pudding course, a gungy mountain of meringue with chocolate spilling over the bowl, Rita took a mouthful, then announced with a sigh, 'This is almost as good as an oral orgasm.' Ray and I looked at each other in disbelief. No one else batted an eyelid. I guess not many here would be shocked nowadays, but that was 20 years ago. Are we always this far behind the Yanks? Whom Ray Westwood loves to describe thus: 'Ball busters, with more shit than a Christmas goose!'

Back at the Wickwar Factory of Supervision, the men who would operate the plant in Spain had arrived for training. I was introduced to Manuel, Brian Mannering's close friend and partner in the Spanish venture, who would manage the factory there. The workforce would consist of Miguel, Pepe, Fernando and Angel, (pronounced Ankel in Spanish). They would stay in England for three months, and undergo man-to-man training with the operators here. I was to look after their technical education.

A s the Boeing 727 of Iberian Airways made its approach to Alicante airport, from the window I could see how similar the landscape looked to that of Portugal's Algarve, where I, together with Joyce and Rachel, had been on holiday earlier in the year. It was now October 1980. Gordon Shutt and I had travelled here to assemble the CRT rebuilding plant, which had been sent in advance from England by road. Manuel was at the airport to greet us. 'Welcome to Spain. It is good to see you both. I have waited a long time for this moment,' he said as he warmly shook us by the hand.

He continued, only now in a sombre mood, 'We have a big problem, Señor Jim. The lorry you sent with all the equipment on has been impounded by our Customs Officers, and is in their compound on the docks. They will not release it.' Manuel explained that the inventory of goods we had given to the driver did not match the goods themselves. Simply, it was a head count. The inventory said 130 parcels and there were 134. Manuel arranged for me to go to the Customs Office with him to try and sort things out. We solved the problem after a few hours. A piece of equipment had been logged on the inventory as one item; being extra bulky it had been dismantled and repacked in five pieces before loading. No one had made the adjustment to the inventory.

The Spanish authorities were still not completely happy with our story. By now the lorry and its contents had been in the Customs shed for four days. They eventually agreed to release the lorry but not the contents. The days dragged by. Gordon and I were staying in Hotel Tanit in the old part of Benidorm. Each morning we rose early, dressed for work, then waited in the foyer for Manuel to appear. He would duly arrive, and with upturned palms say, 'No luck yet.' A week passed and, unable to start work, we spent most of our time on the beach. Manuel had already suffered several setbacks with the building of the factory at Campello. He still had no electricity connected and no telephone. Also, despite having spent three months in England training, two of the staff he had had recruited (Fernando and Angel) had now decided against a career move and returned to hotel work.

It was a brighter but still concerned Manuel that greeted us at the hotel one morning. 'Good news?' I asked. 'I hope so. We can get the machinery from customs in a few days. But we have to pay,' Manuel responded. It transpired that providing we paid storage for the time it had been impounded, they would release it. 'Why didn't they say this a week ago when we went to see them?' I inquired. 'Then they wouldn't have been able to charge as much,' Manuel informed me. 'That is the way it is here. If the authorities can find an excuse to fine you or make you pay excess, they will. We can argue, but there is no guarantee we will win, and all the time the storage will mount up.' 'How much?' I asked. 'They want £3,000 said Manuel. 'We will have to get a bank draft from England, it will take time,' I replied. Manuel came back with, 'No bank draft; they want cash.' I was flabbergasted. Somehow, Brian who was back in the UK managed to get the cash to us. Manuel paid it over to Customs, then adding insult to injury, had to hire a lorry to take our machinery and equipment to the factory. We had wasted 10 days. Gordon had come over with me to help assemble the plant; now he only had two days left before he was due to fly home.

Spain was still only five years post-Franco (El Caudillo) and many Spaniards were still very much pro the dictator. Especially those in the Guardia Civil (Civil Guard) you know, the ones with the green uniforms and black shiny tri-corn hats. I certainly wasn't in awe of them; in fact I thought they looked amusing, whereas the Spanish shrunk in their presence. 'They still wield a lot of power my friend,' confided Manuel, and went on to tell us that you could still buy your way in or out of favour with money; also many Spanish businessmen preferred the Franco regime. They knew where they stood with it. It did have its good points, like no war since the civil unrest, and low crime. A girl could walk anywhere in the middle of the night without fear. The penalties meted out for those who broke laws were so intimidating few transgressed. One could be arrested on suspicion and kept in prison indefinitely without a charge being brought; then released without the right of redress or apology. The regime in Spanish prisons was harsh and conditions appalling, not fit for animals. I don't think it's much better now. And the 'black economy' still thrives! I will demonstrate this later in the book.

Joyce, Rachel and my wife's mother and father-in-law came to Spain for a two-week holiday. The plan had been for them to go to the beach and so on during the day, and I would take them out evenings and at the weekend. Because of the delay at the factory, sadly, I had to let them down a bit. But I did take them out at the weekend. Manuel kindly loaned us his car and we drove up to Denia, which is about 40 miles north of Benidorm.

My sister Stella owned a bungalow there, about a mile out of town at Las Marinas, in a small complex called El Palmeral. Built around a pool, with landscaped gardens, the gleaming white chalet-style bungalows, each with their own veranda, nestled in the Mediterranean sun. Stella had asked me to visit Bill Hancock, and pay him some money she owed for items he had purchased on her behalf for her bungalow.

Bill Hancock lived in number 9. I didn't have to knock on the door; he had already observed me walking through the palms towards his bungalow and stood outside waiting. He was just as Stella had described. About 5 feet 6inches, a little portly, with hair receding from a golden crown. Stripped to the waist, his torso had the appearance of an ancient brown leather suitcase. Battered and creased, but with plenty of mileage left in it. When he spoke, his face moved with a rhythm crossed between a waltz and a samba. Behind his pure blue sparkling eyes was a fascinating story; I would hear it one day soon.

I introduced myself thus. 'Bill Hancock? I'm Jim Ruston, Stella Bond's brother.' 'Ohh Stella, she is so lovely, so kind. Pleased to meet you Jim, is that your family over there?' He replied pointing towards where I had parked the car. 'Yes,' I answered, at the same time beckoning them over to meet Bill. 'It's so nice to have company. Not many people come out this time of year,' he informed us. Bill wasted no time in asking, 'Not going up to Guadalest I don't suppose, are you?' 'Not today Bill, but if you want to go, I will be here most of next year and will come and take you.' This simple gesture secured for me the friendship of an extraordinary man. It would last a decade.

Gordon Shutt worked his socks off during the limited time he had left in Spain. Together, and with the help of the Spanish lads, we had managed to assemble most of the machinery before I had to say goodbye to Gordon. He had enjoyed the experience, but was glad to go home. Laden down with presents for his wife and kids, Manuel took him to the airport. You learn a lot about people when you share a room with them. No intellectual, but Gordon had many other qualities that I admired, among which were loyalty and integrity. He also possessed a fund of amusing stories, a comfort when things are not going well. We laughed a lot.

There was still a great deal for me to do, though. My problems were compounded by the absence of electricity. Manuel spoke with the owner of the factory adjacent to ours. When I say adjacent I mean about 30yds away. Our neighbour agreed to run a cable with a supply sufficient to power my soldering iron. This was a great help, although it did have its drawbacks. At midday when our neighbour closed his factory for lunch, he switched me off; also if he was late opening in the mornings I had to wait. It was frustrating to say the least when in the middle of joining two wires together to find the solder refusing to melt, then realising the iron was getting cold because the electricity supply had been turned off. I cursed and swore, and blamed everyone.

We got as far as we could, but still with no power. Eventually we came to a standstill. Our working relationship, although fractious at times, was better than I had imagined. Manuel, Pepe and Miguel were solid. They would see this through, come what may, and I admired them for it. Through the passage of time I learned as much from them as they did from me.

The Spanish still believe in fundamental education. They don't need a calculator to do their sums. They know their history and are fiercely proud of their country. Schoolchildren, despite their age have to reach a set standard before moving up to the next grade. Ever conscious of the stigma attached failing to reach the standard, they study long and hard.

'I Manuel, I come from Barcelona, I know nothing!' Was the catchphrase that helped to make the TV comedy *Fawlty Towers* such an enormous success. Some prats took this seriously, and thought because the Spanish waiters they encountered during their fortnight on the Costa del whatever did not always understand their requests immediately, then they must be stupid. This amused the Spanish enormously; they took every presented opportunity to take the piss. Constantly repeating, 'Que. I no understand. Sorry.'

Miguel, who could speak, read and write English better than most of the customers he served during his years as a waiter, was a past master of the wind-up. If he had a bunch of obnoxious louts to serve, he would bring everything but what they asked for, and all the time calling them every swear word in his colourful Spanish vocabulary, of which they could not understand one word. His colleagues would often have to leave the room in haste for fear of collapsing in fits of laughter.

It's amazing what fun you can have with language. My niece June taught a Belgian croupier to say 'Good evening, bollocks,' when greeting clients that entered the casino in Charleroi. It was months before anyone put him right. I have spent many hours in meetings where several interpreters have been required to translate the different languages of those present. It is so easy to be misled. It can also be extremely difficult to appraise the intellect or integrity of those with whom one is negotiating. 'Is that really his view? Has he understood what I meant? Or has the question been misinterpreted?'

A single-track narrow gauge railway runs from Alicante to Denia. It is called the Limon Express, although there is nothing express about it or the fare for that matter. It cost 100 pesetas (about 50p) the engine runs on diesel and the faded blue coaches are ancient. There are passing places on the line, allowing the on- coming train to proceed, whilst the outward one waits patiently in a siding. The Limon Express winds its way from Benidorm, through Altea, then on to Calpe, gently swaying as it passes through a number of tunnels hewn out of the mountainside. The final destination is Denia. The station is in the middle of the town.

SUN SAND AND A SLEDGE

The main thoroughfare through the picturesque town of Denia is named Generalissimo – a palm tree lined avenue, with street cafes spilling out on to the pavement. An altogether affluent place is Denia, and I felt Stella's presence there. This would be her choice. From a phone on the corner of the street I called her home in England and told her so. 'Glad you like it Jim. Stay in my bungalow as often as you wish, and say hello to Bill for me,' she replied. I walked out of the town and headed toward Las Marinas. The dusty road was almost deserted, the sun shining without interruption from a sky so blue you couldn't paint it. In a pair of blue jeans with matching shirt, and canvass shoes on my feet, I gulped down the unpolluted air, thinking, 'I may never go home.' With the heady smell of orange blossom from groves going off to my left, and reflections on the sea to my right playing tricks with my eyes, rounding a slow bend I could see in the distance a group of palm trees surrounded by a white wall.

I had sent a Christmas card to Bill Hancock, in which I had written, 'See you in January'. There was not a sole in sight as I entered the small complex. I walked around the deserted pool but could find no one. Bill held the key to my sister's place, so I could only sit and wait. After a while I heard a voice calling, 'Is that you Jim?' Standing up, I could see Bill pushing his bicycle with a shopping bag over the handlebars through the entrance to the bungalows. His eagle eye had instantly spotted a stranger. I went over to greet him, but before I could say anything, and with a serious expression on his face he said 'Ohh, the chickens have gawn up.' This I found to be his only concern, the price of the spit roasted chickens they sold in the town. He bought one every Saturday. He informed me that for some time they had been 300 pesetas (then about £1.50) and now they were 350 pesetas. Such inflation!

Bill's bungalow was an Aladdin's cave. He held keys for a number of his neighbours, who in return gave him all manner of items. Not least of all, on leaving after their stay, they showered him with half-full bottles of wines and spirits. He had the best, and most varied stock of alcohol of anyone I know. Bill boiled some potatoes to go with the chicken, and with fresh bread, a mixed salad and a choice of wine, we had a meal fit for a king. All the produce was grown locally, organically. A taste I could only remember from childhood.

After eating, and as evening drew in, the air was still warm as Bill and I walked along a beach that stretched for miles. The sea was flat and calm, and I could feel the stillness hugging my body. January is a favourite month with many Spanish. '*Sin touristos, y la mar esta en calma, todo tranquilo.*' No tourists, the sea is calm, all is tranquil. For me, the second half of the 70s had been stressful. Now, for the first time in years, I felt at peace.

I asked Bill what brought him to Spain. He replied: 'Well, I came out on holiday, and stayed in one of the bungalows, and loved it. Bungalow number 9 was for sale, and I didn't think twice. Within a couple of months, I had sold my home at Frinton-on-Sea [in Essex], and moved out here. There was nothing to keep me in England. My wife had been dead for some time and we didn't have any children, although I do have a niece I keep in touch with.'

Bill said he left school at 14 and got a job at Sainsbury's in London. He lived in the store's staff hostel, which, in his words, was:

Strictly run, and short on comfort, but after a long and arduous day at the shop, I was glad of somewhere to lay my weary bones. We started work at 7am and got everything ready to open at 8am. This included cleaning the windows and washing down the tiled formwork at the front of the building. In winter the water froze on the cloth as you wiped. Competition was fierce; you dare not open later then your rival across the road for fear of losing a customer, and you would not close before him either. It was a cat and mouse game played out by the store managers, each watching the other furtively, from across the street.

I worked on different counters, learning the grocery business. Well that was what they said was supposed to happen; I was a slave really. We all were. After closing a 6pm we had to clean all the counters down, and sweep the floors; the one in the butchery dept had to be washed. They expected an awful lot for very little and we never got away before 7pm. We were paid weekly; there was no such thing as paid overtime. I got 5 shillings a week plus my keep. They told me I was lucky to have a job. It was the 1930's and there was a slump, so I supposed I was.

Little wonder Sainsbury's became such a successful business. At the time Bill was recounting his memories of the big store to me, Stella's son Grahame was working with Camilla Sainsbury, a descendant of the famous family. It's a funny old life. Bill continued:

War broke out so I was called up. I met and married a lovely girl; she was very timid though, and often ill. This continued throughout our married life; she was unable to have children, which saddened us both. I was put in the newly formed REME, and went over to France a few days after D-day. I wasn't bothered; I was with a lot of good blokes who I knew I could count on, but I did worry about leaving my dear frail wife, and for who knows how long.

I drove a recovery vehicle and pulled all sorts of transport out of rivers and craters, as we pushed on towards Germany. The war was as good as won, but Gerry was fighting to the bitter end.

Later the next day, a passing dispatch rider stopped. The day before the cease-fire was finally declared, I was driving an officer in a Jeep along a battle-torn road near Berlin when there was a mighty explosion. I felt myself spinning through the air, saw a kaleidoscope of coloured lights, then blackness. The Jeep had been blown to bits, the officer badly wounded and me dead. Or so they thought. They took the Captain off to the field hospital, and left me in the crater the Jeep had made. I lay there for hours, during which time I had been reported killed in action. Luckily, a dispatch rider stopped for a smoke right next to where I lay and staring at the remains of the Jeep thought he saw something move, and cautiously went over to investigate. He summoned a medic who at first declared it was hopeless. I was a good as dead. An ambulance took me to a field hospital where they operated on me. I had broken most of the bones in my body, and my jaw was badly smashed. My battledress blouse had been totally destroyed. In it had been my ID card and Army pay book. They had no idea who I was and I couldn't tell them; I was in a coma.

My poor wife received a telegram telling her I had been killed. She was distraught. Well she would be, wouldn't she? I eventually regained consciousness and told them who I was. 'You can't be,' they argued 'He's dead, the records show he is.' In Army language if it's on record then it's so, end of the argument. I was sent back to the north of England, where I convalesced, and managed to get in touch with my dear wife, who was so relieved that I wasn't dead. Thousands of soldiers were being de-mobbed every day, and I patiently waited my turn. When it didn't come I went to the office to complain. 'It's the paperwork, Hancock,' they told me. 'It says your dead. How can we de-mob a dead man?'

It was nine months after war ended that I finally got my discharge and went home. Paperwork! They had fixed me up pretty good though, so I suppose I mustn't grumble. I still have quite a lot of shrapnel floating around my body, which does give me a bit of gip now and then. My jaw took quite a lot of fixing; there are still a few wires in it, and it does have a mind of its own!
I look alright for my age though don't I Jim?'

I placed my arm around his shoulder, and said with sincerity; 'Bill, you look a million dollars.'

After a brief visit home, I returned to Alicante via Barcelona, where I had to change planes. I was informed that my suitcase would be transferred on to the Alicante flight so there would be no need to collect it from the carousel. Fine with me, but when I got to Alicante, no suitcase. Normally I wouldn't panic, but this time my suitcase contained a quantity of electron guns, which I intended using for trials. Plus a few more! When I informed Manuel that my suitcase would be delayed, he went white. 'It they open it Jim, we will be in big trouble. We don't have an import licence yet for this equipment,' he said with some alarm. The next day Manuel and I drove to the airport at Alicante. Gingerly we approached the Customs Office, and I waited while Manuel spoke to a police officer who immediately pointed to an area that had been roped off. The officer explained that when the suitcase had passed through the X-ray showing a quantity of foreign objects. All hell broke loose.

The Guardia were summoned, and an area was sealed off, as they thought the contents could be dangerous. After the customary shouting and waving of arms between Manuel and the officials, I was called over to explain why I had these items in my suitcase. Eventually, and then only after much chastisement from Customs officials, we were sent away and told to come back tomorrow. More delays. 'What do you think will happen?' I asked a very fed-up Manuel. 'I know what will happen. It will be a question of paying. It just depends how much,' he replied. And so the next day armed with a bundle of pesetas Manuel went back to the airport. After a couple of hours he returned with my suitcase plus contents, intact. Handing it to me he smiled saying simply, 'Don't ask.' It later transpired that the officials let the electron guns pass through Customs under the apron of *Regalos* – souvenirs, gifts and so on!

The electricity was connected at last and we were able to test all the equipment. I never normally keep a diary, but for some reason I kept one for 1981 and in it wrote: Monday 23 May. Built first monochrome tube at the Spanish plant. Also today there was an attempted *coup* on the new Spanish democratic government in Madrid!

Guards led by Lieutenant Colonel Antonio Tejero de Molina, an ex Franco sympathiser, had burst into the Cortes, the Spanish parliament, and firing a sub-machine gun into the ceiling, took the cabinet and some 350 Members of Parliament hostage. Francoist General, Jaime Milans del Bosch, who appeared to be behind the *coup*, had earlier declared a state of emergency in eastern Spain. However he soon had second thoughts and quickly ordered his troops to stand down – but only after King Juan Carlos had broadcast to the nation, via television, condemning the attempted *coup*. It was a much closer thing than the press made of it.

Tanks and armoured troop carriers were out on the street in Valencia, where the General's cronies were based, and the Guardia were closing bars everywhere and sending people off the streets. Benidorm was deserted. Manuel suggested I fly out. 'Why?' I reasoned, 'They won't harm me.' They didn't enter into the last conflict, so why would they now? They won't want a problem with the Brits. Franco didn't.' Manuel said that some of his close friends, who had always been anti-Franco and who strongly supported the new democracy, were packing rucksacks in readiness to get out via the Pyrenees. That's how serious the Spanish were taking it.

It was a huge triumph for the new Spanish democratic government. It had been seriously challenged, and had won. As I said previously, there are still plenty of supporters for the past Franco regime. Especially amongst the 'old money'.

The following day, unperturbed by the political trauma, we built the first colour picture tube. In my diary I wrote: 'All cathodes with even emission, zero gas, excellent purity and convergence. Lunchtime we celebrated.'

Back in the UK the whole family descended upon us for the marriage of Stella's daughter Janine to Kenny Gardiner, my son-in-law Eddie's brother. Janine had met Kenny at Jane and Eddie's wedding, where he was best man. Now the two girls, as well as being first cousins, would also be sisters-in-law. It was the first time we had all been together since Dad's funeral, and it was marvellous to have so much family around. A photo was taken of me and my brother and sisters, the first and only one of all eight of us together.

Rachel and I rode in St Catherine's valley on the Sunday morning. Some years hence we had sold a lovely 12.2hh bay pony mare to Stella for her son Grahame. Now outgrown, the pony was being ridden regularly by Rachel, who would soon take on Grahame's bigger pony, Mr Bumble, a 14.1hh chestnut the like of which you only come across once during a lifetime. These two ponies saw Rachel right through pony club, shows, cross country events and hunting with me. Six weeks later, and with some reluctance, I returned to Spain.

My daughter Karen was to marry Gordon Stephenson whom she had met at Stars and Stripes. The wedding would take place at St Mary's Yate, where Jane had been married. Surely nothing would go wrong this time. Joyce and Karen had organised everything, so I was confident there would be no hiccups. All I had to do was get myself back to England in plenty of time for the big day. The Saturday morning of the wedding arrived, and I stood in the sitting room at Wisteria looking at my beautiful daughter in her wedding dress, and reflected. When she was 16, I paid for her to go on a modelling course, where she was coached by Gill Moran, better known as TV's 'Green Goddess,' Gill had done a good job. Thanks to her, Karen has wonderful deportment and instinctively carries herself with confidence.

We opened a bottle of champagne, sharing it with Joyce, who had already done so much, and now had to escort the bridesmaids, Rachel and Rebecca. In a relaxed mood we waited for the limousines. We waited and waited, and becoming anxious as time was running out, I phoned Pendock's, the specialist car hire firm Joyce had booked. To my horror all I got was an answering machine, with a message, which stated that in the event of a problem, you should phone again on Monday! By now Karen, quite naturally, was getting upset. Putting on a brave face I said, 'If we leave now, we will still be late at the church, so we had best not delay any longer. Karen, I will take you in your mum's Colt Sigma Estate,' – a lovely car, but in desperate need of a clean! 'Joyce you will have to take the bridesmaids in Karen's car' – a little Hillman Avenger.

I drove as quickly as I dare, all the time keeping Joyce in my view, until finally we pulled up in the car park shared by St Mary's Church and junior school, which both Karen and Jane had attended. Already in the car park stood my Datsun Coupe, black with lots of chrome. It gleamed. I had loaned it to Gordon for him and his best man to ride in. Sod's law! Joyce helped to get Karen out of the car, and as my daughter and I stood together under the Lych gate, I looked at her and said: 'Trust us Oakley; let's face it, you and I are a bloody disaster, always in trouble!

Most years I took Karen with me to the radio shows, now no longer in Earls Court but staged in the top London hotels. I took her to the East End to show her where her ancestors lived, and out to Loughton to see her Uncle Roy. He loved her free spirit. Roy doesn't attend many family gatherings, but he had travelled down to see Karen married. Wherever we went I showed her off; all my friends and colleagues made a fuss of her. We were close. She followed me to Belgium. A few years hence she would follow me to Spain. She currently worked in the office at Supervision in Wickwar; when we finally got the phone installed in the Spanish factory, we spoke together most days.

With the bridesmaids and Joyce following behind us, Karen and I giggled as together we walked towards the church door. The congregation were relieved to say the least, and some of my mates were laying bets that Karen had bolted! Gordon was worried sick. Deep inside we were furious that Pendock's had let us down, but we didn't let it spoil what otherwise was a wonderful day.

The car hire firm Pendock's are also well known as funeral directors. I will make sure their services are excluded from my will. I would hate to be late for my own funeral!

Karen and Gordon honeymooned in Spain, staying at Hotel Tanit, now my second home. Accompanied by Joyce and Rachel, I returned to Spain during the newlyweds' honeymoon. Manuel had rented an apartment for us at Villajoyosa, about halfway between the factory and Benidorm. It was August and the temperature was in the high 90s. I was getting up at 6am and leaving for the factory soon after. We were only working until noon, then resting until 3pm and closing at 5pm. Because of the heat generated by the ovens we only ran them once each day – for four hours.

The apartment, although new and nicely furnished, was incredibly hot without the benefit of air conditioning. When I arrived after work each day, Rachel was waiting patiently for me to take her swimming in the sea. It was the only time in the day that I didn't feel hot. Often in the middle of the night I got up to go to the kitchen, only to find Rachel standing inside the open fridge door, trying to get cool. My intention too, only she had got there before me!

It was a Saturday, and we were sunbathing on the beach with Karen and Gordon at Villajoyosa. I went over to the bar at the edge of the beach to get some drinks. It was scorching. In the bar was a small black and white portable television, which was tuned in to the BBC's coverage of the royal wedding. It all seemed surreal. The crowds were cheering Charles and Diana as they drove away from St. Paul's Cathedral. I was transfixed; it was compelling viewing. Thinking of everyone back in England in party mood crowded around TV sets, with champagne flowing, I admit to a pang of homesickness. When I got back with the drinks, I had to explain what had taken me so long. At least I had seen some of the pageantry on this historic day.

My work in Spain was coming to an end – at least that is the way I saw it. The licences I held for the Stars and Stripes were to be transferred on 11 December, when the arrangement I had with Brian Mannering and the investment company would come to and end. I had more than fulfilled my part of the bargain; once the licences had been transferred and the residue of the money still owed to me paid, that would be it. I went up to Denia to contemplate the future. Bill was alone in the complex and he greeted me in the way I was now familiar with. 'Ohh Jim, the chickens have gawn up, they are now 400 pesetas. I commiserated with Bill, then sat on the terrace of Stella's bungalow with one of the many books I had read during the last year here. What of the future? I had had a taste of it, and now craved periods of solitude. I desperately need to be alone on a regular basis. How can I think with so many distractions? Whatever I did in the future, it would have to accommodate this criterion.

My dear friend Bill Hancock asked, 'Jim, can you come to the shoe repairers with me? I can't get any sense out of the old bloke there. When I ask him when my shoes will be ready, he calls be a loony. He's had them for months.' I went with Bill to the shoe menders, which turned out to be a hole in the wall, and not much more. There we found the ancient cobbler, bent and wizened, standing among a shoe mountain. How he knew which shoes belonged to whom, I will never know. Perhaps he didn't. I asked in Spanish, (I could now speak a little), '*Dónde están las zapatos de mi amigo?*' Looking straight at Bill he replied, '*Lunes.*' 'There you are, he's calling me a loony again. I've a good mind to punch him,' countered Bill angrily. Hastily I said, 'Bill, my friend, he is not calling you a loony, he is saying *Lunes* – which is Spanish for Monday! Despite my intervention, it still took Bill a further few weeks to get his shoes back, and even then he wasn't at all sure they were actually his, but as they fitted, he thought it best to keep them. By the way, the day he collected them was in fact a Monday – *Lunes*!

The video boom had hit the UK, and I was considering going back into TV retail to cash in on the demand there was sure to be. Whilst Brian at Supervision in Wickwar understood my feelings, he wasn't exactly happy at my intended departure. Ray Westwood asked if I would be interested in joining his outfit as a consultant. It would mean travelling all over the UK and abroad – wherever people were rebuilding CRTs. He said John McQueen was keen for me to join them. I freely admit I was flattered. If only I knew where Jenkins, my old maths teacher at Nailsea Secondary lived, I would take this invitation offering me a chance to work with one of the finest scientists in the world of electronics and shove it down his throat, or maybe up his arse! I was tempted to accept the offer, saying I would give it serious thought.

Meanwhile life at home was sweet. My daughter Jane gave birth to her second child, a girl, Natalie Ruth. I would continue to be surrounded by females, no bad thing! We always looked forward to Sunday lunch at Wisteria. It was customary for Eddie, Gordon, Karen and me to go to the local pub, The Fox and Hounds, which now had a new landlord by the name of Brian Hedge. The previous tenants John and Peggy Hickson, had recently retired after many years as publicans. They have a daughter whose stage name is Jaquie Voltaire; she lives in Mexico where she is quite a star. On one of her visits to Acton Turville, I got her to sing for me at Stars and Stripes, and introduced her to Alan Wells, who gave her a booking at the Webbington. I asked Jaquie how she got along with Alan. She replied, 'Darling, he spent most of the time trying to get me into his bed, would you believe?' Yes I would, Jaquie.

After our liquid lunch at the Fox, we enjoyed a traditional Sunday roast beautifully prepared as always by Joyce. As we sat chatting over a few bottles of wine (only a glass or two for me) I became aware that it was incredibly still outside, and could smell snow. After tea and to the delight of Rachel and Rebecca, a few snowflakes fell, and then it got heavier. Joyce was becoming anxious about the girls and fellows getting home, and suggested they make a move before conditions got any worse. Jane, Eddie and Rebecca, with baby Natalie only six weeks old, wrapped snugly in blankets, set off in their little van. Karen and Gordon followed closely behind in their car. It was now snowing heavily.

In good weather it was a 15-minute journey to Jane's flat in Yate. I decided to give them a half-hour then ring to check they had arrived safely. I waited, then rang, no reply. Another 15 minutes, and another, still no reply. Joyce was becoming more than anxious. Looking at my worried wife, and getting on my feet I said. 'I'm going out to find them.' 'How?' she replied. 'Don't worry, I will find a way.' I replied confidently. I put on a good warm coat and cap, and dragging the sledge I had bought for Rachel, set off down the road. I freely admit at that moment I hadn't a clue how I expected to find them, other than walking in the general direction they must have taken. The snow was deep and now covered everything, I couldn't even see the road. I thought 'I'll take a line', as when hunting. I knew the area like the back of my hand, every gate, every hedge, and every wall. I headed off up the slope and out of the village in the general direction of Old Sodbury.

On reaching higher ground I got a shock. Stretching as far through the blizzard as I could see was a white blanket of snow. I could not identify anything, no hedgerows, no landmarks, no anything. I felt helpless. My kids and grandkids were out there somewhere. They would never have got through. It had all happened so quickly. My chest was tight, and with snow driving into my mouth, I had difficulty breathing. I knew I had to get help. Reluctantly, I turned back, and now with the blizzard behind me and propelling me along, dragging the sledge I fairly flew down back the slope, around the corner and into Barry Minty's farmyard. 'What's all the hurry Rushabout [his name for me]? Slow down,' my neighbour said. I told Barry of my anxiety, and climbing on his tractor he urged, 'Let's go Jim.' I scrambled up beside him and we set off. I soon realised that there was no way I could have made it on foot.

We drove for about a mile, not much more, when the tractor's headlights picked up two vehicles almost completely buried in snow. 'There they are mate,' said Barry. I could just about make out a figure standing by the vehicles. It was Eddie; he had noticed the headlights and got out of the van to attract our attention. I never saw anyone happier to see me. We managed to squeeze the girls, and children inside the cab on the tractor. It had stopped snowing, and save for the reassuring throb of the tractor's engine, everything was silent once more. Barry set off for home, and Eddie, Gordon and I followed behind in the tracks left by the tractor's tyres.

When we got back to the house, we men via the pub, the lost souls told their story. Driving home, visibility got steadily worse, until they could no longer see the road. They stopped to confer, and the driving blizzard swept the snow around their vehicles forming a drift. They all got into Eddie's van for warmth. He decided to try to make it back to the village to get help, leaving Gordon to stay with the girls and kids. His vision impaired by the driving snow, Eddie could neither see nor find his way back to the village. Left with little option, reluctantly, he returned to his van.

Eddie and Gordon told me how worried they had been by their situation. But Jane and Karen, although concerned, were not panicking. They just kept saying, 'Dad will come and find us.' 'How can you be so sure?' Eddie asked. They replied, 'Because we know our dad. He will have checked by phone that we never got home, and any minute will come across the fields looking for us.' Blind faith. I was so proud of them. I have never let them down. In an emergency, if I held out my arms and said jump, I am confident they would. We were all quite naturally worried about six week old Natalie, but need not have been. Wrapped in a blanket, she was as 'snug as a bug in a rug'.

The village was snowed in for three days; it was like the war years, with everyone sharing. A local farmer delivered a churn of milk to the village shop, and we helped our selves, which was most thoughtful and generous of him. The village menfolk spent most of their time in the pub; Karen came too of course! We were all sad when the road was finally cleared. HM The Queen was in the vicinity at the time – in fact about one mile from where our children were stranded. She had to seek refuge at Cross Hands Hotel in Old Sodbury. They have displayed a plaque to commemorate her enforced visit. They now advertise that you can sleep in the room she slept in. It will cost you, though!

I flew back to Spain for the last time, with Supervision that is, and Brian Mannering came with me. Manuel and his colleagues Miguel, Pepe and Juan who had joined them in place of Fernando, were running the factory most efficiently; this gave me a great deal of satisfaction. I spent the most relaxed week I had had in Spain to date. Brian bought me a bottle of vintage wine as a Christmas present, and I also managed to slip up to Denia for a day to have lunch with Bill. For once the chickens had not 'gawn up'. I gave Bill a camera and told him I would return some day to see the results of his 'snapping'.

Over lunch, Bill and I talked of the future. He said he was writing a book and showed me a manuscript written in his beautiful hand. After reading it, I urged him finish it and offered to find a publisher when it was complete. It was not until then I discovered that he was a cousin of the great comic genius Tony Hancock. 'A nice enough man, but prone to bouts of severe depression. Always amiable when we met at family gatherings though,' said Bill. Who was himself extremely amusing without realising it. Looking back over my shoulder, as I trod the road back to Denia, and the Limon Express, I could see Bill waving goodbye from where he stood at the gate to El Palmeral. It would be much longer than I had intended before I would see him again. I am saddened by it now.

Brian and I left Alicante on a Boeing 727 belonging to Iberian airways, bound for Heathrow via Barcelona. When travelling from Alicante to Barcelona by air, the plane is generally routed along the coastline. From the window I could see the factory; it looked so distant, but I could visualise the layout – the mezzanine floor where the office was, and where I had my workshop; the loading bay where we often had our lunch, on a wooden box, in the shade by the door, where my hosts introduced me to everything Spanish, and where we argued about any and everything, historical and topical. If you expect to find a fool in Spain, you had better bring one with you. Whether I like it or not, a piece of my life is inextricably theirs.

We landed at Barcelona and were told there would be a delay. For the second time this month it had been snowing heavily in England. I worried for Joyce in Acton Turville. The airports in England were closed; we would have to stay in Barcelona. The airline put us up in a four star hotel. Fine, but it was Christmas week, and we would rather get home than spend the festivities here. After a couple of days, we were told that Bristol airport at Lulsgate had opened its runway. If we chose to, we could fly to Schiphol Airport in Amsterdam, and catch a plane from there to Bristol.

A COCKNEY KID IN GREEN WELLIES

On landing at Schiphol we only had 20 minutes to catch the Bristol plane. We got to the departure gate just in time, walked out onto the tarmac, and climbed the steps of quite the smallest commercial passenger aircraft I have ever flown in, about 30 seats. In fact, it was even smaller than the one in which Bill Parker and I flew to Amsterdam a few years earlier. On that occasion, bemused by the ancient-looking plane, as we entered the cabin Bill said to the smiling air hostess, 'Just don't start playing any Glen Miller music!'

Once airborne, and with a complimentary drink for our inconvenience, we settled. On approaching Lulsgate, the Captain spoke on the intercom telling us not to worry if the plane slid a little sideways on landing, 'It's icy down there,' he announced'. Gee thanks, I thought, another bloody Tucson landing! On making contact with the tarmac the antique aircraft slid and slithered its way, not an unpleasant sensation, to a halt. When my feet made contact with Mother Earth, the ground was so slippery I could hardly keep my balance. Everything was frozen, so it was surprising that the runway was in use. I was pleased to be home though. Dad always said, 'On stage make a grand entrance, and an even bigger exit.' I seem to do that with alarming regularity, even without a stage!

FLOODLIGHTS FOR BADMINTON

There was a shop in New Road Chippenham for rent. It looked ideal. Joyce was against me going back into retail, but as usual went along with things. I took the lease on the premises, one end of a row of three shops with a flat overhead, and with help from son-in-law Eddie, set about fitting out the shop.

I opened my new shop, which boasted the latest video library in town. Business was brisk. The video recorder boom had begun in earnest. In the beginning there were three video systems, VHS, Betamax and Phillips. Phillips was the first to go, leaving the remaining two to battle it out. Sony and Sanyo were the Beta champions, whilst the remaining manufacturers favoured VHS the latter being cheaper to produce and maintain, but inferior in picture quality.

However, it would be the major rental companies that would dictate the outcome. If they favoured VHS, which they did, then the software makers would follow. The customer would buy or rent whichever format had the best selection of Films on offer. Simple really; Joe public is rarely in the race. Consumers generally end up with a product at a price determined by the giant conglomerates.

I bought a new horse and kept it with Bob Brastock at his yard in Badminton. Bob had employed a girl called Linley from New Zealand to look after his horses and those of his clients who had horses with him at livery, one of whom was Charles Morrison the MP. I first met Bob when I bought a horsebox from him in the early 70s; he lived in Bath, then, having married the daughter of Bert Perry who farmed, at Lansdown. Bob had since divorced and got himself married to Wendy Payne, whose father John I knew well. He had a farm close to mine at Wickwar. John's daughter Wendy was at school at Horton Hall with my daughter Jane. They were the same age, but Bob was only a year younger than me. Good luck to you mate!

In the mid-70s Bob and I enjoyed many good hunts together, one in particular being quite memorable. It was at West Kington, and Bob was riding a big grade A show jumper called Jim, that would jump anything. I was cantering along about a 100 yards behind him as he approached a wall, not over big, but big enough for me on Sax. Bob leapt the wall with ease, and once landed I could see him standing in his stirrups waving to me. I couldn't make head nor tail of what he was trying to convey, so just kept going. With a mighty grunt Sax jumped the wall, clearing it with little to spare. Looking back, I could now see what Bob had been waving about; standing under the wall, out of the rain, was a bloody great Hereford-cross store, fat enough for market. We had jumped right over him! Bob was laughing his socks off! I needed a drink and took a large pull on my flask.

A COCKNEY KID IN GREEN WELLIES

The horse I now had was called Noble Emblem (whom I called Nobby), a thoroughbred by the American racehorse Swing Easy. He had a tremendous turn of speed but was not really suitable as a hunter. I really don't know why I bought him; he was a poor jumper and could get both of us into a lot of trouble. I suppose it was the exhilaration I felt when galloping across open country that appealed. There is nothing quite like a thoroughbred under you. Ask anyone.

However, it came to pass that in my exuberance traversing a swollen river, poor Nobby got himself staked on an unseen stout piece of wood, and remained chronically lame for several months. In the meantime, Bob very kindly loaned me a succession of horses to ride. There was Jim the show jumper, grey 17hh, whom I could steer but couldn't hold. None the less he was the best jumper I ever sat on. George, a 16.3hh ex-steeplechaser, pulled like a train but covered a lot of ground quickly, jumping everything he was placed at. I couldn't stop him either; and in the end neither could Bob, so he got the chop. Then there was Lady, a 16.2hh light chestnut mare, strong but manageable, with a lovely nature. I had many joyous days on her.

Linley, Rachel and I, spent wonderful frosty mornings exercising around the roads. When she wasn't riding with us, Wendy, Bob's wife, came out in her car meeting us half way with a flask of hot coffee laced with a little something. Bob and Wendy looked after both my horse and me superbly during my time at their yard, and also kept an eye out for Rachel in the hunting-field – for which I will be eternally grateful. So I was extremely saddened when Bob had a nasty fall, which broke his neck. I don't think he ever hunted again.

When Bob split up with his first wife, Bert Perry's daughter Jenny, he had to find somewhere to live. My secretary Connie Vacher told him of an empty cottage on the Sodbury Road at Badminton, saying she would have a word with the then agent to the Beaufort Estate, Tim Mitchell. She introduced Bob, and The Duke was delighted at the prospect of having an ex-hunt servant coming to live in Badminton, but told Bob he would have to wait until the litter of fox cubs that were living in the grounds of the cottage had left! Bob has lived at Withymoor Cottage ever since – although he and Wendy divorced some years ago.

I kept a horse with Marjorie Richardson at her stables in Grittleton for a while. Marjorie looked after Nobby brilliantly whilst he recovered from surgery. Both she and her husband Alistair were exceedingly kind to me. Marjorie makes the best chips in the country!

It was around 8pm on a dark winter's evening. Karen and Gordon had only just left us to go home to Bristol when a knock came at the door. I opened it to find to find Rita Akerman, with whom I had hunted for many years, standing there. With a worried look on her face she said; 'Jim, I don't want to frighten you, but there has been an accident at Tormarton crossroads, and your daughter is laying on the verge with a blanket over her.' The blood drained from my body as I asked Rita if there was anything further she could tell me. She said she knew nothing more. I thanked her, and as she left, she said in a most sincere way, 'Oh I do hope she is alright Jim.' Joyce was trembling, and asked for a stiff drink. Getting Joyce a drink with one hand, I donned shoes and coat with the other, and almost with one movement swept out of the door and into my car.

When I got to Tormarton crossroads, a mile away, I could see an Ambulance with lights flashing. I leapt out of my car, but before I got very far on foot, I was stopped by a policeman who asked, 'Are you looking for a young girl?' My heart sank, but quickly recovered when he continued, 'She's alright, she's in the ambulance.' I 'through one up' to the Almighty, thanking Him. I then asked, 'What about her husband?' I was informed that he too was OK, and in the ambulance with Karen, which by now was leaving the scene on it's way to Frenchay Hospital. I sped back along the road to give Joyce the news. Relieved, all she could say was, 'Her face, her lovely face.'

I arrived at Frenchay, and Karen was far from OK. She had cuts on her beautiful face, and was badly bruised and shaken. Gordon had faired better, and I asked him what had happened. He said they were both lucky to be alive; in fact it was nothing short of a miracle. They were travelling home along the Tormarton Road in their Ford Escort, when a car came straight over the crossroads hitting them broadside on. The Escort did a summersault and Gordon went through the driver's door, which had sprung open. The seat on which Karen was sitting was ripped from its anchor points and hurtled backwards, and out through the rear window, with Karen still on it; luckily the seat had come out in one piece. Karen landed a few feet away from the rear of the vehicle.

Unconscious and drenched in petrol from the burst fuel tank of the Escort, Karen was totally obscured from view. Gordon couldn't find her, and was frantic. The car landed upside down on a stone wall. The roof of the car on the passenger side was completely crushed on impact. If Karen had been wearing a seat belt she would definitely have been killed. A spark could have also ignited her petrol-soaked clothes; it doesn't bare thinking about. She took a long time to recover, and suffered further from the effects of whiplash for some years.

I rang Rita to tell her Karen and Gordon were OK, and to thank her for her concern. The driver of the car that caused the accident, was banned from driving for a year and fined a paltry sum. Karen and

Gordon had a long and protracted battle with insurance companies before eventually getting a far from adequate settlement.

I took Joyce and Rachel to America for a holiday. We had a great time in San Francisco and went out to the island of Alcatraz. Rachel sat in the cell made famous by Clint Eastwood, in the film *Escape from Alcatraz*. We flew on down to Tucson, and I went trail riding with Jose, whilst Joyce and Rachel were entertained by Jose's wife, Rita, who was doing exceptionally well in the county shows. At the Houston show, her horse Bou became the 10-day circuit ground champion. We were all thrilled for her. We went shopping in an out-of-town mall, a new experience for us; it would be 15 years before a Mall opened in Bristol.

John and Peggy McQueen made us very welcome. Rachel and I swam in their pool, and Peggy asked if Rachel could stay for a few months with her. She wanted to show off this English rose with a beautiful accent to her friends! John asked why I hadn't taken up his offer to join Southwest Vacuum. I explained that ultimately I wanted a complete change, leaving the technology behind. He understood and wished me every success. We corresponded with Rita and Jose for a few more years then lost touch, which is a shame. I continue this habit of leaving friends scattered around the world. From time to time I think of, and miss, them all.

For the first time in my life, I entered a period of indecision. The bubble had already burst in the video business. Stocks were now plentiful and prices were tumbling. It had been a mistake going back into retail; I was bored with it already. Joyce had been right. I bought a video camera and recorder, and started to film weddings and other functions. One of the first was 'An evening with Arthur Negas'. Caroline Somerset asked me if I could fix up a microphone and TV link in the ballroom at Badminton House for the forthcoming function, a cheese and wine party with a talk on antiques by Arthur Negas, in aid of the Conservative Party.

The TV link was needed for those who could not get into the ballroom. As people arrived they were given a form on which was listed a number of antiques. These had been laid out in the vicinity of the hall and the idea was to value them. Someone shoved a form in my hand. I tried to give it back saying I was there in a professional capacity, but they insisted I have a go. It was a marvellous evening. The Duke and Duchess were sitting right at the front, with the Duchess insisting my daughter Rachel sit beside her.

Arthur was his usual showman self, and had his audience captivated. Then came the result of the competition. Arthur declared how difficult it had been, but there was one clear winner: 'Far and away in front of you all is Mr Jim Ruston,' he declared. I could have died. I was behind the camera and just poked my head around the side, and nodding and smiling like an automaton, said 'Thankyou'. In her obvious pleasure at the result, Caroline Somerset waltzed over to shake my hand. Halfway to me she slipped on the polished floor, throwing her arms and legs around in what looked like something between a Highland fling and a tango. But she somehow kept her balance and there was rapturous applause, for her of course, not me!

In early February 1984 I received a call from Major Gundry. We had long since buried our differences, and now got along famously. 'Jim have you heard the terrible news?' 'Yes Major,' I replied, 'I heard it on the radio this morning.' The morning news had announced that the 10th Duke of Beaufort, known affectionately by those who hunted with him as Master, had died in his sleep. The Major continued, 'The church at Badminton will never hold the amount of people who will want to attend the funeral. We will have to erect a marquee to accommodate those who won't be able to get inside. Can you relay the service by sound to the tent, Jim?' 'It will be an honour,' I replied with sincerity.

The Duke had left instructions that his staff and villagers should take priority in the church, except that is for the Royal family whom he adored, though I doubt mentioned in his arrangements. The very epitome of correctness, I doubt he would want to be seen to presume that they would attend his funeral. He would desperately wish it though. (Now I'm assuming.) The press would be excluded, and not allowed anywhere near the church.

The marquee was erected and I made a visit to see what equipment I would need to relay the sound. I entered the church and was surprised to see a coffin in front of the altar. No one had told me that the Duke was laying at rest there. There were a few people milling about outside, but none challenged me. I fetched my toolbox, a reel of cable and an audio amplifier from my car. It took two trips but still no challenge came. I must have been in the church for at least an hour installing microphones and an amplifier. Running a cable from the amplifier past where the Duke lay, at one point I was on my hands and knees and had to reach under the trestle on which the coffin was placed in order to route the wire. I fixed the speakers in the marquee and did a sound check.

Come the day of the funeral the police were everywhere, and they kept the media outside of the gate. Already having left my toolbox under the pew where I had decided to control the sound from, I had agreed to walk to the church with Brian Higham, and met him in his office as arranged. Brian took a bottle of whisky from a cupboard saying, 'We had better have a drop. Jim, to mark the end of an era.

Things will never be the same again, I promise you.' The staff and villagers filed into the church, and I took up my position on the pew where I had installed my gear. Checking underneath, my old blue toolbox was still there. Had anyone looked in it? No. It was locked, I had the key, and it had not been forced open.

Without warning, from my left the Royal party appeared. They had come along the private passage that connects the house to the church, and passed just a few feet in front of me. This was the first time I had seen Princess Diana in person. She looked pale, thin, but so elegant, and once seated looked straight ahead seemingly oblivious of those around her.   HM The Queen was accompanied by Prince Phillip. Prince Charles, Princess Anne, Princess Margaret, the Queen Mother and other Royals were also present. The Duke's wife, Mary Duchess of Beaufort, had been reluctant to come out of her room, and it was her lifelong friend, the Queen Mum, who coaxed her saying, 'Mary, you must come with me.' She obeyed instantly. The Royal family could not possibly have had two more loyal subjects than the 10th Duke and Duchess of Beaufort.

Our local policeman, Mike Earle, came in quietly and sat by me. We were the only two on a pew no more than a couple of strides away from the entire Royal family. After the service the procession left by the main entrance, whilst I slipped out of the side door and stood with a few others at a discreet distance, but close enough to observe. The Royal family stood around the grave with the Duke's family. The Union flag was removed from the coffin and handed to Leslie Vacher, the Duke's devoted butler of 40 years. As the coffin was lowered into the ground I recall thinking how unreal it all seemed. Did I really witness this? Once the Royal party had moved away, Brian Gupwell and Brian Higham stood by the graveside with heads bowed in reverence.

Later that same day, Brian Gupwell told me that he had his hunting horn in his jacket pocket, and had intended blowing 'Going home' at the graveside, but unsure of the reception it might get, didn't. I think he should have; surely the late Duke would have loved it. I am reliably informed that the Queen rarely attends interments. Memorial services, yes. Clearly demonstrating the esteem in which she held the late 10th Duke of Beaufort.

I waited for everyone to leave the church and grounds, then walked quietly back in to retrieve my old blue toolbox. Not one person had asked to see inside it. I was never challenged by a policeman, or asked to identify myself by anyone. OK, Mike Earle probably pointed me out as 'Jim Ruston, local man, hunts with the Duke, well known by all, lives in the same village as me.' But that is not the top-class security that befits our Royal Family. Someone should have searched my equipment; a third party could have tampered with my toolbox.

The first wedding I filmed was that of my niece, Sharon – my sister Maud's youngest daughter. Sharon was born a few days before my eldest daughter Jane, and had stayed with us in the West Country on a number of occasions. She also stayed with us in the 70s at Shortwood farm, when on that occasion she was trying to escape from a volatile relationship she had with a fellow who was threatening violence.

Now Sharon was marrying Chris, a Greek with an unpronounceable last name, for me that is. She looked stunning in a dress that cost the earth. Maud and Joe were so proud of her. At the reception a live band played for dancing, and needless to say Maud insisted that I sing with them. I did, and thoroughly enjoyed the experience. They were a fine bunch of musicians. Some friends of Maud and Joe asked if they could book me for a function. I think Maud expected me to say yes, but I declined, politely saying I had given it all up.

Sadly after around 15 years of marriage, Sharon and Chris split up. They have a son Anthony. Sharon is an extrovert, a free spirit. A kind generous girl who follows her heart, often to her chagrin. A real party animal with lashings of style.

I filmed Anton Smith's wedding, my old friend Tom's son. Also, Anne Somerset's marriage to Mathew Carr, and the christening of the new Duke's first grandchild, Francesca. On a more sombre note, the laying up ceremony of the late Duke of Beaufort's flag in Badminton church, and on a lighter one, an Anne Summers naughty underwear show at a nightclub in Chippenham. When I wasn't filming, I was out with my Nikon 35mm camera.

Virginia Holgate (now Leng – later Elliot the famous three-day eventer) had moved with her horses to Acton Turville. Her mother Heather had bought a place with a few acres on the Littleton Drew road. Ginny and her horse Priceless had won both Silver and Bronze medals at the 1984 Olympics held in Los Angeles. The local bobby Mike Earle and his wife Jean, together with George and Anne Beesely who ran the local shop, were determined to organise a homecoming for the Olympic star. Mike asked me if I could help in any way. I said I would be delighted, and organised some loudspeakers through which to play music to welcome Ginny back to the West Country. The Earles made a supreme effort with banners and bunting, but Mike was having a problem making the five Olympic rings. I suggested he use pieces of hosepipe to from a hoop, but he only had enough for three, so I popped home and cut a length from Joyce's garden hose. Some weeks later, as she was watering the garden, and I overheard her saying, 'I'm sure this pipe used to reach further than this.' I kept out of the way! They also got the Acton Turville junior school involved asking the children to form a lines each side on the lane to welcome home their local hero.

Everything was set. We had taken up our positions in the lane when a Land Rover appeared; as it passed by, leaning from the window, a girl with a plumy voice called out, 'Keep back off the lane. The media will be all up this road shortly.' I felt so sorry for Mike and Jean who had done so much and all the small children lining the road, who were told to 'shoo'. It was a bloody good job we ignored this pompous tart. The 'Media' consisted of local radio, one guy with a tape recorder, Chris Vacher from BBC West, and HTV with 'one man and his dog'. I don't think it even made the network. If it hadn't been for the Earles and Beeselys there wouldn't have been a welcome home for our Olympic Girl with the only medals won by anyone from the West Country. She was overwhelmed with emotion and gratitude, but then she is a top bird. They don't come much better than Ginny! And the look on her face when her horse Priceless, who had got home before her, was brought out for a reunion was pure magic.

Can you imagine the welcome an American Olympian receives, not just from his country, but his state and hometown too. It's little wonder our athletes struggle. We don't give them much encouragement and support, do we? I filmed the homecoming, and gave it to Ginny, who next day wrote me a moving note, one I treasure. I operated the sound gear at a couple of her demonstrations of training horses, organised by her mother Heather. Ginny was a delight to work with.

When Virginia, returned from Australia in 1986 where she became World Champion, there were even fewer people to welcome her home. Jean and Mike Earle rallied the troops once more, and made banners to stretch across the road. From the media, I think only local radio and newspaper attended. The only person there with a film camera was me. It beggars belief.

I was fortunate indeed to be asked one year to act as starter for the cross-country section at the Gatcombe Horse Trials. Alan Walter and I shared the duty, with me starting the first half of the entries. Even more fortunate, I had the honour of starting both Ginny Leng and Jane Holderness Roddam, easily my two favourite equestrians. The starter's job is crucial and calls for a calm but positive approach. Often, only a second splits competitors. Indecisive starters can cost a rider that, and there is little redress. I hope I didn't fail them. A cocktail party is held before the event, and Princess Ann and Mark Philips always attend. Olivia 'Olly' Bush organises the canapés, and delicious they are too. My daughter Rachel was one of her helpers. When I asked Rachel if the

Princess had come into the kitchen during the preparation of the food, She casually replied, 'Yes, she came over and had a stir of a pot I was minding.'

The new joint master and huntsman Ian Farquhar's 40th birthday was looming. There was to be a lawn meet of hounds at Sir Peter's his father's place. His brother Michael asked me to film the meet. They hired a strip-o-gram in a policewomen's uniform, who, after convincing Ian get down from his horse, undressed down to a basque. And as they say 'she was a big girl'. The look of horror on Sir Peter's face, one of the late Duke's closest and most respected friends, said it all. Brian Higham was right; things had changed.

Another lawn meet, this time at the home of the film star Jane Seymour. She owns St Catherines Court near Bath. Jane only ever rode with us twice. Unfortunately, on one occasion hounds killed a cat. It made headlines in the national papers, which also featured the star's picture, although it was really nothing to do with her. If she had been any further from the incident, she would not have been with the followers at all. To add fuel to the already raging fire, out of kindness, she offered to give the distraught cat owner a kitten. This went down like a lead breakfast. I felt sorry for her; we all did. She got most of the flak because she is a name. I sent Jane a copy of the film of her lawn meet, showing her helping to serve drinks. She was very complimentary, responding with an invitation to 'Come up and see me sometime'. I never did. Fool.

It was Margaret Thatcher's second term. The economy was upwardly mobile and technology was moving at breakneck speed. A mobile phone emerged, one that could be fitted into you car, although at around £1,500 it was expensive. I sold a few, but it would be some time before there would be volume sales. (Excuse the pun). Someone said karaoke was all the rage in Japan. 'Kari what?' I asked the Hitachi rep. I ordered one and gave it a whirl; I could see the potential, but it would have to stay on ice for a few years, as there wasn't the software available. Copyright to words and music needed addressing before backing tapes could be produced, the only ones available were pretty old tunes. I sold a few of the new machines but got fed up with the type of person that bought them fancying themselves as singers, but not good enough to sing with a live band. There are plenty of 'Walters' (Mitty that is) out there still doing it.

I was quite heavily involved in the Beaufort Hunt Club. Each year at the famous three-day event horse trials the hunt have a tent, in which there is a members bar. My friend Bert Perry from Lansdown introduced this facility in the early 70s, and by now it had grown quite considerably making a valuable contribution to hunt funds. I helped Bert almost from the outset, along with John and June Bishop and Jean Bush. There were others of course, but forgive me if I don't mention you all. The Beaufort Hunt Club is the only club I have ever belonged to that holds an AGM without an election of officers. I think the latter is mandatory in a club where membership is by subscription. At the time of his untimely death, Dick Horton was chairman of the Hunt Club. Major Gundry got up at the meeting and said 'I have spoken with Tony Keen, and he has agreed to be chairman.' Round of applause. Treasurers and secretaries were seconded, not elected. When they thought they had served long enough, they made their intention to stand down clear, and a suitable replacement was 'found'. It does run extremely smoothly though. I can't recall a conflict worth talking about. 'It's our club, and we run it our way!'

I was made a life member of the Hunt Club when Dick Horton was chairman, in appreciation for some PA equipment that I had donated. I first encountered Dick at a hunt near Bushton, the Thursday country where he was field master (the land over which the Beaufort hounds hunt is divided in to four and called by the day on which that area is hunted Monday, Wednesday, Thursday and Saturday). He had been thrown from his horse, which had galloped off. I rode after it and brought it back for him. It was a hard fall but he shook it off, and was still in the saddle when I left for home.

It was at Bushton where for my first time I witnessed a fox being killed by hounds. I admit to it being a bit of a shock seeing an animal broken up in that way, but it was a quick death. With hunting the outcome is always definite. Either the quarry gets away or is killed, unlike other methods of control.

The Farming community is the very fabric of the countryside, and much of what they do to conserve it tends to go unnoticed. If I were ever in a tight corner, I would be very pleased to see some of these folk coming over the brow of a hill. At the outbreak of the Second World War although not required to do so, farming had been classified a reserved occupation. Many enlisted immediately, some serving with distinction.

Dick's wife Jim (I guess Jemima) had died. His son David, who farmed at West Kington, where I had got unbelievably drunk one Boxing Day, (that's a story I am ashamed of) asked me to relay sound and vision to a barn for those unable to get in the small church for the funeral service. I had everything arranged, when David rang to say I had better bring plenty of gear, it would now be a double funeral. The day after his wife had died, Dick passed away quietly. Caroline,

David's former wife, now married to Bill Walter, said she wasn't at all surprised. She told me that Jim had an incredibly strong will, and would have insisted, 'I'm not going alone, come along Dick,' and so he went. She really believed that.

A man named John Clark had visited my shop in Chippenham, leaving a message asking whether I would consider going down to La Manga in Spain to film some apartments he and his wife Cooka were selling. This was to be my introduction to the Spanish estate agency business; although I didn't know it then, it would change my life quite a bit.

La Manga is about 70 miles south of Alicante, a peninsula that sticks out into the Mediterranean, about four miles long. On the side nearest land is the Mar Menor, or little sea. It is very salty and easy to swim in. Shallow for the first few hundred metres, makes an ideal place to practise water sports of all kinds. At the head of the peninsula are two golf courses. Sevvy Ballesteros' brother was the professional there during my time.

John Clark was English through and through, with a classical public school accent. I think his father was a vicar. A tennis fanatic, whenever and wherever you stood waiting with him, John practised back and forehand volleys with an imaginary tennis racquet. Cooka was Spanish, but spoke excellent English – an ideal foil for John as his partner in the Spanish property business.

Whilst filming I learnt of the method of selling they had adopted. First they held exhibitions in the UK, at which they would hope to persuade people to travel to Spain to look at the properties they were offering. The trip, during which they hoped to make sales, was heavily subsidised by the Clarks. There would normally be three or four couples on each trip, and with luck they would have a trip every two to three weeks. The inspection tours, as they were described, lasted for four days. During this time you would be shown a selection of finished properties, in the price range you had indicated when you booked your place on the tour. Having selected a property, you were asked for a holding deposit of £500, then taken to open bank accounts. One account necessary for you to own a property in Spain, and another, a convertible account, used for the transfer of money from your UK funds to pay for the property you had agreed to purchase. A contract was signed and you were handed the keys. Simple.

I returned from Spain and edited the film I had made; impressed by La Manga and the property on offer, I showed a copy of it to my daughter Karen. Oakley wasted no time at all. She and Gordon booked a trip with John and his wife, loved La Manga and the property on offer

– an apartment right on the beach. Trust Karen, the smallest, but the boldest.

Through the film, I introduced my bank manager David Jenkins to La Manga. David had moved to Calne, the next town up the A4 from Chippenham, and now managed a tiny branch of Barclays Bank, next door to the Harris sausage factory. Closed and standing empty, the factory, instead of the asset it once was employing hundreds of local people, had become a scar on the landscape.

David, a fine sailor, he had served in the Royal Navy, and now kept a sailing boat in partnership with a colleague down at Newton Ferris in Devon. I sailed with him on a number of occasions and always enjoyed it. Fiercely patriotic, he would say as we navigated the coastline, 'Do you know Jim, we are so lucky and privileged to live in this wonderful country. It's no wonder so many thought it worth dying for.' I know of no better view, than the one of the English coast from a sail boat, with a light wind pushing you along on a clear sunny day; another form of solitude.

Suitably impressed with the video film of La Manga, I arranged for David and Pam to meet John and Cooka, after which I accompanied them on an inspection tour. They bought a two-bed bungalow close to a small beach where David could sail. They were delighted with it. I didn't ask for any gratuity from John for the introductions. It never crossed my mind, although he did pay my airfare to go out with David and Pam. On reflection, and now that I know of the enormous commissions involved in Spanish property sales, I should have asked for an introduction fee. They would have paid it. Quietly, they were making a small fortune. On the way down to La Manga we had passed through a busy town. 'This is Torrevieja,' Cooka informed me.

'We could sell here, but prefer La Manga.' I took no more than a cursory glance at the ancient Spanish town, but didn't forget its name.

I was embroiled in village life. Two villages really, Acton Turville and Badminton share much, with very little going on in one without the other being involved. I performed the duties of commentator at the local horse show, and also at the hunt terrier show. I was a member of the Badminton branch of the Royal British Legion, where Tom Smith was Chairman, Bill Walter Vice, and Mike Earle Secretary.

Each November, with the Duke as our President leading the parade, behind the branch's standard bearer Don Lane we marched from the park gates to the church. Our vicar Tom Gibson, who could deliver a real 'fire and brimstone' sermon, if the occasion warranted, had served in the Second World War 'Dad's Army' was alive and well in Badminton.

FLOODLIGHTS FOR BADMINTON

It is an insular existence for many whose lives revolve around the village; it was easy to get sucked in. There really is nowhere on this planet like it. The wife of a one-time proprietor of Drewett's store in Badminton left her husband citing 'bringing her to the back end of nowhere' as one of the reasons. Brian Higham's wife Audrey, to whom he had been married for 28 years, left returning to her native county unable to stand living eating and breathing Badminton any longer. Brian's daughter Catherine, who had been a good friend of my daughter Karen, followed her mother. In those days Brian was much more reserved than he is now. So much so that at Catherine's 18th birthday party, Brian asked me if I would publicly thank all their friends for coming. Few would believe that of him today.

Audrey laid on a marvellous buffet, but stayed in the kitchen all evening. Introvert by nature, she became ever more so. I liked Audrey a lot, and for a long time, so did Joyce, but she became difficult to communicate with. Her departure devastated Brian, who fell into spells of deep depression, and became extremely angry at times his closest friends feeling the brunt.

Later though, Brian met a lovely women named Hilary Forster. She worked for the British Horse Society and they had met at a function where Brian had been asked to speak. At first he wanted to keep the friendship under wraps and asked if Hilary could stay over with us at Wisteria when she came to visit. We were delighted to have her, and after a while Brian stayed too.

Hunt Balls are great fun where everyone lets their hair down; it was customary for the Beaufort Hunt to have two: The Farmer's Hunt Ball in May and the traditional Hunt Ball in December. The former used to take place in Chippenham Town Hall but under the direction of David and Mary Hibbard, it moved to a marquee on Badminton recreation field. This was a huge success. It was always oversubscribed. With a top-class live dance band, breakfast served from 1am and plenty of champagne, it was the highlight of the social hunting calendar. The latter changed venues a number of times, but during the period of which I am talking it with was at Grittleton House School. It started at 10pm, breakfast at 1am, carriages at 4am. Most civilised. The classrooms in the school were used to accommodate a steel band and a disco. The assembly hall was used for the main dance area, where a live band played. A seedy night-club scene was recreated in an upstairs room, something for everyone.

Grittleton School quite naturally shares an excellent relationship with the Beaufort Hunt; many of the children who attend it, including my daughter Rachel, are from farming families that hunt. Rachel loved it

L-R. Jane on Shandy, Heather on Prince, Karen on Whisky, at Tanhouse Lane.

Jane on April Chimes. Joyce's brother Michael is riding Sax. I am on Carnaby Street at Shortwood Farm

Top: Joyce with Moulton Khalifa at Malvern Stallion Show
Mid: Joyce with Kimari and Biff with Rebecca at AHS Kempton Park
Bot: Carnaby Street. Paradise with her foal Cockney Rebel
(Both above foals were by Carnaby)

L.R. Top: Janine, Karen, Jim Davidson, Val and Norman. Dino is in backround.   Self in cabaret with pony Express.
Mid: Tom and Sue (Bright and Breeze). Billy Parker.
Bot: Me, Dave Pitt and Colin, Victorian nights at the Randolph.
My 'chromium plated' palace.

Top: Wanna buy a Villa?
Mid: Karen Joyce and her Mum - early days in Spain.
Me and Joyce – a blissful moment on the beach at Guardamar.
Bot: Joyce in her Spanish garden.

L.R. Chris, Heather, Michael, and Joyce, with their mother Eva.

L.R. Maisie, Stella, Jim, Eve and Betty

L-R A private word.   Our first tented exhibition at Cheltenham.
Chris Dowling, Leo Cooper, Jack and Patrick Shervington at the Islington Exhibition.
Jack and me in the gallery. Lili Ghibon the school teacher from Romania

Top. Badminton House Floodlit.
L-R. Jack Russell, Chris Reeve (mounted), and Brian Higham. My last days in the saddle.
Rachel in the hunting field on Bumble. Caroline Duchess of Beaufort presenting a cup at
the Badminton Horse Show.

Our Girls – Karen, Rachel and Jane (seated)

there. The teachers were flexible on hunting days, especially when there was a lawn meet. If some kids were absent no questions were asked. Rachel was also a member of the under 13's Wiltshire county hockey team that won the cup the year she represented them. As well as her sporting achievement she also put up a very creditable performance as Blousy Brown in the school adaptation of the musical *Bugsy Malone*. She both acted and sang beautifully, I was so proud of her.

It was at the Hunt Ball of December 85 that I was approached by David Beaufort, now the 11th Duke. He said, not to me but to Joyce, 'Your husband could install floodlighting at Badminton house, couldn't he?' Turning to me he continued, 'Would you Jim? I know you would make a splendid job of it.' 'Yes I could,' I responded, at once thinking, 'What am I taking on here!' David replied, 'Splendid,' then moved off to talk to the numerous people who were trying as always to get his attention. I reckon he should make them hold on to the tail of his coat as at Eaton? and wait their turn! People have been known to sprint a hundred yards down Badminton High Street to get noticed by the Duke.

It was March 1986 and freezing. I fixed two sodium floodlights to each of the four fronts of Badminton House. I did the wiring alone, but enlisted the help of my son-in-law Eddie to haul the light fittings into place, and screw them down; I couldn't have done it without him. We froze together. Making the connections with frozen fingers is bad enough, but more frustrating, the cold was making my eye, the one that doesn't blink, run, and the tears were freezing on my cheek, my vision impaired.

One weekend, the Duke caught sight of me up a ladder and called out, 'We will be switched on for three-day event won't we Jim?' 'Yes,' I assured thinking I hope so, but I still had much to do. It was really too big a task for one person and I don't know why I gave myself so much pain, but I completed the installation in time. I even managed to find time to devise a circuit to bring all the lights on instantly, which could be activated by a switch from the side of Caroline's bed. She told me it was a great comfort to her when alone in the house, which she often was.

The Duke was delighted with the effect of the floodlighting and told me so, adding, 'Send me the bill.' I did, and he sent his cheque by return of post. He is incredibly thoughtful in that direction. Historically, I had always dealt direct with him and his wife since their days at the cottage, much to the annoyance of their agent Richard Wood, who worked for Humbert's, the estate's agent. I suppose my bypassing him rankled, and although polite when we met, I got the feeling he never liked me. I don't suppose I helped by never telling him anything. When he enquired as to what I was doing, all I would ever say was that 'The Duke has instructed me to...'

When the Duke and Duchess's eldest son Harry married Tracy Ward, because the wedding would not take place at Badminton, two parties were organised to accommodate their many friends. When Caroline Beaufort asked me to which party I was going, I replied 'I haven't been invited.' 'You most certainly have,' she responded. 'I remember clearly putting your name on the list. I just can't be sure which party that's all.' With that she picked up the phone and I heard her say 'Mr Wood, will you please come and see me. Right now, please.' Apologetically, she turned to me saying 'I will have your invitation sent round to your house Jim.' I had never seen her so cross. I couldn't have been home more than 20 minutes when Richard Wood walked up the path and knocked at the door. 'I do apologise, I'm terribly sorry, somehow I had overlooked your invite. Of course you had been invited,' he said in mitigation. I would love to have known what Caroline said to him. It gave me a quiet satisfaction, but did nothing for our relationship. Not that I gave a flying f--- about that!

I decided to try to capture what goes on behind the scenes at the Badminton Horse Trials. I enlisted the help of Brian Higham's lady friend Hilary Forster to do some pieces to camera. I don't really know what I thought I would do with the end result. I was shooting with a domestic camera and recorder, albeit top of the range. The quality, once edited and reproduced, would never be good enough commercially.

Although extremely wet, it was a marvellous three-day event. Brian Higham had a house full of visitors staying for the trials. His Mum came down from Yorkshire with Len, a lifetime farmer friend of theirs. Mick and Jilly Connors and family from southern Ireland, whom Brian thinks the world of, and has bought many horses from, were also staying. Hilary was the perfect host and they all made for a great house party. Something Brian could never have done during his time married to Audrey. We lunched in the competitors and grooms canteen, and went to the cocktail party in the house, by invitation only, an event, most like to be seen at! Those who attended the cocktail party and saw Badminton House floodlit for the first time were complimentary, and congratulated the Duke. He was extremely pleased, and told me so. On the Saturday night after the cross country we had a great bash at Brians. He was happier than I had seen him for years. That year Ian Stark won the prestigious competition on Sir Wattie and took the Whitbread Trophy home with him to Scotland. I filmed him as he left.

A COCKNEY KID IN GREEN WELLIES

There was an incident involving a car being driven by young men who were guests at the Badminton House, and a horse on the cross country course, which put a bit of a damper on our jollity. It could have been worse, had not the Beaufort Brigade closed ranks, and although it had been witnessed by quite a few, nothing leaked. On the Sunday evening, travelling near Badminton I noticed the house was in darkness. Worried that something had gone wrong with the new lights I telephoned the Duchess. 'No, there is nothing wrong with the lights,' she responded. 'It's just that in the circumstances, I thought it best to keep a low profile, so I switched them off!'

On the Monday morning I said farewell to the Connors family as they left to catch the ferry back to Ireland. Hilary had already left at first light. Brian and I stood in the lane outside of his house. 'Will there ever be a better four days than these Brian?' I asked. 'I doubt it Jim, it would want some following,' he replied. As she was leaving, Jilly Connors asked me to keep and eye on Brian. She worried he might slip into depression after we had all gone. I told her that I already intended to do just that.

I spent weeks in my studio editing my film and recording the voiceover. The content was OK and those who saw it were complimentary, but it was far from professional. Miles too long and poor picture quality. However, I am glad that I did it. So many of the people who helped to create the famous trials and appear in my film are now dead. Colonel Weldon, Major Gundry, Tom Smith, Jack Windell, Jack Tuck, Charlie Chapel, Bert Perry, Bill Walter and of course the 10th Duke of Beaufort who first conceived the idea, then put it into practice in 1949. Looking at the list now it's hard to believe that so many good men could have expired in a period of no more than five years. Five of them were involved in the very first trial in 1946. It can never be the same again. That doesn't mean not as good, just different.

Meanwhile things within my family were to change again. My sister Stella's marriage had been rocky for some time, but it all came to head when she found out her husband Grahame was seeing another woman. She had suspected something of this nature for some time but had no proof. This was provided by her son Grahame who, with friends, followed his father over a succession of evenings before eventually discovering the location of his lover. It was a coincidence that I happened to be visiting when Stella's son arrived home with the news confirming his father's illicit affair. In those days I drove a vintage MGC 3 litre sports car, and had recently offered to lend it to Grahame, Stella's husband. I now realised why he was so keen to borrow it. To take his girlfriend out in of course! Grahame never showed his face for ages, and my sister filed for divorce on the grounds of his admitted adultery.

During a lengthy legal argument, over who would get what, which financially only the lawyers won, Grahame proffered three alternative settlement 'packages'. Stella and I sat at her kitchen table where she had laid out paperwork from the lawyers describing the offers. 'Look Jim, she said. I'm a "package", just like the Telebond adverts in the papers' – Which currently read: 'Rent a TV and Video Package.' She saw the funny side of it, and we both had a bloody good laugh.

I had bought the MG from Terry Crook, a car dealer from Melksham. I first met Terry in 1975 when he started selling Colt cars. He was one of the first dealers to be appointed. I appeared in Cabaret with Cardew Robinson at a gala reception to launch the dealership, and Terry and I became instant friends. He had a penchant for motor cruisers, floating gin palaces really, and kept a boat down on the Wareham River. I boated, I can't say sailed – there isn't a sign of canvass on such a vessel – with Terry often. It was a completely different nautical experience to the one I was used to with David Jenkins. Both had their own merits. You wouldn't catch David in what he described as something between a sun lounge and a greenhouse. 'Grow nice tomatoes in that one Jim,' he would say as a gleaming white vessel, with powerful engines throbbing, pushed his workmanlike yacht sideways in its wake as it passed. A boat with sails would be far too sedate for Terry. No place for the sun deck and cocktail cabinet!

They were each perfectly suited to their chosen role. David, a bank manager and dedicated sailor, knowledgeable and serious about seamanship. Terry, a car dealer, a rough diamond who loved the glitzy life, whose boat was aptly named Bossman. I had some wonderful times with Terry. We often cruised around to Studland; well known now for its nudist beach, we anchored and went ashore in a dinghy, joining pals on the beach for a barbecue. We cruised the coastline, sleeping on the boat and popping into harbours that looked inviting.

Terry, his wife Valerie, and Joyce and I went to Portugal, in 1976 just as the revolution had ended. There were burned-out fighter planes still on the runway as we landed. We stayed in Prah de Luz; we were the only ones on the beach. It was my birthday, 17 May and we celebrated it in a bar that had been shot up by terrorists, and a man killed. 'Everything is OK now my friends,' said the convivial John Coffee, Terry's Portuguese friend, who was the local 'mister fix it'. He worked in the fish market in Lagos, and took us all over the place. We had lunch in the hills with a bullfighter, and spent the week in alcoholic oblivion. In the mid-80s Terry sold everything he owned in the UK and moved to Portugal, where he still resides.

Len Harvey, who had owned the Takeaway next to my old TV shop on the Yate shopping centre, had split up with his wife Sylvia. After 28 years of marriage, she had left him for someone else. He was heart-broken. To add to his injury, his businesses failed and he also lost his home. I offered him a job as a salesman, and said he could live in the flat above the shop. He didn't have a car, and when he arrived at my shop everything he owned was in the two suitcases he was carrying. I felt deep compassion for him.

Len wasn't giving up on his wife and thought he could win her back. He went through periods of extreme optimism, followed by others of deep depression, and during these highs and lows hit the bottle hard. He wanted desperately to get back into the catering-licensed trade; it's what he knew best. Although his wife had now divorced him, he remained ever hopeful of a reunion. 'If I could get back on my feet and get a job managing a pub, I could get her back.'

On occasion Len would disappear during the day, and I would find him in his flat, in tears. I sat for hours on end with Len trying to encourage him. Eventually he got a job as head barman in a Bristol pub. From there he became manager of a lovely country pub at Mark in Somerset. Sylvia, now parted from the man she left Len for, who had gone back to his wife, moved into the pub, but would not share a room with Len. She had a number of men friends. Her behaviour tore Len apart, but at least while they remained friends, he thought he still had a chance. When Len was offered the tenancy of the pub, he applied for the licence in joint names with Sylvia, putting her name in front of his own above the door. 'What we do for love?'

A few years later, Len Harvey had a massive heart attack from which he never recovered. Sylvia was there at his bedside. Throughout his life he had been devoted to her. I think he died of a broken heart. I loved that man, as did many, many others.

Mum had been poorly for some time and was taken into hospital in a critical condition. She had suffered for some years with angina and a number of other related complaints. My sister Eve was on holiday abroad and had to be summoned. Now with her 'five' gathered around her, our mum had a smile on her face, but she was so frail, like a leaf in autumn waiting to fall.

We set up a vigil and vowed never to leave her for one moment. Stella and I did the night shifts, where we sat in the room next door to mum, talking over endless cups of tea until the early hours. We spoke of our childhood, and the harsh life mum had had to endure. After dad died she never really had the will to continue. We argued, 'Of course you have mum, you have all of us.' I didn't understand then, but I think I do now. As you grow old, life passes you by. Your peers are extinct and most of your generation has passed on. Your life, the one you cherished, is in the past, there isn't much left to live for.

I telephoned Maud in London and asked if she was coming to see mum. I was distraught when she replied, 'Mine isn't the face she wants to see.' I don't know where she got that from. My mother had brought up Maud's daughter, June, from a baby, treating her as her own, and now when mum lay dying, she wouldn't come to say thankyou. I said 'Maud if you don't come to see mum, I know she was your stepmother, but she has shown you kindness far beyond that which you have earned – neither I nor the other four will speak to you again.' I meant it. When I replaced the receiver, I wept. What had happened to the Maud we idolised? When dad died she relied on us all so much to help her through it; we relied on each other, and I thought we were inseparable.

Mum was fading. The last thing I remember her saying to me was, 'Jimmy, I could murder a cup of tea.' Betty held a cup to her lips. She could only sip a little, but there was a sheer look of joy on her face when she tasted the nectar. We all smiled. Eve came in so that Stella and I could go home and get into a change of clothes. Betty too slipped away for an hour. Later, Stella phoned me to say that mum had passed away, with just Eve by her side and holding her hand. Although annoyed with myself that I wasn't with mum when she died, I thought it fitting that it was Eve. My lovely sister now has that moment, which is hers privately. Until recently Eve had never thought of herself as particularly close to Mum. Once Eve had married, she never lived at home again, as Betty, Stella, and Maisie had done.

We rushed back to the hospital and consoled each other. The five plus one, June. Stella and I sat in the little chapel and prayed, I said words of thanks for the best mother a son could have; I was hardly worthy of her. She fought tooth and nail for us during the hardest times. 'Over my dead body,' she would say if we were threatened. I wish I had done more for her. She took very little from a life, where she walked in the shadow of her husband.

During the funeral service at Failand church, my head kept turning towards the door expecting at any moment that Maud would walk through it. As mum was lowered into the grave where dad had previously been buried, Maud came running through the churchyard, followed close behind by my brother Roy. When the internment was over, Stella as courteous as ever, invited Maud, Roy, June and her husband Jimmy, who by now had joined the mourners, back to her house. Maud declined and they went back to London. When I next saw Roy I asked him why the three of them had come to mum's funeral. They didn't come while mum was alive, although they had adequate warning that her condition was serious. Why turn up now? I could see he was embarrassed as he replied, 'It's a matter of respect bruv. I was very fond of her.' It's a pity he didn't tell her so whilst she was still alive.

Sister June never lived with mum. Our grandparents brought her up, so it wasn't expected of her. But Maud, she obviously had a guilty conscience. Her faith should tell her that it can't be eased that simply, she has to live with it. Sadly her prejudice against her own granddaughter remains. I was so upset at the time that I went to see our local vicar Tom Gibson, and explained the whole scenario to him. Was it my sister's Jewish religion that prompted this attitude? If anyone should understand about prejudice, surely it is the Jews? Tom listened carefully and sympathetically. He could see I was distraught. He said he could see no sound reasoning for her behaviour, which he called disgraceful, and un-Godly. The rift continues till this day. Prejudice closes more doors that it opens.

I joined the parade at Badminton on Remembrance Day as normal. It was three weeks after mum's funeral, and after the service I went alone to Failand church and stood by her grave. I always place poppies on dad's grave every year. He used to observe the silence on the 11th with great reverence, and expected everyone else to. I now placed poppies for both of them, and some fresh flowers for mum. As I did, my 49 years flashed before me; I could see them when we were young, the music, the parties, dad the entertainer, and all-time kidder. Mum laughing, and with tears rolling down her cheeks saying 'Stop it Jim.'

The 1950s were probably their best years. Mum followed dad around the venues where he played as often as she could. One of the places he often played piano at was The Langford Arms in Somerset. There was a local, who was a sandwich short of a picnic so to speak, but a good darts player. One night in collaboration with the landlord and others, dad turned up in a black cloak, big hat and, wearing a sinister looking moustache, announced himself as Count Stanislav Piesemendrick, and challenged the dart player to a game. God knows where he got the name. He then stated that he was 'Grand Champion Darts Player of all Transylvania'. Dad couldn't play darts to save his life, so the local man beat him easily. Then came 'the sting'. Dad accused his opponent on cheating, and demanded satisfaction, 'a duel'.

Dad had taken with him two old air pistols, ones I had acquired in one of my legendary swaps. The challenger and the challenged, followed by the rest of the pub, went out into the car park. The seconds 'loaded' the pistols, one of whom also had a cap gun that he would fire at the given time for effect. The 'duellists' stood back to back, then walked 10 paces, turned and fired. A loud bang came from the cap gun as dad fell to the ground, mortally wounded.

The local darts player was ushered back inside, while conspirators in the charade pledged their silence, saying they would 'get rid of the body'. Meanwhile dad had gone back to his car, changed clothes and slipped back into the pub as though he had been there all the time. I don't think anyone ever told the poor local man the truth. It was legend there for years. Dad was always getting up to things of this nature. Were they both really gone? It was hard to bear. It still is.

I thought I might get planning permission to build a house in the garden on the west side of Wisteria. I called at the planning office of the local council. They told me I might get approval when the new village boundaries were drawn up.

Business at the shop in Chippenham was on the decline. I put the premises on the market and after a few months found a buyer. What would I do now? I retreated to my small workshop where I languished for months. Joyce was pleased that I had got rid of the shop, but was apprehensive as to what I would do next. With my track record, wouldn't you be?

Joyce and Rachel, who then still rode to hounds, had found another hobby, dog showing. Joyce had bought a Welsh springer spaniel called Lady, whom at first my dear wife looked upon as a pet that could do with some obedience training. With this in mind, she took the dog to a training class in Malmesbury, where both Lady and Rachel could receive tuition. A few weeks later, with not a little encouragement from others, mother and daughter took their little spaniel to a local dog show, where the judge gave further encouragement saying Lady showed promise. They now had 'dog show fever', leaving home in the early hours travelling the length and breadth of the country, winning prizes all over the place. Not only did Lady qualify for Crufts in her breed class, but also after beating a Class of 52 at the NEC in Birmingham, Rachel and her little spaniel won through to the final of the Junior Handler of the Year, at the Earls Court Show. Joyce was brilliant both at turning out and showing horses, and now she had turned her talent to the canine variety, she was achieving the success she had previously enjoyed. I was so proud of them both.

The planning consent to build a house in the garden of Wisteria was granted. This opened up a few options, it was time to reflect and appraise the situation.

I don't deny that I had had a great deal of fun during the last few years, but commercially I had slid backwards, although I hadn't intended to. It had occurred whilst I thought I was standing still; I had been overtaken, more than going in reverse. My main activity had been the video business and photography, and whilst enormously satisfying it hadn't been profitable.

I had spent much of my time filming events of interest connected with hunting. The Yeomanry race which hadn't taken place in years, was re-kindled, so I filmed it for posterity. The Hunt Club Revue at Sodbury Hall, where Brian and Hilary recited poetry, and Anthony Brassey the Hunt Chairman, Pammy Jane Farquhar and Camilla DeFerranti, dressed as the Supremes, danced and mimed to the hit record 'Stop in the name of Love'. I had spent a few hours several weeks before the revue at the cottage where Ian and Pammy Farquhar now lived, putting the three through a dance routine. On the night they were sensational.

Ronnie Dallas retired, and I filmed a Meet of hounds and presentation to him in front of Badminton House. Ronnie had been Hunt secretary for 30 years, and he and his wife Sylvia had always been kind to me. Sylvia was one of the first people with whom I spoke in the hunting field and we always acknowledged each other thereafter. She shows a genuine interest in everyone, and what they are doing. Sylvia is descended from the Cubitt family, the civil engineering and construction dynasty who laid out many of the squares in London, and much of Bloomsbury in Victorian times. Cubitt Town on the Isle of Dogs, where I once lived, is named after them.

For a few years I did the announcing at the Beaufort Hunt point-to-point races. At the one that took place following Ronnie's retirement, and during a break from my duties, I was summoned by the Duke of Beaufort, who had caught sight of me standing by the weighing in tent, 'Jim, I have a bone to pick with you.' Thinking it was something light-hearted, I smiled as I walked over to him, but in serious tone he continued, 'I have had a number of complaints from people who could not hear the proceedings at Ronnie Dallas' presentation. The sound was not loud enough.' I responded with, 'That was the best I could do with the equipment; it was flat out.' To my astonishment he replied, 'Well bloody well get some bigger speakers then,' and walked off. I was both upset and hurt by his outburst. The equipment he was referring to was that which I had donated to the Hunt some years before. In the very many years that I loaned all sorts of electrical equipment for hunt functions, I had never ever made a charge. I thought that without knowing the facts, the Duke's criticism was unjust. I told Anthony Brassey of the incident; visibly embarrassed, he said he would 'have a word'.

On a number of occasions I filmed the Duke's lady friend and confidante, Miranda Morley, being coached by Ferdie Eielberg, the dressage expert in the indoor school at Badminton. Miranda rode two good horses at the time, Max and Monkey. I spent hours on end filming the three of them. She had an exceptionally competent groom in Mac, a Dutch girl, who was also interested in photography. Eventually I persuaded Miranda to buy a camcorder for Mac to use; she became very adept at the art.

I got along very well with Miranda, and would like to think we were friends. Christmas day she always attended to her horses herself so that Mac could have the day with her family. One year, a couple of days before Christmas, Miranda left a message on my answering machine saying if I happened to be around on Christmas morning to pop into her stables for a drink, she would be pleased to see me. I did, and over a drink and a mince pie, we shared our hopes and fears for the future. I realised then that although I had hunted with her for around 15 years, I hardly knew her. Once you break through the exterior shell of a most private person, you'll find a warm, genuine and sincere human being.

Miranda had had her horses stabled at Badminton for some time, and now that David, now Beaufort had inherited the estate, she moved into a cottage that had been extensively refurbished for her at Little Badminton. There is a lovely little cottage next door to it, which was ideal for Mac to live in. Miranda still worked in London during the week, where she ran her own garden design business, but now had a permanent base at Badminton.

Mac was leaving Badminton to follow the man she hoped one day to marry. Miranda wanted to give her a going-away present and asked me to glaze some pictures she had taken of Max, Monkey and the cottage where Mac had lived, on to some fine china plates from her personal tableware. She further asked if I would present them to Mac on her behalf, saying, 'Jim, I know you will do it properly.' I don't know why Miranda asked me to do it. I can only assume that she thought it too emotional to do herself. She thought an awful lot of Mac. Both women and horses' had been a great team and it was sad to see it split up. I invited Mac to Wisteria and made the presentation; the dear girl burst into tears.

It was 1987, and a Christmas show planned by Jane Holderness Roddam took place in the Badminton indoor riding school. Michael

Tucker performed the duties of MC and eventers including Ginny Leng took part in pony club games. Mounted, girls from the Hunt formed a quadrille and gave a marvellous display set to music. Jane, riding sidesaddle and looking so elegant, gave a display set to the music from the TV hit series *Upstairs Downstairs*. It was a moment to remember. It was a fun evening and greatly enjoyed by everyone. The finale included not only those who had taken part, but also local children dressed in costume, forming a nativity pageant. With the main lights off, leaving just the parade floodlit, it looked spectacular. Hilary Forster read a moving message of thanksgiving.

I supplied the sound system, produced the music for the rides and also captured the proceedings on video. Jane was demonstrably grateful for my efforts. I assured her I had enjoyed it as much as anyone. Still she wrote to thank me formally saying they hoped to stage a similar event the next year, and would I help. I said I would, not realising then that by next Christmas I would be occupied elsewhere. I don't think there ever was another Badminton Christmas show. Pity.

In the past, and for a number of years, at Christmas, the late Duke and Duchess held a fancy dress party at Badminton House for the local children. The parents accompanying them also dressed up, and I reckon we had a better time than the kids did. Lady Caroline Somerset as she was then always dressed as a Cossack; late Duke wore a long striped nightshirt. Major Gundry got the party going with a swing and danced with all the children. There was a prize for the best dressed. Some went to great lengths and their costumes were magnificent. They were magic times for us all, incredibly special.

Despite this I felt the urge to move on. But where? Should I build a house in the garden of Wisteria? Whatever I did I would have to consider Rachel, who was now at Bath College studying English and Geography. I remembered that the deeds of Wisteria showed a covenant forbidding construction on the garden to the west side of the house without first obtaining consent of the Somerset Trust who held the covenant on the piece of land on which I now had planning consent. I thought little of it when I purchased the property.

I made an appointment to see David Beaufort and told him of my dilemma. He assured me he wanted nothing from me, but that I would have to deal with his agent over the paperwork. This meant approaching Richard Wood, which I did. Richard informed me that the present Duke had no jurisdiction over the covenant. The piece of land in question had long since passed into the Somerset Trust. However, the covenant could be bought out, for a price. He would let me know. A few weeks later I got a letter from him saying the Trust wanted £20,000, but in view of

my long association with the Beaufort family they would accept
£19,000. I was flabbergasted. Richard stressed that the Duke had no
desire to make this charge. I could continue to build the house
proposed, but the covenant would have to remain.

I was over a barrel so to speak. How much would the trustees want in
a few years time, should I want to sell, with a house built on the land? I
gave it a great deal of thought and eventually saw I had no option but to
pay, if I wanted to execute my plans. At this point, I could not help
drawing a parallel. The figure they wanted from me to release the
covenant was about the same as I had charged the Duke and Duchess
for the rental of TVs and video recorders over the past 18years! It had
been entirely due to my own initiative that I had procured planning
consent, and now the Somerset Trust just sat back and said, 'Thanks,
that's nineteen grand you owe us.' At first I was bitter, and decided to
sell up and move on, and although I never changed my mind about
selling and moving, the bitterness faded.

It had been a matter of business being business, and nothing personal.
'Good business' is how the Beauforts got their millions. I took the
lesson on board, and vowed to learn from it. When the Duchess's
learned, not from me I add in haste, about the deal, she asked, 'Are you
one of our tenants then, Jim?' She didn't understand. I doubt she had a
clue what they did or did not own.

Joyce, with her eagle eye, saw an advert in the *Western Daily Press*,
and read it to me: 'Overseas property estate agents require a manager
for a new office they are opening shortly in Clifton, Bristol.' You know
a bit about the overseas property business so why don't you apply Jim?
It would do until you make up your mind just what it is you want to do
next,' she reasoned. Could I work for someone else? It had been
different with the tube building business; that was an arrangement, a
definite term. I thought long and hard. Joyce was eager for me to give it
a try. I really had no excuse, nothing else was on the horizon, and I was
in limbo.

I arrived at an empty shop in Alma Road in Clifton, Bristol, where the
round-faced, ebullient character I came to know as Bob Shepherd,
entrepreneur, super salesman and current sales director of Eurochoice
Properties, waited to greet me. 'Jim Ruston?' 'Yes,' I replied. He
continued, 'I could tell it was you by your letter; charismatic, and full of
quality.' I was taken back to say the least, thinking, what a load of
flannel! I was soon to learn that this was Bob's way. He was like it with
almost everyone, especially the firm's clients, or Billy Bunter's, punters
– or just plain Billies, as he preferred to call them.

VIVA ESPANA

My interview was without doubt the most unusual I have ever attended, not that I attended many in my career. Others present were Eric Cartright, managing director, and Malcolm Harrison, finance director. The big guns were out in force to choose their new manager. It wasn't so much a case of them interviewing me, more the other way around. An hour or so later I was offered and accepted the job to manage their new branch. A few days after that a letter arrived confirming my appointment, and informing me of travel arrangements they had made for a group of new employees to visit their office, and properties they were selling in southern Spain. 'Our Spanish office is in Torrevieja Jim. Have you heard of it?' Eric Cartwright asked. I told him I had driven through it once.

Joyce was more than pleased that I had found a new interest; and I, having taken the plunge into a new cause, would give my all. When I returned from my visit to Spain, where I had spent a hectic week meeting developers and viewing properties, I was filled with enthusiasm. I suggested to Joyce that we sell up and buy a house in Spain. 'What about Rachel?' Joyce countered. 'She has to finish her education.' We discussed it with our daughter, and she assured us that providing we leave her with a decent house in which to live and a car, she would be OK. She would still have her sisters close by, and would visit us during her holidays.

I put Wisteria, with the benefit of planning permission for a further dwelling, in the hands of Alan Walter, my vet friend Bill's son. Alan is a surveyor, and at the time worked for an estate agent in Tetbury, where he put things in motion to find a client for my property.

Together with help from my assistant Julie, who had recently been appointed, I opened the Bristol office. Bob Shepherd arranged the advertising which had an immediate effect, we were swamped with enquires. We offered four-day inspection tours to Spain at a cost of £150 per couple one of whom to be the prospective buyer. If you were not careful, some would try to bring kids along for a cheap holiday. The tours, which included flights, hotel, all transport and meals, were, needless to say, heavily subsidised. On average around eight couples made up each tour. Sometimes we flew them into Alicante, other times Murcia. The latter we later adopted as the more flexible. Although called Murcia it is nowhere near the ancient cathedral city, which itself is inland, whereas the airport of the same name is on the coast, near Los Alcazares. When flying into this airport one gets a spectacular view of La Manga, which from the air is breathtaking. The punters' first impression of the area we were taking them to, no bad thing.

A COCKNEY KID IN GREEN WELLIES

The man in charge of sales on the Spanish side was Paul Mangel. A scholar with a degree in English gained at Exeter University. (I could do with him now!) Once the inspection tour had landed, Paul organised their itinerary. After booking into the hotel, the clients attended a welcome meeting, where they were introduced to the representatives who would take them around during their stay, one rep for each couple. Over-manned you might say, but it worked. Everyone met up at lunchtime, then again in the evening at restaurants that had been pre-booked. A Spanish beauty named Carlotta took care of this task. Tall, slim, with dark flashing eyes, she had most of the male clients in a spin from day one, but she was lazy. Surprisingly, most females also seemed like her. Carlotta, a socialite, worked for an interest and a little pin money. She could be unreliable, but was tolerated as entertainment value. Observing her hips swaying to and fro as she left you confirmed her worth!

We were booking them up in the UK, and Paul and his team were signing them up in Spain. I had introduced a couple I knew well, Gordon and Leila Yeomans. Suitably impressed, they bought an apartment on a small up-market complex at Cabo Roig, where Terry Wogan has a house. To have made a sale at the outset was a feather in my cap. It also gave me confidence in what I was promoting, I valued the Yeomans's opinion, Gordon has been in the building trade all his life.

Christmas came, and Joyce and I took stock of our situation. Alan had not yet found a buyer for Wisteria, although he said he had had a number of interested parties. I was offered the opportunity to work in Spain, and this appealed to me, to be at the sharp end, where you only had four days in which to clinch a deal. The percentage of people who bought after they had returned from their tour was no more than about 1 per cent. I was confident with what we were selling, and anxious to prove I could match the best.

In January 1989 I flew to Spain. I had left Joyce with the task of finding a small semi to leave behind for Rachel. Joyce would join me in Spain once Wisteria had sold. After a few weeks, and getting anxious, my wife phoned to say there was still no sale. Before I left for Spain, I had been contacted by an estate agent from Wooton-under-Edge, who had seen Wisteria advertised, and offered to try to sell it for me. I told him that it was already under instruction. Joyce, who was trying hard to find a house for Rachel, was beginning to panic. There was very little for sale; we were still in the property boom. Eventually my wife found a house in Warmley, a suburb on the north side of Bristol, and not far from Bath. It was ideally situated. The owners wanted a quick decision.

I rang the agent in Wooton telling him if he had a client for Wisteria, to sell it. Within two weeks he found an interested party and secured a sale. Alan Walter was upset that I had introduced a competitor, and could not understand why. He said he had worked so hard trying to sell my property, and produced a list of some 40 people who had shown interest. The new agent had in fact sold Wisteria to someone that Alan had already shown around the property himself, but never clinched a deal. I have no doubt that Alan is a competent surveyor, but a salesman he wasn't.

The laws of average of finding so much interest in a property in a buoyant market and not securing a sale from 40 interested parties must be small. As it turned out, the market was on the cusp of decline. Two months after completion of the sale of Wisteria, the price of property started to fall, gathering speed daily. The property market collapse of 89/90 was unprecedented. If I hadn't made the decision to bring in another agent, it would have cost me thousands, and I would probably have had to abort the Spanish venture. I took no pleasure in dumping Alan, for I know that is how he must have felt, but I had lost confidence in him. I have listened, not for long I might add, throughout my life, to salesman telling me why they haven't made a sale. And if I sat and waited for clients who said they would 'get back to me' I would have moss growing between the cheeks of my bum!

The last I heard of Alan Walter was that he gave up working in the estate agency business, moved to Devon and was working with horses. Alan is a superb horseman, and has ridden quite a few times in the Grand National. I have much admiration for him, and still like him a lot. Alan's father, Bill Walter, divorced Caroline and for a time lived with Veronica Fairmudge, eventually leaving her to marry Jane Clayton, whom he wooed from her husband Michael, the editor of the Huntsman's bible *Horse and Hound*. Michael had broken his arm, and now to add insult to injury his wife had left him for another. A wag of a journalist wrote something about poor Michael Clayton nursing a broken heart, as well as a broken arm.

I was relieved to have sold Wisteria, and Joyce was looking forward to living in Spain. It hadn't been the best decade for her. Her father had died early on from a heart attack, leaving her with the added responsibility of her mother, whom she was now apprehensive of leaving. Joyce is a wonderful mother to our children, and was quite naturally devoted to her own. Joyce moved with Rachel into the little semi she had bought in Warmley, and once settled, prepared to fly to Spain to join me.

A COCKNEY KID IN GREEN WELLIES

Spain is a country steeped in history, sharing its past with so many different cultures. From the time of Roman domination to the empire created by Charles V in the 16th century, various peoples and cultures passed through Spain leaving their mark on the land, and on the sentiments of the population. Everywhere you turn there are signs of the Muslim domination, and their battles with the Christians. Six hundred years of occupation, wars and mutual influences, with hundreds of castles and fortified towns to defend territories conquered from the enemy. Many of these defensive structures can still be admired today, such as the castles of La Mota, Alicante, Alcazar de San Juan and the walled city of Avila.

However, not everything revolved around war. Everyday life, religious sentiment, and a love of art also found a time and place in history. Cathedrals, commemorative monuments and frescoes pay tribute to the richness of artistic expression visited upon this country, by those bringing with them diverse and challenging cultures.

The Costa Blanca (White Coast) stretches from Denia in the north to Los Alcazares in the south. The area enjoys an average temperature ranging from 15 degrees centigrade in winter to 30 degrees centigrade in summer. If you love the sun, then with an average 340 days of it each year, this is for you. Acre upon acre of orange, lemon and almond trees decorate the landscape, whilst ground crops of avocado, artichoke and asparagus carpet the ground. Flora and fauna of so many varieties produce a breathtaking kaleidoscope of colour. So much colour, contrasting with the brilliant white of the houses, against a backdrop of deep blue sky, is a vision hard to compare. And one that can be enjoyed most days, and it's free! General Franco once said of his fellow countrymen: 'They have the cheap wine, food, cigarettes and beautiful sunshine; what more do they want!' I know people who will settle for this. I need a little more though.

Since its earliest times, Torrevieja has been a producer and exporter of salt. The massive salt beds have been the basis of the town's economy. In the early days the inhabitants had to travel by sea to wherever they wanted to sell the product. This led to them becoming skilful sailors with eye for trade. The salt industry remains, and they still build small boats on the beach to the south of the town. About 100 years ago the clipper *Pasquale Florres* was built there, to haul salt. She became famous through the TV drama series The *Onedin Line*. An attempt was made to refurbish her, which looked most promising when I visited her.

I took my colleagues from Eurochoice and some of their European agents aboard her, and at the time much of the restoration work had been completed. Sadly the refurbishment programmes fell foul to funding failure, and now in decay, she languishes in Bristol docks, where I recently saw her. I don't think there are many sadder sights than a classic vessel moored to a quay and left to rot. But some good news, plans are afoot to take her back to Torrevieja where she will be refitted, and I think put on show. I am reliably informed she will receive a huge Spanish welcome. If I can, I will go over for it, and drink to her health and survival.

It was early January 1989. I was standing outside Casa Vicente, a restaurant we often used at lunchtime for our clients, when a car pulled up close by me, and out of the drivers window popped the head of my son-in-law Gordon. He had driven right across Spain on his way to La Manga where he and Karen had their apartment. The chances of him finding me standing at the side of the road as he drove by must be quite slim. I knew he was on his way, he and Karen had sold up in UK and were moving to Spain. Karen and her two children Daniel and Jade were flying over with Joyce. Gordon had arranged to pick them up from Alicante later that evening.

I had purchased a lovely plot of land some 1,200 square metres on a development called Ciudad Quesada, about five miles inland from Torrevieja. Quesada is a family name; Ciudad means city, although it was hardly that, the development had been named after the Quesada family who built it. The head of the family, Justo, developed the site with land he had purchased years ago for about 100 pesetas (50p) per Square metre; he was still building on it. His daughter Pepita is married to Antonio, also with the name of Quesada – hence the name of their firm, Quesada y Quesada. It was from them that I purchased the plot of land on which they agreed to build a large villa for Joyce and me. Eurochoice, the company I now worked for, sold a lot of houses on this development, which I thought was the nicest in the area. Many people like to be close to the beach. This is fine for holidays, but not for long periods. It gets much too noisy.

The villa we were having built was called a Luz – light. It had a small tower built into the roof from where light pours into a huge sitting room, hence its name. With a large fitted kitchen three bedrooms and two bathrooms it was both spacious and luxurious. I watched it being built brick by brick. It was the photograph of a finished Luz that I had sent to Joyce that had kept her spirits up until she was in a position join me. At that time I hadn't really taken too much notice of the name of the road in which our villa was being built. It was Goya, an omen?

It would be sometime yet before our house would be ready for us to move into. In the meantime, Joyce would stay with Karen and Gordon at La Manga, I would remain busy night and day with the Billies. We were now receiving clients on Tuesdays and Saturdays. Quite often, an extra tour arrived on Thursdays. We were flat out. I slept in the same hotel as the clients, but was eager to have my own place and much-needed space.

Torrevieja (Old Tower) is a typical Spanish town. Although there is naturally an influx of tourists during July and August, there are no package holidays. The reason for this is the lack of hotels. There are few, and even these are small. The vast majority of accommodation available consists mainly of apartments and villas, which are privately owned. It is very much a Spanish holiday resort, and a favourite with many who live in the 'dust bowl' that is Madrid; the capital is unbearable in mid-summer. In August, when temperatures reach the 90s, Spain's commerce virtually closes it doors, and everyone flocks to the coast.

We were selling on a number of developments, besides Ciudad Quesada. There was Marsol (sea/sun), a collection of bungalows near the sand dunes, through which a path led to the beach. I sold one to Eileen Donnelley from Bristol. Eileen, now in her 60s, had been recently widowed. After a few conversations it transpired that I knew her husband Jim, from the days when he was with the BBC's outside broadcast unit. Jim was a sound engineer and had spent his entire career with the Beeb. On one of my rare visits to Bristol, Eileen's daughter, who lived in the City, got in touch with me to ask about her mother, saying she hadn't heard from her for quite a while and was worried. I was able to assure her that her mum was fine. When I spoke to Eileen about her daughter's concern, all she said was, 'They worry too much,' Eileen had a little car, which she drove everywhere. With her widow's allowance, plus Jim's pension from the Beeb, she was in clover.

The development called Lago Jardine (Garden Lake) was close to one of the big salt lakes with bungalows built around a historic building. Although in decay, the intention was to restore it to accommodate a fitness and medical centre. An eminent doctor from the World Health Organization had visited Lago Jardine and given it a glowing accolade, as a place where health benefits, due to its location near the salt lake, could be gained. This was huge selling point, and many bought on that very premise. Needless to say, Bob Shepherd made capital of this!

A schoolteacher from Bath, a spinster, who reminded me of Miss Morris my old junior school teacher, drew my attention on an inspection tour with her penchant for fine liquor. I had one or two with her. Having bought a bungalow, without fuss, she moved to Spain. When I next saw her, she had been living in her new home for a few months, and was hobbling around with a stick, telling me she had fallen down and broken her leg, but wasn't bothered by it.

This lady had a wonderfully happy disposition, which I gathered was largely due to a liberal consumption of alcohol. Some months later, whilst sitting on her sun drenched terrace, with a book in one hand and a glass of Spain's finest brandy in the other, she quietly passed from one paradise into the next. There must be worse ways of making the transition.

There are so many stories of people wanting to change their lifestyle for such diverse reasons they would fill an almanac. One thing I learned, if you have problems, moving abroad will rarely solve them. You won't believe how few think things through properly. The two most common reasons for failure are: missing the family back home (especially children and grandchildren) and, as common, insufficient funds on which to live. The latter causes a great deal of stress. Age and experience do not go hand in glove. The Cavalier attitude displayed by some towards money matters never ceased to amaze me. As Pepita Quesada often said, 'People come to Spain looking for a house. They bring with them their cheque book and leave behind their brain.' The reverse would be more advisable.

We were a very professional team I can assure you, and did not miss too many sales. But, there were times when a client's circumstances simply didn't add up. You would think they would welcome our advice to give some more thought to buying. As they say in the famous 'Street', 'Did they Eck as like.' On the contrary, a client would often become indignant that we had the affront to question his/her ability to furnish the necessary funds.

The property market in the UK was in decline, and it was beginning to filter through to Spain. The 80s had seen UK property more than double in value. In turn this had a two- pronged effect on the Spanish market. On the one hand, the added value highlighted the considerable equity the owner had in their home. So bombarded by financial 'advisers' – there was little control then, as many have since found to their chagrin – people were being encouraged to release this equity for home improvements and so on. Some used the money released to put a deposit on a house in Spain.

Those who purchased wisely with no mortgage would fare much better than those who did not. When the market collapsed, the former Cavaliers now had two mortgaged properties, often one with negative equity. The peseta had also plummeted from a fairly steady 190 – 200 to the pound to 165 – 70. Suddenly, the poor mortgagee had to find extra money each month to pay the Spanish bank with whom they had their overseas mortgage. And those with a mortgage also on their UK house, as many had, were now in dire straits. As interest rates leapt to curb inflation, their repayments spiralled. It was years before the market started to recover. Millions of pounds were lost both sides of the Atlantic, leaving many Brits in poverty under the sun. Sadly, they blamed everyone except themselves, and we came in for our share of criticism, as if we controlled the economy of Europe!

Joyce and I rented a small villa not far from where our house was being built, and I was both surprised and pleased that Joyce settled into the way of life so quickly. I was still working long hours, which meant she had to spend quite a lot of time on her own, but she never complained. A colleague, Paul Cleveland, who had been with the firm for a while, brought his wife Elaine and two year old son Darren out to set up home in Spain. We all became firm friends, and ended up living quite close together, which was nice for Joyce. Elaine is a cracking girl.

We had recently taken on a new site about 70 kilometres down the coast from Torrevieja at Puerto de Mazarron, where the developers Eurosol were building a range of properties in four different locations, all within four miles of each other.

Mazarron is on the Costa Calida 'the warm coast', and is in the province of Murcia, the smallest autonomous government in Spain. The journey from Torrevieja takes you through Cartegena. This beautiful city derives its name from the ancient settlement of Carthage in North Africa. Part of its original boundary still survives, and is said to date from Biblical times. I visited Carthage in 1972, whilst on holiday in Tunisia. Founded in 800 bc, destroyed and then re-built by Rome, then razed by the Arabs in 679 ad, I was amazed to see how much of the early settlement survives. More moving still, are the gravestones, more than 1,000 years old with readable dates on.

As you leave the city, the road becomes narrow, winding its way between the hills. An odd house is dotted here and there, and goat-herders tend a motley bunch of creatures grazing at the roadside. The terrain is rugged, and one is dwarfed by the solid rock rising steeply several hundred feet on both sides of the road. A double bend switching back viciously is negotiated, and as if out of nowhere, beyond a seemingly never-ending downwardly spiralling road, the port of Mazarron comes into view. Breathtaking. At first it looked like acres of glistening water, an illusion that momentarily fools all newcomers to the area. In reality it's the sun's reflection on the acres of polythene tunnels under which millions of tomato plants are growing. For this is tomato country. The next time you buy Spanish tomatoes in your supermarket look on the box. There is a better than even chance they came from Mazarron.

Puerto de Mazarron is a working fishing village, which really comes to life in July and August when it becomes a retreat for the Spanish holidaymaker. I loved it instantly and could have easily lived there, but apart from the two summer months it was much too quiet for Joyce. She never liked it one bit. A new hotel had been built on the beach, small by tourist standards. A lady of generous proportions, named Natalie ran Hotel Playa Grande. Friendly and businesslike, she did not speak a word of English – neither did any of her staff for that matter. 'Everyone in Spain speaks English' is pure mythology almost anywhere apart from the major tourist resorts. Mazarron is just one example.

Clients on the first inspection tour who stayed in Playa Grande were somewhat bemused when confronted with the menu at their first meal. Nati, God bless her, had done her best. Using a dictionary to translate the menu she had come up with the following: For canaloni – drainpipes. I don't know why she didn't realise it didn't need a translation! For emperador – shite fish. God knows where she got that from. And no one could understand why flan translated as a 'cake with fruit' arrived as crème caramel (Spanish for flan). It caused a great deal of amusement among our clients. We should have left it as a permanent feature of the menu; it certainly broke the ice on the clients' first night.

To say we were premature taking clients to Mazarron is an understatement. Of the four sites Eurosol had planned to develop, only two had been started: one called Puertosol (two-storey bungalows built around a pool, and another similar and closer to the beach, but with no pool), named Bel Mazarron. Apart from those two projects all we had to show clients were plans of the future developments at San Gines and Los Azohia, both on the outskirts of the port. Needing more variety, we took on a development of detached villas already under construction on a hillside overlooking the beach and sea, quite small but pretty, and each on a 500 square meter plot. These sold like hot cakes.

By now we were receiving clients from Finland, Norway and France – with agents in Sweden and Germany soon to follow suit. Disappointed with what was on offer in Mazarron, the directors of Eurochoice decided to concentrate more on Torrevieja, where there was a much wider choice of property. This suited Paul and me as we both lived there, and the travelling was getting tedious. The inevitable happened, Eurosol were not happy with the sales of their properties and broke off relations with Eurochoice. By now, living in Spain, I had become friendly with Roberto Bergonzi, the boss of Eurosol, and after much deliberation decided to join him as his sales manager. Paul Cleveland came with me. Paul and his family moved temporarily to Mazarron and I would commute from Torrevieja, staying the occasional night in Hotel Playa Grande. It was on one of these nights that I encountered 'Rocky'.

Paul and I were doing our bi-weekly airport run, dropping off one tour and collecting the next, among whom was Mr Smith. Dressed from head to toe in black, and clutching a plastic carrier bag in his hand, he plonked himself down in the seat opposite the one Paul sat in to welcome the new clients on board. The man in black remained silent during the trip to the hotel, and it wasn't until we all gathered for dinner that he spoke. Looking me straight in the eye, with a twitch, he said 'Hey Champ, I've got 20 grand to spend. Am I in with a chance? You don't get a more direct approach than that, do you! Throughout the meal I sat next to Rocky, my name for him, because he reminded me of an old fighter friend of my dad's who was 'punch drunk'.

After dinner, Rocky invited me to have a drink with him. 'I like you Champ, you seem honest,' he said as he patted me on the back with a paw the size of a dinner plate. During my night-club days, I came across plenty of serious drinkers, but none of them would have lived with Rocky. He was drinking four San Miguels to my one. The clients had all gone to bed; even Paul had said goodnight and drifted away. 'Hey where is the night life, Champ?' Rocky asked. 'Can we go to a night-club?

Not wanting to let him think there would be nothing much in Mazarron for him, regretfully, I took him to the Pyramid Disco. A consortium of tomato growers wanting to cash in on the growing tourist industry had funded the new night-spot; it would be dead in winter of course! The Pyramid was quite something. It had the best sound and light show I had ever seen; it really was spectacular. Rocky enthused, 'Would you look at that Champ, this is a fast town. I'm gonna like it here. Twenty grand. Am I in with a chance, Champ? asked Rocky, a little shakily.

I eventually got Rocky back to the Playa Grande and pushed him into his room. Exhausted, I stripped off my clothes and fell into bed. It was about 3am. I had just dozed off, when there was a loud knock at my door. '*Señor Jim, por favor.*' It was Nati's voice. I jumped out of bed, put on my trousers, and opened the door to a very irate hotelier. '*Que pasa Nati?*' She replied, '*La problema esta con El hombre en Negro*'.

Nati beckoned me to follow, as she hastened towards the ballroom. There sitting in reverse on a chair in the middle of the dance floor was Rocky. As soon as he caught sight of me he exclaimed. 'Hey Champ, I thought you had deserted me. Pull up a chair and watch these Spanish girls dance.' It was a private party, and the guests, all Spanish were not amused. The guys were posturing, whilst the senoritas were enjoying the attention of Rocky. Nati was becoming extremely cross, and threatened to call the police unless I removed him from the hotel.

Where do you go at 3am in the morning? Rocky couldn't understand, what had he done? Well he hadn't actually done anything. Nati had over reacted, but I didn't want to risk her calling the police; the Guardia might have turned up instead of the locals, then it would have been curtains for Rocky, and anyway I wanted his 20 grand! Although I had no idea what I could do I convinced Rocky to follow me, it was a beautiful night and bloody nuisance though he was, and I liked him. We were walking towards the harbour when a car pulled up. Unbeknown to me, Rocky, walking behind me, was thumbing a lift!

'Come on, Champ,' Rocky shouted as he ran forward to where the car had stopped. I lingered, as Rocky with much waving of his arms, signalled to me to get in the car. I didn't fancy it and shouted to him to go on, I would follow. Rocky got in the car and it sped off. I had no idea where he would end up. I jogged back to the hotel, and was greeted by Nati who looked relieved to see I was alone. Knackered, I crashed once more into bed.

The next morning during breakfast Nati came to get me saying two policemen had arrived with a very subdued Rocky. 'Hey Champ, where did you get to?' he enquired of me. 'Never mind me mate, what have you been up to?' I asked. It transpired that he had been to a party with some Spanish guys and had got completely legless. His compadres left him in the street, where the police found him and brought him to the Hotel. Nati would not let him stay, so I had to give my assurance to the police that I would take him to Torrevieja, and have someone look after him until he flew out.

I booked Rocky into a hotel in Torrevieja, leaving him in the care of Colin, our salesman who lived there, saying, 'Don't let him out of your sight,' Two days later I walked into Departures at Murcia airport, and there sitting among other clients was the man in black, and what a sorry sight he looked. Wearing the same clothes he had arrived in, he was nursing a heavily bandaged head. A trickle of blood leaking from under the bandage was running down the side of his cheek. I noticed that in one hand he clutched an A4 envelope, the very ones we used for contracts of sale, and thought, 'I don't believe it. Someone has signed him up!' As soon as he caught sight of me his face brightened, and then went serious. 'You left me Champ. I missed you,' he said, in a pathetic sort of way. Apologising immediately I said' 'Sorry Rocky, but I had a lot to do, other clients to deal with.'

A COCKNEY KID IN GREEN WELLIES

Apparently, Rocky had left the hotel in Torrevieja late that night, and got into a fight with some Spaniards, ending up in hospital where he needed 14 stitches in is head. The next day Colin, at Rocky's insistence, took him to look at property, selling him an apartment on Villas Del Mar. Of course Rocky hadn't parted with any money, he was skint, but he did sign a contract! Within two weeks of his return to the UK, the man in black paid the deposit on his purchase, and subsequently met all his obligations under the contract. The last I heard he had exchanged his small apartment for a bigger one. You can never tell who are buyers, and who are not. He obviously had more than 20 grand!

When I returned to Hotel Playa Grande I was confronted by Nati, who complained that '*El hombre en negro*' had offered her 1000 pesetas (£5) to sleep with him. I could hardly contain myself and replied, in English I hasten to add, that she should have offered him a fiver to sleep with her! Every tour had its characters; they would fill a book on their own! We once did 17 tours back to back, without a break.

PAN EUROPEAN

I was dividing my time between the office of Eurosol in Torrevieja and the one we had in Puerto de Mazarron. Between mid-July and the end of August we didn't plan to receive any clients. It was too hot to show people around property, and in any case the whole area was awash with tourists. And of course flights were far more expensive; it wouldn't be economically viable to arrange inspection tours during this period.

The boss at Eurosol, Roberto Bergonzi, had decided to take a holiday for the whole of August. He, together with his brother Marco, their sister Maria and their respective spouses would make a trip to Canada; the three Bergonzis' had been born and raised in Montreal. They were multi-lingual, fluent both spoken and written in French, Italian and Spanish. Their father Renzo was Italian and their mother Swiss. The Bergonzis' had originated from San Remo in Italy where they still had strong family ties, Renzo's cousin is the famous opera singer Carlo Bergonzi.

Roberto's pretty secretary Yolande was to be married in the Church Parroquial Inmaculada Conception, in the centre of Torrevieja, and we were all invited to the wedding. A wedding is a huge occasion in a Spanish family. You may say 'It is here too', but somehow I feel we have lost our way on these occasions. I hate to generalise because there are always exceptions, but evermore I hear of wedding guest lists that exclude many. At some, no children are invited. The Spanish would be horrified at this suggestion. At others members of the family are excluded to make way for friends, in order to keep numbers at an economic level. This does little to promote, especially in the young, the institution of marriage and the sense of family. Of course not everyone has a deep pocket, and it is a very expensive time, but for me, if the economic choice lay between a sit down affair for 50 or a buffet for 100, there would be no contest, the latter would get my vote. To exclude family on these occasions can cause lasting rifts. Respect for one's kinfolk should never be sacrificed for splendour.

Our office in Mazarron was opposite the beach, about half a mile from the harbour. In the off season it was pure tranquility. One balmy day I was sitting at my desk, talking to the two Spanish girls Anna and Carmen, both of whom worked for Eurosol. Anna spoke a little English, but Carmen spoke none. From where I sat, I could see a woman I guessed to be English, and in her early 40s, walking towards the office door. With a massive smile on her round face she said 'Got any jobs?' Her name was Joan Ensor, who not only proved to be an asset to the firm, but also a more loyal colleague I would never find.

A COCKNEY KID IN GREEN WELLIES

Joan had moved with her husband Roy to Mazarron 17 years previously. She was fond of telling me, 'There were few tourists then Jim, it was just a small village. We used to by our veg from a man with a donkey and cart.' Joan loved Spain and was well respected locally. Continually struggling with her weight, she would promise to diet regularly, breaking it frequently! I owe her so much; she taught me a great deal about Spanish customs, the common laws of the country and how to integrate. If I ever had an altercation with the Spanish, Joan would back me up unconditionally, and even if I was at fault. Joan joined my sales team and was hugely successful at her job. The clients felt very comfortable being shown around by an English woman who had made her home in the country they were considering migrating to.

Joan had only lived in Spain for a short time, when she had a serious car accident in which she nearly died, It took months of care and much plastic surgery to restore her good looks. Quite naturally she had the greatest admiration for Spanish physicians. Tragically, Joan's daughter Kelly was savaged by an Alsation dog who bit half her face away, which distressed Joan so. And then as though that she had not suffered enough, this lovely woman died suddenly from a massive heart attack, while waiting for her parents, who often came over on holiday, at Alicante airport. She was just 49 years old.

The temperature in August was in the high 90s degrees F. and close to unbearable. I had enrolled in a language school for a month of intensive tuition in Spanish. Lessons started at 8am until 2pm, six days each week. Then there was at least three hours' homework. Each day at 2pm I went home for lunch, after which I went to work in the office until six. It was the longest month I have ever known. The small classroom only had one inadequately sized window and a couple of electric fans to circulate the air. In the first week the tutor Miguel would pause in between tuition and say, 'In ten days…' I thought ah, in ten days all will become clear, perhaps I could cut this torture short. Once I had learned a little more of the language I realised he was in fact saying, '*Intiendais?*' ('Do you understand?') Quite clearly I hadn't! I had a lot of fun though, despite sitting up half the night naked, in front of a massive fan, doing all the homework.

The Bergonzis family returned from Canada. There was to be a conference in Milan, organised by a group of financial institutions, specialising on property investment in Europe. Roberto thought it a good idea that Eurosol be represented there, and invited some of our European agents to attend. Roberto and I would travel to Italy by road. I left my poor wife to cope on her own in the villa, and early one morning set off for Milan with Roberto in his Mercedes Coupe.

PAN EUROPEAN

We were booked into Hotel Michaelangelo, an imposing building in the centre of Milan. Roberto, who always did everything in style, had arranged a suite, and it was magnificent. 'You have travelled a long way Jim, and have much to do. You need to be comfortable, no?' 'Thanks, yes I do,' I gratefully replied. We met up with the agents and had a meal, most convivial.

We were joined in Milan by Nicolas Ghanem, who is Lebanese and a distinguished civil engineer. Together with a colleague, he had formed Iberian Construction Company, which contracted all the building work from Eurosol. Nicolas is highly educated, a perfect gentleman with an engaging manner, with whom I got on tremendously. Worried for the safety of his family, Nicolas had moved them to Spain, to get away from the trouble in the Lebanon. He has a beautiful wife, three sons and a daughter; the family had left a substantial house and other assets in their homeland, always intending to return at the first possible opportunity. Nicolas was truly international, as were the Bergonzis of course, always thinking global, whereas I had never considered much outside the UK.

Nicolas seemed to have family connections everywhere, and even the worldly Roberto was impressed when Nicolas arranged for us to visit a cousin. His relation had the most prestigious antique and fine art gallery I have ever entered. I once spent a couple of days in Helsinki with Nicolas; he had family there too. There was much to this man that I never learned, although I did learn of his apprehension of flying in small aircraft.

With a view to putting together a new sales brochure, I had selected photographs of the areas where we operated in Spain. This was quite an ambitious project in as much as it would be translated from English into seven languages. I needed some more aerial shots of Mazarron and its coastline, so I arranged with Antonio Quesada to fly me, as he had done many times previously. I told Roberto of my plans, and he thought it a good idea if he came too, as he had never seen his developments in Mazarron from the air, suggesting also that Nicolas should accompany us.

When we got to the airfield and Nicolas saw the plane, a four- seater Cessna, he all but collapsed. After falling to his knees and praying to his maker, he asked, 'Jim, do I really have to go with you?' Roberto shrugged his shoulders, but made no comment, so it was left to me to persuade poor Nicolas that he would be OK, and that I had made countless trips in this very aircraft and returned safely. He did not enjoy the flight one bit saying, 'It is only my loyalty to you both that I am in this plane. Is it big enough to be called a plane?' I have a wonderful photo of my Lebanese friend standing by the Cessna. If a picture tells a story!

At lunchtime on the second day of the conference, Roberto was approached by the event organiser who offered a 15-minute slot for Eurosol to make a presentation. We had no previous warning of this; they made the offer because we were so well represented, there were 10 of us present. Roberto turned to me saying. 'What do you think Jim, can you do it?' This presented the perfect opportunity for Nicolas Ghanem to get his own back for the flying incident. 'Of course he can,' he proclaimed boldly. 'If he can convince me to fly for two hours in a sardine can, then he can convince these people here that Eurosol is the best developer in all of Spain!' I had one hour to prepare my address, then I made my presentation, which although nerve-racking for me, was well received. At the end of the conference I was interviewed by the Milan *Financial Times*. The next day Roberto bought a copy of the paper and read it to me. It mentioned me saying, Jim Ruston said this, and Jim Ruston said that. My boss, visibly pleased, said 'You did well for us Jim, and now the work is over, we will take a little leisure time.'

We drove to San Remo, where Roberto's family were visibly excited to see him, and welcomed me warmly. After some refreshment, Roberto toured the shops, some of which were owned by his relations, buying cold meats, cheese, coffee and so on. 'You can't get this, or that, in Spain Jim,' he would say as he loaded yet another box of goodies into the boot of his Mercedes.

Reluctantly we left Italy and drove down to Leon in France. Our French agent Michel Lorthios, who had also been at the conference, had persuaded us to view a potential site for Ski holiday chalets he had his eye on in the French Alps, close to Grenoble. We met with Michel and stayed overnight in Leon before setting off to look at his project. When we got to the Alps we found it buzzing with activity as they prepared for the winter Olympics. The ski jump was under construction and I stood under it thinking, 'You have to be slightly mad to jump off of this; what kind of person does this crazy event?' Then reflecting for a moment, I recalled the previous winter Olympics in Calgary Canada. There he was, hovering like an eggbound crow in a gale, Eddie the Eagle! We never did pursue the ski chalet project.

Our first Christmas in Spain was spent with Karen, Gordon, and our grandchildren Jade and Daniel. It was different having cocktails on the beach before the traditional Xmas fare. Christmas Eve was spent with friends of Karen and Gordon in a bar. It was all very jolly but lacked completely the spirit of Christmas that I was used to back home. Sitting on the beach watching Jade and Daniel paddle in the sea, I had an overwhelming feeling of nostalgia. My thoughts turned to Jane and Rachel, Beckie and Natalie, and I knew Joyce was missing her mum. I had now spent so much time in the sun I longed for a frosty morning, and the smell of England. The Spanish don't really make much fuss of Christmas preferring to celebrate the three Kings on the 6 January.

During our Christmas break Joyce made the decision to return to England. Rachel was at Bath College taking A levels and had endured an unpleasant relationship with a boyfriend, and now lived alone in our house in the suburbs of Bristol. I would soldier on for a while longer, although with the declining demand for our properties, I wondered how much longer it would be before we would have to severely curtail our activities. The whole of Europe was suffering a downturn in the economy. People had far more to worry about in their own country than contemplating purchasing a holiday home in another.

I had done my best to stimulate and encourage our agents to be more proactive, and had great hopes for both the Swedish and German agents to come through. To this end I agreed to visit each agent and attend an exhibition whilst with them. I flew to Norway, and with our agent Robert Larson held quite a successful event. On to Sweden where Stig Gustafsen had a four-day event in Hotel Gothenborg, in the city of that name. I stayed in the hotel as a guest of Stig, a successful businessman who was prepared to back his judgement with finance.

In the reception area of the hotel I noticed a sign that said Brostrom Rom. The name was familiar, so I followed the way the sign pointed until I found the room where on the wall by the door leading into it was an oil painting of a distinguished looking man; underneath, a plaque read: 'Dom Axel Brostrom – founder of Sweden's modern shipping industry.' I thought I had recognised the name. His grandson also Axel, was at Millfield with Stella's son Grahame. Axel spent most of his holidays with Stella at Cold Ashton and I got to know this complex, patrician, gentle boy, quite well. In fact my whole family liked him. His devotion to Grahame puzzled me at first, then later, the obvious became obvious.

After leaving Millfield, Axel bought a flat in Bath. He had become heavily dependant on drink, and sadly whilst still in his early 20s, died alone at home. There were no suspicious circumstances. His mother Annabella Brostrom was an absolute nightmare. She drove a dark red Rolls Continental with her initials emblazoned in gold on the doors. She bought a flat in Bath, but eventually bolted leaving debts all over the place.

Stefan Kohl and his partner Otto had their office in Hamburg, where I visited them at the precise time of the tearing down of the Berlin Wall.

A COCKNEY KID IN GREEN WELLIES

It was difficult for them to concentrate on what I was saying as their minds were elsewhere. People had been filtering in from East Berlin before the official opening of the barrier. Trabants, the three cylinder East German cars, were seen outside of supermarkets, where affluent West Germans were hanging bags, laden with shopping, on the wing mirrors; some even stuck Deuchmarks under the cars' windscreen wipers. It must have been a huge culture shock for the East, or GDRs as Stefan referred to them.

Stefan and Otto were already looking for opportunities in the East, and now they could only speculate on the economic effect unification would have on their country. I never saw much of them after that. They didn't bring any clients to Spain during the remainder of my time there.

Just before I left Hamburg, I stood in a street with Otto who pointed out two buildings standing on opposite corners saying, 'Those are the only two original buildings that remain in this area. Your RAF flattened the rest during the war.' Putting his arm around my shoulder he said 'Why did we try to kill each other? What a waste, all those brave young men. You will always be welcome in my home Jim.' I didn't know quite how to respond. I will send him a copy of this book, and hopefully he will understand.

When I visited our agent Petri Rienne in Helsinki, I was surprised to learn that he had organised an exhibition of our property in a bank. The national bank of Finland, Postabanki, had agreed to allow Petri to set up his display in the foyer. It was a marvellous opportunity for him to talk to the many clients of the bank; I just can't imagine that happening in the UK. Each day I went with Petri to help where I could, but have you ever tried speaking Finnish? It's an impossible language.

When they visited Spain on an inspection tour, Paul Cleveland was allotted the task of looking after the clients from Finland, which he did in his own inimitable style. Appearing casual and laid back, with a gesture of 'No pressure, take your time', Paul would wait until he spotted an opening, then move in and close a deal as swift as you would close a door. The Finns were always accompanied by a representative, often Petri himself, and Paul was informed that it would be useless to show them any property for the first two days, as most of them would be the worse for drink! At that time beer in Finland was £4 a pint – in Spain 100 pesetas 50p! In Finland a bottle of whisky was £36. A bottle of brandy in Spain was only £3.

There was also a fair amount of flirting between the group, often leading to all sorts of complications. If one considers they had left Finland in the dead of winter, with only a few hours of daylight, arriving on the Costa Blanca in brilliant sunshine, where the wine was flowing like water, the combination of sun, sea and sangria, played havoc with their libido! You could actually buy a bottle of wine in Spain for the same price as a bottle of Evian water. Admittedly at that price the wine wouldn't be up to much, but enough of it still got you drunk!

The Finns bought a lot of property on the Costas but it didn't do Petri much good. He somehow got himself into financial difficulties and one day just disappeared from the face of the earth, leaving many clients in limbo, and equally as many debts in his native country. Postabanki were none too pleased either, finding themselves with generous amounts of egg on their face. The last I heard was of a group of out of pocket clients taking action against Postabanki, claiming they thought Petri Rienne had the bank's backing. As it transpired, the only connection Petri had with the bank was an overdraft! Caveat Emptor.

The Costas have become multi-national, but although there has been some integration, there is colonisation. The Swedes and the Germans put up flags to show where they are, Nordic emblems fluttering in the breeze are commonplace. Thank goodness the Brits don't follow this trend, although like the rest they tend to stick together. The only thing they all have in common is 340 days of sunshine each year and the shits if they eat too much paella!

If you had asked me in the late 80s if I agreed with scrapping the pound in favour of the Euro, I would have said yes, I felt totally integrated into Europe. Now living back in the UK, I have again adopted the John Bull posture: 'Don't you dare touch our pound.' During my time in Spain the peseta fluctuated between 170 to 200 to the pound. When the slump came, it remained fixed around the lower figure. Even Roberto said we will never see the pound at 200ptas again, but as I write it is 260! Great for tourists, and those wishing to buy property in Spain, but what of their economy? In just about every Escritura (title deed) created, the property value is written down to reduce the IVA (VAT). When the property is resold the same thing happens, and the difference is paid in black money (undeclared cash). This is common knowledge. The authorities turn a 'blind eye'. How can we possibly have a single economic policy throughout Europe?

I can't leave Spain without recording the following event, or rather tragedy. Whilst for most of the time the sun shines, when it rains it pours. Paul, Joan and I were in the Hotel Playa Grande with one or two of our English agents when it started to rain. Joan frowned and with a little chuckle said, 'It looks like it could be a good one. It has been threatening for days and the forecast said rain.' It rained none stop throughout the day, getting heavier all the time. Joan went home and I followed her in my Renualt 11 to collect some paperwork from her house. I took one of salesgirls with me to show her for future reference where Joan lived. Joan was our lynchpin in Mazarron, so I always told all new staff how to contact her should they find themselves with a problem.

We stayed and chatted over coffee with Joan and Roy, until Joan said, 'Jim I think you should make tracks. I don't think this rain will let up.' Joan and Roy had a lovely villa, built on a hill at Isla Plana to the north of Mazarron, where the view over the bay is spectacular. The road from their villa is quite steep and by now it was dark, and with torrential rain lashing the windscreen I had a job to see where the edge of the road was. My companion looked terrified. I told her not to worry, but I had spoken too soon. As we rounded the bend, where the road started to level before it joined the main coast road, we hit floodwater around a foot deep; bringing the car to a halt, I reversed and waited. The rising water was now coming in through the bottom of the car door on my side. What should I do? By now my young colleague was so frightened she didn't even answer when I spoke to her.

I made a snap decision, which with the benefit of hindsight was foolhardy to say the least. I whacked the Renault into second gear and driving gently forward I could feel the bow wave the car was making, causing the vehicle to sway gently from side to side, not unlike a boat rolling. The road sloped so I drove the car on to the high side, and kept the engine revs steady. I must have thought I was back in 57 and aboard my DUKW! Lady luck was with me as gingerly I made my way back to Playa Grande, where the surface water was still no more than a foot deep. Why I didn't just go back to Joan's I don't know. I was never worried for myself, but I should have had more consideration for my colleague.

It rained all night, then disaster struck. There is a huge reservoir at Totana about 15 miles in land from Mazarron, but at much higher altitude. The civic engineers, in fear that the reservoir might burst causing untold damage in its locality, decided, after much consultation, or so they said, to release the pressure of water into the Rambla (a natural dry river bed which takes excess storm water). This Rambla runs all the way down the valley and under a bridge at Bolneuvo west of the port of Mazarron, and into the sea. The Rambla was near full when the water in the dam was released.

The result was devastating. The Rambla overflowed as it approached Bolnuevo, the unstoppable torrent of water, now taking its own line having knocked out the bridge, swept right on through a caravan and camping site. Hundreds of campers, many still asleep in their caravans and tents, were swept out to sea. We stood on the balcony of the Playa Grande in a stupor. We could not believe our eyes. First one, then a whole line of them floating behind each other as in convoy. It was surreal. Soon there were some 20 to 30 caravans floating out to sea! What of all those poor souls in the tents. Whole families were there.

There was nothing we could do. The emergency services alerted fishing boats in the harbour. In the tradition of fishermen and sailors around the world, they did their level best to launch a rescue mission. They hooked up the caravans, then tried in vain to tow them round to the harbour; most broke up. A trawler towing a caravan is an eerie sight, pathetic actually. We all had tears in our eyes. When the flood finally subsided, Joan joined us. Try as she might, she could not get anyone to admit to the number of casualties. The next day the regional newspapers admitted to finding three bodies, but locals said there were in excess of 40, some hinted at many more. There were tourists of all nationalities on that camping sight, but nothing was reported in the English papers. To us it smacked of a cover-up, and we tried to get a look at the campsite ourselves, but the police had the area sealed off. However, we did explore the beach where so much debris had been washed ashore. In amongst the bits of plywood were personal belongings, all manner of possessions, battered and torn. It reminded me of the things we found on bombsites I played on in the East End. The campsite is still there, so is the Rambla, and the Dam.

The property market in Europe had almost come to a standstill, now just a trickle of people filtered through looking for property in Spain. Eurochoice had ceased to trade in the UK, and the directors had gone their separate ways. Bob Shepherd, the ever- optimistic sales director of Eurochoice, started a new venture. He had come to an agreement with Pepita Quesada to sell exclusively on their development. To this end Bob, together with Derek Drake and Jeff Christmas, formed a new company based in Southampton called La Vissa. Bob invited me to join them and head up a team of agents, who would vigorously, through regular exhibitions, try to stimulate the interest in Spanish property.

With Joyce now back in England it wouldn't be long before Karen and her family would follow. I was living between my house in Spain, hotels with clients, and Karen at La Manga. My grandson Daniel had now been at school for two years and spoke fluent Spanish, and both he and his sister Jade swam like fish. They were fully integrated into the Spanish way of life. My son-in-law Gordon had also fitted in very well, and now had a small building maintenance business going. Karen, though, had been there, done that, got the tee shirt and was bored with it.

A COCKNEY KID IN GREEN WELLIES

Father and daughter stood together in the Mediterranean, and with the surf gently lapping around our legs, looked towards the distant horizon. The deep blue cloudless sky was our canopy, and the ocean shimmered like a billion diamante on a velvet dress. This was the paradise most people only ever dream of. The rest of the world seemed a million miles away. Karen spoke first. 'Dad, this is doing my head in. I have had enough sun and sand to last me a lifetime. We are thinking of selling up and moving back. What do you think?' I replied, 'There are thousands who would change places with us, few would understand, but I do of course. If it's time to move on – you know the rest luv.'

The piece of me that remained in Spain in 1982 would be joined by another piece that I was about leave. I eventually sold my house in 1995, and in so doing, ended my 15-year affair with this fascinating country and its people. I will return. I can't say when or why. I simply know that I will.

Karen and Gordon, having arrived back England bought a house in Yate, where they also opened a small art and framing business. I was still channel hopping, and on one of my customary visits to their shop I noticed on the floor propped against a wall, a rather large framed picture of a cricket scene. I knelt to examine it and found it was of a test match that had taken place in the West Indies; a limited edition print, signed and numbered by the artist, Jack Russell. Equally of interest to me were the signatures of the team that had played in the game, countersigned on the border. I have to admit that it wasn't immediately apparent to me that the artist Jack Russell and the cricketer with an identical name was same person. I hadn't followed cricket for years – they don't take a lot of interest in the game in Spain – and couldn't have named the current England team. Although some of the of the signatures on the print were familiar.

I asked Karen how she came by the picture, and she told me that the wife of the artist had brought it in to have a new piece of glass fitted, adding that the lady also bought brushes and paints from her shop. Karen and Gordon knew little about cricket, so hadn't made the connection either. I have collected signed limited edition prints, mainly equestrian scenes by Lionel Edwards Cecil Aldin and Snaffles, for years. Snaffles prints bought in the early '70s for £30 were now worth upwards of £1,000. So with this in mind, I asked Karen if she could speak to Mrs Russell when she came in to collect the picture and ask if there were any of these prints for sale. Providing they bore all the signatures of the England team, I would like to buy one or two.

A few days later Karen rang to say my prints were at the shop. I showed them to my sports-loving wife, to say Joyce loves sport is a bit of an understatement; she would watch two flies walking up a window pane to see which one reached the top first!

Viewing the picture, it took Joyce about 10 seconds to make the connection between the artist and cricketer. I did feel a fool. She had been following the cricket all summer on TV and was familiar with all the names of the England players.' I showed the picture to a few friends who like me, thought it not only a very good piece of art, but also potentially a good investment. Some asked if I could get more, so I ordered another 10 prints.

Mrs Russell had told Karen that her husband was very keen to paint a scene of a blacksmith's shop, one with some history if possible. Karen said that her dad had been around horses most of his life, and might be able to help. I met Mrs Russell for the first time in my daughter's shop, which Karen arranged, and there greeted a demure bubbly blond lady, with a huge smile, and a north country accent. This was Aileen Russell, Jack's wife. I liked her instantly, it would be difficult not to. Aileen told me of Jack's quest, and I in turn informed her that I knew the very forge I was sure would be ideal. Aileen responded, 'Jack would like to meet you anyway. He wants to meet the man who can sell more of his prints in seven days than we can manage in as many months.'

I first met Jack Russell in my daughter Karen's art shop in Yate. He arrived one morning as previously arranged by his wife Aileen. 'Jack Russell, how are you doing?' he greeted. 'Jim Ruston, fine thanks,' I responded. I asked Jack about his painting called 'Moment of Victory'. He said it was his first painting in oils of a cricket scene; the match had been memorable. We discussed Jack's idea of a painting of a blacksmith's forge and I told him briefly of one I knew at Crudwell in Malmesbury. I said I would telephone Bernie Tidmarsh who owned the forge, to arrange a visit.

As we parted I asked, 'How can I contact you Jack?' We had no address or telephone number for him. At first he pondered, then saying 'Follow me, please', sped off, with me hard on his heels. We pulled up outside a detached house on an estate on the North side of Yate, and Jack invited me in, where once again I met Aileen. Two small girls were playing in a well and truly lived-in sitting room. Jack introduced me to Elizabeth the eldest, and Victoria, commenting he also had a baby son named Charles, and an adopted son from Aileen's first marriage, whose name is Marcus.

'Cup of tea Jim,' Jack offered. 'You have found my weakness already Jack, I drink gallons of the stuff,' I laughed. Smiling, Aileen said, 'Join the club' and pointing at Jack continued, 'He practically lives on tea.' I had never met anyone who drank more tea than me until now, but compared with Jack I'm a novice! Jack showed me his 'studio'; a small room you could barely swing a cat in. However cramped it may have been, Jack had managed to produce some fine work from there.

I now knew Jack Russell's address to which he added a telephone number. 'I don't tell people where I live, and hardly anyone has my phone number' he said. 'Its OK, I understand, I won't pass it on,' I assured.

I rang Bernie Tidmarsh and arranged for Jack and myself to visit him at his forge the following Friday. I first met Bernie when I delivered a colour TV set to his father, who lived in the cottage by the forge; Bernie was just 20 years old then and still living at home. He worked long hours for very little. Bernie never complained, he loved the work. When Princess Ann married Mark Phillips, Bernie's dad went to the wedding, as did Bernie some years later when Prince Charles married Diana. Bernie met and married Mary, Prince Charles's much-valued groom, and the Prince threatened to have Bernie thrown in the tower for taking his prized possession. (A story Bernie loves to tell.) A coach and horses carried Mary from Highgrove to the church on her wedding day.

When Mr Tidmarsh died, Bernie, who had been doing the lion's share of the work for some years, took the reins. He had started in the forge as a boy working after school; he rode on the back of his father's bike to visit out laying farms. He made his first set of shoes at 9 years old (they are still hanging in the forge) and nailed his first set on at 12 years. Whereas most farriers prefer to have the sole of the horse's foot facing them, and then nail the shoe on downwards, Bernie leaves the foot in the natural position, and nails the shoe on from underneath, upwards. 'Well you can't see where the nail is going if you hammer it in downwards, can you?' he explains. It must be much more difficult to do. That's probably why few so adopt the method. Bernie makes nothing of it though.

Bernie is farrier to the Duke of Beaufort, and looks after the feet of all the horses in the Badminton stables. He is also honorary farrier at the Badminton three-day event, Gatcombe Park horse trials, and is on hand for the British Equestrian team when they train at Badminton. He is also entrusted with the horses of Prince Charles, Princess Ann and Princess Michael, plus many more of our top horsemen/women.

The forge at Crudwell is 400 years old, during which time it has been in the same family, albeit through a mix of both maternal and paternal ancestry.

As we drove out to Malmesbury I showed Jack parts of the country he had never seen before. 'The only place to live Jack,' I stated. He nodded back. I asked him about his art career, and he told me what he had done so far. He had first started sketching at Worcester on a wet day when play was ruled out. He drew a man sitting under a tree reading a newspaper. Selected for the England tour of Pakistan, he had gone as reserve keeper. He didn't get the chance to play much cricket, but did find plenty of time to sketch.

When Jack returned from the tour with some 40 or so sketches under his belt, a helpful gallery owner in Bristol arranged an exhibition for him. It was a sell-out. Although it has to be said prices were on the low side. I know Jack was unknown as an artist, but he was known, especially in Bristol and throughout Gloucestershire, as a cricketer. Add intrinsic value to some exceptional works of art, they should have been priced much higher. Those who own these early sketches are fortunate indeed. No art teacher ever spoiled Jack; he never had a lesson from one! Look at the sketch of The Blind Beggar drawn in 1988, when Jack had been drawing for just a year.

Bernie was bending over his anvil as we entered his forge. Hearing us, he paused, lifted his head and said, 'Hello Jim.' Then glancing briefly at Jack added, 'Mornin'.' Bernie never changes his routine. He starts making shoes at 6.30am. His apprentices – he is always training at least two at any one time – start at 8am. Bernie sets them to their tasks, then retires to the cottage next door for breakfast with his mum. I have sat down for breakfast with Bernie and his dear mother on a number of occasions, memories I will always cherish. Taking no more than a half hour for his breakfast, he returns to the forge, leaving at around 9am to go on his rounds. With two lads assisting, Bernie would look to shoe around 6 – 8 horses each day.

Jack chatted away to Bernie and told him he would like to paint a scene in the forge. 'No problem at all. Jim will tell you my movements,' Bernie responded. On the way back to Yate Jack thanked me, and said 'Bernie Tidmarsh is something else, isn't he Jim?' It would be some time before I came to realise, how very much a like Jack and Bernie are; each totally dedicated to his profession.

I asked Jack what finished work he had for sale, and he said he had a few originals, 'Moment of Victory' prints, and also a small quantity of black and white prints; The prints had been published by a company that had subsequently wound up owing Jack unpaid royalties, although much of the printed stock was recovered. We discussed the possibilities of my taking over the marketing of this unsold work, but Jack wasn't keen to enter into any kind of contract, and neither for that matter was I.

I could not make a permanent commitment to Jack Russell at this stage because I was still helping out with property exhibitions for La Vissa. Also, Bob Shepherd had asked me to accompany a TV crew who wanted to make a documentary on Brits migrating to the Costas. They would film clients on an inspection tour, insisting on doing a 'warts and all' job. I would be there to make sure there weren't too many warts!

Jack had been selected to tour New Zealand with the England cricket team. They would leave on Boxing Day 1991. So initially, we had very little time together with which to discuss a business plan. We talked about increasing the range of pictures for sale, and agreed to make limited edition prints from Jack's painting of the forge once he had finished painting it. I also had another project on my mind, but would we have time before Jack left to complete it?

I had been considering commissioning an artist to paint a picture of the commando raid on St Nazaire, which took place on 28 March 1942, and had in fact gone as far as lining up a painter I knew to carry out the task. I wanted to do the painting for my brother Roy. It was his commando, No 2, from which the majority of the assault troops on the audacious and daring raid were drawn. I grew up with the story of the raid. The 50th anniversary would be on 28 March 1992.

When I shared my thoughts with Jack, his response was instantaneous. 'It has been my burning ambition to paint a military picture.' I told Jack the brief facts of the raid saying. 'You will have to read a book titled *The Greatest Raid of All* by Lucas Phillips. I have a copy you can borrow.' The copy I loaned him was in paperback. I had bought it in a second-hand bookshop in Spain just a few weeks before my first meeting with Jack. Until then I didn't know a book on the raid existed. This grubby little paperback rekindled not only my interest, but also a desire to commission a painting for my brother.

Without any formal agreement, I began to put into motion a plan to promote the art of Jack Russell. I would work on a commission-only basis, whilst Jack for his part would endeavour to complete the paintings he had agreed to undertake, a tall order on both counts.

Jack created a painting of the forge without much fuss; in fact he painted two. One was purchased by Bernie. The other – aptly named by Mary Tidmarsh 'The Shoe to Fit the Foot' – we published as a limited edition. The original, despite many offers from clients who wish to own it, still hangs in the Jack Russell Gallery. It is special to both Jack and me in that it marks the beginning of our collaboration.

It was after midnight when the phone rang. It was Jack. He was reading the book on the St Nazaire raid, and had come to a passage from which he thought a scene could be painted. He had reached the page where the convoy is first discovered by enemy searchlights sweeping the Loire estuary and enthused, 'This is the moment, trust me Jim. It has everything I need to create atmosphere in the painting.' We continued talking, we were buzzing, and neither of us got much sleep.

Could Jack paint the picture before Christmas? Could I find the necessary people to ratify its authenticity? Could I get it printed in a limited edition by 28 March to coincide with the anniversary? Roy had not kept in contact with anyone. He had heard there was a group of veterans calling themselves the St Nazaire Society, but didn't have a contact for them. I tried to telephone the Commando Association but could get no reply. I telephoned directory inquires and got the number for the Royal British Legion in Falmouth. I thought the raid embarked from the harbour there. Surely they must still have some contact with veterans.

'Oh you want Johnny Johnson or Frank Axford,' answered the friendly voice on the telephone. It's Remembrance Day next week. Why don't you come down? You will be made most welcome, and Johnny and Frank will be here for sure. Johnny always lays a wreath for the St Nazaire boys.' I thanked him profusely and assured him we would try our best to be there. I rang Jack, and he was ecstatic.

Jack had painted a small colour note of the scene he had outlined to me during that midnight call. We would go down to Falmouth for the parade, and show the rough picture to the interested parties. Jack picked me up at an unearthly hour on Remembrance Sunday, and armed with flasks of tea we set off for Falmouth. Half-way down we stopped briefly for a swig of tea. 'Want a sandwich mate,' said Jack opening a tinfoil package containing cheese and pickle sandwiches. 'Too early for me Jack, but thanks for the offer,' I answered. This was our first 'meal together'. Through the ensuing years there would be countless stops on journeys, and apart from one brief period when Jack changed his diet, following a discipline to enable him to get into a 'zone', when the sandwiches were tuna and something indescribable, it was always cheese and pickle. I enjoy the former, but the tuna jobs were virtually inedible.

Meeting Johnny and Frank was a wonderful moment. Roy had told me of Johnny, and he was everything my brother described. Johnny was in 5 Commando, and responsible for demolition on the raid, when he carried a pack of explosives on his back. He was badly injured, and nearly died. Ironically it was a German medic who saved his life with an injection of adrenaline into the heart. He was a POW for the rest of the war. Frank was Navy, a wireless telegrapher. Whilst Johnny had gone into St Nazaire on the Campbeltown, Frank was on one of the ill-fated motor launches that accompanied the destroyer.

Both Jack and I have a lasting memory of dear Frank Axford, sadly no longer with us, whom, each year on Remembrance Day, whilst everyone else was hurrying from the cold, eager for the warmth of the Legion Club, remained in the street outside selling poppies.

We could not have been made more welcome. People are always pleased to have Jack in their midst, particularly those interested in the noble game. We sat in the committee room with Johnny, Frank and a few others, looking at Jack's small painting. Everyone present was most complimentary, with both Johnny and Frank saying that it evoked many memories. Before we departed, Frank gave us the name and phone number of the secretary of the St. Nazaire society, Eric de la Torre.

Eric was delighted to hear of our intentions, saying it would answer the prayers of the Society. They had been struggling with ideas for the very same thing I was now proposing, a commemorative painting of the famous raid, from which prints could be made, thus enabling the Society to make various presentations on the date of the anniversary. The Society's concern had been the cost of commissioning and publishing. I put Eric at ease immediately, telling him that there would be no cost to his Society Jack would paint the original, which he would retain, and he and I would donate six framed limited edition prints for use by them.

Eric arranged an unforgettable meeting for us at the Special Forces Club in Knightsbridge. Stepping inside of the impressive entrance hall, we were greeted by a small party. An incredibly fit- looking man I estimated to be in his 60s, thrust out a hand, at the same time exclaiming, 'Jack, my hero, I have long wanted to meet you.' This attitude endeared Jack and I to this amazing band of men, always praising someone else, never themselves. The greeting had come from Major General Corran Purdon, (he had written a book called *List the Bugle* I helped with the publication and marketing of it) who held the rank of Lieutenant in No 12 Commando at the time of the raid. He was awarded a Military Cross for his deeds. This brought an immediate response from Jack. 'You are the heroes,' he insisted. 'I just play cricket.'

With Corran at that first meeting was: Robbie Barron ex No2 Commando and now treasurer of the Society; Eric de la Torre ex No 3 Commando; Hugh Arnold ex Sub Lt RNVR (he had won the DSC on the raid), Len Ball DSM, Ex-Navy; and John May, ex-Sub Lt RNVR.

As we walked up the stairs, I noticed the photographs fixed to the walls. Odette Churchill, her husband Peter, Violet Szabo (immortalised by the film *Carve her name with Pride*), Maurice Buckmaster. More pictures of British agents of the SOE, Members of the French resistance, and others were there. On the landing was a glass cabinet, in which various artefacts from the clandestine world of secret agents were displayed. The whole place had an atmosphere the like of which I have never before experienced. We entered a large lounge. In one corner was a bar behind which an immaculate steward in a white jacket with brass buttons served drinks with a smile. Sitting on a stool by the bar, I swear to God this is true, was a lady dressed in an off-white full-length raincoat, complete with black beret pulled down over one eye. She must have been in her 70s. Who was she? An open fire beckoned, and on the breast wall above it was a wonderful painting of an agent being dropped by parachute at night. I turned to Jack, who also was looking at the picture. No words passed between us; one look was enough. Did we want some of this, or what?

An adjustment here and there to Jack's picture was suggested, but generally all those present applauded it. Jack had painted a swastika on the flag flown on the destroyer; it had been flown as subterfuge, to deceive the enemy into thinking for as long as possible the raiders were a friendly force. After consultation with the veterans, it was agreed that whilst accurate, no one really wanted a picture of HM ships flying a swastika hanging on their wall. Jack changed it for the ensign.

Standing on the pavement once more, pointing back to the very ordinary looking terrace we had just left, as if in disbelief Jack asked, 'Were we really in there Jim? It just makes you wonder what was going on in England, in secret, during the war years,' I responded, shaking my head as we walked.

Jack painted a more detailed picture of the flotilla proceeding up the Loire River lit by searchlights. It would need to be shown to the St Nazaire committee before he could embark on the definitive painting, so I made arrangements once again to meet up with the veterans. The evening before the planned meeting in London, I became ill. Undaunted, Jack attended the meeting, where his latest creation was well received by the St Nazaire Committee. Jack was delighted, but I had missed out on another visit to the Special Forces Club. Gutted!

Jack was now in a position to paint the final picture. A large canvas was selected, at 5 feet x 3 feet this would be his largest painting so far. The finished painting is a fine work of art, and really captures the imagination. An amazing achievement, considering what little reference Jack had to work from, and the tiny room he worked in, with the canvas taking up most of it! After the printer had finished copying it, I had it at home for a while, and just kept looking at it. I took the painting to London for Roy to see, and propping it on his kitchen table said with confidence, 'We will see this picture on TV soon.' My brother was visibly moved.

The printer made 850 prints. These would have to be signed and numbered by Jack, and countersigned by six veterans of the St Nazaire raid. Christmas was approaching rapidly, and Jack would leave for New Zealand the day after.

Eric de la Torre had booked the committee room at the Victory Services Club near Marble Arch for the 20 December 1991 to accommodate the signing session. Time was at a premium so we certainly couldn't afford any delay in the printing process. Fortunately there were none. Barry and Roy, the principals at APB Printers in Bristol, delivered on time, as they promised they would, and with Jack's car loaded to the roof, we set off for London.

We always try to arrive everywhere early, and on this occasion it was as well we did. The committee room is on the first floor, and only one tiny lift, just about big enough for two people, was available. The lift, a wooden affair, not much better than a kitchen service lift, creaked and groaned as we loaded the prints on board. I squeezed in with them whilst Jack ran up the stairs. We made six difficult trips, but we did it in time. The long table normally used for meetings suited our purpose perfectly, and Jack and I set about laying out a production system, whereby the prints could be passed down the line for signing by the six people who had so generously agreed to do it.

Our signatories arrived: Michael Burn MC (Capt 2 Commando); Bob Montgomery MC (Capt Royal Engineers); Don Randall DCM (L/Sgt 2 Commando); Micky Wynn (Lord Newborough DSC RNVR); Hugh Arnold DSC (RNVR) and Len Ball DSM (RN). Eric and Robbie from the Society were also there to help us. I'm not sure whether it was Bob Montgomery or Don Randall who noticed it first, but one of them pointed out that some of the decorations were printed incorrectly. Horror of horrors, the printers, despite having received correct copy from us, had inadvertently printed Navy decorations against the Army names. Embarrassed, both Jack and I assured all present that it would be corrected before any of the prints were distributed. A lesson learned, it has never happened since.

The signing went along fine, and when we broke for dinner Micky Burn approached me asking, 'Jim, I see your surname is Ruston. Are you related to Audrey Hepburn? Her father's name was Hepburn-Ruston, I also knew her mother Ella van Heemstra.' I replied that I wasn't aware of any connection, but I would look into it and let him know. He then told me the following story.

Audrey's Dutch mother, Baroness Ella van Heemstra, was a very dear friend of mine. By the autumn of 1939 her marriage was at an end. Audrey was nine and living on a farm near Folkestone (at that time she was known to the people she lived with and her school chums as Audrey Ruston) whilst I was stationed nearby in the Army, and at her mother's request went to see her. Soon after, Ella took Audrey with her back to Holland, where she was then living. Holland was invaded and occupied, and it seemed to me that they were now out of all reach. I was captured during our raid on St Nazaire, and not long after I had been in my first POW camp, and to my surprise, I received a Red Cross parcel, but no sender was indicated. This puzzled me, as at the time I hadn't had any contact with my family, or anyone else for that matter. It wasn't until after the war I learnt who had sent the mystery parcel.

Audrey's mother Ella had gone to the movies in Haarlem, her home town, where the German newsreel showed a propaganda version of our raid, purporting it to be a fiasco, when in fact it had been a brilliant success. Ella watched intently, when suddenly, I appeared being marched through the streets into captivity with a bayonet in my back and my hands raised making a V sign with my fingers for the benefit of British intelligence. Ella recognised me, and in her excitement grabbed the arm of the person next to her, who just happened to be a German officer, and shouted 'It's Micky!'

Ella knew the owner of the cinema, a Jewish lady, who although the cinema had been confiscated, still had a set of keys for it. At the dead of night, these two courageous ladies entered the cinema, got into the projectionist's box, and ran the newsreel through. When they got to the bit that showed me, they stopped the projector, cut out two of the frames, spliced the film back together and made their exit. Hence she knew of my captivity, and sent an anonymous parcel via the Red Cross.

At the end of the war Holland was on its knees. Ella wrote to me saying that Audrey, now 15 years old, was desperately ill and needed the new drug penicillin. It was extremely scarce, but could be bought if one had enough money. Cigarettes were also at a premium in Holland. If I could send some she would sell them on the black market and buy penicillin. I sent bundles of fags. Ella wrote back saying the penicillin she bought with the cigarette money had saved Audrey's life. After the war, Ella came to London and gave me the frames she had cut from the newsreel, which I still treasure. I remember Audrey through all the glitter of stardom, as I first saw her more than 50 years ago, as a fragile, exquisite, patrician child.

It was not until January 1993 whilst in Spain, where I saw a glossy magazine with Audrey Hepburn's picture on the front declaring that she had died, did I begin my family research; even then not really in earnest, but Micky had lit the flame.

After lunch at the Victory Club we continued with the print signing. Suddenly to the surprise of all present, Lord Newborough, known to his family and friends as Micky, announced that he had to leave for another engagement. A look of embarrassment spread over the faces of the other signatories, so to ease the situation, addressing his Lordship I said, 'No problem, I can bring the unsigned prints to your house when it's convenient.' He smiled and left. The others were not too happy that I would have to make such a journey. Lord Newborough lived in North Wales. By now Jack and I had been together for just three and a half months. Would we continue at this pace?

With Christmas over, Jack left for New Zealand; after a short festive break, I left for Spain to make the film with TVS. The TVS presenter Sandy, and cameraman Brian and I got on splendidly. The film that evolved was well received, and did much to enlighten prospective candidates on both the merits and de-merits of living in Spain. (I still have a copy.)

Despite frantic activity holding Spanish property exhibitions all over England, we were fighting a losing battle. The promotion costs outweighed the profit from sales. I thought it prudent to withdraw from the market until the UK domestic situation was in recovery, thinking it foolhardy to chase a downward spiral. Others did not agree and continued to pursue the ever-fading rainbow. The inevitable happened. La Vissa collapsed with Bob and Jeff going their separate ways. Some years later when the market started to improve they formed a new firm called Prestige Villas, based once again in Bournemouth. The venture is currently enjoying a great deal of success. Coincidentally, Eric Cartwright, Bob's erstwhile MD at Eurochoice, has an office just around the corner, also selling Spanish property. I have to give them all 10 out of 10 for perseverance. I really do believe they genuinely love the business.

I now took every opportunity to show Jack's pictures wherever I could. We had a small display in Karen and Gordon's art shop, and even with limited space it was amazing how much attention the pictures received from the public. I took a few prints on the road, holding small exhibitions at cricket clubs, schools and so on. I also arranged private viewings. Jack always tells everyone, 'We started the art business from the boot of Jim's car.' In a way we did.

Although Jack had played extremely well in New Zealand, he wasn't selected to play in the forthcoming world cup series taking place in Australia. This was a blow for Jack, although he had half expected it. Jack told me he had played 20 tests in a row for England, establishing himself as first choice keeper, until he was dropped during the previous tour to Australia, where Graham Gooch had said, 'It's no reflection on you Jack, but we feel the need to play an extra bowler. So Alec Stewart will play a dual role as batsman/keeper.' Ironically, come the next world cup series in 1996, the roles were reversed.

Although Jack eventually got to play in 54 test matches, his path was dogged along the route by the indecision of the selectors as to what was England's best side. Since the retirement of Ian Botham, no true all-rounder has been found, and in an attempt to pad out weak batting, or sometimes bowling, Jack was sacrificed for the option. Crazy. It has hardly ever worked, but it was successful in mucking two careers around, namely those of Jack Russell and Alec Stewart. Both suffered because of it.

Although I was disappointed for Jack at being left out of the squad to go on to Australia, it was a bonus for me. It meant he could attend the official launch of 'The Greatest Raid of All' and more exciting still, travel with the veterans to St Nazaire for the 50th anniversary reunion.

The committee members of the Society were delighted that Jack and I would be able to accompany them.

Although at that time, I had no contact at the Imperial War Museum, I addressed a letter to the Director General, offering to loan Jack's painting of the St Nazaire raid to them. The response came from the Museum's publicity guru, Dr Christopher Dowling, who said the IWM would be delighted to hang the painting. And what about an official presentation where we could invite the press? And so I entered into a dialogue with Christopher, himself a keen supporter of cricket, who was equally keen to meet Jack Russell. It was arranged that the St Nazaire Society would invite some of their members to attend the event, to which Christopher and I would add our lists. The presentation was arranged for 27 March, we were due to leave for Falmouth to meet veterans there on the 1 April, a tight schedule.

Jack's New Zealand tour had not gone without incident. Sadly it had signalled the end of the career of his closest friend in cricket, David 'Syd' Lawrence. Jack and Syd had played together since the Gloucestershire Federation under 11s, and came right through the system, making their debut for England in the same game. They had dreams of a test scorecard reading 'Caught Russell, bowled Lawrence', and achieved their dream.

It was the final day of the test at Wellington, where the game was petering to a draw. As Syd ran in to bowl, an almighty crack was heard by those standing close to him as down he went writhing in agony; he had shattered his kneecap. Jack, distraught beyond words, tried to give encouragement by holding his friend's hand as he was carried from the field of play. On reaching the gate at the edge of the field, their path was barred by the media. Camermen, photographers and reporters were all over the place. Micky Stewart, the England coach, tried to push them away, but with little effect. One over-exuberant cameraman from New Zealand TV just wouldn't go away, and kept pushing his camera into Syd's face to get a close-up of the poor man's agony. This was all too much for Jack, who finished up chasing the media man up the steps to the stand shouting abuse at him. Unbelievably the NZ TV company wanted Jack Russell and Micky Stewart to apologise to them! Jack would have none of that, and told them so, saying, 'It's Syd who deserves the apology.'

The whole thing was caught on camera and shown on TV. Of course the film had been edited to make it look as though Jack and his colleagues were the aggressors. My brother Roy, far from a cricket lover himself, saw it on the news. 'You're mate's got some guts Jim, pity he hadn't caught the guy. He could have given him a righthander!'

He suggested. (Or maybe a left in Jack's case.) Syd's injury cast a shadow over an otherwise hugely successful tour. As hard as he tried, Syd never made a return to first class cricket. He now owns a successful night-club in Bristol. David Lawrence is, without any doubt, one of the most popular guys around.

I journeyed to North Wales driving through Llangollen, famous as the home of the Eisteddfod. Lord Newborough's estate was just a few miles further on. I swung past a lodge cottage into the driveway of the 2,000-acre estate, stopping at the office where I was told his Lordship would meet me. Extending his hand in a warm and friendly manner the peer said, 'Welcome Jim, I'm so pleased to see you, and sorry that I have caused you such a journey. Would you like some tea or coffee, or would you rather me kick on with the signing, and then we can have lunch? By the way, please call me Micky.' I thanked him, and opted for getting the job done first.

Having finished the signing, we walked towards the house, then entered the Palladian-style mansion. In a large kitchen, Lady Newborough served up a delicious lunch. As we ate, we chatted about farming and the difficult times approaching it. We knew nothing then of BSE and the devastating effect it would have on the agricultural economy. I asked Micky about his role in the St Nazaire raid. He had commanded the MTB 74 and was to fire his torpedoes into the mighty lock if *Campbeltown* failed to reach it. However, *Campbeltown* did her job to perfection so Micky fired his torpedoes into the old lock entrance. With delayed fuses, they caused even more havoc when the Germans had thought there was nothing more to fear.

Micky would have got clean away from St Nazaire – his MTB was the fastest vessel in the British Navy at the time, if he hadn't slowed to pick up survivors of a launch and been hit amidships by a shell, which blew his MTB apart. His life was saved by his engineer Bill Lovegrove, who fished him out of the river unconscious, and with an eye hanging out. This the Germans skilfully removed without anaesthetic!

As I was about to take my leave, Micky showed me a shell, the sort that would fit a cannon, the end of which could be unscrewed. He had it made especially to contain his ashes when he died, and left instructions for his remains to be placed in this shell, and then fired out to sea. As I write I can confirm that on his death, which was quite recent, Micky's wishes were carried out! A remarkable man.

Jack and I arrived at the Imperial War Museum in good time for the presentation. As we lifted the painting from Jack's car I grinned and said, 'You do realise don't you Jack, that as yet no-one at the Museum has seen this painting, or even a photo of it.' He gasped. I continued

'Don't worry mate, it is everything I have described. They will love it. But I do admit they must have a great deal of faith in you.'

Without doubt, the presentation at the Imperial War Museum launched the painting of the raid on St Nazaire and Jack Russell's artistic career simultaneously. The painting was shown on national TV (Roy, I told you it would be) and also made the *Times* court page. That was just the start, after which it seemed to appear everywhere. We made two more important contacts at the launch. Leo Cooper, a book publisher whose imprint is Pen and Sword, a very well-known name specialising in military subjects, approached me. Leo said that he was in the process of publishing a book on Bill Sparks, which they intended to call *The Last of the Cockleshell Heroes*. Would Jack consider a commemorative painting, and would I call him to discuss it further?

The second approach was from a hugely charming man who introduced himself as Patrick Shervington. He said he would like to commission Jack to paint a picture of the fusilier statue that stands in Holborn. He went on to tell me that he had recently retired as Colonel of the Royal Regiment of Fusiliers, whose HQ is in HM Tower of London, and that he had recently accepted a post as Director of The Lord's Taveners – the charity whose aim it has been since its inception in 1950 to raise money to give youngsters, especially those disadvantaged or disabled, a sporting chance. Another invitation to meet and explore possibilities for a major painting. We had lift-off.

Five days later we found ourselves on the road to Cornwall once more. We went straight to the harbour where we had been informed the present-day *Campbeltown*, a frigate, would be moored, a high-tech man of war. The Navy does know how to welcome you, and we were no exception. After a tour of the ship we were invited to the wardroom for a drink. Jack is practically teetotal, but is tactful enough to go through the motions when required; it's pretty hard trying to tell a matlot you don't drink!

In the early evening we entered the lobby of The Royal Duchy Hotel clutching two framed prints of the 'Greatest Raid'. I quickly slipped the prints from their frames and laid them on a table, where the many veterans who had gathered would countersign them in readiness for presentation to the town of Falmouth and the town of St Nazaire. This was the start of the 50th anniversary of their epic exploits. Many had not seen each other since the 40th reunion when the Queen loaned the Society the Royal Yacht *Britannia* to take them back to France. That must have been something, I was sure this was going to be as well.

At dinner we sat next to 'Nosher' Brown, an ex-commando. When the food was over, and before the speakers got to their feet, Nosher announced that he wasn't going to listen to any boring bloody speeches, instead he was off to the Legion Club. 'Any one coming with me?' he called as he disappeared through the door. Jack and I followed at as respectful a time as we thought proper; after all, we did have a long drive home. Thereafter, if we ever need to make an early exit from a function, we excuse ourselves by saying 'Nosher is waiting for us'.

The next afternoon we set off for Plymouth, arriving at the Brittany Ferry Terminal at around 11pm, and almost immediately drove on board. The boat was due to land on the French coast at Roscoff at 6am. Jack and I wasted no time in locating the cabin we had booked and getting our heads down. He was lighter and fitter than me so he took the top bunk. It was still dark when we arrived, and we thought we were up and out sharply, but when we got to the car deck it was amazing how many were already in their cars waiting for the off.

We drove, with Jack at the wheel, non-stop to St Nazaire, a journey of some five hours. I kept Jack going with barley sugar. I discovered its worth in my Army days and it has served me well ever since. Approaching St Nazaire by the coast road, we passed the Old Mole, looking every bit as ominous as we had both imagined. A concrete jetty that was heavily fortified in 1942, and where many of the fragile motor launches and their brave men met their fate. We stopped and looked across the river. The sky was grey, the water foreboding. We, who had taken no part in the raid, could feel a sense of compassion for those who had lost their lives in the inky darkness of the water surrounding this jetty.

Silently, we drove on, together, yet alone in our thoughts. Making for the harbour, we rounded a bend and looming before us was HMS *Campbeltown*. She was tied alongside, and we could see a hive of activity taking place on board. A huge canvas canopy had been erected above the fore deck, and naval ratings were scurrying around with buckets and brushes, making everything ship shape, dare I say, Bristol Fashion, in readiness for the reception on board that evening. We turned our attention to the huge dry dock nearby. This was the dock that was breached by Campbeltown in 1942. So much damage was caused that the dock was unable to function again until 10 years after the war. Some 169 were killed on that wild night 50 years ago. More than 200 were taken prisoner. Five Victoria Crosses and 100-plus other medals were awarded for bravery.

Jack and I climbed the gangway, and joined the throng of veterans and invited guests now gathered on board. Patron of the St Nazaire Society, HRH The Duke of Edinburgh, was moving from group to group, chatting informally with those he had met before, and being introduced to those he hadn't. He was visibly pleased to see Jack Russell, greeted him warmly and asked about England's recent cricket tour of New Zealand. The Duke is very keen on cricket, having played the game pretty well himself.

I wandered over to the port side of the ship and stood watching the Band of the Royal Marines, who were playing on the quayside. As they struck up 'Land of Hope and Glory', I could feel the build-up of people around me. Soon, most of those on board were stood to attention with glasses raised in salute. It was a spontaneous reaction, which made it all the more magical. The hair stood up on the back of my neck. Nobody does it better than us Brits!

After the Duke had been piped off the ship, people began to make their way back to their hotels. Jack went ahead of me to get his car. In front of me, carefully making their way down the gangway, were three ladies, one of whom had had just a wee bit more to drink than some. She was almost at the bottom, when she slipped, and in an effort to steady herself, grabbed the handrail. This action caused her to release the grip she had on her handbag, which sailed over the side and into the murky water. One of two smart Navy ratings, who were stood to attention at the bottom of the gangway, with split second reaction, removed his cap and jumped in water after the bag, grabbing it just as it was about to disappear beneath the surface. Climbing out, he replaced his cap, and gave the handbag back to a most grateful lady. The age of chivalry is still with us, thank God. Those of us who witnessed the deed gave forth a hearty Bravo!

The next morning, travelling by coach with the veterans Jack and I attended the Service of Remembrance at the memorial to those who fell at St Nazaire. There was a parade, and Society members marched passed. After this moving occasion, we were to move on to a reception being given by the Mayor of St Nazaire. At this function it had been organised for the Mayor to receive on behalf of the town of St Nazaire a limited edition print of 'The Greatest Raid of All', countersigned by more than 80 veterans. The Duke of Edinburgh would make the presentation.

We got to our got to our destination eventually, but time was getting tight to say the least. I had placed the picture to be presented in the luggage compartment of the coach. Retrieving it, with Jack on one end and me on the other, we scurried off, zigzagging as we went in and out of the crowds of people who had gathered in front of the building where the reception was to take place. To compound our problem, two lines of standard-bearers were stood to attention each side of the wide concrete steps at the front of the building. The eyes of the public were focused on the entrance, all waiting for the Duke of Edinburgh to arrive.

Jack said, 'It's no good Jim, we can't do it, there isn't time. We can't just walk across in front of everyone.' 'No mate,' I replied. 'But we can walk around the back of them. Follow me.' Holding the picture between us and with myself in the lead we squeezed our way behind the standard-bearers.' And with a 'Sorry mate, excuse me mate', as we jostled them, we reached the steps and tore up them two at a time. Approaching the main door, we were challenged by two uniformed officers, one of whom spoke to us in French. I know very little French, Jack knows even less, so I replied in Spanish and kept walking. We entered the main hall, now full of people, and there to our relief standing at one end of the room, was a big wooden easel on which we hastily placed the picture. There was just time – a few seconds, no more – to stand back out of the way before the Duke's party walked in.

On the way into the hall I had deposited my old grey bag, in which I carry my camera, on a table just feet from where the presentation was to be made. I had been informed by a French PR girl that flash photography was not allowed. Ignoring the order, I chanced one, and got a great picture, plus a few black looks! I left the old grey bag on the table for at least a half-hour, during which time no one asked to look inside it. I have since left this bag close to politicians and Royalty on many occasions without it coming under scrutiny. It appears little has changed security wise, despite the deaths of Lord Mountbatten and Airey Neave.

It had been a wonderful weekend, one that neither Jack nor I will ever forget. For me the saddest moment came when we visited the cemetery, in which many of those who fell on that daring raid in 1942 were laid to rest. The Duke of Edinburgh laid a wreath, and buglers sounded the Last Post, but it was the sadness in the faces of those who had lost loved ones that made the biggest impression on me. Later I put my thoughts into poetry. Corran Purdon sent a copy of it to Alfred Hemery, then French president of the St. Nazaire Society. He was a young man in the French resistance at the time of the raid. Alfred translated my poem into French, and circulated it to schools and colleges teaching Second World War history to add to their curriculum. I feel humble to say the least.

On the way home Jack said, 'Puts things into perspective doesn't it Jim? I mean, my being dropped from the England squad is a trifle compared with what the St Nazaire boys had to endure. I will view things differently from here on.'

Gordon Holman, a war correspondent and extremely brave man himself, who with a colleague accompanied the raiders on that epic voyage, wrote: 'I lived with the Commandos for some days before the raid. No man has ever been in better company.' I share his sentiment.

A few months later, Jack and I received a package containing two ties from the St Nazaire Society, inviting us to wear them as honorary members. We wear them with pride.

With his new commando attitude Jack felt he could climb any mountain. He was in great form with both bat and gloves, so his selection to play in the forthcoming test series against Pakistan was no surprise. However, try as he may he could not get much success with the bat. It was more or less the beginning of the batsman/keeper era, where to keep brilliantly just wasn't enough, you had to make plenty of runs too. Harsh, when you consider the value of a specialist 'keeper'; one half-chance stumping, or a low diving catch, often turns the tide of a game. Jack has proved it many times, but there it was. The gloves were handed to Alec Stewart, who was in good nick with the bat.

I saw my first test match during that series; Jack invited me to Edgbaston, and arranged lunch for me in the Pavilion with the other guests of players and officials. With Waquar Younis at one end and Wassim Akram at the other, both in devastating form, Jack faced some awesome deliveries. It was unforgettable for me though.

Disappointed Jack may have been, but downhearted, no. I had now become involved with Jack's cricketing career as well as his artistic one. Cricket would always take precedence, but it was essential that I knew what was going on to enable me to plan things between the domestic season and winter tours. I had attended a few games at Bristol and met the Secretary, Phillip August, whom I found most agreeable. Dickie Rossiter was chairman of a committee made up mainly of volunteers. Norman Walters was honorary Treasurer, and, aided by his capable wife Janet, also ran the county shop. Maggie, Debbie, and Diane ran the office. The marketing team comprised Andy Brassington with one assistant, Rachel. Altogether a fraction of the administrative staff they employ today. Andy, the Club's wicketkeeper before Jack, was extremely helpful to me.

It was Norman who suggested I hire a small tent to display Jack's works of art at Cheltenham during the cricket festival. The festival lasts for 12 days, and is the longest running of its kind in the country. The event is well attended and often the ground is full to capacity. I arranged the hire of a tent with Chris Coley, a Gloucestershire County Cricket Club committee member, who organises such things at the festival. He does a brilliant job. I looked forward to my first tented exhibition.

A TESTING TIME

With a little research, I discovered that a major exhibition of art was being scheduled to take place in September at Olympia in London. Unfortunately it would coincide with the last three days of the county cricket season, so Jack wouldn't be able to attend. I booked a space I thought adequate for our first exhibition; with this and a marquee at Cheltenham, I was beginning to get somewhere.

In brilliant sunshine I arrived at the College ground in Cheltenham to set up my art display. I had just three colour prints on show, the remainder being the black and white pictures that I had inherited. The display looked attractive enough though, and almost from the first day interest was high. Very few people had seen any of their cricketing hero's artistic work, and even fewer had had the opportunity to buy anything. Business was brisk during the first few days, and Jack was delighted. 'Can I see you after the game Jim? I need to talk to you.'

I would have a long wait; I had learned by now that Jack is always last to emerge from the dressing room after play, and when he did he stated, 'Jim, if I want to get back into the England side for the winter tour, I feel I need to make a statement. I need the selectors to be looking at me. I'm playing well enough, but I need that something extra. What do you think?' I pondered for a while before answering 'How do you fancy arriving at the ground by helicopter?' 'Yea, Yea,' he replied grinning. 'It might upset the management but I'll risk that.'

Don Collins, my old mate from the club and pub days, has a son, Rick, an airline pilot. At that time, Rick was flying small private jets out of Bristol Airport. I phoned Rick and he organised a small chopper to take Jack to Cheltenham. Jack was cautious. He hadn't flown in a helicopter before, and I told him the one I had organised was a trifle small. Known for telling everyone how big everything is, when I indicate small, it's time to worry! There wouldn't even be enough room for his kit, which I intended to take in my car. We decided to pull the stunt on the Sunday Gloucestershire were playing Yorkshire in a one-day game. There is always a big crowd on Sundays, especially so when a clash with the Yorkshire Tykes is on offer. On the Saturday, I spread a rumour to watch for something special the next morning. It had the desired effect. Everyone looked skywards as the helicopter hovered. When it landed and Jack climbed out, a huge cheer went up. Warning the media in advance, the stunt made both TV and newspapers.

After Jack had changed and returned to the pitch for practise, I wandered out on the field. When I got close, Jack confided 'I caused a bit of a stir, not least with Billy, (Tony Wright the captain at that time), so will have to justify it.' No one could possible have done so with more aplomb. It was the last over of the game, with Gloucestershire needing 14 runs to win. Jack was facing the bowling. Yorkshire's Paul Jarvis ran in; crack, Jack hit him for six, and a huge cheer went up, then silence. The tension was electric.

The next ball came and Jack hit that for four, to another round of applause. By now, I was out of my tent and standing on a chair, craning my neck to see what was going on. The bowler ran in for the third time that over; wallop, Jack sent the ball racing towards the boundary boards, and before it arrived, strode off the field with his bat under his arm. The crowd went wild. He had wanted to show them, and he did! To quote the immortal words of movie mogul Sam Goldwyn: 'Make a big entrance, and an even bigger exit.'

With success on both sides at Cheltenham – Jack with the cricket and me with the pictures, I was itching to push things along. I wanted to hold an exhibition in the Chipping Sodbury area. I thought I could use my many contacts there, and if I could get media coverage, who knows what might happen. I vaguely knew the proprietors of the Sodbury House Hotel, David and Margaret Warren, so called on them to discuss the possibilities of staging a show at their hotel. My visit was fortuitous in more ways than one; they had recently completed the refurbishment of an old coachhouse adjoining the hotel, which looked ideal for exhibitions. I hired the facility for the last week of October, deciding this would be the last show that year.

The exhibition at Olympia was exhausting. My dear wife Joyce came with me the day before the event was due to take place, to help set up the stand. There were so many exhibitors wanting to use the two available lifts, we decided not to wait in the queue, and instead lugged everything up the stairs. The following day I returned to London alone, and manned my stand. Come the end of the show I would have to dismantle it on my own, then carry everything back down the stairs, a daunting prospect. Each night I stayed at the Victory Services Club, where I had now become a member. During the three-day show I had what I would call, moderate success. I made a few useful contacts. A PR girl named Nim, from the Business Design Centre in Islington, approached me saying she was touring the exhibition promoting an event her Design Centre were holding in mid-November, called Art Mart. I told her that I was fully committed, and didn't think I could fit it in, even if I wanted to.

Nim, impressed by my display, told me she had asked Jeffrey Archer to open their exhibition. I asked if she knew that Jeffrey was a mad keen follower of cricket, and she admitted that she didn't. Then an idea suddenly struck me. I could try, they might go for it. 'Nim', I started, 'I might be encouraged to exhibit at Art Mart if you give me a free stand (they were asking about £2,500 for the space I would need). 'I know Jeffrey would be pleased to see Jack Russell there. Think of the publicity,' I continued. I now had my teeth into this one and would not let go, without giving any consideration as to how I would find the time to do it all.

With the Olympia Exhibition behind me, I could concentrate on family matters. Rachel had been walking out with a charming young man from Shirehampton. They had discussed marriage, but as so many young couples these days tend to do, they bought a house and lived together for a period. Now they were to marry. Rachel's fiancé, David Gentry, had been educated at Bristol Cathedral School, and so was entitled to marry in the cathedral.

Rachel and David liased with Joyce over the wedding arrangements, leaving me to do little more than turn up on the day. It was an absolutely splendid occasion. A vintage car conveyed Rachel and me to the cathedral, where we arrived in brilliant sunshine, and made our entrance. From the mighty Organ at the far end, the Wedding March hit the high vaulted ceiling, and cascaded down upon the congregation. Walking down the aisle of the magnificent cathedral with family and friends to the left and right and my beautiful daughter on my arm was a wonderful moment in my life. The third and last of my daughters to marry. This time everything went without a hitch. It had been a case of third time lucky! (They now have two children, Emma and Sophie.)

I travelled to London and met with the exhibition organisers at the Business Design Centre, and after a few rounds of the customary shadow boxing one always has with PR people (I should know), a deal was struck. They could now use Jack Russell's name in their promotion of the event, and in return we would be allocated stand space free of charge.

On my way back through London, still buzzing, I called upon Patrick Shervington to discuss his fusilier project. We agreed that Jack and I should attend the Remembrance Parade in Holborn in November.

For the first time, the Test and County Cricket Board took an unprecedented step in awarding contracts well in advance of the forthcoming tour. I think they awarded five in all, to senior players, the élite if you like, and Jack was among them. With a contract guaranteeing payment now in his hand, he quite naturally thought it signalled his inclusion on the winter tour to India and Pakistan. So you can imagine his disappointment when Graham Gooch phoned him to say he hadn't been selected, but instead asked him to act as Vice Captain on the England 'A' tour to Australia. Alec Stewart would keep wicket on the main tour, and Yorkshire's Richard Blakey would deputise. The selectors had also left out David Gower.

The media had a field day, criticising the wisdom of leaving out specialist keeper Russell, and top batsman, especially in the conditions expected on the sub-continent, David Gower. Jack was arguably the best wicket keeper in the world, and without any doubt at all the best when standing up to the wicket. With David Gower's ability to play spin, of which one could expect a good dose in the forthcoming contest. The omission of the pair was a scandal, and one chairman of selectors, Ted Dexter, would not live down in a hurry.

Jack resigned himself to his fate. I would have a little more access to him than I had expected – cricket's loss, my gain – and I wasted no time in piling him up with commissioned work.

The selectors' controversial decision had the media clamouring for interviews. I knew Jack would never say anything derogatory about the selectors, but I also knew he would do his level best to use the exposure to promote our forthcoming art exhibition at Sodbury House Hotel. Although I was a new boy on the block in the world of cricket, the media had already come to expect that I would always want something in return.

I informed our local TV station that they could interview Jack in a cornfield in Old Sodbury, where he had gone to paint and reflect on the challenge ahead. 'Just what did he have to do to regain his rightful place in the England team?' The interview came over marvellously well, and with the camera pointed for the most part at what Jack was painting, and sympathy from the interviewer, Alistair Hignall, on Jack's non-selection, it was a great show piece. 'What do you intend doing with the picture you are painting Jack,' asked Alistair. 'I expect Jim will display it in the exhibition we are holding at the Sodbury House Hotel in October,' replied Jack. This format of interview would work for us time and time again, but you have to take it on the chin when you are out of favour. If you court the media, don't get upset when they turn on you; don't hide, face them up. Always remember it's nothing personal (although some overstep the mark). Journalists have an editor to answer to, it's reportage.

Brian Higham rang to tell me that a film unit was at Dyrham House (a National Trust property) making a new production. The title for the film was *The Remains of the Day*, in which Anthony Hopkins, James Fox and Christopher Reeve were starring. Brian thought I might like to get some photographs. The film company had asked the Beaufort Hunt to organise a meet of hounds in front of Dyrham House as part of scene.

Jack studied the scene whilst I shot a couple of rolls of film. We spent a very interesting couple of hours watching the proceedings.

When I got home, I rang Brian to say Jack had decided to paint the scene we had witnessed at Dyrham. Brian suggested we visit Badminton the next day and meet Christopher Reeve, who was staying locally and riding out each morning from Badminton stables. I said we would come. Next morning we met Christopher. What a charming man he is. I took photographs of him and Brian, and some with Jack. I asked the caped hero, if, when back in the States, he rode western style. He answered indignantly, 'No I don't. I'm an eventer; or at least I am trying to become one.' I thought it best not to make any comment. I observed Christopher riding away from us; sitting a trifle forward, with feet turning outward. He didn't look balanced on the horse. As you will have heard Chris Reeve, or Superman as he is better known, had a very bad fall from a horse, leaving him totally paralysed. He deserves our sympathy.

Jack completed a wonderful painting of the scene we had witnessed at Dyrham House, and it took pride of place at our exhibition at Sodbury House Hotel. The preview had been a huge success, and just as the last person left, and I was about to lock up and go home, two young women walked in. 'We saw the lights on, can we have a quick look,' they asked. 'Sure,' I replied. In conversation I learned that I was talking to Jay Steel, who at that time was the ladies' clay shot world champion. So impressed by Jack's paintings was she that she bought the Dyrham picture which he had named 'The Remains of the Day' after the film we had watched being made. Jay and her colleague had travelled down from Scotland to collect a Spaniel they had purchased through an advertisement in the Shooting Times, and were staying overnight in the hotel.

Jay became a firm friend of both Jack and me. I did some publicity work for her, in which I featured Jack and Mervyn Barrett, the Duke of Beaufort's gamekeeper. I photographed the two of them outside Mervyn's cottage on the Duke's estate. Jack in his cricketing whites, with hat and keepers gloves, and Mervyn in his gamekeeper garb, with two spaniels at his heel. My caption read 'All the best keepers choose RC cartridges'. Jay was the UK importer of the brand. The advert appeared in all the leading country sports magazines, and made Mervyn quite famous! Jack didn't go unnoticed either. Had I not lingered in the exhibition I would have missed Jay. She left early next morning. So you could say it was my 'Remains of the Day'. (By coincidence, a motto in Latin attributed to my ancestor Joseph John Ruston – roughly translated – amounts to the same.)

A COCKNEY KID IN GREEN WELLIES

The paintings looked wonderful in the old coachouse, and the local TV station and newspaper journalists' came along to report on the artistic talent of Jack Russell. The press attention Jack was getting nationally in support of both him and Gower went much in our favour. It seemed just about everyone wanted to air his or her views on the subject. Patsy Yorston, a newsreader at HTV, did a piece to camera saying unconditionally, 'This is a wonderful display of paintings. If I were you I would hurry down here and buy one before they are all sold out'. The next day we were mobbed. The exhibition was a huge success, during which we sold £10,000 worth of paintings – a great deal for us then. (God bless you, Patsy)

Once Jack and I had come down off the ceiling, I said, 'This is exactly the type of venue I have in mind for your work, Jack. Period, with character, and if possible, somewhere in this area.' He replied 'I agree mate, my paintings did look right in this setting'. There was nothing much locally for rent at the time, and we were not ready to consider purchase, even supposing the right premises were on offer.

Jack and Aileen had at last found a property that would suit them; it had been a frustrating time for them both. The house they found had been extended a number of times during the past, and was a bit of a hotch-potch affair. But it had the three essential ingredients all estate agents crow about: position, position, and position! Set in two acres with a modern stable block, it had all the potential one could ask for.

Jack and I discussed the alterations that needed to be made to his new acquisition before he and his family could move in and my son-in-law Eddie carried them out. Jack wanted to move in before Christmas. It would be a scrabble, but hopefully it could be achieved. I spent every spare moment I had, tearing around organising building materials. Jack wanted some oak beams, I found some, and I know it will be difficult for you to believe, but I collected them in my Renault hatchback; there was a considerable overhang! I also collected a huge Victorian flagstone from Bath Reclamation, to lay in the hearth of the natural stone fireplace that Eddie was building in the sitting room. It was a good thing that a director of the reclamation firm, Bath and Scotland rugby star Damien Cronin, was on hand to load it for me. I couldn't even move it; Damien just picked it up!   During the period of alterations to Jack's house, my poor Renault was severely abused.

With the fusilier project foremost in our minds, we journeyed to London to take a look at the statue in Holborn. Having parked the car, loaded with paints, brushes, canvas and easel, we walked to the spot where the memorial stands on an island in the middle of the road.   It was a lovely late October day, and The Fusilier was silhouetted against an almost cloudless blue sky. We read the inscription on the huge stone plinth on which the statue stands. It said it was to remember the 22,000 men of the Royal Regiment of Fusiliers who fell in two world wars. It is at times like this that you realise the scale of the loss of human life in conflict.

I became aware that we were not alone on our island, I was standing immediately behind Jack, and people were crossing from the pavement to look over my shoulder at what he was painting. Soon there were so many of us on a tiny space, it resembled a scene from Monty Python.

With Jack's colour notes, and my photographs, we were ready to attend the Remembrance Day Parade in Holborn on 8 November, to witness proceedings first hand. We arrived early for the 11am homage. A few people were beginning to gather and take up positions on the pavements from where they could get the best view; Jack and I positioned ourselves among them and waited.

By now the crowd of onlookers had built up, and there was little room to manoeuvre. However, I managed to get myself in a position where during the wreath-laying ceremony I was able to creep forward and take the pictures that needed. The Parade, and homage, which followed, were executed with the military precision we have all come to admire from our Armed Forces, spectacular yet moving, as the sense of occasion deserves. Jack and I walked back to the car in silence, each savouring the moments we had experienced for as long as possible, when Jack broke his silence saying, 'Jim, when you walked forward to take the photos, you got so close I thought you were going to lay a wreath!'

Jack had intended to paint a portrait-shaped picture of the fusilier, incorporating just those around the memorial; this is the scene we had discussed with Patrick and what he was expecting. However, inspired by the whole occasion of remembrance, Jack used artistic licence to create a magnificent painting of the whole parade. Instead of a picture measuring around 24 inches by 36 inches it was now 48 inches by 72 inches. You can imagine the surprise Patrick had when he caught his first glimpse of this enormous canvas. After the initial shock, he exclaimed, 'It's wonderful Jack, I'm so thrilled.'

The paint on the canvas was hardly dry as we headed once more up the M4 to set up our stand at the Design Centre in Islington.

The Business Design Centre is quite a large venue and the four-day show called Art Mart, had been advertised as a chance for the art-loving public to see the works of 40 artists all under one roof. The painting of the fusilier, now titled, 'We will remember them', formed the centrepiece on our stand. As is customary on these occasions, a preview would take place for invited guests the evening before the official opening to the public. We had invited Patrick Shervington, Leo Cooper and Christopher Dowling as our guests. Patrick spent most of his time, walking down the aisle opposite our display, viewing the picture he commissioned from every possible angle!

The VIP party, invited by the Design Centre, included local dignitaries, and headed by Lord Archer, walked down the aisle to where we had our stand. As the party reached us, Jeffrey Archer bounded on to our stand, and grabbing Jack by the hand, exclaimed, 'Jack, what are the selectors thinking? Leaving out Russell and Archer!' This caused a huge roar of laughter, breaking what had otherwise been a fairly sombre atmosphere. Jeffrey Archer, immaculate as always, chatted enthusiastically with Jack. I was standing with our three invited guests at the edge of the stand, when Leo Cooper, nudging and nodding towards Lord Archer, said, 'He's got style hasn't he.' It broadened my grin, but I was feeling pretty pleased with myself anyway.

We had a successful four days at the Design Centre, made the more enjoyable with the unexpected appearance of an old friend. Artist and sculptor Jonathan Wylder had painted portraits of my daughters, Karen and Rachel, in the early 80s. I hadn't seen him since, so I was delighted to meet him once more. He told me he had a permanent exhibition on the mezzanine floor at the Design Centre, and invited me to view it. His activities were now concentrated on sculpture, the pieces I saw were staggeringly beautiful, the prices were equally so. I did promise to keep in touch, but haven't. Remiss of me.

It had been a hectic year. Jack was scheduled to leave for Australia on 25 January 1993. Would there be time for just one more project before then? A painting Jack had wanted to do, when time allowed, was a scene of Lord's cricket ground. A painting of Lord's, by Jack Russell, from which we could make limited edition prints, was an attractive prospect. If Jack could do the painting before his departure, leaving me to organise the prints, it would be most beneficial to our progress.

Lt Colonel John Stephenson was then Secretary of the MCC, so it was to him that I wrote, on Jack's behalf, telling of our plans for a painting of Lord's. Adding our wish to approach one or two former England players asking if they would be willing to countersign a quantity of prints, I asked whether we could come to London to discuss it. The answer affirmative, we decided on a plan of positive action, in as much as Jack would paint the picture before the meeting with the Colonel. This way we could get some feedback on the painting at the same time as discussing possible signatories.

A TESTING TIME

After a couple off recces of Lord's ground, where Jack made colour notes and I took photographs, Jack set about putting paint on canvas. With time running out for Jack, bearing in mind his commitment to the fitness programme all England players selected to tour must strictly adhere to, yet again we headed up the M4 with a painting barely dry.

Colonel John Stephenson greeted us warmly, as, carrying a large canvas, we edged our way into his office. The Colonel's face lit up as he viewed the scene Jack had painted. 'Here I am in my office at Lord's, in winter, and I am watching a test match, on this very ground; it's splendid Jack,' He praised.

The meeting was most productive. It was decided we should approach Sir Colin Cowdrey, Dickie Bird, Godfrey Evans, Brian Johnston and Denis Compton to countersign the prints we were to publish. We also asked Colonel Stephenson if, he, too, would do us the honour of signing. 'Delighted to, the honour is all mine,' he responded. We met the deadlines we had created for ourselves, but we were far from out of the woods. Thus far, we had pushed everything along at a cracking pace, but this time we would take it to the wire.

Jack flew to Australia, whilst I wrote to the celebrities we had chosen to countersign the prints of Lord's. I contacted our printer, APB in Bristol, and set in motion the production of a limited edition of 850 prints

To my delight, all but Denis Compton replied to say they would be delighted to sign prints of Lord's for Jack. With hindsight, it was a tall order, expecting they would all be available on the same day. Miraculously they were. We decided to arrange the launch, on the evening of the same day as the signing. Whoa! There were so many ifs: Jack not getting back on time, or the signing over running, to name just two. Undaunted, we went for it, and set the date. I had still to hear from Denis Compton, so I wrote him another letter. Without a reply and as a last resort, I telephoned the legendary batsman. Now this can be quite unnerving when one is not used to talking to legends. I mean you don't meet them every day, do you? 'Hello, who is that,' said a voice down the phone. I answered 'I am Jim Ruston, and I wrote to you asking if you would sign some prints for Jack Russell.' 'Jack who?' came the response. 'Jack Russell, he keeps wicket for England.' I hurriedly replied. 'England, cricket, what England cricket? I didn't know there was any. Have they got a cricket team?' The words from the great man came in an unhurried, almost vague tone. Try as I might, I could not get any sense whatsoever from one of my heroes.

I tried once more, this time speaking to Mrs Compton, who apologised, saying she couldn't understand why Denis hadn't replied;

he had been unwell, but she would ask him to. I told the charming lady not to worry, and certainly not to apologise. It was us who were asking the favour. And so, regretfully, the print went to press minus the name of Denis Compton. A great pity. However, later the same year he signed another of our limited editions, called The Old Tavern, Lord's.

Jack left for Australia whilst I took stock of the progress we had made in the art business. We had come a long way in a very short space of time. The exhibition, at Sodbury House Hotel endorsed my belief in getting the right venue to exhibit Jack's work; I had discussed this with him before he left. The limited display space we had in my daughter's shop, whilst generous of her and her husband to provide, would not be sufficient for our future ideas. I began to look for suitable premises.

The road from Yate to the A46 has a bypass, so unless you take the old road, you will miss the market town of Chipping Sodbury completely. With little optimism I drove into the small town, which boasts one of the widest main streets in England. Driving down the high street, I could barely believe my eyes when I saw an estate agent's board over a shop advertising first floor office space to let. The premises were those of Worthington's, a traditional soft furnishing and clothing store. Typical of most of the buildings in Chipping Sodbury, the property dates back hundreds of years. I stood on the pavement and, looking up, tried to imagine what the interior was like. The shape of the roof told me that unless a false ceiling had been installed, the interior should have similar features to those in the coachouse at Sodbury House Hotel.

I telephoned the agent's and ask to view. A tall blond young man, who met me on the pavement outside of Worthington's, introduced himself as Richard Horne from Chesterton's. The interior had everything I had dreamed of, high oak beamed ceilings, period windows and an atmosphere of quality. I told Richard Horne of my reason for wanting the premises, and that we would take them subject to contract. A keen amateur cricketer himself, he was delighted. So was I, having found exactly the right venue, the position, the style, it couldn't possible be more suitable if we had built it ourselves. My fingers literally danced across the keyboard, as I typed a letter to send by fax, to Jack in Australia.

The reply I received from Jack was not the one I had been expecting. Instead of the, 'Go for it mate, let's get in there', I got a cautious 'Sounds OK, but wait for me to return before making a decision'. His main concern, he said, was being tied to a five-year lease. For a moment I was deflated. For the past 16 months I had risked a great deal personally, spending far more than I was earning, promoting the art of

Jack Russell to the exclusion of all else. An art gallery, displaying Jack's work in a solo permanent exhibition, would be the turning point. If we didn't take this opportunity, where would we go from here? We couldn't risk losing these perfect premises. The owners said that whilst they were quite happy to have Jack Russell, (by now a limited company) as a tenant, they were not prepared to hold the deal open until his return.

I sat down, put my head in my hands, and thought of my next move. I could take the premises in my own name, and display Jack's work in what would be my gallery, as I had been doing in my daughter's shop. This option, in the long term, I thought unwise for Jack. I was quite prepared to pay half of the rent, and all running costs involved. The terms of the lease were advantageous to say the least; there would be no in-going payment, and I had even got them to agree a three-month rent-free period to allow time for decoration before opening.

I wrote back to Jack in the strongest terms, reminding him that when we first began working together, he expressed a wish to keep control of things, no matter what transpired, and I had agreed. That is why I had started the negotiations for the premises in the name of Jack Russell Limited. Had I other intentions, I would simply have taken them in my own name, informing him that I was moving my office. Until now, the only business address we had was the one at Station Road, my daughter's shop, where I had limited space and a phone line, the expenses of both being met by me.

We had already agreed to move in this direction as soon as the opportunity arrived, and here it was. I did of course appreciate Jack's position; he was 13,000 miles away. But I hoped he could trust me to make the right decision. After some thought he did. Just how right the move turned out will be revealed later in the story.

I took possession of our new premises, and son-in-law Eddie, in his spare time, redecorated them. I hung all the pictures I had available and made everything look as presentable as I could in readiness for Jack's return from down under. I kept things quiet as far as the media were concerned, so as not to pre-empt the publicity I intended to attract when Jack got back.

Whilst the England 'A' team had a successful tour, with Jack in particular in top form – he had captained the 'A' side for three games, winning two of them – the senior squad had had a nightmare of a tour in India. Chairman of selectors, Ted Dexter, admitted that he had made a mistake by leaving Russell and Gower out of the team, particularly Russell. Instead they had relied on Alec Stewart as a batsman keeper, taking Yorkshire's inexperienced Richard Blakey, to deputise. Alec got injured and poor Blakey was called upon. Not only was his keeping less than average, he also failed miserably with the bat, scoring just six runs in four innings. The legendary wicket keeper Godfrey Evans went on record saying: 'The Gower non-selection was a disgrace, and leaving out the best wicket keeper in the world, Jack Russell, is beyond me.'

On entering his own gallery for the first time, Jack's eyes lit up, and he enthused, 'It's everything you described to me Jim, and more. I can see now why you were so excited about it. You were right mate we couldn't let this pass us by.'

Jack would soon have to start training in readiness for the County cricket season, so there wouldn't be much time for him to paint or help with the art business. Loaded down with prints from Jack's painting of Lord's, Jack, Eddie and I arrived at St John's Wood, where with the co-operation of Colonel Stephenson, we had arranged a signing session in the committee room, adjacent to the hallowed Long Room. It was the first time Eddie and I had been in the historic pavilion. For anyone who loves sport, it is an awe-inspiring experience just to stand there and reflect on the great names who have walked through this room and out onto the lush green turf. Grace, Hammond, Bradman, Larwood, Compton, Cowdrey, Bedser, Laker and Hutton, and Evans of course! I could go on and on. But who will future generations be regaling? The modern game is sadly lacking in 'characters'.

Sitting at a long table with prints in front of them, were Godfrey Evans, Dickie Bird, Colin Cowdrey, Brian Johnston and John Stephenson. There were 850 to sign, and it should have taken about three hours, but every so often Dickie told a story, which brought the system to a halt! It was hilarious. Brian Johnston kept looking at his watch; he didn't want to miss *Neighbours* (a favourite programme of his) on the telly. (Brian lived just around the corner.) Godfrey discussed England's recent tour of India with Colin Cowdrey saying, 'How could they leave Russell out, he's the best there is. I've always thought Ted Dexter's judgement to be quite sound on cricketing matters, but when I next see him, I shall tell him how wrong he his'. Sir Colin nodded in agreement. All this was taking place with Jack in the room; they were referring to him as though he wasn't there! Jack looked at me, and I could see he was visibly amused. If only we had recorded the conversations that day. Pure magic, a privilege to be there.

Fours hours later, and with the last print signed, we gathered our belongings and raced over to Lillywhites in Piccadilly for the launch of Jack's Lord's painting. Patrick Shervington and Christopher Dowling supported us once more. Bob Willis, the fast bowler, who played a vital role in the 1981 test match where England reclaimed the Ashes (more often referred to as the Botham Ashes) paid us a visit. I liked Bob once, and appreciated his support, but his constant carping, and slagging of Jack during the West Indies series in both 1994 and 1998 was unforgivable. Former pro-cricketers turned broadcasters should know better. Sadly many of them don't.

Away from cricket my sister Stella phoned, to say the ladies who were staying in the house she lets asked her if there were any quality horses around that they could view. She told them of me, and was now asking if I could take them to Badminton stables. I said I would try to arrange it and rang my friend Brian Higham to ask if he would mind showing a couple of women around the horses. 'Be glad to Jim. Are they nice? I mean nice looking that is?' he enquired. I told him I hadn't yet met them, and that all I knew was they were Americans.

Brian's relationship with Hilary had come to an end. I'm not totally sure why; I never asked, and Brian never said. With his divorce from his former wife Audrey now absolute, Brian was once more a single man. Stella introduced me to the two Americans, and one, whose name was Sherry, accompanied me in my car whilst the others followed in a hire car. On the way, Sherry asked me a few questions about where I was taking her, and I tried to explain the Badminton set-up. This is virtually impossible to anyone not familiar with big estates. She asked, 'Are the estate workers like the slaves we once had in America?' Laughing, fit to drop, I replied, 'Brian Higham is going to love you!' I didn't realise just how true that statement would turn out to be.

Brian showed the ladies the stables at Badminton, and whilst they were walking around the horses, pointed discreetly towards Sherry, whispering, 'She's nice, isn't she?' 'Very nice, Brian,' I agreed. At Brian's invitation, we all went back to his cottage for a slow gin, a speciality of his. Brian and Sherry got along famously well, and within a short time they were courting. They were married by the end of the year. I was so pleased for them both. Sherry is a lovely lady, I'm proud to have introduced her to my dear friend.

A few days after the launch at Lillywhites, Brian Johnston phoned me saying, 'I seem somehow to have volunteered to help Paul Getty to organise cricket at Wormsley in Buckinghamshire. Would Jack Russell do us the honour of playing in Paul's team this summer? It will be splendid if he can.' Brian, the consummate professional, had as always done his homework making sure the fixture he had in mind for Jack to play in did not clash with county commitments. I asked Jack if he wanted to accept the invitation and he said he would love to. When I phoned to tell Brian this, he replied, 'Splendid. By the way, Paul may ask Jack if he can paint a cricket scene at Wormsley for him. He had one painted recently, disliked it and wouldn't hang it.'

The county had moved their traditional Gloucester Cricket Festival from the old Waggon Works, to Archdeacon Meadow, the latter being the King's School sports ground, and in fairness an altogether nicer venue than the former one at Tuffley. With the success I had enjoyed at Cheltenham Festival the previous year, I decided to exhibit at Gloucester. Rain ruined the first two days, although the weather did improve, and with a bigger crowd I did some business. Jack was eagerly awaiting the announcement of the team to play in the first test against the visiting Australians. He had started the new season well, and with his performance with England 'A' not long in the record books, thought he had a very good chance of regaining his place behind the stumps for the forthcoming Ashes tour.

When the team to play Australia was announced, Jack's name was not in it. Once again the selectors had gone for batsman keeper Alec Stewart, despite the effect keeping wicket was having on Alec's batting. Jack was averaging 27.17 runs with the bat in test matches whilst Alec, a class batsman, was averaging only 20 when having to keep wicket as well. It didn't work; it never really has. Effectively, two careers were being harmed, Alec's as an opening batsman, and Jack's as a specialist keeper. England lost the series. Australia retained the Ashes.

Visiting my daughter Karen, in her shop, I could see by the look on her face that something was troubling her. She greeted me without a smile, unusual for her. Karen's husband Gordon, standing nearby, also had a sombre look about him. In fact, they both looked awkward. For a few moments we stood in silence, then Karen said, 'Dad, I really don't know how to tell you this.' I hate that phrase; my legs went like jelly. She continued, 'Rene Parker phoned a short while ago to say that her husband Bill has passed away.' The blood drained from my body. With tears welling up in my eyes, I replied, 'No, not Bill. We promised each other not to do this. He can't just go and leave me'. I will never forget the look of sadness in Karen's eyes, as she replied, 'I know he meant an awful lot to you, Dad. I was very fond of him too.'

I last called to see Bill a few weeks before. I had heard he was unwell, but he wasn't the sort of bloke to mention it himself. So when I asked him how he was, his reply was typical. 'Oh I'm alright. It's lovely to see you mate.' We sat in the sitting room of the bungalow he shared with his lovely wife Rene, and their daughter Debbie, and recounted old times. We had a little drop of Scotch together, and put the world to rights. When Rene walked in on the two has-beens, her smile said everything. Both she and Bill always made me so welcome; we are friends of long standing.

I rang Rene, intending to say how devastated I was, and offer my support to her and her family, but when she picked up the phone, neither of us could speak, we were too choked up.

A few days later, I attended Bill's funeral service at Canford Cemetery in Bristol. Driving through an avenue of trees to where I could see cars and people gathering, I was about to park when for no reason I can explain, I drove to another spot further on. Having parked there, I reached into the inside pocket of my jacket for the comb I usually carry, but this time had not. Resigning myself to the fact that my hair looked untidy, I stepped out of the car and immediately felt something underfoot. Looking down to see what I had trod on, I discovered it to be a small black comb. Bill had left it for me, hadn't he? I still have it.

A great many people turned up to pay their last respects to a much loved man, and those who had served in the Armed Forces, wore their military ties. Bill was a man's man, and there were some fine men here, men I would be glad to have beside me in a crisis. There was no greater tribute to our friend than to pay homage to him. Few weeks pass that I don't think of Bill, and the wonderful times we had. They were some of the best days of my life, and I thank you for them dear friend.

We had another successful exhibition at the Cheltenham Festival, after which Jack managed to find a free day to visit Wormsley. Having played for the Paul Getty XI some weeks previously where the man himself asked Jack if he would consider painting a cricket scene for him, I was pleased he was able to find a 'window' in his hectic schedule to get the project underway.

Paul Getty's (now Sir) cricket ground, on his estate in Buckinghamshire is spectator-friendly. A raised bank on which striped deck chairs are placed, give the cricket lover an unobstructed view over the whole playing area. With wonderful views of the surrounding farm and parkland, where animals graze contentedly, the location is idyllic. Jack set up his easel and went to work on a canvas. Like all accomplished artists, he works very quickly, and soon the basic structure of the picture emerged.

A few weeks later I visited Wormsley for the third time, now to take the action pictures Jack would need to complete his painting. It was 15 August, Jack's birthday. In aid of The Lord's Taveners charity, an old England XI were playing and old Australian XI. It was wonderful to see so many legendary cricketers in one place. Brian Johnston was talking to Denis Compton and the Bedser twins. Godfrey Evans was sitting with Peter May and Denis Lillee. Greg Chappell and Bobby Simpson were bantering with Mike Denness and Colin Cowdrey.

But perhaps the most magical moment was when Patrick Shervington caught sight of Leslie Crowther, who was at his first cricket match since the horrendous car crash that almost killed him. Leslie was standing on the balcony of the wonderful thatched pavilion when Patrick greeted him. The look of sheer joy that spread across the face of both men said a thousand words. Leslie Crowther had been a tireless President of the Lord's Taveners for the previous two years, and had struck up a close friendship with Patrick and his wife Vicky. The couple had given endless support and encouragement to Leslie and his wife Jean through the black days, when Leslie had cheated death, and after, when he made a miraculous recovery. Now he was here, the great entertainer, doing what he was so passionately fond of, watching cricket with his friends.

Jack had informed me when first we met that in a year or so he would get a Benefit. This, he explained, was a year during which functions were held, to the financial benefit of the player nominated. The award of a benefit generally came after a player had been with his county for 10 years or more. Of course there have been exceptions. The system is unique in sport and seems only to apply to cricket (footballers are sometimes awarded a testimonial match). A precedent was set before the war years where a group of supporters got together to raise money for a loyal county cricketer, whose financial benefits from his career had been minimal. The taxman tried to take his cut of the bounty, but objections were raised and the matter went before a court, where the outcome was favourable to the recipient. It was decreed that as a gift from admirers, in appreciation of the person who had benefited, it was not taxable. The system continues to this day.

Jack said he had been told to expect a Benefit in 1994, although it must not be officially announced until the end of the year proceeding. I had established a good working relationship with the management of Gloucestershire CCC and offered to negotiate a new contract for Jack. Not so long ago, County Cricket Clubs were not at all used to their players having agents other, that is, than the players from overseas, whose contracts were generally negotiated by an agent specialising in that field. I was one of a new breed, but the management at Jack's club had no problem at all in accepting my involvement. It has worked well since.

The England team to tour the West Indies the coming winter was announced. Newspaper hacks to a man had been rooting for Jack's re-selection, and cheered on by his fellow professionals, surely the selectors wouldn't dare leave him out any longer. They didn't, and Jack was back in the England squad. He had earned his recall. With a benefit year now only months away, Jack signed a new four-year deal with Gloucestershire.

The finished painting of Paul Getty's cricket ground looked stunning. I contacted Paul's PA Sally Munton to arrange delivery, saying that Jack would be happy to transport the picture personally. Sally informed me that Mr Getty was delighted the picture was finished, and could Jack bring it to his London home in St James' Place. I freely admit, both Jack and I were excited at the prospect of a visit to the London home of the billionaire.

On our arrival we were shown down to the underground garage, where we parked the car and took the lift. With the painting, now in its ornate frame, looking even larger than it had done on the easel, clutched between us, we emerged from the lift and were met by a butler. 'Please come this way,' he gestured. 'I will tell Mr Getty you have arrived.' We stood in a beautifully furnished hall, admiring the superb décor, when an extremely attractive lady appeared from an adjoining door, and introduced herself as Victoria. She then led us into a huge sitting room and bade us sit down. Victoria, she later married Paul, asked if we would like some tea, saying she would make it, and that Paul would be with us shortly.

Victoria returned with the tea, and almost at once Paul Getty himself walked in to greet us. 'Jack I'm so pleased to see you,' he said extending his hand. Jack responded and introduced me, as he never fails to do. 'So this is the picture of Wormsley. It's splendid Jack, simply splendid. I will keep it here for now, having decided to hang it in my bedroom,' he said with enthusiasm. 'Would you like me to hang it for you, Mr Getty?' I offered. 'Could you? It wouldn't be putting you to too much trouble would it?' he asked with concern. 'Not at all, I have come prepared to do just that,' I said, pointing to the small toolbox I had brought with me.

I followed Mr Getty into his bedroom, where he showed me the place he had in mind for the picture to hang, on the wall opposite the foot of his four-poster bed. He then returned to the sitting room to talk with Jack, leaving me to hang the painting. After hanging the painting I joined the others telling them it was ready for approval. The look on Paul Getty's face was a picture in itself, as he sat on his bed to make sure the painting was at a height he was comfortable with. I made a few adjustments until he said 'That's it, now I can watch cricket at Wormsley when I'm in London, even in winter!'

I had been invited by the Royal Regiment of Fusiliers to attend a luncheon in HM Tower of London, where the guest of honour would be

the Lord Mayor of London. Jack and I had been to the Tower recently
to present the painting of the fusilier in Holborn, which now hangs in
the entrance of the Regiment's Museum. We were privileged to drive
over the bridge between the Ramparts and across the huge courtyard to
the Museum. I had only ever visited the Tower years ago as a teenager,
and seeing as how I was born in the Borough of Tower Hamlets, I felt
especially proud. Had I lived in London at the time of my National
Service, I would almost certainly have served my time there – as did
Michael Caine, and The Kray twins; please, I am not drawing a parallel
here! Now I was to dine with the Mayor, a bevy of politicians, high-
ranking Army Officers, and the like. I said to myself, 'Pleased to meet
you, I'm Jim Ruston, ex-Craftsman REME!'   It was a memorable
occasion. My dad would have been so proud. As in the words of the
song, 'If they could see me now…'

I had a nice letter from Sally Munton, Paul Getty's PA, to say that
Brian Johnston had been invited by Paul to view Jack's painting of
Wormsley. And how Brian had admired it so. Naturally it came as quite
a shock when not long after receiving the letter from Sally, at a sporting
lunch in Bristol, where Graham Gooch, David Lloyd and Brian
Johnston were billed as guest speakers, I heard that Brian Johnston,
about to board the Bristol train at Paddington, had collapsed. Sadly, he
died, and will be forever missed.

On my one visit to Wormsley, I had talked with Brian at some length
about his time as presenter of *In Town To-night*. He was amused to hear
the stories of my dad, and when I showed him the cigarette card from
the popular series, he exclaimed, 'I have a set of those myself.' The last
time I spoke to him was as a result of request asking if he could write an
article for a brochure I was compiling in advance of Jack's benefit year.
He phoned to say he was terribly busy, and in the middle of recording
talking books for the blind, going on to say, 'Use anything from any of
my books dear boy. Give my very best wishes to Jack. Congratulate
him for me on his return to the England team. He's where he belongs,
and should never have been left out.' Johnners – irreplaceable.

Through the offices of Leo Cooper, Jack and I had met up with Bill
Sparks. We paid a flying visit to his bungalow in Crowborough, where
we met both Bill and his wife Renie, who is normally very protective of
her husband, but when Leo told her it was Jack Russell who wanted to
visit, the barrier was lifted. Bill loves his cricket, and was as thrilled to
meet Jack as both of us were to meet him. Jack showed Bill the sketches
he had made, and a small colour note he had painted in preparation for
the final picture. Now complete, our friends at the Imperial War

A TESTING TIME

Museum were offering to present Jack Russell's latest work to the media at a party they would sponsor.

It was another great day at the War Museum. Leo Cooper had just published Bill Sparks' book, The Last of the *Cockleshell Heroes*. The timing for Jack's painting *'Cockleshell Heroes'* couldn't have been better, and it was well received. The Royal Marines sent some of their top brass, and they were very complimentary about the picture. It was agreed that the painting would hang for a period of two years in the Royal Marine's Museum at Southsea. Whilst it would be added artistic exposure, and indeed an honour for Jack, Bill Sparks had mixed feelings. At this time, neither Jack nor myself had any knowledge of the conflict between Bill and his Corp's Museum; nor did we foresee the close friendship that was about to develop between myself and Bill and Renie Sparks.

Back at home there was another wedding in the family. My niece June's daughter Claire, was marrying a local man from my old wartime village Nailsea, where she now lived with her mother. I agreed to help with the photography. It was a really beautiful wedding and the reception that followed was magic. My sister Betty and husband Roy's daughters' Debbie and Stella, looked lovely. Stella and her son Grahame came. To watch my sister Maisie dancing with our brother Roy was a moment of sheer joy. Wild horses would not normally drag Roy to a wedding, yet here he was. With the benefit of hindsight, he must have guessed that for him the sands of time were running low and took this opportunity to spend some time with all us all. Cliff Stock played keyboard, while my brother sang his favourite song, 'Georgia'.

June was so proud of Claire, who had done much to help organise things. It is the saddest thing that my sister Maud was not there to see her granddaughter get married. She was still not prepared to accept Claire and her daughter, the stunningly beautiful Niaomi (who has recently won a place at the prestigious Northern School of Contemporary Dance). My dad would have been heartbroken at this rift. He was devoted to Claire, and he would have loved Niaomi, as did my mother, so deeply. They were also immensely proud of June and her achievements(if only they had been alive to see her presented with her Master of Science degree from Bristol university). Before he left his home in Essex, Roy rang Maud telling her he was going to her granddaughter's wedding, and asking her to go with him. With vitriol she said, 'I have divorced myself from that family.' Her response brought tears to his eyes. Roy, never, ever, got involved in domestic matters, but must have thought this his last chance to try and bridge the gap. Sadly it failed. The gap widens.

FAREWELL MY HERO

A committee was formed to organise functions during Jack Russell's forthcoming benefit year. Steve Patch, Jack's car sponsor, agreed to take the Chair. The first function, would be a dinner at the Grand Hotel in Bristol to launch the benefit year. We invited a bevvy of cricketing personalities, including the three top ex-England keepers Godfrey Evans, Alan Knott and Bob Taylor. TV star and avid cricket fan Rory Bremner provided the after-dinner entertainment. He was magnificent. Tributes were paid by those qualified to state 'Jack Russell, the best wicket keeper in the world.' It was indeed a Gala evening, and one I would have enjoyed more had I not been suffering an attack of gout in my right foot! I must have looked odd, dressed in a smart lounge suit, whilst on my feet were sandy coloured beach shoes – the only pair I could get my poor feet into. I struggled, feeling faint much of the time.

My sister Stella, a wizard with figures, agreed to act as treasurer for Jack's fundraising year. Not a job to be envied, it's a lot of work and responsibility, and it's unpaid. During the function, a raffle and an auction were held raising thousands of pounds, which gave a wonderful start to the benefit year. Jack was both joyous and grateful, and with his lovely wife Aileen making one of her rare appearances in public (she prefers to stay out of the limelight), his night was complete. Two days later he left with the England squad to tour the West Indies.

Joyce and I were also about to embark on our long promised visit to Australia. A few months earlier, Keith Logan had paid us a flying visit; he was in England to attend the funeral of his father Reg. The year before when Queenie, his mum, died, he sent a fax asking if I could pick him up at Heathrow. On that occasion I was tied up with one of the London exhibitions, so regretfully had little time to spend with him. Keith brought us up to date with his news, which sadly included a divorce from his wife Sue. On a lighter note, he confided that he had met a girl called Prue, on whom he was quite keen. Now for Logan to admit that is quite something. After all they are all keen on him aren't they? He just waits and chooses – in his dreams!

Keith had said to me, 'If I ask Prue to marry me, and she says yes, will you and Joyce come to the wedding? Our answer had been a spontaneous 'Yes', and now the wedding invitation had arrived saying Keith and Prue were to be married at 6pm on 25 January at the Royal Sydney Yacht Squadron. Dress – Black Tie. That was enough for me to say to my excited wife, 'Book the tickets.'

Joyce and I went Australia House in London to get our Visa's, returning home via Dagenham to see cousin Cissy, and Loughton to visit my brother. Roy had not been well for a while, it was his old trouble, hardening of the arteries, plus a few more problems he evaded when asked. He was full of enthusiasm about our forthcoming trip down under, which was typical of him, finding joy in your joy, I never heard him utter a negative phrase in his life. I promised that on our return, I would visit and tell him all that we had seen. Although he had difficulty walking, it didn't stop him coming out to the car to see us off. Glancing back as we pulled away, I could see his frail figure standing at the gate waving, looking a shadow of his former self. For the first time in my life, I worried for him, and it brought a lump to my throat.

We flew with Quantas via Bankok to Sydney. As we came through arrivals, we could see Keith standing by the exit. 'Welcome to Australia, it's only taken you 25years to get here!' he said as he hugged Joyce, then slapped me on the back.

As we drove across the Harbour Bridge Keith told us of his first impression as a young boy, all those years ago, when he sailed into Sydney Harbour with his parents. He had thought. 'What kind of place is this? It looks like a paradise. Am I dreaming?' Glancing out across the harbour, I could see right there and then why he had made his home here. Joyce always loved Australia, and wanted to emigrate in the early 60s. She even sent for application forms. A television engineer, I would have had no trouble at all finding a suitable position, but it was me rather than her who decided against it. Had we, the book I now write may have told very different story.

Installed in our hotel on Sydney's northside, we arranged to meet Keith later, then flaked out on the bed for an hour or so. That evening, over dinner at a lovely fish restaurant, and in full view of the famous opera house, Keith introduced us to Prue, his bride to be. Joyce and I took to her immediately. In my wife's eyes, Logan can't do anything wrong; if Prue was to be his wife, then we would take her to our hearts. An astute businesswoman, Prue owns a school of colour and design in Sydney, where pupils attend courses in both disciplines. A hugely successful venture, which as I write has expanded considerably.

During the next few days, Joyce and I became typical tourists. We visited the Opera House. Whilst the exterior is spectacular, we found the interior disappointing. The overuse of timber cladding gives the feel of a giant Swedish sauna. The design had left much to be desired acoustically, so deflectors, looking like satellite dishes, had to be suspended from the ceiling to improve the sound quality. We took an excursion around the harbour on a huge catamaran, during which coffee and biscuits were served. We were like a couple of kids, wide-eyed, in the fascinating city. The following few days were enchanting. One was Australia Day, so we visited a park where groups gathered, many were in the national dress of their ancestors – Scots, Welsh, Irish and so on. There was a bandstand where a diverse programme of entertainment continued throughout the day, enjoyed as we lay on the grass with the sun shining down from a cloudless sky. We watched various species of exotic birds – parrots, budgerigars, cockatoos – flying free in their natural habitat, a new experience for both of us.

Music from a string quartet filled the air and champagne flowed, as we walked into the grounds of the Royal Sydney Yacht Squadron. Joyce dressed in a pale blue two-piece suit looked her usual lovely self, whilst I tried to look as comfortable as I could in an ever tightening dinner suit. The figure has spread a little since I bought it. With other guests, we gathered around the lawn, from where there is a perfect view of the Opera House and Harbour Bridge. With a lady vicar in the lead, the wedding party arrived. Keith looked as happy as I had ever seen him, and Prue, so elegant, in a beautiful dress. With the Bride and Groom, were their three children: Sarah from Keith's previous marriage, and Nicholas and Jeremy from Prue's. The kids played an important part in the ceremony, so special.

Afterwards, the Yacht Club, with the sun sinking slowly over the harbour, created the perfect atmosphere for dinner.

The best man made a speech, in which he told where he had first met with Keith; it was in a yacht race, when Keith had bumped his boat. 'Quite within the rules,' he hastened to add. 'I liked this gutsy pom at once. Cheeky bastard, coming over here, and having the nerve to elbow us Aussies out of the way, he seemed to know the rules better than we did.' He then went on to pay tribute to Joyce and me for travelling 13,000 miles to be at the wedding of a friend, saying. 'He must be some kind of friend,' (That got a round of applause, which made us feel quite humble.) He is indeed. I looked across at my old mate sitting next to his lovely bride, thinking, 'You've done yourself proud Keith. Good luck, you old git!'

I telephoned the Sydney Cricket Ground, to say I had brought over a picture of Lord's, as a gift from Jack, and I would like to visit the stadium. They invited us to join one of the organised tours, which take place daily. I asked whether I could bring my wife and a few friends. They said, 'No worries mate.' What answer did I expect? Imagine trying this at Lord's! The conducted tour of Sydney Cricket Ground is probably the best of any sports stadium in the world. It includes programmed animation, and spectra vision, the first I had seen. The latter took the form of a small female figure, about 12 inches tall in Victorian dress, walking around inside a glass display case pointing out various items of cricketing memorabilia, explaining to whom it once belonged. The image is created with four laser beams, a technique that will be used here to create 3D television they say by the year 2003. I could not take my eyes off it.

Keith never misses a chance to score points off me, always tongue in cheek, and I am quick to reverse the situation when I can. Now was a good time. 'Keith, it comes to something when I have to travel 13,000 miles to show you around your own cricket ground,' I said with a smirk. 'I wondered when you were going to mention that, I guessed you would you miserable pom. But you can't get your bloody Ashes back though, can you?' he roared. Smart arse, he's always got an answer.

Joyce and I were invited by the manager at the Sydney Cricket Ground to attend a limited overs day-night game between Australia and South Africa. I think it was the first international the South Africans played, post apartheid. It was our first experience of cricket under floodlights, and we found the atmosphere electrifying. Australia won, but it was a tight game, the South Africans played brilliantly, in particular Hansie Conje, who was outstanding. Thinking then, 'We will see a lot more of this guy,' we have, and sadly his downfall too.

Most people who visit Australia want to see the barrier reef. I spoke to Keith about it and he said he had a friend in the travel business. She would sort out some flights for us. 'Flights,' I said. 'How far away is it'? 'Oh just up the coast a bit,' he replied. I was beginning to discover just how big this country is. The charming girl in the travel agents told us Keith had rang, and that she had a few options for us to consider. She then went on to tell us she would be eternally grateful to Keith for saving her brother's life, and revealed the following story.

Her brother was crewing with Keith on a catamaran in heavy weather when the vessel capsized. Keith surfaced, but could see no sign of his colleague having done so. Diving under the boat he found his mate caught up in the rigging, but try as he may, he could not free him. Coming to the surface, Keith waved frantically to other craft in the immediate vicinity; realising at once it would take precious minutes for anyone to come to his aid, he dived again to check on his pal.

Keith placed his mouth over that of his mate, and expelled every last drop of his air into his lungs. Screaming for air himself he surfaced, inhaled deeply, then dived again to repeat the process. Keith kept this up until help arrived. No one expected his mate to survive, at least not without serious brain damage. Miraculously he did, and went on the make a complete recovery. Keith had never mentioned the incident to me. I didn't know he was a bleedin' hero, or I would have made him a badge or something!

From Cairns, we went everywhere. The barrier reef. Into the rain forest, where the heaven's opened and we got a soaking. I bought myself a nice green bush hat, and thought I looked the business in it. When we returned to England Jack asked to borrow it, I haven't seen it since! Although hot, wet and humid, it had been a wonderful trip. Back in Sydney, Keith greeted us thus: 'I meant to tell you before you left sport, it's the rainy season up there, sorry!'

We still had a few days left before flying back to the UK, so I talked Joyce into taking the train out to the home town of the great Australian cricketer Sir Don Bradman. The cricket ground at Bowral is named 'The Bradman Oval' in honour of the legend. The pavilion was being used as a museum; a new one has since been built. Among the artefacts on display is a painting of the Bowral Oval by Jack Russell; it was commissioned a year or two before our visit. As we viewed it, Joyce reminded me that it was she who took the parcel containing this painting to Bristol Airport for its dispatch to Australia. 'It's nice to see it arrived safely,' she smiled. Before we left Bowral, I went into a stationer's and bought a visitor's book to use in our Gallery. Now, with so many famous signatures in, it is part of the Gallery's history. Tomorrow's history begins today.

Keith took us all out on his boat. As we sailed, he pointed out the various inlets in the coastline. We rafted up beside a yacht belonging to friends of Keith and Prue. Keith, Sarah and I, dived off the boat and swam ashore, whilst back on board, our hosts prepared a sumptuous feast, with a nice Chardonnay to wash it all down. I was leaning on the cabin roof, looking forward, when I blinked, thinking, 'Am I seeing things?' I took another good look, then asked, 'Keith, is that the *QE2* heading this way?' Keith looked up from his plate of nosh, and without so much as a glimmer of enthusiasm, confirmed. 'Yea, the old girl sails in every couple of years. I guess she is about due again.' I was dumbstruck; there we were having lunch on board a boat on a perfect day in Sydney Harbour, and the *QE2* sails by. Given half a chance, Logan would have claimed he organised it just for me!

We said our goodbyes to Prue and the kids, and Keith took us to the airport. It had been the best holiday Joyce and I had ever had, but it was over all too soon. We thanked Keith warmly, then said farewell to our dear friend who, with a trace of a tear in his eye, responded, 'You two finally made it here; I always hoped you would.' We promised not to leave it so long next time, to which he replied, 'I hope not, I might well be bloody dead if you do!'

The art business was building, and with the added strain of a benefit year, and Jack out of the country for at least the first quarter, I knew I would struggle to continue doing everything myself. My daughter Jane had agreed to help out on a part-time basis. She had done a magnificent job whilst Joyce and I were in Australia. Jane, like her mother, is a diligent and accomplished bookkeeper. With Jack Russell Art now a limited company, there would be extra responsibility. Jack agreed that I needed help to enable me to push on with our plans.

My sister-in-law Josie rang to say my brother had been taken into hospital with his old trouble, thrombosis and so on. I regretted I hadn't yet seen him since returning from my holiday, but I had been busy preparing for a sporting lunch the committee had organised for Jack's benefit. I arranged for a large screen TV to be installed for the function to show the cricket between England and the West Indies live on the 2 March. Sky Sports agreed to send a taped interview they made with Jack in the West Indies that we could show at the start of the function.

I sent a fax to Jack telling him about Roy, and that the way things looked he may not survive. Although incredibly weak, my brother still had his old fighting spirit, but he had had two heart attacks and his kidneys were failing. After one of the heart attacks, a doctor asked Roy a lot of routine questions to see if he was still 'with us'. Roy told him not to talk so much bollocks, and to f--- off!

I was at Roy's bedside with Stella's son Don, in Harlow General hospital, when a nurse brought in a fax sent by Jack. It read 'To Mr Roy Ruston – Commando, from Jack Russell, and The England Cricket Team in the West Indies...Dear Roy, Here's wishing you very speedy recovery.' Every player signed it. It caused a stir among the doctors and nurses, and Roy loved it. There was a copy of the *Sun* newspaper on Roy's bed. On the back page was a picture of Jack leaping in the air from a Courtney Walsh delivery, with the caption underneath reading: 'The jumping bean machine versus the mean machine'. Roy laughed at this saying, 'Your mate should have been with me and Fletch at Salerno; we were jumping around a bit!

My nephew Don went down to the cafeteria, which gave Roy and I some time alone. We spoke of dad, and the early days. He pointed down to his legs, like the rest of him painfully thin, saying, 'To think what these have carried me through bruv. Now look at them, bloody useless.' His feet were cold, so I put socks on them. He wanted a fag. He knew he shouldn't, but what did it mater now? I helped him out of bed and across the small room to a window, where he lit a hand-rolled cigarette, and took a few puffs. For a while he looked distant, alone with his thoughts. I stayed with him until late, and he kept reminding me of the long journey I had before me. He was worried I would be too tired to make it, but I didn't want to leave him. With our hands firmly locked together, we said our farewell. The look that passed between us told no lies.

The sporting luncheon got away to a fine start. After a good meal we settled to watch cricket on the big screen. The interview with Jack was much appreciated by those present. I thought, 'If I follow this with the auction before the live coverage, with Jack still fresh in their minds, one or two may find a deeper pocket.' We were about to draw the raffle when my nephew Don, who had been helping at the function, relayed the sad news of my brother's death. A numbing feeling spread though my body as I switched to auto pilot, and continued with the task at hand. I was like a zombie, as though I had been programmed.

When finally I got home, my pent-up feelings emerged and I broke down. I had lost not only my brother, but also my hero. My thoughts turned to the lovely Josie she would be heartbroken – and their daughter Georgia, whom Roy worshipped. Both would be inconsolable. His four sons – Roy, Stephen, Danny and Lee – all fine men, would comfort their mother and sister. Our sisters Maud and June would feel as though they had lost an arm, or worse. June's daughter Teresa worshipped her Uncle Roy and turned to him more often than her own father. The whole family would feel the pain.

The next day I sent this fax to Jack: 'I am full of sadness, Roy died at 5pm yesterday. I am finding it hard to bear; you will understand that more than most. Everything went well at the function. We made five plus. Will elaborate later. After hearing about Roy the going got tough. I'm wearing my St Nazaire tie it's helping. Give the lads this message from Roy – Re The Windies' 'The bigger they are, the Bigger they are!'

Jack faxed back from Room 866 at the Trinidad Hilton: 'I'm so sorry to hear about Roy. What can I say? You know where my thoughts are.' I did.

The funeral at St John's, Loughton was a moving occasion. Roy left his home of more than 40 years for the last time. The family was out in strength, and the cortège, led by a hearse adorned with flowers, slowly made its way to the church. As we sat in prayer, a tape of Nat King Cole singing 'Unforgettable' was played. I could think of no better song, and I would love to have sung it for him. But I don't think I would have been able to get one word out, I was too choked up. Around 200 people came to pay their last respects. Ex-Commandos from No 1, 2, and 3 stood to attention at the grave. Doug Fletcher, who had been with Roy at Scilly, Salerno and Vis Island in the Adriatic, where he and Roy were part of a protection squad for Field Marshall Tito, and fought side by side with the Partisans. The recent conflict in the former Yugoslavia upset Roy. He said, 'We lost a lot of good men helping them fight for their freedom. Now they are bloody well killing each other. What a waste.'

Now Doug was saying his farewell. He had brought a floral tribute in the shape of a Green Beret, complete with the silver dagger cap badge of No 2 Commando, which he placed on the coffin of his comrade as it was lowered. What special times they must have shared. Roy had once said to me, 'No offence bruv, but Fletch is more than a brother to me.' I understood what he meant. Commandos in full combat dress blew the Last Post. My floral tribute was in the shape of a piano. Jack and Aileen sent a wreath, which I laid next to mine. There were so many flowers; my brother was obviously much revered in his community.

Jack experienced a great deal of pain in Trinidad. The West Indies XI bowled out the England team for just 46 runs. The second lowest score by a touring England team in history. The press had a field day. Calling them turnips, one newspaper had superimposed a picture of each player on a turnip. It must have been humiliating for those involved. Jack, who had not been in the best of form on the tour thus far, was at an all-time low. Curtly Ambrose, the giant Windies fast bowler, virtually destroyed the England team single-handed.

Talk about coming back from the dead, the England team of 94 will go down in the history books for their re-group and attack attitude, putting up a magnificent performance to win the next match in Barbados. Without doubt, Alec Stewart's century in both innings was a major contributory factor. Had he been keeping wicket also it might have been a very different story. Mike Atherton had put his faith in this team and they eventually came good for him, although too late to win the series.

The last test was played in Antigua. Brian Lara, batting for the West Indies, broke the world record by making 375 runs in an innings, beating the previous record of 365 made by Sir Gary Sobers, which had stood for a number of years. Jack eventually caught Lara behind the wicket. The innings is recorded: Lara bowled Caddick, caught Russell 375. England played well, forcing a draw in which Jack played his part with a stubborn knock of 62, put on in a stand with Chris Lewis.

But the writing was on the wall. Jack hadn't performed well, and there had been a change in the Chairman of Selectors. The ex-Yorkshire and England Captain and bowler, Ray Illingworth, had been appointed. He was making it clear, from his villa in Spain, that he would make changes. Everyone knew he favoured Steve Rhodes, who kept wicket for Yorkshire, over Jack. Jack's lack lustre performance in the Windies had sealed his fate. But Illingworth might have had the decency to wait for the England team to return before announcing his decision. He effectively dropped both Jack and Chris Lewis whilst they were at the crease on the final day of a test match, where their performance had gained us a draw. Anyone reading a newspaper knew the pair had been dropped before they did! Man management? Scandalous.

I organised a special showing of the paintings Jack had brought back from the Caribbean. The media interview with Jack had a double edge, for every question about the recent tour, Jack, having answered, countered by saying how much the painting had helped him come through a difficult period. In future interviews, cricket, always given priority, and the painting, would go hand in hand. The public were now becoming increasingly aware of Jack Russell, 'the cricketer who paints'. The paintings from the tour sold rapidly, which was encouraging. Now, Jack would have to get his head down and play like a demon through the summer in an effort to regain his test place.

I had conceded that with the gallery to run, and a benefit year to co-ordinate, there would be little time for much else. I certainly had not considered any form of expansion at this stage when out of the blue came a phone call that would further complicate an already complicated year. The voice on the phone said, 'Is that the Jim Ruston who had a TV shop in Yate about 20 years ago?' 'Yes,' I replied, 'Who wants to know?' 'Derek Hutchings, remember me?' 'Derek you old bugger,' I shouted back at him. 'How are you? Or should I say where are you?' After some mild banter and not a little nostalgia, 'We were young and handsome then', and all that bollocks, Derek went on to say he now lived in Tenerife where he had a hotel, but had been in Bristol for the last two weeks negotiating with Carlsberg Tetley to buy three public houses they were offering for sale. One of these was The Bell Inn, Chipping Sodbury, right next door to where I was sitting. He said that Richard Horne of Chesterton's had told him that I had made enquiries about the freehold of the old pub.

I told Derek that I had inquired some months before; they were asking £160,000, and I thought it too much, and at the wrong time for us. Derek then made an offer I felt we could not refuse. 'What if I could sell it to you, for a little over half of that? Would you be interested? 'Is the Pope Catholic?' I answered. 'You don't change do you mate,' he laughed. Derek levelled with me saying he needed to get a deal agreed on The Bell immediately, to enable him to complete the purchase of the three pubs, he really only wanted one, but buying them in a package was financially advantageous. 'You don't change either, Derek,' I commented. I told my old acquaintance that I would give him a decision in 12 hours. He said his offer was subject to us being able to complete in tandem with his deal with Carlsberg.

A COCKNEY KID IN GREEN WELLIES

Luckily, the call from Derek had come on a rare day off for Jack. Together we entered the old premises of The Bell. It dated back to the early 1500s. Like many of the buildings in Chipping Sodbury, one is deceived by their outward appearance They are much bigger than you expect, and this was no exception. There would be room for a substantial showroom, offices, storeroom, kitchen, toilets and so on. Added to which, at the rear of the premises, was skittle alley, ideal for further storage and a workshop for picture framing. And what about considerable space on the first floor? We could let this as offices.

Once the initial excitement had subsided, we took stock of the condition of the building. I was confident it was OK structurally, but also conscious of the enormous amount of refurbishment it required. I said to Jack, 'This is your Shortwood Farm (I had told him of my good fortune in buying that.) We could do with this offer being made in 18 months' time, but here it is in our faces. It will be a hard uphill struggle, both physically and financially, but take it, and you will never look back,' I recommended. This time Jack needed no persuasion, saying 'I agree with you Jim, as long as you think you have the time to cope with it all.'

I rang Derek, and told him we would complete on 25 July as requested. By coincidence, he had been invited to watch Gloucestershire play South Africa on 7 July, in two days' time. I said I would meet up with him there. In the meanwhile I got the wheels rolling our end. We had less than three weeks to organise the finance and so on. Jack was busy with his cricketing commitments so it was left to me. It was great to see Derek Hutchings again after so many years, I told him, if these premises were as successful as the last I had taken over from him, I would be a happy man. I don't think Jack ever got to meet Derek, which was a pity. Derek is one of life's characters. Wherever he is, you can bet something is going down. I haven't seen him since, but I guess he is laying in the sun somewhere, and a beautiful girl won't be too far away!

If I hadn't found the premises above Worthington's, I wouldn't have met Richard Horne, who in turn could not have given Derek Hutchings my phone number. Small world, becoming even smaller, when you spread your wings, essential in business.

The coming summer, England would play host to two test nations: New Zealand and South Africa. For the latter, it would be their first visit here to play cricket since the damnable Apartheid. Jack and I considered a commemorative painting of the South Africa team walking out at Lord's. To this end Jack arranged, through Dennis Silk, then President of MCC, permission for me to enter the Pavilion and Long

Room on the day of the test to take photographs. Cameras are forbidden in the hallowed Pavilion; the rule is strictly enforced. I had some difficulty convincing one over-zealous steward, even with the letter signed by Dennis Silk, that I had permission to take pictures. I got some lovely shots, especially of the two opening batsmen for SA walking through the Long Room, to great applause from the members. Then I watched whilst the England lads walked through. When Steve Rhodes, in wicket-keeping garb passed me, it hurt. I thought 'Enjoy it Bumpy, [his nickname] Jack is right up your bum. Drop a catch, and your mate Illy will drop you.' Jack was playing out of his skin for his county, and I was confident he would get his England place back.

The Cheltenham Festival seems to come around quicker each year; soon I was in my space once more, only now with a slightly larger tent and a more varied display of pictures. We were on the verge of exchanging contracts on The Bell Inn, and Jack and I had devised a signalling system whereby I could indicate that we had exchanged. I waited for Giles Woodward, our solicitor, to call my mobile phone with news. Time was running out, there was only one week left before the completion date.

Gloucestershire were fielding, and after each over, as they changed ends, Jack looked towards my tent for a signal. I responded by shaking my head. I wore a distinctive blue hat then, which Jack said was always easy for him to spot. The day wore on; I rang Giles. 'Not yet. I'll let you know when I have,' he said with a sigh. When the call eventually came, Giles said simply, 'It's yours.' Looking out across the pitch I could see Jack was at my end, and in his customary crouching position. Impatiently, I waited for the end of the over, and for him to look towards me before walking to the far end. When the end of the over came, instead of looking my way, he trotted off down the pitch chatting with a couple of players as they ran. He was too far away to see me properly, and I was near to bursting. At the end of the next over he strolled back down the wicket looking directly towards me. I waited and waited, then nodded my head vigorously. Jack leapt, punching the air as he did so, and everyone looked to see what had caused his moment of exuberance. Only he and I knew that a milestone had been reached and turned, in our collaboration and his business future.

We had a great Cheltenham Cricket Festival. What with the new property deal secured, and a benefit cricket match where Jack's Gloucestershire Greats XI played a Rest of the World XI featuring Brian Lara, whom everyone wanted to see. Taking nothing away from the wonderful turnout of past and present cricket stars, who also came to honour Jack. The game attracted a capacity crowd, the atmosphere was wonderful, and it did the benefit coffers no harm either.

It was down to Eddie once more to make a start on getting our newly acquired premises fit to move into. This time it wouldn't be just a lick of paint. We were talking major repairs. Eddie was about a month into the refurbishment, and was working in very difficult conditions, where cold, damp and dust, were beginning to tell on him. He soldiered on without complaint, but I was concerned for him. I had just left him when a phone call came asking me to get an urgent message to my son-in-law. The message was concerning Eddie's brother Terry. It was serious. He had had a heart attack, and maybe died, the informant was uncertain. In semi darkness, and thinking of what to say, I groped my way into the bowels of the old Bell Inn where Eddie was hacking plaster from the wall, and told him to go at once to his mother's house. Eddie's family are very close. Terry was the eldest. Eddie had lost his dad in 1980. His mother Kay, an independent and thoroughly capable lady, now headed the family; she is a lovely woman, for whom I have the highest respect. Sadly the news was black. Terry had died in his sleep; his son Neil, failing to get any response from calling to his father, went into his room and found him laying peacefully in his bed. Eddie, despite pleas from me to take some time off, carried on working in the 'black hole', alone with his sorrow. As with everything, he dealt with the loss of his brother in his own way.

A local children's charity, which was involved in raising funds for an orphanage and hospital in Romania, asked me if I would consider taking a series of photographs in that country. These they would use in a slide presentation in their attempt to increase public awareness of plight of the children and the extreme shortages that existed in Romania. Despite the pressure of work, I agreed to go for a week; I really found it hard to refuse. The charity arranged a return flight and accommodation, and I gave my services, including all photographic materials, free. I flew out with a small party of volunteers. On arrival, we were met by an English-speaking Romanian guy, who drove us to the mining town of Petrosani.

Throughout the journey in the minibus, I soaked up the vast expanse of countryside. It was common to see a group of children walking along a road, which seemed to have no horizon. To where were they walking? I pondered. On driving through a small village, it became obvious that the children were on their way home from school; just how far they had walked remained a mystery.

After a four-hour drive we arrived in Petrosani, in darkness, and were shown into a small hotel in the centre of the town, where we met two more volunteers who had flown out the week previous. I was introduced to Paul Alan and Richard Gibson. The latter was, in fact the actor who played Herr Flick of the Gestapo in the TV series *'Allo, 'Allo*. Richard was in Romania to gather material for a possible TV documentary on the orphans' and their predicament. Richard and I built an instant rapport, and roomed together.

Richard opened the door on a sparsely furnished double room, which did have the luxury of an on en-suite facility, although there was no hot water, the toilet had no seat and the bath hadn't seen water for a decade. Richard raised his eyebrows and asked, 'Coffee Jim?' For the first of many times, I witnessed Richard's antics in conjuring up the magic brew. He placed a chair on the small rickety dressing table, on top of which he placed a biscuit tin, on top of which he rested an electric jug he had filled with water. Gingerly he removed the light bulb from its socket, into which he fiddled an adapter, then climbed down from his perch. We sat in darkness waiting for the jug to boil. Richard had brought the jug, coffee and biscuits, with him. Both the liquid and solid were welcome, albeit coffee without milk. There were practically no dairy products available in that region, or for that matter anywhere else in Romania.

'I hope you like omelettes, Jim,' said Richard, as we drank our coffee. 'There is precious little else to eat here.' The next morning at breakfast I saw what he meant. An omelette, a piece of grey bread, some jam, and to drink, a cup of hot sweet water. Richard had been drinking this all week, and had yet to discover what it was that made the water so sweet! Definitely not sugar, there wasn't any. The room where we ate also served as a restaurant and bar. The place was packed, mostly with miners having worked the night shift, and now taking a glass of something before going home. They eyed us with curiosity more than suspicion. The air was so thick with smoke it was almost impossible to see across the room. The stable diet appeared to be Vodka, very large glasses of the stuff consumed in silence.

The trustees of the charity were to meet the mayor of the town to discuss the problem of distribution of the aid they had sent. There seemed to be quite a discrepancy in the volume dispatched from UK to that which had arrived here. An English-speaking translator would be at the meeting to act as interpreter. Whilst we were assembled in the foyer of the town hall waiting for our audience with the mayor, an attractive young women walked through the door and joined us. Wearing a brown jacket with fur trimmed collar, matching skirt and knee-length boots, a chiffon scarf hugged her slender neck, as in perfect English, almost without a trace of an accent, she said, 'Hello, I am Lili Ghibon. I have come to translate for you.' In amongst the drab, grey, lifeless surroundings, she shone like a new pin.

The meeting went around in circles. The trustees were trying to establish exactly what had happened to the bulk of the aid they had sent, with the under-Mayor (the Mayor was tied up and could not see them) evading the issue as skilfully as any of our own politicians. To put it simple, there was a general acceptance that only 75 per cent of all aid coming into the country was getting through, 25 per cent was being ripped off. Later the same day, we met Adrienne, a feisty journalist with the local paper, who informed us that in fact the figures for the distribution of aid were the reverse. Only 25 per cent gets through the remainder is diverted. 'By whom?' we enquired. With a cynical laugh she replied. 'Anyone in authority, mostly those to whom the charities have entrusted it with in the first place.' Everyone in our party became deflated. We thought of all those people back home, who did so much to collect and donate items for the benefit of the orphaned children.

Lili said she was ashamed, and apologised for the way the charity was being treated. We assured her that she was not at fault, and not to take the blame for the unscrupulous, who took advantage of the situation. Lili told us she was a schoolteacher and that she had studied English at university, and now taught it at one of the big schools in the town. Her classes were overcrowded, and the school day long; material and books in particular were very scarce. She tried to photocopy as much as she could, but paper was short, and she had to pay for each copy. I said we could get her a photocopier. She said that would be wonderful, then added, 'But my headmaster will take it, and sell copies to others.' 'How can he, if you own it?' I asked. For a moment she became subservient, and looking down at her clasped hands, said, 'He can.' Now, I wanted to apologise to her, for mankind.

Lili said she had never been to England, but hoped one day she would make it. 'What would you most like to see,' I asked. 'As much as I can. The England of literature, places the writers and poets I studied wrote of', she replied. I thought immediately of Helene Hanff, who had wanted to visit England for 20 years before she finally made it, for the very same reasons as Lili. I thought it an injustice that this young woman was devoting her life to teaching English, and talking of England in this way, without ever having the chance of visiting. She earned around £12 per week, from which she could save practically nothing. 'I know it's just a dream,' she said.

I learned much during my brief visit to this incredibly poor country. The rich get richer, the poor poorer, but worst of all the weak weaker. Some doctors were taking medical sundries, syringes, vaccines, surgical gloves, bandages, ointments and so on. which had been donated by charities to the hospital where they worked, and using them on their private patients. I couldn't believe this could be true, when one of the aid workers confirmed it saying, 'We sent 12 gross of rubber gloves. The carton went in one door of the hospital and within minutes was out of the other.' On visiting the hospital in question we found the nurses without a rubber glove between them. The aid worker said that when she handed over a box of syringes, she had kept one back for herself, just in case. Sensible women. Had she needed an injection in an emergency, she would have had to buy one of the donated syringes back!

Visiting the orphanages was traumatic. Dozens of kids of all ages up to 16, when they have to leave, whether they have somewhere to go or not. I found it easier not to focus on any one child, but instead to look at a group. I kept my camera close to my face most of the time to hide my anxiety. Many of these kids have parents who have simply abandoned them. I do know what it is to have nothing; I don't know what it is to be unloved; it must be 10 times worse.

One morning in the early hours, we took the train to Bucharest. Having queued for our tickets the previous day (you think you've been in a queue? stand in one of theirs for several hours for a loaf of bread), which were just like the ones we had here just after the war, oblong cardboard things, we made our way to the station. The long single platform was crammed with travellers, many of whom were carrying battered cases; some carried boxes, others pickaxes, shovels and various tools of trade. A wire-fronted box containing chickens; another with ducks. One with rabbits. I have never before witnessed such a diverse colourful and interesting group of travellers. A huge engine, pulling a seemingly endless line of carriages, entered the station, and with an ear-shattering clatter screeched to a halt. We boarded the train and moved towards the sleeping carriages, and as we struggled through the aisle of the ancient coaches, you can imagine our surprise when we entered a brand new sleeper. I slid back the door of a compartment with two bunk beds, central heating and a basin with hot water, the first I had encountered since arriving here. It was dark, so unable to enjoy the landscape I got my head down.

We were met by Alexander, a friend of the charity, and a charming man, who took us to his flat, where his wife served us eggs, bacon and coffee with milk. Alexander worked at one of the best hotels in the capital, and by Romanian standards was quite well off. In his small but nicely furnished flat stood a quality colour television with satellite, and a hi-fi system. He also had a car. Thanking our host for the lovely meal,

I said, 'So you can in fact get most things here in Bucharest.' 'Yes James, if you have plenty...' He gestured rubbing the forefingers on his right hand against his thumb. Capitalism, working at its best, right here in Eastern Europe!

I have recently learned that Alexander was killed in a road accident. It is with a sense of sorrow and compassion that I write of this. Alexander had a beautiful wife and two lovely children, whom he obviously adored. He spoke with great optimism about their future. He very generously gave me a wristwatch, similar to the one I got for my 18th birthday. There was no way I could refuse his gesture. Rest in peace, Alex. Forget fairness, there just isn't any.

We had an audience with the British Consul who denied our allegations about the proportions of aid being ripped off, although he conceded that is was probably higher than that which the Romanian government admitted. Their attitude, in general terms were thus: 'People in the UK are sending aid to Romania for our people, and one way or another they are getting it. Where's the problem?' There's not much you can say to that!

Bucharest is a beautiful city. The palace built by the zealot Nicolae Ceausescu is stunning. There are as many floors under the ground as there are above it. It also houses an underground car park for 2,000 cars. This was his HQ from where he directed his secret police force of torturers and murderers. Apart from Adrienne, who as a journalist was out to expose all wrong doings, the average Romanian, even now with the new 'openness', was still not prepared to talk against the authorities, other than in a whisper. It will take years before they stop looking over their shoulders.' Alexander told us that before Ceausescu was executed for crimes against his people, they were not allowed to have more than two friends at any one time in their apartment. If they did they could be accused of holding a meeting, which was strictly forbidden. One can't imagine living under such oppression.

We returned to Petrosani, and made ready to leave via a different airport. Richard and I had got on marvellously well together, and with others visited an area where gypsies dwelled. We parked the minibus nearby and went into a bar. I say a bar; more a few tables and chairs with a counter. We talked with a dark-haired young man, every inch a Romany, and looking not a little villainous. He told us, in broken English, that he was a musician. He had had the chance to go to America, but the authorities would not give him a passport. 'You see, I am gypsy, they don't like us,' he confided. 'What instrument do you play' asked Richard. 'Saxophone,' he replied. 'Would you play for us? We would pay some money,' Richard offered. At this suggestion the young man got quite indignant, and gesturing with both hands said he would play for nothing, then with a sad look on his face and looking down at his feet continued, 'But my saxophone is no good.'

After much encouragement, coming mainly from Richard, the young musician sent a boy off to fetch his instrument. He was clearly embarrassed when it arrived. It was really only fit for the scrap heap. Bruised and dented, and with no tension left on the keys (rubber bands were needed to hold them down on the pads), the musician handed the instrument to Richard, who had said he could play the sax, for appraisal. Richard Gibson is as game as they come, but try as he might, all he could get from the instrument was a squeak. Turning to me he said, 'No bugger can play this bloody awful thing, Jim. I wished I hadn't insisted he fetch it. Now I'm embarrassed.' With that, Richard handed back the sax.

Our young Romanian friend, eager to please, took the reed from the instrument and dipped it in brandy to soften it. Then he stood, and after a few scales, played the most wonderful music I have ever heard played on a saxophone. I asked Richard, 'How good is he?' He replied. 'Better than anyone I've ever heard. Just what would this guy sound like with a decent instrument.' Think of the suppressed talent there must be in this and other countries, where people have lived for so long under the cosh. Let us pray one day this talent will emerge.

On our way out of Petrosani, we dropped the lovely Lili off at her home, a block of flats among a whole lot of blocks of flats, grey and foreboding. She looked a vision of hope against a backdrop of sadness. I took a photograph of her, and as I did, made a conscious pledge that some day soon I would get her to England. Then when her pupils ask, 'Have you ever been to England Miss?' she can look them in the eye and say 'Of course,' and tell them of her visit

On the way to the airport, we stayed overnight with the parents of one of the Romanian friends of the charity, on their small farm, a single-storey dwelling, a few sheds and a field. I can say without hesitation, that we were shown the finest hospitality, and enjoyed a meal fit for a king. The bread was freshly baked, right there in the oven; the milk came from a cow tied outside; and the vegetables were from the garden. The outside loo, a shed with a hole in the ground, reminded me of Kingston Seymour. Richard and the others were a bit shocked by it, though. In fact this farm had electricity, which we never had when we were evacuees. It was October and getting colder by the day, and I wondered what it was like here in winter when the snow came. A shiver went down my spine at the prospect.

A COCKNEY KID IN GREEN WELLIES

The Romanians I met were fiercely proud, but many were also angry that they had been misled into thinking communism was the ideal. With a new freedom of movement slowly dawning, they now compared their living standards with those of the Western world. 'How long will it take for us to catch up. Will we ever? they asked. I also found the 'dog eat dog' syndrome far more obvious, and without shame, than it is anywhere else I have been.

At the airport we spent what Romanian money we had left on large Vodkas, By now I was getting a taste for it. With a little vermouth, one had a very nice Vodka martini. My everlasting image of Richard 'Herr Flick' Gibson was of him sitting up in bed in his striped nightgown on a freezing cold morning. There was no heating, the town communal boiler, from which everyone gets their heating and hot water, had not yet been fired. Richard, clasping a cup of coffee between his hands, said, 'Jim, isn't this bloody desperate? It's much too grown up for me. I want to go home!'

The England cricket team to tour Australia the coming winter had been announced, but Jack was not among those selected. Steve Rhodes would keep his place as England's, or should I say Ilingworth's, first choice wicket keeper. Alec Stewart would deputise if Bumpy either got injured or lost form. In fairness to Rhode's he had played quite well through the summer; first against New Zealand, who then were not up to much, followed by South Africa, who played some exciting cricket, looked promising, but still needed more competition after such a long time away from the test arena.

Jack had been thrown a lifeline in the guise of a standby contract. He would be paid a fee to keep himself match fit in readiness to fly out to Australia should the call come. Jack said with optimism, 'At least no one else is in the frame for the keepers job. My time will come again.' It did. But it wasn't Steve Rhodes who got injured, it was Alec Stewart. He broke a finger and, whilst he could still bat, could not risk keeping if called upon to do so. Jack was called up. It was a marvellous Christmas present, doubly so because it meant he could enjoy the celebrations at home for the first time in eight years, then fly out to Sydney. Once back in the squad, he wouldn't feel so isolated from the international scene, and would snatch his chance when it came.

LILI IN LONDON

Whilst Jack languished in Australia waiting for the opportunity to put on the gloves and stand once more behind the wicket in a test match, I filled my days running between our existing gallery and the property that we had acquired next door. Occupying two lots of premises is expensive, so I was anxious to push the refurbishment along as fast as possible. Whilst I had discussed costs with Jack before he left, he was naturally concerned about expenditure; I was keeping him informed of progress by fax. In some instances he was beginning to 'nit pick'. Normally, this is not Jack's style, and I suspected it was largely due to his frustration in not getting any cricket. After a few differences of opinion I sent a vitriolic message which read: 'I can always stop work on everything until you return, if you're unhappy with things here.' 'No, no,' came his instant reply. 'I am sure you know you what are doing.'

I thought 'Thanks for the vote of confidence. Please, please, somebody give him a bloody game to shut him up!' Unfortunately it wasn't to be, despite what had been a below average tour for Rhodes, Illy stuck with him. The critics were screaming for Jack to be given the gloves but to no avail. I was equally frustrated, not just for Jack, but because of the transition I was trying to bring about. I had to re-let our present premises, then try to arrange the move so as not to disrupt business too much. I knew that with the best will in the world, there would be a loss of trading whilst this took place. Juggling with three balls in the air, just for good measure, I threw up another two trying to co-ordinate the letting of the new offices we had refurbished on the first floor of our new premises at the same time. The rental income would help our depleted cash flow. Inevitably, there was a period of about six weeks after moving out of our old premises before our new gallery was open to the public. It was a difficult period for all of us, not least of all me; if I don't sell, I don't earn!

Jack returned from Australia with one or two small paintings. I would like to dispel a myth: Jack does not, and never has, painted or sketched during a cricket match that he is involved in, even if only as 12th man. He uses his artistic skills as therapy on days off, and is most productive when playing well. One discipline effects the other. If the cricket is turning pear shaped, his painting lacks heart. The two instances that demonstrate this best are the tours of South Africa 1995/6 and West Indies 1997/8. The former produced a flourish of paintings with expressive images, capturing an atmosphere of lightness and contentment. The latter quite the opposite. One can sense the torment symbolised in dark moody scenes, as the artist laid bare his emotion on canvas.

A COCKNEY KID IN GREEN WELLIES

Before the domestic season got under way, from colour notes made on his recent tour, and the previous one to the West Indies, Jack painted two stunning pictures: one of the win in Barbados, the other of the win in Adelaide. The Barbados painting captures the moment when Curtly Ambrose's stumps are sent flying from the ball delivered by Chris Lewis that won the match. The one of Adelaide shows Devon Malcolm taking the wicket, which won us the fourth test. Sadly, and yet again, we lost a series, with Australia keeping the Ashes.

We made limited edition prints from both paintings, and I trotted off around the counties to get them signed by the players that had played in the matches they commemorated. This was no mean task, as it meant visiting 14 different county cricket grounds. Jack had previously contacted the players concerned, and got their agreement to sign. Whilst it was a lot of fun, it was tiring. First I went to the indoor school at Finchley, where Middlesex train to get Mike Gatting, Angus Fraser, Phil Tufnell and Mark Ramprakash to sign. Gatt was captain then, and he was marvellous rallying his colleagues around so as not to delay me any more than possible, a real gentleman. There are 350 prints in each edition, so players who had taken part in both games were asked to sign 700 prints!

Up to Old Trafford for Atherton and Crawley. To Derby for Devon Malcolm and Phil DeFreitus. Taunton for Caddick. The Oval for Graham Thorpe and Alec Stewart. Goochie at Chelmsford, and Trent Bridge for Chris Lewis. Chris, who would have to sign both editions, seemed pre-occupied, and kept getting up from the table and walking out of the room. I thought this strange. Feeling awkward, I said I was sorry if it was inconvenient for him. He told me that he had just been given news that someone had set fire to his mother's house! Little wonder he appeared edgy, I would have been climbing the wall. Thankfully, no one was injured in the blaze. What's wrong with the world?

When I got down to Southampton for Robin (Judge) Smith to sign, I was aghast to find a pre-season friendly game about to start. The schedule had changed, with Robin padded up ready to bat at No 3. I resigned myself to having to wait until the end of play. However, Judge had other ideas. I laid the prints out on tables in the Pavilion, and Judge signed away saying: 'Jim, if we lose a wicket I will have to run'. As he signed the last print, the familiar shout of 'Ow is ee' went up. Judge shook my hand, at the same time saying 'Give my best to Jack', and scuttled off to the wicket. A lovely man, one of Jack's closest friends in cricket. Both editions are almost sold out, making them real collectors items.

Caroline Duchess of Beaufort died. With her family and many friends, I attended the funeral in the church at Badminton, and sitting in the pew where I had sat so many times before, my mind filled with wonderful memories of this warm, yet feisty Lady. I recalled the day of her daughter Anne's wedding. I was filming it on video, and immediately after the service Caroline approached me saying, 'You didn't film me grabbing my granddaughter and marching her into the vestry did you Jim?' 'No,' I replied. 'I didn't see you do it.' She continued, 'The only child behaving badly would have to be ours. I got a black look from one woman, and thought yes, just say something and I'll give you one too!' I truly believe she would have done so!

After the internment we were all invited into the house for a drink. Even though filled with sadness, her family knew she would have wished it. Such is the kindness and generosity of the Beauforts.

Caroline had been diagnosed as having cancer of the bowel. Having suffered something much milder, although still life threatening, with my pancreas, I felt deep compassion for her. She had been so sympathetic towards me at the time of my own illness saying, 'You turned to an old friend, and it let you down. She was referring to my fondness of the whisky bottle then. What could I say to her now? I vowed not to mention it, but she referred to it as a 'bore'.

With the passing of the duchess, would things change much at Badminton, I wonder? Given time, would the Duke marry Miranda? She has certainly been a most patient and loyal friend to him, for 25years to my knowledge. (He did)

With the West Indies due to tour the coming summer, it meant Courtney Walsh would not be available to play for Gloucestershire. Having taken the captaincy the previous year, with Jack in the role of Vice-Captain, the press had dubbed the formidable duo Little and Large. In the absence of Large, the captaincy was handed to Jack. He relished the challenge realising that it would be for one year only, which suited him. Courtney would take over on his return. Jack had previously made it clear that he did not want the captaincy. Captaincy is demanding, and he thought he would struggle to give his best in the role whilst still playing for England. He was ever confident that it was only a matter of time before he would be re-called to international duty.

Having accepted the challenge, Jack formulated a plan of action. He sent directives to each player at Gloucestershire CCC outlining his plan for the season, making it clear he wanted 100 per cent effort to create a winning attitude. 'If we believe it, we can achieve it' was his motto. He managed to persuade eight of the players to join him training in March instead of waiting until April, as they were contracted to do. More would have but for existing commitments. His method was to pay off.

With the 50th anniversary of VE Day being celebrated everywhere, I drove to London and stood outside my gran's old flat in Stepney, more or less on the spot where the Five, with our cousins, had a bonfire all those years ago. Filled with nostalgia, my emotions ran wild as I recalled the events and relations to whom we were so close, who were now out of touch. We had shared so much in an effort to survive, then almost unnoticed, gradually drifted apart. Tearing myself away, I hurried back to Nailsea where I had arranged to meet Stella and our niece June. The village, now more a town, held a bonfire and firework display to mark the ending of hostilities 50 years ago. It felt strange, somehow flat, to those of us who lived through it. I don't know what I expected to feel. Stella looked at me and said, 'The important thing is that you and I are here with our memories Jim, and I'm glad we came.'

Amidst headlines on the sporting pages of various newspapers,' such as 'Jack's men never say die', 'Gutsy Glo'shire win nail biter', 'Russell steers his boys to last ball victory' and 'Last Gap Russell is The Hero', we opened the new gallery to both press and public.

I was so proud of the way the gallery looked. Eddy had done a magnificent job on all the building work, and the interior decoration carried out by Gordon put the finishing touch. Both are superb tradesmen, the gallery is a tribute to their skill.

It was a glorious summer, in which Jack got his long-awaited recall to the England Test Team. He did it in true 'Boy's Own' fashion, straight from the pages of childhood fantasy. Gloucestershire were playing Lancashire at Cheltenham. It was Jack's chance to show England captain Mike Atherton he meant business. Chairman of Selectors Ray Illingworth was also watching the game from the committee tent. He had travelled down from the north to watch the cricket, and to meet with his fellow Selectors at the Queen's Head Hotel to select the side to represent England in the fourth test at Old Trafford.

Leading from the front, Jack steered the Glo'shire lads to a 10- wicket win over the visitors. With Lancashire wicket's falling faster than shares on Black Monday (22 March 1973), Illingworth was heard to say, 'It can't be the pitch, Russell made it look easy enough.' Such praise from one who had said Jack couldn't bat! At this stage in the season Jack was averaging 47.

As was now customary for me at Cheltenham, I watched and cheered from my tent. It was so hot I didn't know whether to stand inside or out of it. Jack's England call was Gloucestershire's loss; with three tests left, he would hope to play in them all. During the second week of the festival Jack was at Old Trafford with the England team, facing Courtney, Curtly and the rest. England needed just 94 runs to win the game and level the series. Wickets were falling rapidly. Surely not another batting collapse, echoing Trinidad the previous year?

When Jack joined John Crawley at the wicket, 47 runs were still needed. 'Creepy' had been there for an hour, and was stuck on 13. Jack, in great form with the bat, took the game to the Windies, and jollying his partner along, ran some quick-fire singles. Then he hit Kenny Benjamin to the boundary twice, and when Curtly Ambrose returned to the attack, the cheeky little terrier pulled him with a mighty swing. Curtly wasn't amused, but it was too late, England were home.

Michael Parkinson rang and asked if I could arrange an interview with Jack. Although Jack had met Michael before, I had not. I was not disappointed when I did. Unpretentious, he introduced himself with hand outstretched saying: 'Michael Parkinson, pleased to meet you Jim. Thanks for organising this for me. What a lovely gallery, and what fantastic pictures, so varied. I knew Jack painted, but had no idea he was so prolific.' Jack told Michael during his interview how, when playing at The Oval, before a game started, he usually slipped along to the Imperial War Museum and sat in the World War One Trench Experience for inspiration. With the final test in the current series about to take place at The Oval, he hoped to repeat this.

Michael was excited at the prospect, and asked if photographs could be taken of Jack in the mock-up trench. Our friends at the IWM were as helpful as ever, and agreed to it. We arrived at the museum towards the end of the day, just as the public were leaving. It was quite a struggle for Jack to get himself over the wire and into the trench. Chris Dowling held the barbed wire down, whilst I pushed Jack over the top. 'Sorry mate,' I apologised, as Jack sprawled among the life-like figures of soldiers in the trench. He grinned back at me as he took up his position amongst the soldiers about to go 'over the top'. He was in his element. The interview with Parkinson, complete with the pictures at the War Museum appeared in *The Telegraph*, the day after Jack's heroic stand against the Windies fast bowlers. The headline read: Battle Hardened Russell Sticks to his Guns – In The Line of Fire. Chris Lander in the *Mirror* wrote: Jack Puts Knife In. *The News of the World* said: Man Of War.

In the final test at The Oval Jack Invited Norman and Janet Walters as his guests, and I sat next to them. Despite having been at Gloucestershire CCC for so many years, it was the first time either of them had watched Jack, a favourite of them both, in a test match. They were not to be disappointed. It was yet another pressure situation for him. There was about an hour of play left, and the West Indian pacemen threw everything they could at both Jack and his partner Graeme Hick. I swear I saw a kitchen sink flying through the air! Jack stood defiant in his crab-like stance. He was getting hit about the body, but deftly avoiding a 'beamer' from Ambrose, managed to keep him at bay. When play resumed the next day, Jack went on the make 91 before Ambrose finally got him with a real good un.

Courtney Walsh, Jack's Gloucestershire team mate, took his 300th test wicket during this match, thereby joining the ranks of those with a similar claim – such as Marshall, Botham, Khan, Hadlee, Trueman etc. There would be much for the Glos supporters to talk about.

After the match I congratulated Jack on his magnificent performance. His response was typical: 'With the article and pictures of me at the War Museum about to appear in the press, I had to do something, didn't I? The timing of both had been perfect – copybook stuff. Michael Parkinson, in glowing terms, had praised Jack's performance. Jack is justly proud of this; the more so coming from one he admires

I was equally proud of Jack. And as I strolled in the failing light through the streets of London on my way back to the Victory Club, quite a walk, I stopped for a moment on Westminster Bridge to admire the floodlit Houses of Parliament and Big Ben, the symbol of London personified. My mind was buzzing. I would have to turn in a sales performance to match Jack's effort. And so began the ongoing duel between us, each trying, in his own sphere, to outperform the other, for the benefit of both. A challenge eagerly accepted, and enjoyed.

It was no surprise, although history tells me never to assume, that Jack's name was announced in the England party to tour South Africa the coming winter. 'Keep this up Jack, and you will challenge Frank Sinatra for the most comebacks!' I joked.

The season drew to a close. Gloucestershire, under Jack's captaincy finished fifth in the County Championship, the highest placing for some years.

We held a most successful going away party at the gallery for Jack, at which we sold quite a few pictures. Time and commitments permitting, Jack would paint and bring back a number of scenes from South Africa. We had commissions for wildlife, landscapes and, of course Cape Town and Table Mountain. Chris Coley and his partner Audrey George would be in SA at the same time as Jack. Audrey's son Cuan is a ranger on a reserve in Zimbabwe, and had agreed to show Jack around the 130,000 acre Humani ranch where he works. The prospect to be among the first England Cricket Team to tour SA since the end of Apartheid, and the chance to capture wonderful images on canvas, fired Jack's imagination. 'If you meet President Mandela Jack, get me a signed copy of his book, *Long Walk to Freedom'*, I requested with tongue in cheek.

The weeks went by then a hushed voice came over the telephone, 'Jim it's Jack. I can't speak any louder, listen carefully. Guess who is sitting not six feet away from me? It's only the great man himself Nelson Mandela. I just had to ring you.' 'Thanks a million mate, this may be the closest I ever get to him. I wish I were there beside you,' I answered. Jack went on to tell me how when he was introduced to the President he said, 'It is an honour to meet you Jack.' Jack replied the honour was all his. 'By the way Jim, don't worry about a signed book. It is arranged. The President is going to sign one for each of the team and I will get an extra one for you.' We said our goodbyes, for a while I stood inanimate, with the phone still in my hand. It had been so unexpected. Jack was thousands of miles away, close to my hero, someone I consider the greatest statesman of all time, and he instinctively thought of me. I cherished the book when it arrived.

Jane hadn't arrived for work, and there was no phone call explaining why. Although father and daughter, Jane and I have a very professional relationship, separated from family life. Time went by and I got anxious. Eventually Eddy phoned to say Jane had had an accident. The roads were icy and a car travelling towards her skidded across the road into her path crashing into her car. She was badly bruised, suffering from whiplash, and traumatised by the accident. Her car was a write off. It was more than three months before she was fit to work regularly again. It took a further three years and the threat of court action, before the other driver's insurance company agreed compensation for Jane's injuries, although he was 100 per cent at fault. Now when it's icy, she leaves her car at home.

We were extremely busy in the gallery at the time of Jane's accident, so life became difficult for me to say the least. Jack had already completed a few small paintings in SA, and sent them back via John Edrich. Light and vibrant, the images portrayed the exuberant mood Jack was in. He was batting like a demon, and the South African's were unable to get him out. Thus far he had batted for 621 minutes without being dismissed, during which he made his highest first class score to date, 129 not out. The press headings read: 'Boks Can't Crack Jack' and 'Duracell Man Russell Bats On and On'.

The first test in Centurion Park was spectacular. Not the cricket I hasten to add, but the electrical storm and huge downpour that washed everything out. It was a shame, both for England who were in a good position when the umpires pulled the plug on safety grounds (they feared a player might get struck by lightning), and for Jack who having done much to put England in a winning situation was currently on 50 not out in the second innings. The press headings read: 'Jack Has A Stormer', 'Electric Russell Hits Out'. A draw was announced, but had the storm not prevailed, the series outcome could have been very different.

The second test match, which took place in Johannesburg, will go down in the history books of great English sporting achievements on more than one count. On a hiding to nothing, only a supreme effort would save the match and prevent England going one down in the series. Skipper Mike Atherton played one of the greatest innings of all time; his unbeaten 185 runs spanned 11 hours at the crease. When Robin Smith went, after a stoic performance, it was left to Jack to partner his skipper until the end of play, and so force a draw. This he did, for 4 hours and 37 minutes, in the most defiant mood of his career. During his long innings Jack made just 29 runs. He was there to support his captain, not take chances. An uplifting moment in English cricket; one surely confined to folklore. For years to come lovers of sport will talk of Atherton and Russell in Jo'Burg 95.

Unprecedented in cricket history (save, I think, for the controversial Bodyline series) an early motion, tabled by Liberal MPs Nigel Jones (Cheltenham) and Don Foster (Bath) was brought in the House of Commons congratulating the two cricketers on their epic stand, and was unanimously applauded. This could only happen in England, the mother of democracy. During the same game, Jack took the world record of 11 dismissals in a test match, beating Bob Taylor's previous standing of 10. Co-incidentally Bob was there to witness it, and presented Jack with an award. Furthermore, the two heroes of the moment jointly picked up the Man of the Match award. Telegrams of congratulations flooded in to the gallery. One from Sir Paul Getty read: Jack – 'Thankyou for enriching my life. Paul.' I sent this message to Jack by fax:

It was Rorke's drift again. Any moment they would throw spears, and jab with assegais; after all they had tried everything else! You and Athers alias the two VCs Melville and Coghill, rescued the British flag. What a scrap! I will take great pleasure in reminding the descenters' of '94 when Glos played SA at Neville Road. Despite bringing the game to a boring draw, you played so defiant an innings as to not let the opposition get any batting. The only time I ever heard anyone boo you. They just didn't understand what you were doing. You won the mind game then, and I bet Cronje is thinking of it right now. You had them beat the day you stepped foot in their country mate.

The press went ballistic. Photos of Jack and Mike covered their pages, with comment like, 'On Top Of The World' describing Jack's world record. Suddenly all the critics loved him, claiming 'I never said he couldn't bat' and 'It wasn't me'. Rats.

It was all heady stuff. What a day Jack had had, but it was far from over yet. Unbeknown to Jack, Paul Romaines, his colleague and coach at Gloucestershire, had booked tickets for Aileen to fly out to SA. This would be the first time Jack's wife had ever flown, let alone been on an England cricket tour. That she arrived on such an epic day was just meant to be. Life is often sweet, but I don't think it gets much sweeter. Aileen was collected from the airport and ushered up to Jack's room, whilst delaying tactics prevented him discovering her sooner. When he finally got away from well wishers and climbed the stairs to his room, opening the door he noticed someone sitting on his bed. He was thinking 'What the...' when Aileen got to her feet saying, 'It's me.' Only they know what happened then!

How could I follow this? I framed up the five canvasses Jack had sent back and sold them in as many days. I had made a start. Now I would organise a preview and open day at the gallery to show the paintings I hoped Jack would return with.

When I returned to work after the Christmas holiday, one of the first things I did was to write to Michael Doggart at the publishers HarperCollins. Jack and I had discussed getting his autobiography published. Although at this stage Jack had written copious notes on his life, there was still much to do before a book could be written. I had noticed that both Ian Botham and David Gower had their books published by CollinsWillow, the sports imprint of HarperCollins, and conceded, if they were good enough for them... The fact that the publisher had a specialist arm for sports books also appealed. My initial phone call produced the name of Michael Doggart as the man to whom I would need to address my proposal.

Jack had always had a good relationship with Peter Hayter the cricket journalist for the *Mail on Sunday*, and we both thought of asking him to co-write Jack's autobiography. Peter agreed at once to do it, saying he was delighted to be asked. With this in place, and armed with scrap books, photographs and publicity on Jack's art, I arrived at the publisher's offices in Fulham Palace Road London.

My meeting with Michael Doggart, although informal, was most productive. I did my usual presentation with much gesticulating, and 'the reason I have chosen you to publish Jack's book' (aren't you lucky and so on). Then, as though an after thought, I threw in the idea of a book of paintings to follow the autobiography. I left content in the knowledge that I had done enough to convince Michael that a book on Jack Russell would be a winner. Three months passed (perhaps they were unsure of success) before I received a letter outlining an offer for the publication of an autobiography, and yet another month before receiving a draft contract. Following this I made an agreement with Peter Hayter to co-write the book. We would have to get the draft manuscript to the publisher by October. Publication was scheduled for May 97.

Jack returned jubilant from SA bringing with him 17 wonderful paintings. His performance on the field of play reflected in the images he had captured on canvas. During the first 36 hours of our exhibition we sold 14 of the paintings. Jack was ecstatic, as was I. It was nice to have Jack back in the gallery, albeit for a short time. Somewhat to his surprise, he had been selected to play for England in the cricket world cup one-day series. Now, as far as Ray Illingworth was concerned, Jack was the *crème de la crème,* and could do no wrong. He determined to have him in the side, whereas skipper Mike Atherton would have preferred Alec Stewart in the batsman/keeper role, which in fairness had worked well in one day cricket. On this all-important occasion, Illy overruled his captain. Not a good decision, it further aggravated an already fragile relationship between the two.

The world cup series was disappointing for England. They failed to adapt to the new style of 'pinch hitting' introduced by the ultimate winners, Sri Lanka. Sri Lanka, who until now were considered an easy touch, took the other teams in the competition by storm. It had worked for them, in that environment, on those pitches. The tactic has not worked since for anyone. When in doubt, play cricket. We were not alone in falling for the three card trick, thinking the one-day game had changed dramatically and adjusting our tactics accordingly. It was a one-off. In the world cup four years on, Sri Lanka finished bottom of the pile.

Jack, always newsworthy, had threatened to quit the series after tournament chiefs tried to ban him from wearing his trade mark floppy hat. He had worn it in every game for both county and country since receiving it from his county, 14 years previously The organiser, Pilcom, demanded he don the blue hat he had been issued with for the series. Faxes flew around between the series technical committee headed by Sunil Gavaskar and Lord's. Common sense prevailed, and Jack was allowed to keep his favourite headgear. A few years later, 'The Hat' came under fire again, with much more serious consequences for Jack.

Captain Muriel Sims of the Salvation Army had been travelling to and from Romania supporting a hospital and an orphanage, since the time of the demise of the despot dictator Ceausescu. I asked her if she could arrange to bring Lilli Ghibon over here for an educational holiday. I would pay her airfare, and she could stay with my wife and me. After going through the necessary procedures, Lili was granted a visa, and arrived at Heathrow. The indefatigable Muriel, now over 70 years old, met Lili at the airport and brought her to Bristol.

Lili was thrilled to be in England, and eagerly absorbed everything she saw. The England cricket team were playing India at Lord's, so I took Lilli with me to see her first cricket match. Like all visitors to this country, she most wanted to see London. I had travelled up on the Thursday. The following day Joyce put Lili on the train at Bristol Parkway. I observed her as she stood wide-eyed on the platform at Paddington in disbelief that she was actually in the city she had longed for so many years to visit. I said, 'Today Lili, I will show you as much of London as we can squeeze in. And tomorrow, you will see a crazy game you will fail to understand.'

We took the sightseeing tour bus. You buy one ticket and can get on and off when you like. We managed to take in the National Art Gallery in Trafalgar Square, and I photographed her feeding pigeons. St Pauls, and St Mary le Bow, where I tried to explain the significance of my cockney heritage. We saw the site where the Globe Theatre stood. Walked down Cornhill. Visited the Tower of London, Houses of Parliament and Buckingham Palace. I took her in cafes, bookshops, museums and for a pot of tea at The Hilton, and photographed her beside a Rolls-Royce. I loaded her down with brochures and magazines about London and its history.

Exhausted, we sat in the restaurant at the Victory Club and browsed over the menu. Lili was not a gourmet by any stretch of the imagination. She was used only to plain and simple cooking, vegetables and meat when available. Omelettes of course! Most of the dishes we consider as 'everyday', she didn't even recognise. 'Have you had a nice day? Is it what you expected? London I mean,' I asked. 'Jim, I am finding it so hard to take everything in, I am overwhelmed. I promised myself not to be. I would take it as it came, with interest, but not surprise. I am embarrassed to admit that I am in a state of shock. No one in my country could imagine this; they would have to see it for themselves.'

We took a taxi to Lord's and found our seats in the Tavern stand. I couldn't have staged it any better for my guest. Jack was on an overnight score of 69 when he walked to the wicket with Graham Thorpe at the start of the day's play. Jack and I had discussed this test match before he left, and he had said 'Jim, I can feel a ton coming on. One is due.' 'If you feel it Jack, you'll get it, and I will be there to watch you.' I responded. There was another reason for my wanting to be in London, apart from Lili that is; Christies in Knightsbridge were conducting a specialist cricket auction that very day. Jack was interested in two of the lots: one a pair of wicket-keeping gloves, the other an England touring blazer, the early pattern you rarely see now. Both belonged to the former England wicket keeper Keith Andrew, who played in the early 60s. The gloves were of extra special interest as they were signed by the legendary keeper Bert Oldfield. 'Somehow, I will get to the auction and try to get them for you mate,' I had promised Jack.

The atmosphere at Lord's was electric, as Jack, sometimes orthodox, sometimes crab-like, nudged and nurdled his way towards 100. I could hardly bear it. I explained briefly to Lili what it meant to make 100 in a test match, and to do it a Lord's was every player's dream. With a flurry of strokes Jack got his ton, and the crowd went wild as he leapt in the air punching skywards with his fist. Everyone in the ground stood in applause. You won't see a better standing ovation than the one we were privileged to witness. I wanted to stay and watch Jack, but time was running out at the auction room. The journey, by taxi via Hyde Park, seemed to take forever, but we finally arrived outside Christies auction room.

There were just three lots to go before ours. Phew, it had been close. I got both lots for a little under both Jack's and my own estimate, then had to wait for the auctioneer to send the list of lots containing ours down to the cashier. Having paid, I cadged a posh Christies carrier bag in which I stuffed the items, then hailed a cab back to Lord's. Lili followed, completely bewildered. She must have been thinking. 'This man is mad.' I suppose I am – a little.

Back at Lord's once more my dilemma widened. How was I going to get the goodies to Jack? I was determined he should have them as a further reward for his century. England's Innings had come to an end with Jack making 124, and people were milling about waiting for play to resume. As I approached the hallowed pavilion I caught sight of Sir Colin Cowdrey. He was standing just inside the door. I rushed up and asked, 'Would you please give this bag to Jack Russell for me?' With a huge grin he replied, 'Ah Russell, batsman isn't he? Keeps wicket as well! I will be delighted to be the courier.' I later learned from Jack, that Sir Colin had burst into the England dressing room in the middle of a team talk from coach David Lloyd. On his way across the room to where Jack was sitting, he tripped over a pile of kit, and almost landed in Jack's lap! Bumble carried on with the talk as though nothing had happened! Jack kidded the rest of the lads saying the MCC had given him a present for getting a ton. He loves a wind- up. He can take one as well.

I took Lili to the airport. I was sad to see her leave. I had so enjoyed being able to show her a little of England. As a parting gift, apart from the case full of clothes and accessories Joyce and the girls had given her, I gave her my trusty portable typewriter. It had served me well for years, and had been my constant companion in Spain.

With the property market in recovery, Joyce and I were desperately seeking to move. We were looking for a needle in a haystack, a cottage to renovate in the Chipping Sodbury area. Jane spotted an advert in a local newspaper for a cottage for sale, about half a mile from our art gallery. Clutching the paper in my hand, I drove out to see it. I needed no more than a cursory glance to know that this was it. It appeared still lived in, just. No price had been mentioned in the advert, so I telephoned the agent in Yate to enquire, and then the fun began. I was informed that offers were being invited for the freehold, and the closing date was in two weeks' time. There were only two days left to view, one of which fell on my birthday, so I booked an appointment thinking 'Lucky Jim?'

The cottage had been in the same family for the best part of the century. It was now being sold to comply with conditions in a will. The sale had caused a certain amount of acrimony between the beneficiaries, so communication was zero. Unable to get a price guide from the agent, I had to make a guess. I made my offer, waited for the closing date to pass, then rang to ask 'Is there a higher offer than ours?' With caution, the agent replied, 'No.' Joyce and I were delighted at having found such a gem of a place, but it would need major refurbishment.

A couple of days later Joyce phoned me at work. She was furious. The estate agent handing the sale of the cottage had rung her to say, 'Sorry, but a higher offer than yours had been received and accepted.' Joyce was upset and near to tears. I stormed into the agents, RA Bennett in Station road Yate, and asked the manager what he thought he was playing at. He sheepishly replied that a late offer had been accepted. I told him that it was his duty to inform all interested parties if the closing date had been revised. I am known to use a sledgehammer to crack a walnut, and so substantially increased my offer saying, 'It is your duty to put this to your client.' Frankly, I thought him out of his depth in a transaction of this nature. Thankfully, our revised offer secured the property. The vagaries of buying and selling property. Reform is long overdue.

The property market was picking up. We sold our house in Warmley in 24 hours, and now had nowhere to live. My sister Stella has a cottage

– I hasten to add in need of repair – and offered it to us for a period. We gladly accepted, but once the refurbishment of our new house began in earnest it was prudent to be on site. We hired a caravan, quite a big touring one. It was autumn, and the weather good. The caravan was fun. It was like being on holiday. Boy, did our view of caravaning change when winter set in. One night, in a storm, the wind was so strong we thought the caravan would take flight. I told Joyce not to worry and that the tall hedge at the bottom of the garden would probably act as a brake, slowing us down before we took off. She was not amused. The only thing that kept our spirits up was the progress on the house. We could see it would be beautiful when completed.

Moments to cherish were sitting in front of a log fire, in what would be our sitting room, in our winter coats eating dinner. A casserole, again! (Posh name for stew, I reckon.) Our only means of cooking was a slow cooker. Once the walls were rendered, the floor fixed, a wall built and a door in the hole we now used as our point of entry, the room would be lovely! This became a regular scenario at meal times, and I haven't fancied casserole since. I wonder why! Anyone want to buy a slow cooker?

My nephew Ashley had joined the Royal Marines, and was undergoing training at the Commando Training Centre in Lympstone, Devon. His grandmother, my sister June, had been ill for some time and was deteriorating. She and her husband Jimmy Wright, a favourite with my mum, had moved from Buckhurst Hill in Essex to Falmouth, primarily because of Jimmy's failing health; he had suffered a stroke. But now it was June who looked the most vulnerable. I made a few trips to see her, and had once stayed overnight. We sat up to 3am talking. We had never been close, I regret that terribly now.

After my dad's first wife, Annie, died, June went to live with her grandparents. Bombed out in the Blitz, they moved to Buckhurst Hill in Essex. June continued to live with them there until she married. I saw quite a lot of her during my teens, and have a lovely photograph of her sitting on a pony called Tango in the garden at Allendale.

Now as I sat on her bed and we talked of those days she said, 'Jim, I only wish I had known you better. I'm sorry I didn't come to see you in hospital when you were a boy.' I had never even thought about that, and she had never mentioned it before. It must have troubled her to be mentioning it now. 'We are together, that's all that counts. I have never loved you less than I do now,' I assured her. I hugged and kissed her, then got up to leave, and as I reached the door, with a lump in my throat, I said 'I will come again soon, Sis,' Our eyes met, and I could see the tears in hers. We both suspected this could be our last moment together. It was.

June's daughters, Teresa and Jamie, had moved to Cornwall not long after their parents. Teresa opened a café in Falmouth, and Jamie a shop in Penzance selling jewellery. Whilst Jamie's business was well established, Teresa's café was in decline. She had spent a great deal of her time nursing her mother, and her business suffered. Soon it closed, leaving poor Teresa close to bankruptcy.

The little church at Stithians was filled with family and friends. Our Sister Maud and her daughter Sharon kept up the charade of not speaking to either Stella or me. Sharon would have loved to but wouldn't dare; her mother would see it as disloyal. None the less we both felt profoundly sad for Maud, being the only one left from the three children of dad's first wife. Maud and June were as close as sisters as Stella and Eve are. Now she was hurting deeply, and we felt her loss as well as our own.

I saw cousins Ivy and Johnny for the first time in years. Johnny was now retired from the prison service and Ivy had not long returned from New Zealand where she had lived for some time. In general conversation I told them about my involvement with Jack Russell and the art business. Johnny told me that his nephew Nicholas was a professional artist, and had recently held a successful exhibition in London. I said I would get in touch with him and arrange to see his work. I did, and both Jack and I bought paintings from him. Nick is a hugely talented artist with a great future. And a Ruston!

Despite all he had done in South Africa, and his ton at Lord's against India, Jack was dropped before the end of the summer series, the reason yet again being to a 'balance' the side, this time to play an extra bowler. 'Sorry Jack,' so it was no great surprise that when the team to tour Zimbabwe and New Zealand was announced, Jack was selected as a reserve keeper. Ever pragmatic, Jack's reaction was, 'I have been selected, I will fight for my place.' It was not to be. Jack played just seven days' cricket during the whole tour. He was devastated, saying, 'The game is kicking me in the teeth at the moment. It has been the most difficult winter yet'.

The *Sunday Times* published a picture titled 'Then and Now' showing Jack and Athers triumphant at Jo'burg, as Then, and a picture of Jack standing behind the scoreboard in Bulawayo with his nameplate, J RUSSELL laying on the ground – discarded – as Now.

Jack's wife Aileen gave birth to a baby girl, Catherine Jane. I took a photograph of them both and the *News of the World* printed it on 22 December, sending a copy down the wire for Jack in Zimbabwe.

Aileen normally shuns publicity, but agreed to this so Jack could get his first glimpse of his new daughter. Jack loved it, so did the public. Jack could have delayed going to Zimbabwe. The consummate professional, he would ask for no preferential treatment. Others do.

I had been having a few communication problems with Peter Hayter on the progress of Jack's autobiography. We were behind the schedule we had agreed with the publisher, and I was becoming concerned. I knew that Reggie (Peter's nickname) agreed to write Ian Botham's autobiography. Did he have a new agenda? I wrote to Jack of my concern, and in the run up to Christmas, Jack responded with following fax.

Dear Jim, Surprise, Surprise!! Reggie told me this afternoon that he CANNOT do the book. It doesn't surprise me really, I knew all along his heart wasn't in it. He says he has too much work, and he has problems at home. He also says he's not doing Beefy's (Botham) book, and he's going to tell him so – we'll see? It's just like being in one of those warehouses at St Nazaire when Col Newman said, 'Sorry lads, transport's let us down, you'll have to do the best you can.' As I see it we have three options: 1) Find another writer. 2) We do it. 3) Not do it. Forget 3; one way or another we are doing it!

I had dinner (he paid) the other night with Pat Murphy. He's done quite a few books including one recently called *'His way – The Brian Clough Story.'* He gave me a copy to read it impressed.
Because Reggie pulled out of the contract, will we get the money back we paid to him? I've spoken to him, but there's no point in trying to persuade him to change his mind Jim. The best person to write it is you –*'The Inside Story'*. You are the only person to get close enough to find out the truth. At least we would have it how we wanted.

I answered saying how disappointed I was with Reggie, and not to worry, I would get back every penny we had paid him – plus. I wrote to Peter Hayter saying how amazed I was, that already having written five chapters, he had abandoned us. Although all the negotiations had been conducted through me, to this day I have never received an explanation as to why he dumped us. I still can't understand that he would let himself down professionally like this. People talk. Whilst we exchange pleasantries when we meet, I have lost faith in him.

I took to Pat Murphy instantly. He told me what he wanted. I agreed. I wasn't in the driving seat. Michael Doggart and Tom Whiting at CollinsWillow co-operated to the full in re-scheduling the dates for the finished manuscript. It was very much in their interest to do so, as they were also publishing Ian Botham's autobiography – written by Peter Hayter! Draw your own conclusions.

However, we were not out of the woods yet. In fact far from it. Jack's winter tour contract with the Test and County Cricket Board provided that all players contemplating writing a book must first obtain permission from the board. Once given, the contents must be passed to them for approval before publication. This applies for a period of two years after the last tour referred to in the book is over. I thought this unreasonable, and was confident it would never stand legal scrutiny. Not to publish during a tour is acceptable, but once concluded, it should be allowed. After all, there's not going to be much controversial that the press hasn't already shared with the public.

It was Jack's criticism of Ray Illingworth's handling of Devon Malcolm that caused most of the flak. Jack had further criticised Mike Atherton and Grahame Gooch on captaincy, and Keith Fletcher as an England coach. The latter trio took it on the chin. It didn't affect their relationship with Jack a jot; they saw his comments as honest and constructive. However Illy was not amused, accusing Jack of having stabbed him in the back, and that he [Jack] apart from cricket and painting had little else in his life, so to get publicity for his book, had 'hammered' a name. Patronising to say the least, and typical of the man. Few would argue that Jack is more famous now than Illingworth; outside cricket, who has heard of Illy? In a recent poll conducted by the *Cricketer* magazine to find the 50 most entertaining players in the last century; it came as no surprise that Ian Botham was number one; Jack was honoured to be in at number 12. Ray Illingworth didn't even make the 50!

Pat Murphy completed the book, and I recovered the advance we had paid Peter Hayter, plus the extra payment we had to make to Pat for taking over at such a late stage.

Things got heated with the TCCB, and they consulted with their legal advisors as to what, if any action they might take against Jack if he published. Tony Brown came on the phone begging me to get Jack to change his mind. When I told him, no go, Jack would not budge, he said, 'So he is going to publish and be damned.' 'No Tony,' I countered. 'He is going to publish and be exonerated!' After his treatment on the recent tour, Jack was fired up. 'If they want a battle in court let them have one, I don't give a stuff.' he said. I was right behind him. At times the board seem to lose sight of the fact that when it comes down to it, they are an employer. Employees have rights, too. Contract or no contract, if something is deemed unreasonable it can be challenged.

A COCKNEY KID IN GREEN WELLIES

I was sitting on the balcony of the pavilion at Nevil Road watching an early season game, when I felt a tap on my shoulder. Turning I could see it was David Graveney. I am never sure which hat he is wearing until he starts to speak. He was Jack's captain at Gloucestershire when he first signed for them. Now he was secretary of the Professional Cricketers' Association, assistant accountant in his brother's firm, who are retained as accountants to Jack Russell Ltd, and more importantly, given the circumstances, the newly appointed Chairman of Selectors of the England cricket team. It can get confusing. 'Jim,' he started, 'You can tell Jack that the board aren't going to take any action over his book, but also advise him that they do not take kindly to threats of court action.' I thanked him for the good news, and assured him we had no intention of deferring to the courts, unless of course the board either disciplined or fined Jack, or suggested he had brought the game into disrepute.

In fairness, it was a difficult situation for David, during which we were glad of his moral support. Ever the diplomat, in my opinion, he would make a good politician.

Common sense prevailed. After referral to Gerard Elias QC, Chairman of the England and Wales cricket board's disciplinary committee, the QC decided that 'No useful purpose would be served in punishing Russell under the strict letter of the law, when he was simply stating his personal opinions on matters of no great secrecy.' I had worked that one out six months before!

Subsequent tour contracts provided that players wouldn't publish anything until the tour had ended. Jack's stand had in fact been something of a watershed in bringing this long overdue reform.

With Courtney Walsh unavailable for the 1997 season, Gloucestershire turned once again to Jack to take the captaincy. Despite pleas from everyone involved, he stood firm in his decision not to. It was one of the few times that we have disagreed. I respected his decision, of course, but could see the writing on the wall regarding his England career, and thought he might struggle to find enthusiasm for the game once his international career was over. I feared he might get bored with the sometimes monotonous drudgery of the county circuit. I was convinced that captaincy, which had proved to suit him so well in '95 and which I feel was a major factor in his personal performance and his return to the England squad, would be the answer now.

Jack and I bashed out fax upon fax between us in an attempt to raise his spirits. He had languished for three and a half months without playing in a test match, and when he finally got a game against a New

Zealand 'A' team, his was the only credible innings (61not out) in a match where England were outclassed by a New Zealand second XI!

The autobiography, *Jack Russell – Unleashed* was launched on 19 May at the Imperial War Museum in London, and was followed by a Bristol launch, which I had got Bristol solicitors Osbourne Clark to sponsor. Over 200 attended, and we sold at least 200 books on the day. The following week the book was serialised in *The Daily Mail*. The media coverage was intense, and followed us around the bookshops where Jack signed copies. In several venues the queues were some 200 people long. The book got into the top 10 best-selling hardback books list, and stayed there for quite a few weeks. We couldn't have hoped for more.

The title for the book had started out as: *Jack Russell – A Wicketkeeper's Life*. Although I made it plain to Michael Doggart that Jack didn't like the title, he had gone ahead with production of the dust jacket. Jack was furious. 'I'm just not having it Jim.' Jack asked his fellow cricketers to come up with something they thought suited him. It was David Lloyd, the England coach, who came up with Jack Russell – Unleashed. Jack liked it, so did I. Now all we had to do was persuade the publisher. Our chance came when we were invited to a party to celebrate 15 years of publishing by CollinsWillow. It was there that Jack had the opportunity to talk to the chairman of HarperCollins, Eddy Bell. When Jack told him he didn't want his book to be called *A Wicketkeepers Life*, Eddy responded with, 'Who thought up that bloody boring title?' 'Um 'er, your firm did,' Jack answered, then went on to tell Eddy what he preferred. The rest is history.

Jack and I had travelled to London early on the day of the CollinsWillow 15th anniversary, which was being held at The Berkeley. But first we went to the London Metropolitan Archive, where I wanted to search the registers of St John's Church in Stepney, where I was christened. The registers are now on film, and Jack watched intently as I wound the reel through the viewer. First I found my sisters Maisie, Stella and Evelyn. On reaching May 1937, before I had chance to study the entry for the 17th Jack burst out laughing. 'George,' he said. 'who is George?' I could hardly believe my eyes; although by birth certificate says I am James Alexander, I was in fact baptised George Alexander! Nothing is straightforward in the Ruston family! There is no longer anyone alive who can tell me how this came to be.

We moved into our new cottage in time for me to celebrate my 60th birthday. The first birthday party I had ever had. We confined it to family only, and I loved it. The house looked splendid. Eddy and Gordon had made another marvellous job of renovation. Joyce, now in her element with as much garden as she could manage, said it would take her five years to get it how she wanted. With little or no help from me, it will take all of that!

In amongst all the book publicity, Jack went to Buckingham Palace where he received a MBE from Prince Charles. It was the proudest moment of his life. The award had been made in the Queen's birthday honours list the year before. When the official looking envelope came, Jack thought it was from the Inland Revenue, so put it to the back of the pile to be looked at last. He eventually opened the ominous piece of mail, drew out the contents, and fell silent. With a look of disbelief on his face and handing the contents to me he said. 'Jim you had better read this, then tell me I'm not dreaming.' Excitedly I responded 'You're not dreaming Jack, you have been offered an MBE. They are asking if you will accept it?

First we celebrated with a cup of tea. Then Jack walked across the road and posted his reply in the box opposite the gallery. Now all we had to do was keep quiet and not tell a soul until the Palace released the information to the press, who are under embargo not to print anything before the official day. I was so pleased for Jack and said, 'Do I get the E, for my 10 per cent commission?' He fell about. He still mentions it.

The summer of 1997 the Australians were back for another Ashes series. Jack was sidelined once more. As had become all too common, once again, we got stuffed. When the touring party visited Bristol to play Gloucestershire, Jack invited a few of them to the gallery. Joyce and our daughter Jane laid on a meal, and Jack and I entertained them. We had a great evening. The Aussie coach said, 'Glad to see you are not in the England side Jack. Well not glad for you mate, but glad for us. This means now we only have to take five English wickets, and it will be all over.'

The Australian wicket keeper Ian Healy (Heals) is a great friend of Jack's, so is the Aussie captain Steve Waugh. It is a friendship of mutual respect. They have both played out some tough matches with him as an opponent. Steve said to me, 'Jack could walk into any test team in the world, I don't understand why he is left out of yours.'

Between us we ferried the lads back to their hotel in Bristol. I had Heals with me, and we joked all the way until I had to turn into the entrance to the hotel, when I completely misjudged the turning and hit the kerb with a thud. I just made it to the hotel entrance as my near-side tyre deflated. I was so mad with myself for hitting the kerb, that I refused all help on offer to change the wheel. 'If you are sure mate, I'll shoot through,' said Heals. But not before berating an obnoxious coach driver who protested at my being in his path. 'What's with you, you arsehole, can't you see the guy has problem with his wheel?' he shouted at the driver. Which somewhat changed his attitude.

I took a photo of the dinner party and sent copies to those that were there. The press would have loved a picture, and of course a story, but it had been a private occasion. However, my old mate Keith in Sydney sent me a fax to say he had seen a photo in Steve Waugh's latest book of the Aussie cricket team having dinner in the Jack Russell gallery. I thought, 'Cheeky bugger, I didn't even get a credit!'

I asked Alan Crompton what the chances were of us having an Australian 'Green Baggy' cap to display in the gallery. He shook his head. They are issued to players when first selected to play for their country. They get only one, and it is numbered. If it becomes damaged or worn, they have to take it in for exchange, and retain the same number. A record is kept of every cap that has ever been issued, and to whom.

Our players can have two or three, or more in a career. Recently the ECB made quite a fuss about a new cap. They said it was better quality, and more comfortable. All existing test players were issued with one, but were allowed to keep their old ones. England caps should be cherished, like the Aussie ones.

HEARTBREAK AND CHANGE

It was a very sad time for Joyce. Her mother died in August. She had been ill for a while, and Joyce had been taking her in and out of the Bristol Royal Infirmary for tests one kind and another, which seemed to leave the poor dear weaker with each visit. It was Sunday, and Joyce and I called to visit her in her little bungalow in Long Ashton, south of Bristol. She looked dreadful. Joyce was deeply anxious, so decided to stay overnight with her. Next morning her mother's condition had worsened considerably, so Joyce called the doctor. It was lunchtime before he came, and the ambulance needed to convey Joyce's mother to hospital didn't arrive until 7.30pm. Joyce arrived home late that night.

The next day, my dear worried wife was up and gone first thing to be with her mum. I waited anxiously for her to return with the latest news. As she walked through the door I asked 'How is your mum?' she answered, 'You don't want to know.' My heart sank. That afternoon a consultant at the Bristol General Hospital had told Joyce's mum in the presence of her daughter that she had cancer, and it was only a matter of time. Joyce asked me, 'What do you think mum said, when she was told she was going to die?' She said, 'Oh well, I've had 81 good years.' I only hope I will be as brave, and as grateful for my life, as this wonderful woman so obviously was.

Joyce's mum was christened Eva Lillian Holway Fry. Holway was her mother's maiden name, which she added to all of her children's Christian names. She married Stanley Goodlife in 1937. They had four children, two of whom she brought up during the war years. She also had evacuees billeted with her. She spoke of them often, and wondered what had become of them. I know some deeply caring human beings, so it is not without a great deal of thought that I single her out as the most caring person I have ever had the privilege to know. When I think of our early relationship, and what a hard time she gave both Joyce and me. We would have split up if we hadn't loved each other so much, especially in view of my absence, due to Army service. But once I had married her daughter, my wife's mother treated me the same as her own children.

The whole family gathered beside her bed, and she seemed to rally. I spent a few precious moments alone with the lady who had been my mother-in-law for 39 years. I held her hand, and for the first time realised what beautiful hands she had. I kissed her gently on the cheek and told her that I loved her. With a wonderful smile, she suddenly appeared much younger, and replied, 'I know you do.' I'm not nearly as nice a person as she was.

Late at night the hospital phoned, and we rushed to her side. With Joyce, her sister Heather, and our daughter Karen, I sat with her as she slipped away. She died as she had lived, quietly and without fuss. You see, she wouldn't want to be any trouble to anyone, least of all her children.

It affected me far more than I could have imagined. Of course I would expect to be upset, but this was much deeper. Weeks later, I realised I was also grieving for Joyce. My sweet wife doesn't wear her heart on her sleeve, but I could see she was terribly hurt. She was devoted to her mother, as was her sister Heather, whom I also love very much. What would they do now?

Joyce, always an early riser, had switched on the TV to catch the Sunday morning news. Suddenly reappearing in the doorway of the bedroom she said, 'Jim, what is happening to me?' I sat up quickly, and looking at her forlorn figure standing misty eyed, responded anxiously, 'What is it darling, what's wrong?' She continued, 'I have just heard that Princess Diana has been killed in a car accident.' We both went downstairs to watch the rest of the news. The nation was already in mourning. With her mother's funeral due to take place the next day, this was too much for my dear wife, who like me, is an old-fashioned patriot and Royalist'– although she never did condone Prince Charles's infidelity. With such sadness all around, it would be difficult for her to grieve in private.

On the day of the funeral, I was standing by Joyce's cousin May, when she turned to me and said, 'Jim, if there is a heaven, then there is a place for my auntie there.' I really don't think there is much I could add to that.

Jack attended the funeral service of the Princess of Wales in Westminster Abbey where he represented Gloucestershire CCC. The Princess had been their patron. Other members of the club walked behind the cortège, with the many representatives of the numerous charities Diana supported. It was an emotional time for Jack, bringing back memories of the day his own brother David died so tragically. He shed tears without shame.

After the funeral Jack sent a fax to Earl Spencer offering him his condolences and understanding, to which he received a grateful reply. He had also written to Diana's sister, Lady Jane Fellowes, praising her stoicism. The nation came to a standstill. I can remember quite vividly the funeral of Winston Churchill and how my dad mourned him; I still have the newspaper cuttings. But his death was expected, her's a tragedy.

A new season dawned, and although Jack never got called up for test duty, he would have loved another crack at the Aussies. He had a great season at county level, passing 1,000 runs in a season for the first time –

although he had come nerverackingly close once or twice before. With England going down yet again to the tourists, the world and his wife were calling for Jack's recall to international duty. An article in the *London Evening Standard* recorded that at 2.73 dismissals per match, Jack had the best strike rate of any keeper in the history of cricket, ahead of all time greats Leslie Ames, Jim Parks, Godfrey Evans, Alan Knott and Bob Taylor.

With the winter of the West Indies imminent, I was confident Jack would be recalled to the England team. He had been stuck on 49 tests for some while now and was desperate to reach 50. I thought once he achieved that landmark, he would look on future tests as a bonus. The evening before the test team was announced to the public, Jack got the all-important phone call from Mike Atherton. Jack had considered his omission from the national team could have been attributed to his open criticism of Athers in his book *Unleashed*, but here he was congratulating Jack on his selection.

Jack and I spent a few lazy autumn days in the Slad valley, three miles from Stroud where Jack grew up. Our idea was to select a number of scenes to paint, not just to sell in the gallery but also to use in a book of paintings we were contemplating. The autobiography had done so well we thought it prudent to follow it soon with another book. HarperCollins had agreed in principle to publish it, so all we had to do now was select the material for inclusion. Although I had been to the Slad valley before, I was not familiar with it. I had read Laurie Lee's classic book *Cider with Rosie*, based on his memories growing up in this valley. Each time Jack named a wood, cottage or meadow, it rang a bell. I would say, 'It's in the book.' So we decided to devote a section of the new book to Slad and the surrounding countryside.

Laurie Lee had died in May 1997, and his grave, still covered with flowers, lay in the churchyard facing the valley and his favourite pub, The Woolpack. He loved both to distraction. Simply writing his name makes me feel like a poacher, who knows what Laurie would have thought of my feeble efforts? No danger, I doubt he would have bothered to read them!

It was during one of our forays into Slad that we noticed a 'For Sale' sign on Ivy cottage. Next door is Rose Cottage, which Laurie bought with some of the proceeds from *Cider with Rosie*, and lived in with his beautiful wife Kathy when they came back to Slad in 1962. Jessy, Laurie's daughter, still uses the cottage (recently I enjoyed a 'scotch on the rocks', with Kathy and Jessy whilst looking out over Laurie's valley, a magic moment). Jack and I gave it a quick look. 'Better not let anyone see you showing undue interest in this property Jack,' I advised.

'The grapevine will buzz and the price will rise!' He laughed, saying, 'You think of everything mate.' I continued, 'When I get home I will give the agent a call and find out the asking price, saying it is me who is interested.

A few days later, Joyce and I, as prospective purchasers, went to view Ivy Cottage. It was in a very poor state of repair. The asking price was £130,000, but I secured the purchase for a lot less. Jack was naturally delighted. Given time, I thought, 'What have I done?' It would be down to me to organise the very substantial refurbishment, and I had only just gotten over the massive work at the gallery. It was a sound investment for Jack though.

Jack completed a wonderful collection of images from the Slad valley, and Eddy and Gordon started work on renovating Ivy Cottage. Our gallery in Chipping Sodbury was flourishing; demand for Jack's work was increasing rapidly. Tempting though it was, we managed to resist selling any of the new landscapes from Slad. These we would want to display at the launch of the Art Book. I had determined that as soon as Christmas was over, and Jack had flown out to the West Indies, I would settle to the task of photographing the paintings we had selected for inclusion in the new book.

Returning from London, where I had visited Cathy Gosling at HarperCollins to discuss the content of the art book, I flopped exhausted in my armchair. Joyce seemed somewhat detached, as she asked what I would like for dinner. Normally she would ask how my day had been. After I had eaten and sat once more in comfort, my wife said, 'Jim, I don't know how to tell you this…' she paused, then continued, 'Teresa is dead.' Putting my head in my hands, I replied 'No, No, No.' I was stunned. I got to my feet, climbed the stairs, and sobbed.

Once I had regained control of my feelings, I telephoned my sister-in-law Josie, who told me of the events as far as she knew them. Teresa my niece had not come to terms with her mother's death a little over a year ago, and to compound her misery, her business failed and she had been declared bankrupt. Her relationship with her father, often volatile, had worsened.

With Christmas only 10 days' away she despaired. Her devoted aunt, Dawn, had pleaded with her to 'Just get in your car and come to me. Don't worry about money I will look after you.' I too had spent hours on the phone to my niece quite recently, offering my support through her bankruptcy. I asked her to come and stay with me, assuring her I would sort everything out, that she was not alone in this. 'How could I?' she had answered. 'I have my dad to look after.' I told her that he was being naughty, and was far more able than he would have her think. He had burdened his sick wife with his ailments during her last years on this earth, and now he was making unacceptable demands on his daughter, at a time when she needed his support.

We will never know what was in the poor girl's mind when she drove into the garage at her father's house, closed the door and sat in her car with the engine running. The inquest returned a verdict of suicide, so we have to live with that. Her sister Jamie was devastated, as was her aunt (and lifelong friend) Dawn. More or less the same age, they were like sisters, growing up together.

Teresa's son Ashley had passed out of the Commando Training Centre at Lympstone in the summer, I was there with my niece to watch him. She was so proud. Now in his Blues, with two of his fellow Marines, and a close friend in the uniform of an Infantryman, he bore the coffin carrying Teresa, towards the very same church in Stithians that we had all walked into the year before to say farewell to my sister June. It was unbearable. I wanted to scream, 'Sorry, Sorry, Trese, I failed you.'

Mother and daughter now lay together in the small cemetery close to the church. I go there whenever I am in Cornwall, and my friend Hazel Hawke, who lives in Truro, places flowers for me at Christmas. I will keep faith until I join them.

My brother-in-law Jimmy Wright (actually his real name is Frederick but I never learned that until it was read out in church at my Sister's funeral), coped very well. He sold the house in Cornwall and moved back to London where he was allocated accommodation in sheltered housing in Chigwell. He often drove the gruelling journey to Penzance to visit his daughter Jamie. It's a pity he could not have been this independent when Teresa was alive. It's best left to the imagination how my dad would have reacted. A man protects his children, if necessary with his life. Teresa's dad just wasn't there for her in her hour of need.

Jimmy Wright had a stroke in 1984, which changed his personality. He became irrational and argumentative, and lost the affection we once had for him. He had recently been diagnosed as having Alzheimer's disease, which, in it's early stages, had probably contributed, in no small way, to his behaviour during the months leading up to the death of his daughter. All terribly sad.

Ashley was stationed at Taunton with 40 Commando, and came to stay with us often. We talk of his mum. It's getting easier. Ashley applied to join the Special Boat Squadron and in May 2000 faced the gruelling selection procedure, which he passed. He now has to do the same course as the SAS – many fail. He will get through. He will do it for his mum.

I have never been so glad to see the back of a year as I was of 1997. As well as losing Joyce's mum and Teresa, my cousin Johnny, whom I had last seen at my sister June's funeral also died, after having had a heart by-pass operation. He was just two years older than I was. Johnny used to visit us in his teens, and go bike riding with my sister Eve. After service in the Parachute Regiment, he married a lovely girl, Rose. My cousin Ivy, Johnny's sister, of whom I am particularly fond, was heartbroken at the loss of her brother. They had the closeness that I share with Stella.

No one can foresee the future, but of one thing I am sure, I will put my family first, above all else. They are so precious to me.

Once Jack had embarked on his winter tour, I set up my photographic equipment in what was once the old skittle alley, and began photographing the paintings we had selected for the new book. Quite a few of the ones we wanted to include had been sold several years ago. I had to embark upon a round robin, visiting clients all over the country. Enjoyable, but time consuming.

There was also the editorial to consider. We enlisted the help of Claire Struthers, a sub-editor on the *London Evening Standard*, whom both Jack and I know. Claire came to stay with my wife and me at the cottage. Where we used the time to collate the notes both Jack and I had made. We were extremely pleased with the result that Claire achieved. Her journalistic talent definitely enhanced the publication.

Jack's tour started off well enough; he was in good nick with both bat and gloves. Then a change of fortune descended upon him. The first test was scheduled to take place at Sabina Park. Both of us had such high hopes, thinking it would be a return to the roller-coaster we had got used to. For my part, I had negotiated the sale of Jack's first ever painting of test cricket, England's win at Sabina Park in 1990 in which Jack played a vital role. I had agreed a price of £25,000 with one of our existing collectors, who asked to remain anonymous. If, in his 50th test match, Jack could play a blinding innings, or do something spectacular behind the stumps on the very same ground and against the same opposition, the press would love it. What a double feature it would make.

This time it wasn't to be. Jack fell miserably ill with a stomach bug, and with foul fluid pouring from both ends, he couldn't even stand, let alone think of playing cricket. Alec Stewart had to don the gloves. Jack was inconsolable, thinking if England won the first test with Alec keeping, they would probably retain the same team for the next game.

No one wants to take the responsibility of changing a winning side. As it turned out the match had to be abandoned after just 56 minutes because the wicket was judged unplayable. Jack breathed a sigh of relief, but not for long.

The ECB (formerly TCCB) dug in their heels on Jack's trusty sunhat declaring it not uniform, it would have to go. This was a huge blow for Jack, and would do him untold damage psychologically. We had discussed what line to take should this arise. David Lloyd had said to me at the Oval in the summer, ' If selected, Jack won't be able to wear that old floppy hat on tour, Jim. The board just won't wear it.' Pardon the pun! I was in favour of suggesting to the management they get a hat made especially for Jack then at least it would fit him properly. However Jack decided to stand firm and was now on the phone to me saying he had been told to wear the hat issued or they wouldn't let him play. The decision was his. It became a case of letting his captain and team-mates down or compromising his game. He had never walked out in a test match without his white floppy, he is famous for it. Once, when drying it, he almost cremated it in an oven! He even panics if he loses sight of it, daring anyone touch it at his or her peril.

Incredibly, the management allowed Jack to 'tailor' the regulation hat to suit him. He hacked away at the brim, and when finished it didn't look so very different from his old one. But try as he might the new hat was uncomfortable. It knocked his confidence. I am not alone in attributing this lack of good common sense by the ECB to the dramatic drop in Jack's form. He had had the heart kicked out of him. I think it was political, and nothing has happened since to change my mind. Not content with mucking his career around as a specialist keeper, they now put the boot into his very personality. If arseholes could fly, Lord's would need a departure lounge.

Jack had a miserable tour, and the critics continued to put the boot in. Anyone who has ever played in the West Indies, including the home teams, will tell you they have the worst playing surfaces on this planet on which to keep wicket. 'Even bounce' is not in the Windies vocabulary. Bumbling Blofield, who makes so many mistakes he irritates, gave Jack a slagging. So did Agnew, another whimp. A self-opinionated individual, by the name of Tim de Lisle had written in Wisden the previous year, 'Alec Stewart should give up the gloves in favour of Jack Russell.' He now wrote, 'On his current form, Jack Russell couldn't keep chickens.' You wouldn't want any of these guys standing behind you in a tight corner! Those who knew better, such as Vic Marks and David Gower, were more understanding.

A COCKNEY KID IN GREEN WELLIES

Jack felt so alone on that tour he phoned his wife more than usual, and Aileen and I spoke far more often than at other times. She was concerned for Jack. I spent a few sleepless nights trying to make up my mind whether to fly out to give my mate moral support. Could I have made a difference? I don't know. I was fully committed with the production of the new art book and running the gallery, but one week wouldn't have hurt. I regret it now. I should have gone. At least I could have made him laugh. I can always do that.

Courtney Walsh asked me to sit on the committee for his Testimonial Year. I said I would be honoured. I have a great deal of respect for him. I was attending a function for Courtney, when 'Three hats Graveney' approached me. 'Has the little keeper topped himself yet?' he enquired. 'If you are talking about Jack, then no he hasn't, and why the f... should he. He could see he had touched a nerve, and forcing a grin said 'Only joking.' 'I don't think it funny,' I replied, and walked away.

A local independent film company had been commissioned by HTV to make a half-hour documentary programme on Jack Russell the cricketing artist. The title chosen was *Brushes with Bats.* Jack enjoyed the film work immensely, and I contributed where I could. HTV were very pleased with the response from the public, screening it for the second time on a Sunday at peak viewing. With the exception of those who previously visited our gallery, it was the first time the general public had had the chance to see the diverse range of Jack's paintings. It was marvellous publicity for us.

Jack was having another good season with his county. His form returning with his hat! However, he wasn't included in the England team to face the South Africans during the summer, although he did get an unexpected call-up. England were to play the tourists in the second test at Lord's, Alec Stewart was suffering with a back problem and, as a precaution, Jack was summoned to Lord's, and stated philosophically. 'At least no one else is in the frame for the job.' I was not expecting to go to Lord's to watch the cricket, but had been thrown an invitation from a most unexpected source. My Aussie friends Keith and Prue had recently paid us a flying visit on their European business tour (smart arses). Returning home, they found they had won a trip in a competition they had entered some time ago. Having forgotten all about the competition, they now found themselves in possession of flights to the UK, hotel accommodation and tickets in the new grandstand for each of the five days of the second test match at Lord's.

Keith phoned to say he couldn't make the trip, but Prue could. I arranged to meet Prue at her hotel and take her to Lord's. She really only wanted to go for one day, just for the experience. The tickets for the remaining days she gave to me. It seemed as though fate had taken a hand once more and I would be there to cheer Jack on. I did manage to get Jack's attention on the balcony of the pavilion before the game began and give him a wave. Alec was passed fit, so Jack wasn't required.

Prue and I had a lovely day, then went to the theatre. I can't remember the name of the play we saw, but I will never ever forget the embarrassment. The language! Every four-letter word in every context imaginable was used liberally. Two Aussie girls sitting to my left were in fits of laughter for the most part, whilst I just didn't know what to do. I didn't know what Prue was thinking; I couldn't look at her. After the performance we went out to eat, neither of us mentioning the play! Thankfully, it was Prue who invited me, not the other way around!

Jack's name was not mentioned when the England squad to tour Australia the coming winter was announced, he was visibly disappointed. Announced at the same time was the team to play in the Wills International tournament on the sub-continent. In an effort to rest some of the players who would soon be off on the tour to Australia, the selectors turned to Jack to keep wicket in the one-day competition. Some consolation I suppose.

The *Art of Jack Russell Caught on Canvas* was launched, amid much publicity and speculation on Jack's England future, at the museum in Lord's cricket ground – ironic really. We were looking for a suitable title for the new book, and it was Aileen who came up with *Caught on Canvas*, absolutely perfect. Once more we did the rounds of the bookshops, where Jack signed copies of his new publication.

'Jim, Jack has resigned from international cricket, you didn't tell me.' It was Joyce calling up the stairs, she had just heard it on the morning news. 'I didn't tell you, because I didn't bloody well know he was going to,' I shouted back, almost choking myself with my toothbrush as I did. In a state of undress, and looking more Rigsby than Redfern, I burst into the sitting room and plonked myself down in an armchair only to find the news was over. 'Look at Teletext and see what it says,' Joyce suggested.

Teletext confirmed that Jack had announced his retirement in Dhaka, Bangladesh, after England had beaten South Africa. He had gone out at the top and told the press:

Everyone has to stop eventually, and I feel that this is the right moment for me to call it a day. I've had 11 years of international cricket, during which I have had experiences money just could not buy. I've been lucky. Now I'll move on. It has been a brilliant time. I started in

A COCKNEY KID IN GREEN WELLIES

Peshawar, and ended in Dhaka, with all stops in between. I had made up my mind that the coming Ashes tour would be my last. When I failed to make the team I decided to go. [Didn't tell me though.] I've been lucky enough to play in 54 test matches, and for a grubby-haired little schoolboy from a council house in Stroud, I can't complain.

That same morning, when I got to the gallery, Jane was holding a fax from Jack telling us he had retired. I thought, 'Cheeky sod, he kept that quiet.' Not even a hint came from him when we last spoke, only days ago. Jack's England status affects the business and me in particular. I act as a buffer between Jack and the media. It would have been nice to be forewarned, so as to make the necessary mental adjustment. I was not amused. We always planned that we would make capital of his retirement from the international scene. Now it was all over in a flash.

It was a weekend when Jack returned from Asia, and Aileen phoned to say he would not do any media interviews until the Monday. I replied, 'Tell Jack there are no interviews. The press have already covered it, it's no longer newsworthy.' I wasn't at all surprised (after all, it's my job), but I think Jack was.

I don't know exactly what he was feeling when we next met, but he appeared downbeat. He became awkward about book signings the publishers were asking for. We had just done a signing in Weston-Super-Mare, and were sitting in Jack's car. And although he had agreed the signing schedule, plus a few 'ribbons' that he had been asked to cut, he was not a happy man. To coin a phrase from an old mate of mine, 'He had his arse in his hand.' 'Success doesn't come alone mate. Where there are benefits there are also demands. It is our book they are selling,' I said. His response was stroppy. 'I may be not be bright, but I'm not that stupid. I am fed up with everyone telling me what to do.' (I took that to mean me.) 'Tell them I will do what I want, when I want.' He named a few people and places that I won't mention here. I am sure what he said was in the heat of the moment. I think it was an after effect, having had time to reflect on his voluntary retirement from the international stage. Had he done the right thing? (My words, not Jack's.)

In between the signings, I saw little of Jack. He immersed himself in his painting. I was more than happy about that! I began thinking maybe the writing is on the wall, perhaps our time was running out. We had been together for seven years, and enjoyed so much success. Now Jack had moved on. Perhaps I should too?

THE MAGIC RETURNS

There had been an acrimonious split between the West Indian fast bowler Courtney Walsh and his county Gloucestershire. Each blaming the other. My good friend Ken Trowbridge acted as agent for Courtney. He is an exceptionally good businessman, and would have had the wishes of his client, close to his heart. As far as I am concerned, Courtney had always made it plain that he wanted to play his final days cricket at the club he loved and had served so well since 1984. It was a great pity to lose the services of a player as talented and loyal as Courtney, whilst still at the very top of his profession. One of the nicest people you will ever meet.

Recently I watched tributes being paid, via television, to the great man, for passing Kapil Dev's record for the most test wickets taken in the history of cricket. Congratulations, World Record Holder Courtney. I am immensely proud to be considered a friend.

I was contacted by Jolyon Armstrong, who acts for Nat West as a consultant on cricketing sponsorship matters, asking if Jack Russell would consider painting a picture for his client of the winning moment in the forthcoming world cup final. I discussed it with Jack, and he agreed to accept the commission. 'Well mate,' I said, 'Right now you are the only professional cricketer who is guaranteed a place in the final at Lord's.' We both laughed.

It was agreed that Jack's painting of the world cup Final would be presented at the Nat West final at Lord's, thus assuring him of a place at that event too! We couldn't possibly have imagined the way things would turn out.

The previous winter, Jack asked me if I would consider acting as literary agent for Alec Stewart. Alec was ready to write his first book, not an autobiography, but a tour diary recording events of England's winter tour of Australia. Brian Murgatroyd, then press officer for the ECB, would act as co-writer. I didn't know Brian, and suggested Alec consider Pat Murphy. There were several other interested parties. After due consideration, Alec decided to go with Murgers. My doubts about him were simple. First he hadn't yet written a book, and second, I thought his tour commitments with the board would be too heavy for him to write 60,000 words. My advice was to go with the tried and trusted Murph. However, I backed Alec's decision and negotiated a deal with CollinsWillow, promising my full support to both him and Murgers.

The book, *Alec Stewart - A Captains Diary*, was completed in time to be launched in April at the National Sporting Club in Piccadilly. The publisher invited Nasser Hussain as a guest. He was one of their authors. With Nasser's omission from the squad to face the visiting test side that summer, we wondered if he would accept. However, 24 hours is a long time in sport, things change, players get injured. Nick Knight who had previously let Alec back in after his omission now made way for Nasser to be recalled. Not only was Nasser Hussain back in the England team, but because of England's poor showing in the World cup series, and their early exit from it, Alec lost the captaincy. Who replaced him? Nasser Hussain. It's a funny old game.

I thought, as did many more qualified than me, that asking Alec Stewart to captain, keep wicket and bat up the order in test cricket was too much to ask. I think the extra burden of keeping wicket cost him the Captaincy.

Jack was having another good season with his county, who were doing surprisingly well in both the Benson & Hedges Cup, and the Nat West Trophy. Jack was desperate to win a medal with Gloucestershire, and at last the prospects of doing so looked real.

The world cup final was approaching, and I was excited at the prospect of attending it with Jack. Jolyon had organised space for us both in the new media centre, which Nat West had sponsored, providing a perfect view straight down the pitch to the pavilion. Jack would paint the backdrop there and then, and I would take photographs of the winning moment for him to add later.

Jolyon called to say he had been speaking to Gerry Francis, a producer at Sunset and Vine, a television company, who wanted to a film Jack painting the picture, for Channel 4. This would be marvellous publicity. Things were improving. Did this signal a return to the old magic?

Viewing the final between Australia and Pakistan from the new media centre at Lord's was a wonderful experience. Jack positioned himself in the corner of the giant 'spaceship' (cruelly described by many as Cherie Booth's mouth), and I sat nearby. It is as well that Jack works quickly; Pakistan batted first, then simply rolled over. With such a low target to chase, the Australians cruised to victory. The game was over with hours to spare. Expecting fireworks, as one is entitled to do given the reputations of the two sides, all we got was a damp squib.

The only highlight of the match for both of us was chatting with Ian Healy, who was covering the game for Channel 9 in Australia. Heals had been dumped by his national side. The two best keepers in the world were spectators, in a final that should have been between England and Australia, with both playing.

On one of my many trips to London, I called at Foyles bookshop in Charing Cross Road, and bought a little book written by Christina Foyle, called *So Much Wisdom*. Described by the author as 'A common place book' I found it to be a charming collection of words of wisdom published by someone my father had greatly admired.

It was the author Barbara Hooper who gave me Christina's address. Barbara had recently written a book on the life of Laurie Lee called *Cider with Laurie – Laurie Lee Remembered*. Jack had given his permission for his painting of Laurie Lee's grave to be used on the front cover and I had taken a series of photographs of the Slad valley for Barbara to use. I also did some photographic copy work for her.

I sent my book off to Christina Foyle with a short note telling her who I was, asking whether she remember my father and if would she sign my copy of her book. The book returned with the inscription, 'To Jim Ruston, With best wishes from Christina Foyle, who has had a wonderfully happy life.' I was delighted. A few weeks later a letter arrived from Christina, asking whether I would care to be her guest at a luncheon she was giving on 17 June at the Grosvenor in Park Lane, to honour Robin Day. She hoped I could accept and 'looked forward immensely to meeting me'. I accepted immediately.

A week before my lunch date with Christina, Barbara Hooper rang. 'Jim, have you seen today's Telegraph.' Christina Foyle had died; her obituary was in the paper. I felt so sad. Why had I left it so long to contact Christina? I could have done so years ago. I remember, from childhood, her name being ever-present in our household.

The luncheon went ahead as scheduled. Christina's family said she would have wanted that. Her nephew Christopher welcomed me, and I sat on the top table beside Frank Foyle. I could feel the presence of the remarkable woman to whom a number of tributes being were made.

My dad had been to many of Christina's luncheons, one in particular on 17 June 1935, to celebrate the publication of *In Town To-night*. Perhaps both he and Christina were present at the luncheon I now attended 64 years later to the day.

Gloucestershire, led by their captain Mark Alleyne, got through to the Benson & Hedges final at Lord's; their opponents were Yorkshire. Jack was ecstatic. We invited our dear friends Bill and Renie Sparks to be our guests on the big day. Joyce and I sat with them in the Mound stand, watching Mark Alleyne play a captain's innings, making 112 runs. With Rob Cunliffe chipping in a brilliant 61, it gave Gloucestershire a first innings total of 291. That was always going to me too many runs for Yorkshire to chase. When they came out to bat they never looked like contenders. All out for 167, Yorkshire went down like a one-legged man in a bum-kicking contest!

Gloucestershire had been magnificent, every player had done his bit, and Coach John Bracewell was justly proud. He had produced a team with a competitive edge as sharp as a razor. No prima donnas, just everyone performing at 100 per cent. Jack intended to paint the winning scene, from which we would make a limited edition, so I took masses of photos to work from.

Incredibly, Gloucestershire had got through to the semi-final of the Nat West trophy. More incredible still, their opponents would be Yorkshire once more.

The semi-final was at Nevil Road Bristol, where I was a guest of Nat West. It was there that I met Barbara Quinn, head of the department of Nat West Sponsorship that Jolyon reported to. With an encouraging 98 from opener Kim Barnett, Gloucestershire, batting first, made 240 runs. Would this be enough? Another 10 would have been nice, I thought. Yorkshire wanted revenge and this time were no push-over. We had lunch in a marquee and I sat with Barbara, Jolyon and my old school chum Mervyn Kitchen. Merv is now a test umpire, and we talked of cricket at Nailsea, when as kids we played imaginary test matches, and how seriously we all took it.

Yorkshire got off to a bold start. Soon they were 161 for 3. But due to some top class bowling from Mike Smith, and Jack standing up to everything, restricting the batsman's play, the run rate was rising. With 10 overs to go, and after a quick fire 27 from 15 balls from Parker, which revitalised the Yorkies, Gloucestershire's new overseas signing Ian Harvey did for them with a magnificent display of accurate bowling. Yorkshire's innings ended with them seven runs short. It was nail-biting stuff. Gloucestershire were through to another Lord's final; the fans went ballistic.

In the other Nat West semi-final, Somerset beat Surrey. It would be an all west-country final, the first in the history of the competition. In fact, archrivals Somerset and Gloucestershire, had never met in a final of any kind before. The media dubbed the forthcoming contest, 'The Cider Final'. This caught the imagination of everyone, and tickets for Lord's were like gold dust. 'Wos fink of ee then' (West Country speak).

Jack had waited so long for a medal, and now he would get two in the same month. Only once before had the two one-day competitions been one by the same county, in the same year. Lancashire, but not in the same month!

Somehow Jack managed to finish the painting Nat West had commissioned. He is magnificent under pressure. Jack would travel to Lord's the day before the final. It would be my job to take the world cup painting for presentation on the day; to say I was excited is an understatement. Jane, my daughter and Jack's secretary, would travel with her mother to London by train. I would drive the van our much valued friend, Steve Patch, had loaned us, with the painting in. Son-in-law Eddy would help carry the painting, which measured 6 feet by 4 feet. We had given ourselves plenty of time in case of delays on the motorway. I'm glad we did. We were diverted off the motorway because there had been a serious car accident. My frustration calmed; at least we were not involved in that. One feels guilty complaining about being delayed, when someone else may have lost his or her life.

The local knowledge I had gained during my Army days in the Reading area became useful. I followed my nose through a maze of country lanes. No other cars were following, I wondered had I lost my way. Then a signpost popped up to the M4 Slough and we rejoined an almost empty carriageway. I phoned Jolyon on my mobile as we drove towards St John's Wood. We arrived at Lord's with time to spare. 'Am I pleased to see you. Barbara has been frantic,' the big man greeted us. I say big man. Eddy is 6 feet five inches. Jolyon is bigger!

Eddy, Jolyon and I, carried the huge painting plus an easel around the edge of the famous outfield. The place was buzzing, the atmosphere electric. I caught sight of Joyce and Jane, who had already taken up their seats, and waved to them. We arrived in front of the Pavilion and set up the picture. The TV cameras were there, plus a gaggle of photographers. Jack came down from the dressing room, and made the presentation to the Chairman of Nat West. We had a few private words, and wishing him good luck, he confided, 'Thanks mate, but don't worry, we are confident, we have a plan.' 'A cunning one I hope – as Baldrick would say,' I replied. 'Believe me mate, it is.' Jack jested.

I could feel something different in Jack's mood that morning. His eyes sparkled. There was a look of steel in them. 'Cross the bridge mate,' (as in St Nazaire) I called as we parted. 'Trust me,' he replied. I did. Eddy and I relocated the world cup painting in the Nat West hospitality suite, then ventured off to find Joyce and Jane, in time for the big game to begin.

Somerset won the toss, and to the amazement of everyone, put Gloucestershire in to bat. If you win the toss at Lord's, you generally elect to bat. It was common knowledge that Gloucestershire didn't fancy a run chase. They are a superb fielding side, more able to contain the opposition rather than out- bat it. Jack told me after the game that the lads couldn't believe the decision Somerset had made. When it was confirmed they hugged one another. They knew right then they had it won; all they had to do was stick to their plan.

Whilst our side was batting, I went on a tour of the ground with Barbara Quinn. I had taken limited edition prints of the world cup picture specially framed to present to various dignitaries. As we traipsed from box to box, I kept my eye on the scoreboard. Kim Barnett and Tim Hancock put on a magnificent opening stand of 125, before Kim was run out. Suddenly we were 5 for180. I began to fret. Would we get enough? Then Jack scored an unbeaten 31. We finished with 230, not a bad score in a one-day game at Lord's, but beatable.

During the interval, the film of Jack painting the world cup picture was shown on the huge TV screen at the nursery end. I knew Jack would see this and feel the added pressure. His fans would expect, and he would not let us down.

Relatives and friends of the players of both sides mostly occupied the section of the Mound stand where we were sitting. We would be good sports, and not join in the rhetoric. Although it became hard not to. Somerset came out to bat. The match was electric, and the contest flowed over into the stands. Somerset lost wickets quickly. Soon they were 4 for 51. Jack was standing up to the bowling, even the quicks. He was performing like a man possessed. He caught Trescothick off Alleyne, then stumped Parsons off Smith in a display of glove work that will go down in history.

Then for a moment Somerset rallied, with Rob Turner, their wicket keeper, who had recently been named in the England 'A' party to tour that winter, putting up a good display of batting. The Somerset supporters began to chant, 'Turner is for England La la a la, La la la la.' Then just as he had passed his half century, Jack had him. A lightning catch off the bowling of Mark Alleyne sent his opposite number back to the dressing room. Now the Gloucestershire fans, struck up their reply, 'Turner is a novice La la la la, La la la la.' The Somerset fans, now silent, felt the cold embrace of defeat. It came in the 45th over with Somerset still 50 runs behind. Graham Rose sent the ball skywards, and the crowd fell silent as they waited for the ball to descend into the safe hands of Matt Windows. Then the place erupted.

Fans ran in from all sides and gathered in front of the dressing room to wait for the victors to come out on to the balcony. I stood and waited hoping to get a glimpse of Jack. I had a pass for the Pavilion, but preferred to stay where I was, in amongst the body of the staunchest of Gloucestershire devotees. The presentations were made. David Gower, one of the few presenters/journalists, who has always kept faith with Jack, was there to adjudicate on the Man of the Match award. He made a speech in which he praised many for their individual performance. Then he turned to Jack and said what pleasure it gave him to make Jack his Man of the Match. And how Jack had just demonstrated the purpose of the specialist wicket keeper. 'Lest we forget the importance of a dying art.'

Tributes to Jack flowed in. Without doubt his performance had been a major factor in Gloucestershire's win. He had dominated, or as one hack wrote, anaesthetised the opposition batsmen, they were frightened to move their feet, else they would perish. The Pakistan fast bowler and former captain Wasim Akram said, 'He is still the best keeper in the world.' A fine tribute from a worthy adversary. The rats of the press ate copious amounts of humble pie saying, 'Russell has returned to his best.' If their performance over a period of 11 years anywhere near equalled that of Jack Russell, they might be worth more than a cursory glance.

Jack painted a wonderful picture of the last seconds of the Nat West Trophy final. We call it 'Winning Double', to commemorate both one-day finals won by the Glorious Glosters. From which we made limited edition prints, signed by Jack's team-mates, who all played magnificently. The Gravy Train was back on the track. We dipped our bread. Two slices!!! (The following year Gloucestershire won both trophy's for a second time. Historic. And for good measure won the one-day title also. Jack had dreamed of winning a medal with Gloucestershire. In a bit over a year he had won five!)

Foyles were organising a literary lunch to coincide with the publication of former Prime Minister John Major's autobiography, *The Major Years*. I decided to take a table and invite a few people whom I liked, and had been helpful to both Jack and me. Barbara Quinn, Jolyon Armstrong, David English, Gerry Francis, Patrick Shervington, Sarah Moger, Claire Struthers, my sister Stella and Jack, made up a table of luncheon guests, as warm, friendly and interesting as any I have ever sat on.

The literary luncheon for John Major, held in the grand ballroom at the Grosvenor in Park Lane, attracted the biggest attendance of any Foyles luncheon on record. It was a swell affair. The top table, as you might guess, read straight out of *Who's Who*. After lunch, we waited in line to get books signed by the author. I had heard him speak previously. One memorable time was at a dinner held at the London Hilton just down the road as part of Courtney Walsh's testimonial. John Major was both engaging and amusing, taking no offence when Rory Bremner did a brilliant impression of him, much to the amusement of us all. In fact, he laughed at himself. I always thought him to be a nice man. Having read his book, I am sure that he is.

For the last five years at the 11th hour an the 11th day of the 11th month we have observed two' minutes silence at the war memorial just up the road from the gallery. The Royal British legion are anxious that the armistice signed at the end of the First World War be observed on the correct day, as it once was. The Legion encourages all their members to do their bit to achieve this. At first it was just Jane and me standing in silence, although a few cars did stop. The second year our numbers had grown to a dozen. This year we had around 50. I invited Bill Sparks and his wife Renie to stay with us, and Bill agreed to stand at the memorial. Patrick Shervington and his wife Vicky came. Charles Patterson, an ex Second World War and much decorated bomber pilot also stood with us. Jack, no longer touring, was able to be there too. The press and TV came to see the Cockleshell Hero. Wearing the green beret of the Royal Marine Commandos, Bill stood ramrod straight, as my 11 year old granddaughter Jade blew the Last Post, then after the two-minute silence, Reveille. I was so proud to stand next to my friend Bill, a living legend, and was moved by the musical competence of one so young.

After our act of remembrance we repaired to the gallery for drinks. Reunited with the painting of the Cockleshell Heroes, Bill chatted with Jack. The two had much to catch up on. They hadn't seen each other for a while. During Bill's stay, Jack painted a wonderful portrait of him sitting in the hall of my cottage.

My grandson Daniel wrote a moving poem of remembrance. *The Bristol Evening post* printed it with a picture of him above. He is a fine young man, quiet and modest. A karate black belt at 15 years old. He looks a lot like me at that age. Oh to change places with him!

With just a few days to go before Christmas, Michael Doggart rang to say Brian Murgatroyd had told them he did not have time to write the extra two chapters for the publication of a paperback edition of Alec Stewart's book. Could I sort it out before Christmas? I managed to get a call through to Alec in South Africa, and he said he would be happy to have Pat Murphy write the extra chapters. With a feeling of déjà vu, I rang Murph on his mobile. Also in South Africa covering England's current test series, he had taken a little time off to accompany his wife Christmas shopping. He was walking through a shopping plaza when his phone rang. 'Jim you old bugger, what can I do for you?' I explained my predicament. 'Yes I can do it, but it will cost.' 'Perhaps next time I will get first call. That's twice I've come to your rescue,' he reminded me. 'I know Murph, thanks mate. Happy Christmas,' I said with some relief. 'Happy Christmas to you too. And don't worry. I'll come through for you.' True to his word, he did.

Mike Newlin of MBN Promotions invited Jack along with a host of sporting celebrities including Henry Cooper, Nobby Stiles, Willy John McBride and Pat Jennings, to be guests of honour at the Reuters Sporting Heroes Millennium Lunch being held at the Grosvenor House Hotel. I was also invited, and was seated next to Henry Cooper.

THE MAGIC RETURNS

More than 1,000 people filled the great ballroom. We enjoyed a traditional Christmas dinner, during which Henry and I talked of our families, and old London.

After the main course, the lights were lowered. Then a team of waiters walked through the room carrying silver platters with flaming Christmas puddings held high above their heads. The effect was stunning. The flames from the brandy flickering in the darkness and sound of festive carols added to a wonderful occasion. As the waiters served the still blazing pudding, the boxing legend touched me on the arm and said, 'Its not a bad old life, is it Jim?' I replied. 'I'll drink to that Henry.' A stark contrast to the many Christmas we struggled through in childhood.